picturing texts

picturing texts

Lester Faigley
University of Texas at Austin

Diana George
Michigan Technological University

Anna Palchik

Cynthia Selfe
Michigan Technological University

W. W. NORTON & COMPANY
New York · London

W. W. Norton & Company has been independent since its founding in 1923, when William Warder Norton and Mary D. Herter Norton first published lectures delivered at the People's Institute, the adult education division of New York City's Cooper Union. The Nortons soon expanded their program beyond the Institute, publishing books by celebrated academics from America and abroad. By mid-century, the two major pillars of Norton's publishing program—trade books and college texts— were firmly established. In the 1950s, the Norton family transferred control of the company to its employees, and today—with a staff of four hundred and a comparable number of trade, college, and professional titles published each year—W. W. Norton & Company stands as the largest and oldest publishing house owned wholly by its employees.

Editor: Marilyn Moller
Assistant Editor: Nicole Netherton
Production Manager: Diane O'Connor
Project Editor: Kim Yi
Managing Editor, College: Marian Johnson
Copy Editor: Kate Lovelady
Photo Researcher: Meredith Coeyman
Front Cover Photo: Kenneth Josephson
Back Cover Photo: Nora Mapp

Design and Layout by Anna Palchik
Composition by Westchester Book Group
Digital art file services by Jay's Publishers Services and Bukva Imaging Group
Manufacturing by R. R. Donnelley & Sons, Inc.

Library of Congress Cataloging-in-Publication Data

Picturing texts / Lester Faigley . . . [et al.].
    p. cm.
   Includes index.
   ISBN 0-393-97912-1 (pbk.)
   1. Visual communication. 2. Rhetoric. I. Faigley, Lester, 1947–

P93.5.P53 2004
302.23—dc22

                     2003063304

W. W. Norton & Company, Inc., 500 Fifth Avenue, New York, N.Y. 10110
www.wwnorton.com

W. W. Norton & Company Ltd., Castle House, 75/76 Wells Street, London W1T 3QT

Effective rhetoric is ... a two-pronged strategy
of verbal/visual persuasion, showing while it tells,
illustrating its claims with powerful examples,
making the listener *see* and not merely *hear*....

—W. J. T. MITCHELL

contents

2 Looking Closer *96*

3 Making Lives Visible *150*

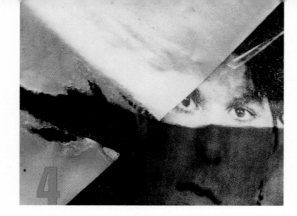

Representing Others *228*

Constructing Realities 316

Picturing Argument 382

Designing Texts *432*

Picturing Texts is written for students living and communicating in a world very different from that of their parents and grandparents—and, dare we say, of many of their teachers. Ours is truly an information-saturated society, and much of the information we encounter daily is visual: billboards, ads, signs, Web pages, television, film, four-color newspapers.

Expectations about what it means to be literate have changed. Students today must be able to read and compose not only conventional print essays but also texts that combine words with images and other graphics. These texts are often highly visual in nature.

Literacy has become literacies, the new piled on top of the old, all challenging and exciting. Students often find themselves leading the way in exploring new kinds of texts—music videos, simulation games, instant messages. Each of these texts allows people to communicate in new ways, across traditional boundaries of time and space and culture and language, using words and images and design.

The challenge for college writing teachers is to expand our concept of writing to include visual as well as verbal texts. College textbooks have not always paid attention to visual texts, let alone kept pace with them—and the great majority still focus on teaching students to read and compose only conventional essays. Even those books that do focus in some way on visual culture teach students only to read and write *about* images, with little or no instruction on how to compose visual texts themselves. As a result, most students receive very little formal instruction on how to read, analyze, interpret, and compose texts that go beyond the alphabetic.

Picturing Texts provides students with ways to understand and evaluate visual texts, along with instruction on how to produce documents that

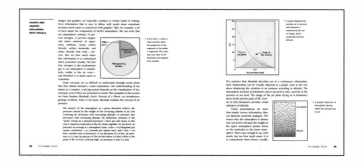

combine words, images, and graphics. Given the way that communication increasingly depends on images as a means of conveying messages, we focus on texts that are highly visual and that often resist conventional genre distinctions. These include texts in print as well as online.

The chapters in *Picturing Texts* are designed so that they can be used on their own or in the sequence presented here. Briefly, the book moves from an introduction to visual and verbal composition (Chapter 1) through lessons on analysis (Chapter 2) and issues of social and cultural representation (Chapters 3, 4, and 5), to instruction in constructing visual texts (Chapters 6 and 7). Each chapter offers students opportunities both to write about texts that contain both verbal and visual elements and also to compose such texts themselves.

HIGHLIGHTS

Presents the visual in the context of composition, teaching students to think of design and images as rhetorically driven, as a means of communication rather than just as decoration.

Teaches students how to use visuals and design in their own writing, showing them how to use photos, charts, tables, headings, colors, and other graphic elements. Throughout the book are practical guidelines that aim to make design and visuals a part of the composing process—to choose appropriate type fonts, include visuals that illustrate a point, and so on.

More than 40 readings, most of them about visual culture and all of them demonstrating good use of visual rhetoric. From David Brooks on *The Sims*

to Michelle Citron on home movies to David Quammen on Dürer's famous woodcut of a rhinoceros, these readings will get students thinking about visual culture and visual rhetoric.

More than 250 images, including paintings, photographs, ads, posters, book jackets, snapshots, and more—famous works of art as well as images composed by students. *Picturing Texts* includes visuals that are models of effective communication *and* models of what students themselves can do. Chapters 2–7 include Galleries of Images that demonstrate key concepts and serve as additional resources for writing and analysis.

Writing assignments ranging from close readings of visual and verbal texts to matters of design. Students are asked to write about visual texts, to compose texts that include visual elements, to make visual arguments, and to design what they write. Although students have many opportunities in *Picturing Texts* to write conventional essays that respond to or analyze images, they are also asked to create texts of their own that rely on the visual as well as the verbal—posters, postcards, menus, brochures, ads, and so on. Each chapter includes a brief Snapshot exercise prompting students to work with a photograph that they choose and also a more extensive project called *Picture This* that invites them to compose film reviews, posters, greeting cards, and many other genres.

Guidelines for evaluating visual texts help students think about the rhetorical effectiveness of images and other visual elements.

User-tested by a team of 12 students at Michigan Tech, who evaluated the readings, pointed out concepts needing more explanation, and suggested writing projects. Some of their work appears in the book.

ACKNOWLEDGMENTS

Like most authors, we are grateful for all the help we have received while writing *Picturing Texts*. Marilyn Moller, first and foremost, has proven to be a rare editor—one as deeply committed to the books she helps create as are the authors and artists who craft them. We thank as well the many other people at Norton who helped make the book happen. Meredith Coeyman has worked tenaciously for many months clearing permissions for hundreds of images; Diane O'Connor has been involved in so many aspects of the production process that this book probably would not even exist without her; and Kim Yi has been a splendid project editor, keeping the book and all of us on course and on schedule. We are grateful to Mandy Brown for the very cool brochure, and to Steve Dunn and Allison Henry for their astute marketing sense. Thanks also to Dan Bartell, Jamie and Scott Berzon, Steve Forman, Katie Hannah, Marian Johnson, Evan Leatherwood, Kate Lovelady, Jim Mairs, Debra Morton-Hoyt, Nicole Netherton, Nathan Odell, Melea Seward, Peter Simon, Katrina Washington, and Brook Wilensky-Lanford. We are grateful to Julia Reidhead, Roby Harrington, and Drake McFeely for supporting this project—and to Libby Miles for first suggesting it. And we thank Laura Gringer of R. R. Donnelley & Sons for seeing the book through a complex printing process.

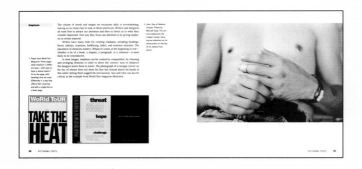

Thanks go as well to the reviewers whose many insights helped us shape *Picturing Texts*: Danielle DeVoss (Michigan State University), Paul Heilker (Virginia Polytechnic Institute and State University), Susan Hilligoss (Clemson University), Melanie Hunter (Tulsa Community College), Elizabeth Losh (University of California at Irvine), Libby Miles (University of Rhode Island), Stephanie Paterson (California State University at Stanislaus), Gardner Rogers (University of Illinois, Urbana-Champaign), and Bronwyn Williams (University of Louisville).

And we want to mention our students at the University of Texas and Michigan Tech, who inspire us to teach and to learn and continually coach us in how to do a better job at both. In particular, we thank the students of HU3910 at Michigan Tech, who served as an incisive and creative user-testing group for this book: Andy Bjorne, Katherine Carlson, Joseph Clairmont, Matthew Hodgman, Melissa Jones, James "Captain" Kirk, Michelle Primeau, Virginia Ruona, Nicole Sarazin, Jody Scheffler, Denny Wagner, and Kristie A. W.

We are especially grateful to the many students and friends whose photos and writing appear here. We say a special thank you to Neil Ryder Hoos, Benjamin Kracauer, and Nora Mapp, whose photographs contribute so much to the tone. Neil's photos of street images, posters, and other public texts open every chapter, demonstrating an artist's eye for the texture of words and images. Benjamin's candid images of friends, family, and buildings reveal his keen sense of structure, light, and the moment. Nora's photographs are good examples of the wonderful visual work that students can do; we thank her for the rubber ducky photo on the back cover and for several other photos as well. In this context, we would be remiss

not to mention our editor, Marilyn Moller, whose images enhance our book with their wit and attention to texture and detail. It is rare to find an editor who is as interested in both word and image as Marilyn. And finally, we thank Yenyi Liu and Sarah Huang (the University of Texas); Katherine Carlson and Matt Hodgman (Michigan Tech); Corianne Daman, Bryan Fisher, Shaun Gingerich, and Andy Wagoner (Ivy Tech State College at South Bend); Carolina Arellano (Fordham University); Rise Axelrod (University of California at Riverside); Charlotte Greenough (University of Michigan); Emily Kracauer and Sam Mapp (Skidmore College); Alison Perry; and Bowie Zunino (Williams College).

In addition, we express appreciation to Cheryl Ball, who took time out from her doctoral work at Michigan Tech to write the Instructor's Guide and the Web site (www.picturingtexts.com), and Benjamin Reynolds, Eileen Connell, and Jack Lamb at Norton for their help on these important parts of this project.

Three of us, of course, could neither teach nor write without the help and support of our departments and universities: the Department of Humanities at Michigan Technological University and the Division of Writing and Rhetoric at the University of Texas at Austin. Both have been most generous in their support of our efforts.

Finally, we are thankful for our partners and families, whose generosity of spirit, and understanding helped and enabled us to compose even when such work challenges our abilities.

Lester Faigley
Diana George
Anna Palchik
Cynthia Selfe

picturing texts

In 1994, while exploring a cave in the South of France, archaeologist Jean-Marie Chauvet and two fellow spelunkers felt a warm draft coming from a pile of stones deep in the cave. Removing enough rubble to squeeze through, they found themselves in a passage that had been sealed for thousands of years. Their lights revealed an extraordinary sight: a series of magnificent wall paintings depicting lions, rhinos, bears, and panthers, over 400 animals in all. The paintings were dated using radiocarbon tests and were found to be over 30,000 years old—by far the oldest known paintings in the world today. The sophistication of the images was also a surprise. The degree of realism is extraordinary, depicting both perspective and motion, artistic techniques that were thought to have developed much later.

As well as overturning assumptions about the beginnings of art, the Chauvet cave paintings force us to think a little differently about ourselves. Anthropologists once defined humans as tool-using or language-using animals, but the Chauvet cave tells us that humans have also long had image-making abilities. Our current era may be called a "visual age," but there is now no known time when people did not create images. We can only guess why the images were painted in the Chauvet cave, but the kinds of artifacts found there, including ancient bear skulls, lead us to believe that the site was of great cultural importance and that the images there said something meaningful.

▶ Chauvet cave, near the village of Vallon-Pont-d'Arc, France.

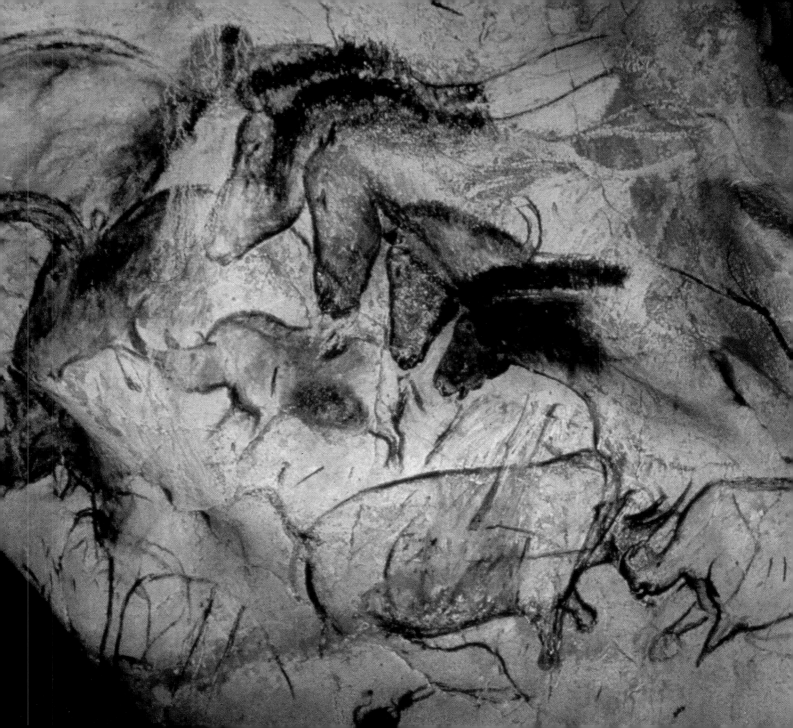

**SURROUNDED BY
IMAGES**

A major difference between image-making in the past and image-making today is that we now have the ability to reproduce and transmit images. Until the development of the printing press (in the 1400s in Europe, earlier in China and Korea), each image had to be made individually, even when it was copied from another image. Printed images were unavailable to most people until the 1800s, when steam presses and cheap paper became widespread. In the twentieth century, the introduction of new electronic technologies resulted in a proliferation of images, starting with moving pictures (movies) at the beginning of the century, then television and video, and most recently the World Wide Web in the 1990s.

All of us today have grown up in a world saturated with images, not only in newspapers, magazines, films, television, and on the Web, but also on signs, buildings, postage stamps, taxis and buses, on the packaging of food and other everyday items, on the clothing we buy and the bags we're given to carry it home—on almost everything. Before personal computers, we interacted with images largely as consumers. We looked at images, bought things adorned with images, wore T-shirts bearing images, and hung pictures and posters on our walls, but few of us created images apart from school art projects, family photo albums, or home movies and videos. Digital technologies and the Internet have greatly expanded our abilities to make images and even to publish them.

5

Words and images have been used together to express ideas since the earliest known writing systems. In ancient and medieval manuscript cultures, texts often included drawings and decorative illustrations. During the early years of printing, printed books competed directly with handwritten manuscripts, and to a large extent they were designed to look like those manuscripts. The earliest printed books were often hybrid texts, combining words and images, in which decoration, illustrations, and colored letters were added by hand after the words had been printed.

In the 1600s, images disappeared from most printed books because two different technologies developed to print words and images, which made books that combined the two very expensive to produce. Words and images came together again in the 1800s, when new technologies allowed high-quality drawings to return to the printed page. By 1900, photographs and cartoons (then a new form of image) became commonplace in newspapers. We've become accustomed today to seeing words and images together everywhere—not only on the printed page but also on signs, logos, television, commercial products, and the Web.

▶ In early printed books, woodcut images were often combined with type to imitate the look of a manuscript. From Ulrich Richental, *Concilium zu Constanz*, printed in Augsburg, Germany, 1483.

▶ Advances in printing and engraving resulted in images of excellent quality in books in the 1880s. From *The Pilgrim's Progress*, illustrated by George Woolliscroft Rhead, Frederick Rhead, and Louis Rhead, 1898.

We often use words and images in combination to present information that could not be conveyed by either one alone. Look, for instance, at the following photograph, which depicts an agricultural landscape with gently curved furrows in deep shadow leading to an abandoned house. At first

▶ Childress County, Texas Panhandle. Photo by Dorothea Lange, 1938.

glance you might guess that the photographer took this picture for its scenic value. However, the date of the photograph might cause you to think further. June 1938 was a time of severe drought on the Great Plains, forcing small farmers to abandon their farms to seek a living elsewhere. The photographer, Dorothea Lange, titled the photograph *Power farming displaces tenants from the land in the Western dry cotton area. Childress County, Texas Panhandle*. At once, the words change how we see the image. The abandoned house is no longer a nostalgic bit of scenery. Lange's title forces us to imagine what the scene looked like when people lived in the house — and to think about what happened to them.

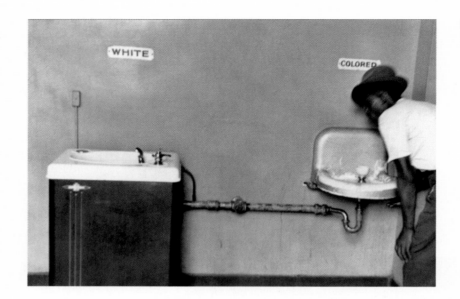

▶ *North Carolina.* Photo by Elliot Erwitt, 1950.

Images can similarly change how we understand words. We know that the South was racially segregated until a series of legislative acts and court decisions in the 1950s and 1960s banned racial discrimination. Before then, African Americans and whites in the South attended separate schools. Theaters and restaurants had separate entrances and separate sections for African Americans or barred them entirely. Though these facts are well known, see how the effects of segregation on the routines of daily life are made more concrete in photographs from the time. Words such as "segregation" often become more meaningful when we can *see* what they mean.

In the era of the Web, we increasingly expect to see words and images together. The Internet has been the star of a new generation of electronic technologies that includes the phenomenal expansion of storage and memory on personal computers and the development of powerful multimedia software. Personal computers, digital cameras, and camcorders have given us the capability of producing texts with images, audio, and video that would have required teams of designers and technicians just a few years ago. As we have more and more need to communicate across geographical, linguistic, and cultural boundaries, the use of images will grow in importance.

**IMAGES FOR
WORDS / WORDS
FOR IMAGES**

On the one hand, images are often used in place of words. Many signs, especially those found along roads, in airports, and on laundry labels, use images without words so they can be understood by speakers of different languages. Brand images—the Nike swoosh, the McDonald's arches, the Energizer Bunny, the Pillsbury Doughboy, the Michelin Man, Colonel Sanders, to name but a few—remind us of their brand names even without accompanying words. Other times, as with the sign about the ship's whistle shown here, words are easier to understand.

On the other hand, many words can bring to mind images. For some of us, the word "Paris" carries an image of the Eiffel Tower, and the common nouns "dog" or "cat" might link to a mental image of your dog or cat.

NON INGRESSO

CAUTION
SHIP'S WHISTLE
IS VERY LOUD

Indeed, there are many words it is difficult to think of without seeing an image. Advertisers are well aware that images can stand for words and words for images, as the ad for Pepsi shown here illustrates. Some clever advertising carries the connection one step further, such as the Red Cross ad on the facing page that says visually that blood is needed.

We have come to expect certain kinds of information to be presented visually. Color weather maps have long been a standard feature of television weathercasts and in turn led to color-coded weather maps in daily newspapers. Color weather maps now seem normal, but not too long ago newspapers reported weather like most other news—with plain words and numbers. Weather maps were first used by meteorologists in the 1870s, who recognized that the complexity of weather patterns across the nation could best be conveyed visually, and it's hard now even to imagine trying to do so with just words or numbers.

Similarly, some explanations require both words and images. For example, a well-designed concert hall delivers rich sound to every seat in the house. The secret to a successful concert hall is how the walls reverberate the fullness of the sound, sometimes for as long as two seconds. It's a concept that's difficult to explain using only words, but relatively easy to show visually— as the drawing on the facing page demonstrates.

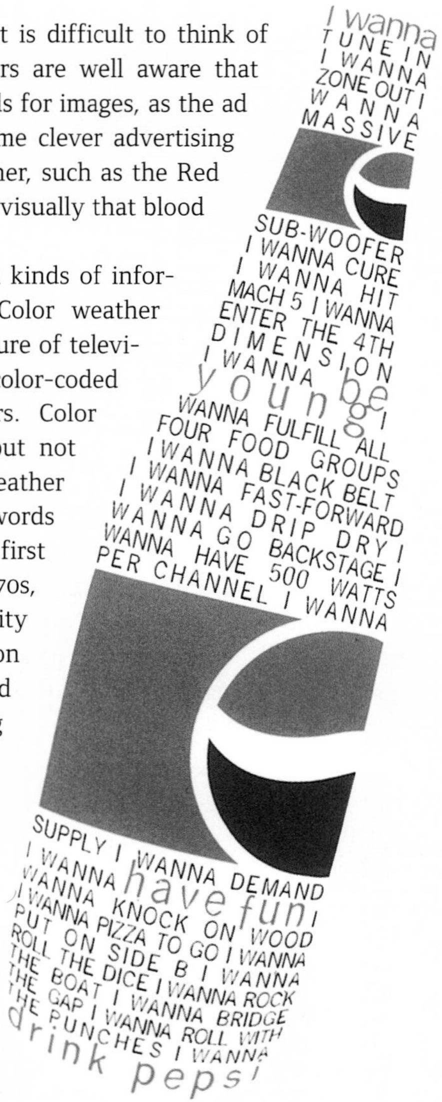

▶ Pepsi ad. Designed by David Carson, a graphic artist whose work has been said to reflect the look and attitude of a generation. This ad was a departure from traditional Pepsi ads that showed attractive models drinking Pepsi, substituting hip language to appeal to a youthful audience.

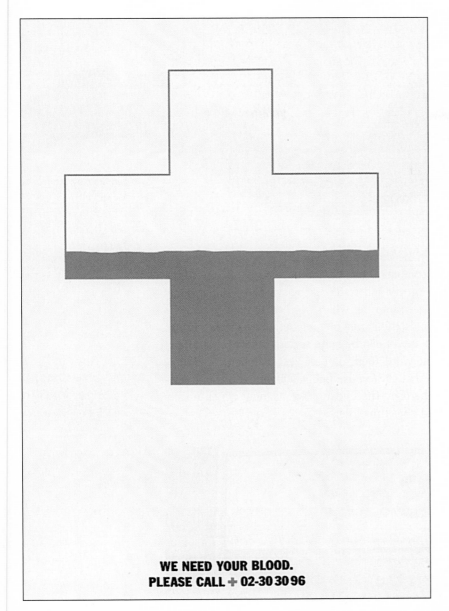
▶ Red Cross ad.

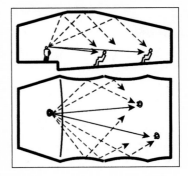

▶ Reverberation (the reflection of sound) prolongs the sounds in a room after the source has stopped. With the same sound-absorbing material, reverberation is determined by the volume of the room: the larger the room, the longer the sound reverberates.

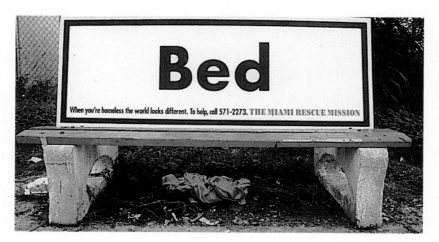

▶ *Sea-Saw*, by Steve Meyer.

Words and images can be combined in ways to get our attention. Sometimes they can be combined for humorous effect—as the three sculptures here by Steve Meyer illustrate. Each is a three-dimensional representation of the words in its title; when we read the image and the words together, the zany translation from one medium into another brings a smile. At other times, the intent can be more serious, as with the Miami ad campaign that pasted the word "Bed" on benches, "Kitchen" on dumpsters, and "House" on bus shelters to raise public awareness of homelessness. We are caught off-guard by the unexpected meaning which results from placing each word and object together.

▶ Ad campaign for the Miami Rescue Mission, Florida.

An Old Cowhand, by Steve Meyer.

Hand-Saw, by Steve Meyer.

Words, images, and other graphics all function as acts of communication. All are texts, and throughout this book we will use the word *text*
to describe all three—words, images, and other graphics—whether
they're used in combination or alone. Photographs, novels, poems, maps,
brochures, advertisements, Web sites, telephone directories, product
labels: all are texts. Similarly, when we talk about *reading* in this book, we
have in mind an extended sense of reading that includes words, images,
and graphics. We assume that a painting or photograph is a text that can
be read.

Whether you're reading an essay or a Web site, there are several
common elements you need to think about. All texts are created by a
person or persons for some purpose. A good way to begin thinking about
a text is to ask who wrote the words or created the image or designed the
graphic, what the subject is, and who the intended audience is. When you
identify this information, you can begin to draw conclusions about what
the author or authors wanted to accomplish and why the text was created.
We will refer to this combination of author, subject, and audience of a text
as the IMMEDIATE CONTEXT.

No text is created in a vacuum. Authors live in particular cultures at
particular times, and we must take the values, beliefs, and circumstances
of those times and cultures into account when we read. For example, we
cannot understand fully the Declaration of Independence without knowing the history that led its signers to endorse separating from England. We
appreciate their extreme courage only if we realize that they might well
have been hanged for treason if the American Revolution had failed. Similarly, Pablo Picasso's best-known painting, *Guernica*, first appeared as the
centerpiece of the Spanish Pavilion at the 1937 World's Fair in Paris.
Picasso had other ideas for this large mural, but when German bombers
annihilated a small Basque town during the Spanish Civil War, Picasso
painted *Guernica* to express his outrage over the atrocity. (You can see a
reproduction of *Guernica* on p. 39.) Think of the social, historical, cultural,
and economic influences surrounding a text as the BROADER CONTEXT. The
relationship between the immediate and broader contexts is illustrated in
the chart on the next page.

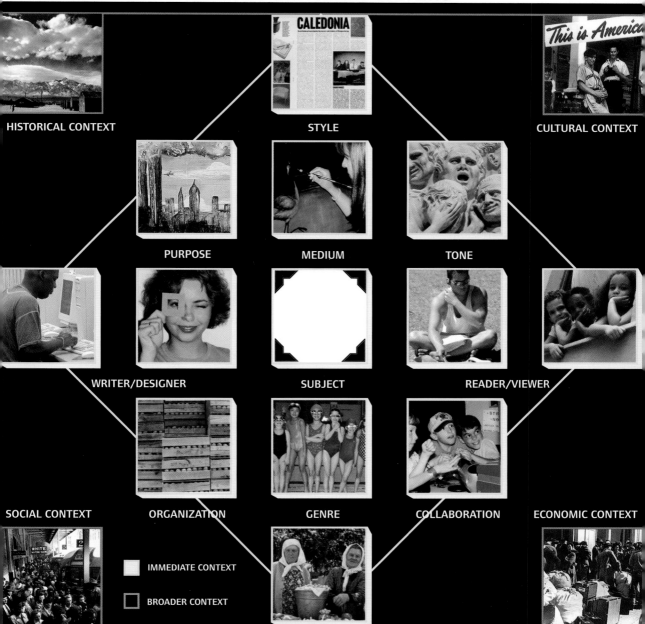

CHARTING RHETORICAL CONTEXTS

HISTORICAL CONTEXT

STYLE

CULTURAL CONTEXT

PURPOSE

MEDIUM

TONE

WRITER/DESIGNER

SUBJECT

READER/VIEWER

SOCIAL CONTEXT

ORGANIZATION

GENRE

COLLABORATION

ECONOMIC CONTEXT

IMMEDIATE CONTEXT

BROADER CONTEXT

In addition to thinking about the immediate and broader contexts, you also need to read with an eye for INTERTEXTUALITY, the way that texts build upon and consciously refer to other texts. The humor in TV ads, for instance, often parodies other texts; think of the Pepsi ad in which Britney Spears imitates Michael Jackson or the Old Navy ads that parody old TV series. Many literary texts refer to passages from the Bible or to ancient Greek myths. Such texts assume that you have knowledge of some other text. Thus, another question to ask when reading a text is what else has been written about or what other images have been made of this subject. You may find that how you read a text depends in this way on your knowledge of other texts.

Readers play a role in determining a text's meaning, and in some cases they construct meanings quite different from those the authors intended. Sometimes such unintended meanings are the result of a lack of knowledge. We have no idea, for example, why some of the oldest poems in English, such as "The Seafarer" and "The Wanderer," were written, whom they were written for, or even what they are about. But sometimes texts are deliberately read differently than their authors intended. In a way, texts are like clothing. Just as caps can be turned backward, shirts can be turned inside out, socks can be mixed, and basketball shoes can be worn with tuxedos, texts can be read in ways that resist intended meanings. Readers may identify with characters who are not depicted as the heroes or may literally write over one text to create another—and in doing so, change its meaning. In the chapters that follow, we'll introduce a few of the many examples on the Web in which texts are rewritten. Sometimes such oppositional reading is turned into art, as when artist Nancy Chunn marked up the front page of the *New York Times* each day in 1996, using ink, pastel colors, and rubber stamps. The images were published in the book *Front Pages,* in which she announced her goal of "getting my two cents in to the power represented by the *New York Times.*"

▶ A page from *Front Pages*, by Nancy Chunn, 1997.

Today we have powerful personal computers, sophisticated software, and the Web, all of which allows us to create texts that include words, pictures, graphics, audio, and video—and to share those texts with people around the world. We now have the potential to create and publish texts that just a few years ago might have required a team of designers. The challenge is that we have much more to do as writers.

The ability to work with images and to design what we write means that we now need to compose more than just words and sentences. Sometimes we need to include photos or charts in an essay, and other times we might choose to make arguments using genres other than essays—in Web logs, in PowerPoint presentations, in email. All call upon us to choose fonts and make it possible to include images. Just as AOL tells us when we've "got mail," it also tells us when we've "got pictures." In a world where we can easily email baby pictures, many birth announcements now include more than just the baby's name and weight—and essays are starting to be more than just black words on white paper. So we've got a lot to learn.

Picturing Texts is designed to help with the choices writers now have, redefining writing to include images and conscious attention to design. It provides tools that you can use to engage critically with texts—those you read and those you compose. There is no simple formula for accomplishing these goals, but there are habits of mind you can develop that will help you think critically about texts—their words, images, designs. On the following two pages are some questions that can help you read and compose texts with insight and depth.

ENGAGING CRITICALLY WITH TEXTS

	As a Reader	**As a Writer or Designer**
Writer/Designer	• Who composed this text? • What else has this person composed? • What social, historical, cultural, or economic influences can you identify? • What point of view does he or she adopt?	• How do you wish to represent yourself in your text? • How can you convince your audience that you are worth taking seriously? • What's your point of view?
Purpose	• What does the author/designer hope to accomplish? • What social, political, or economic influences can you identify?	• What do you want to communicate? • What is your most important goal?
Medium/Genre	• What media are used — print? electronic? handwriting? type? paint? film? • What is the genre — essay? journal? letter? story? poem? ad? painting? photograph? collage? something else?	• What media will you use — print? electronic? handwriting? film? paint? type? • What is the genre — essay? journal? ad? letter? painting? photograph? collage? story? something else?
Subject	• What is the text about? • What statement does the text make, and how is that message supported? • What other texts exist on this topic and what other texts are referred to?	• What is your text about? • What other texts should you refer to? • Where will you find facts, examples, images, and other material?

	As a Reader	As a Writer or Designer
Audience	• What is your initial reaction? • What is the audience assumed to know or believe? • Who is the intended audience? Are you a member of this group?	• Who is your intended audience? • What are they likely to know and believe about your subject? • How can you interest them in your subject?
Organization	• How is the text organized? • Is the arrangement what you would expect or is it a surprise? • What is included? excluded? emphasized? not emphasized?	• How will you organize your text? • Is a particular organization required, or do you have some choice? • What will you emphasize? What then might you pay less attention to?
Style/Tone	• How would you characterize the style — academic? hip? formal? informal? • How would you characterize the tone — serious? humorous? satiric? something else?	• What style are you aiming for — formal? informal? academic? fanciful? • What tone should you adopt — serious? witty? light-hearted? something else?

picturing texts

RIJKS MUSEUM
amsterdam
9 maart - 20 mei 2007

MICHAEL SWEERTS

Alle dagen open van 10 tot 5 uur • Info: 020 6747 047 / www.rijksmuseum.nl • Gratis toegang t/m 18 jaar

When we hear the word "writing," we picture words. Writing brings to mind images of books filled with page after page of written words. Books with many pictures we think of as "picture books," and we expect to find them in the children's and visual arts sections of bookstores. Yet our daily experience with written words tells us something different. On the one hand, stories are often illustrated with drawings; newspaper articles include photos; Web sites are full of written words, images, and sounds. On the other hand, television, which we think of as a *visual* medium, now includes many written words, from bulleted information on news shows to the sports scores that run across the bottom of the screen.

All of these verbal and visual texts have a third important component: DESIGN. If you look up the word *design* in a dictionary, you'll find it means to plan, or create, or "plot out." *By design* means "on purpose." And indeed we can now design every- thing we write, choosing typefaces and fonts, using color, adding images, creating charts and graphs. Computers even allow us to write in genres that used to be the domain of professionals, as word-processing software enables us to compose a brochure almost as easily as a letter.

Design is an important element in communicating our message. How we design a text will determine the response of the reader. The more we understand how texts work, the better we can design our words, images, and graphics to achieve our goals. Sometimes words work best; other times, images; sometimes, both. See, for example, how you might describe a museum with words alone, or with a combination of words and images. Following are three such descriptions of museums on the National Mall between the Capitol and the Washington Monument in Washington, D.C.

A VERBAL description—one using words alone—might simply describe the museums; it might look something like this:

National Museum of American History

Experience the history of the United States in this huge museum. Exhibits range from the flag that inspired Francis Scott Key to write the "Star-Spangled Banner" to Julia Child's kitchen. One popular exhibit is of the First Ladies' inaugural gowns. <www.americanhistory.si.edu>

National Museum of Natural History

Learn about the history of Earth and the creatures that have lived on it. Exhibits include dinosaur skeletons, a life-size model of a blue whale, the famous Hope Diamond, and an insect zoo. Children love the hands-on Discovery Room. <www.mnh.si.edu>

National Air and Space Museum

See historic aircraft—including the Wright Brothers' 1903 flying machine, Charles Lindbergh's *Spirit of St. Louis,* and the *Apollo 11* command module—and a lunar rock that visitors can touch. The museum includes an IMAX theater with four screens and the Albert Einstein Planetarium. <www.nasm.edu>

National Gallery of Art

View one of the world's greatest collections of European and American art, dating from the Middle Ages to the present. A new sculpture garden becomes a popular skating rink in winter. <www.nga.gov>

National Museum of African Art

Housed in this mostly underground building is the only American museum dedicated to art from sub-Saharan Africa, an important resource for the study of African art and culture. <www.nmafa.si.edu>

These verbal descriptions give us a general idea about what is in each museum, but they are not very helpful if we want to know where the museums are located in relation to one another and in what sequence they might best be visited. This information could be conveyed with words alone, but a map provides a much simpler explanation.

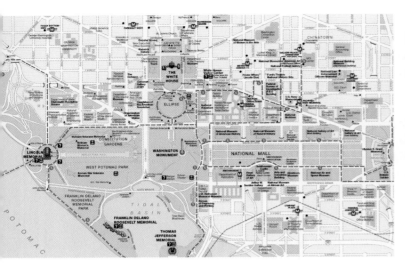

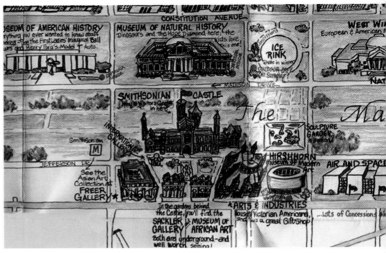

Left: National Park Service Map of the National Mall. Right: From *MapEasy's Guidemap to Washington D.C.*, 2002.

The National Park Service Map of the National Mall on the left shows where the museums are located, but it does not help us to *see* them, or to know what is in their collections. Better than either of the preceeding examples is the *MapEasy's Guidemap to Washington D.C.*, shown on the right, which calls itself "a location map and guidebook in one," and combines a map, verbal information, and sketches of important buildings all in the same text. Using this *Guidemap*, we see where each museum is, what it looks like, and some details about what's inside.

The *MapEasy's Guidemap* is the work of a professional artist, but computers allow all of us to combine verbal and visual texts when we need to. The question now is not if but *when* we should use images and when we should use words. An even more important question is *how* to use each effectively. This chapter tackles those questions and introduces some key words and concepts for working with visual and verbal texts.

We use many of the same terms to talk about verbal and visual texts. Description, comparison, point of view, emphasis: all are concepts that apply to both words and images. These concepts refer to basic decisions we make about how to represent the world. No matter how factual we try to make our words or how faithfully we attempt to take a picture that represents reality, we still must make decisions—ones that affect how and what our text communicates. Very simply, if we point the camera in one direction, we don't point it in another. Likewise, there are many different approaches to writing about a subject. Take jet planes: we can discuss how they fly, describe them from the point of view of a passenger, analyze the economics or the history of air transportation, and so on. And, there are many ways we can represent an airplane visually. We can photograph it taking off in a blur to show its speed, or show its interior as a wide-angle photo with an NBA star stretched out in a seat to show its generous leg room. We can create a bar graph to show that it's more punctual than other airlines—or ads like the ones here seen in a busy subway station showing that even its Web site saves time.

Whether we're working with words or images, there are some key concepts that help us work with text. A brief discussion of some of these concepts follows. The concepts are arranged alphabetically: balance, classification, comparison and contrast, description, emphasis, metaphor, narration, pattern, point of view, proportion, and unity.

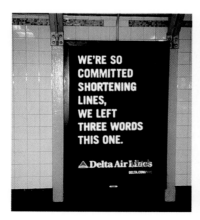

Balance

The notion of balance brings to mind a scale with equal weight on each side. Such balance is called symmetry. Symmetrical sentences tend to be graceful and easy to follow, as we see in John F. Kennedy's famous words: "Ask not what your country can do for you, ask what you can do for your country." At another level, balance in writing means presenting more than one point of view in an argument.

People generally expect balance; indeed, many of us unconsciously rearrange objects to achieve balance. Putting the fork on one side of the plate and the knife on the other seems natural to most people. The Walker Evans photo is an example of symmetry, with the two houses on either side of the image. But balance can be achieved in ways other than the symmetrical placement of objects. Color, contrast, texture, space, line, and movement are also used to achieve visual balance. In an image you might balance a small dark object on one side with a large pale object on the other. The Levi's® SILVERTAB® ad visually balances two boots—one facing left and up, the other, right and down—as well as the Levi's logo on the right with the SILVERTAB® logo on the left.

When a text or an image lacks symmetrical balance, it tends to create a tension that we might find disturbing. But such tension can be visually engaging. The image of the girl looking through the fence, for example, has a deliberate contrast between adult and child, (his hand down, hers up), directing our eyes up-down-up-down. This image is balanced, but assymmetrically balanced.

▶ *Houses, Atlanta.* Photo by Walker Evans, 1936. A perfectly balanced symmetrical background of two houses is tied together by the two movie posters in the foreground.

▶ *Chicago.* Photo by Yasuhiro Ishimoto, 1951/52. This image uses assymetrical balance, the large man on the left with his hand pointing down balanced by the small child in the center whose arm reaches up. Her strong gaze from the center of the image looks directly at the camera—and thus at us, anchoring our focus on the image.

▶ Levi's® SILVERTAB® ad. The two boots are balanced visually, one foot up, one down; and the SILVERTAB® logo on the left balances the Levi's® logo on the right.

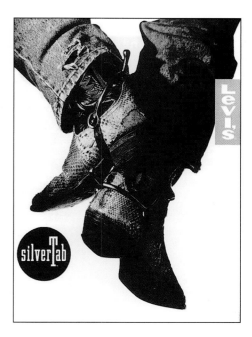

Classification is one means of organizing and analyzing a topic. When we classify, we group things into categories according to their similarities. If we were writing about Greek architecture, for example, we might classify various buildings as Doric, Ionic, or Corinthian. We could do this both verbally and visually.

Often, visual cues are critical for classifying different kinds of animals —for example, the difference between a sockeye and coho salmon—yet we still require names to identify the categories. Many classifications depend entirely on words. The classifications of crimes into felonies and misdemeanors or college courses into lower-division, upper-division, and graduate would be impossible without words.

▶ Greek architecture can be classified as Doric, Ionic, or Corinthian, according to the shapes at the tops of columns.

Doric entablature

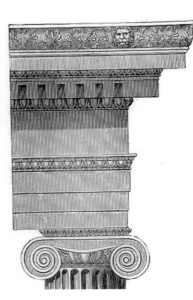

Ionic entablature

Corinthian entablature

▶ Apples classified according to variety.

▶ Our table of contents uses typography to classify parts of the book—one font for chapter titles, another smaller font for headings.

Comparison and Contrast

In both writing and design, we regularly use comparison to explain or demonstrate an idea. Recognizing similarities and differences is basic to thinking and essential to learning. Animals in the same family, for example, have basic similarities (ibises all have long curved bills), but different species also have differences (white-faced ibises have reddish faces surrounded by a white border; glossy ibises have dark faces).

Comparison is a frequent strategy for organizing units of writing. We often can explain something unfamiliar by comparing it to something more familiar, especially when similarities and differences are noted.

Comparison is also a good way of underlining a point. Advertising often uses strong comparisons in this way. Juxtaposing images side by side that either relate to each other or are the opposite of each other is a strategy used regularly in the visual arts. Many elements are used to create contrast in design, including color, focus, scale, texture, and shape. Comparisons are often made with charts and graphs. The performance of an individual stock, for example, is often represented on a graph with the relevant benchmark index, such as the S&P 500 index.

▶ *At the Time of the Louisville Flood.* Photo by Margaret Bourke-White, 1937. The juxtaposition of the poster proclaiming prosperity and the long line of unemployed workers contrasts the American dream with the reality these workers were experiencing.

▶ These signs for men's and women's restrooms compare the ways men and women use a toilet to differentiate one restroom from the other. No words are needed.

Description

The familiar saying that "a picture is worth a thousand words" is often used to claim the superiority of images for description. But although images can show us quickly and often very accurately what something looks like, they cannot tell us what it smells, sounds, or feels like the way that words can. Of course, words and images can work together, with words describing details we may not be able to see.

Close observation of details is the key to successful description, whether verbal or visual. Beginning in the 1600s, microscopes allowed scientists to see things that are too small for the naked eye, but the scientists could describe these details only with drawings. Today, researchers depend on accurate and thorough photographic descriptions made with microscopes, telescopes, and other imaging technologies. Photographic description also has become an important part of daily life, as we are reminded whenever we cash a check or board an airplane.

▶ *General Store, Moundville, Alabama.* Photo by Walker Evans, 1936. Many words would be required to describe everything that is shown in this photograph.

▶ Engraving of a bug. This engraving by Francesco Stelluti (1577–1652) is the earliest known illustration drawn from a microscope.

▶ This Land Rover ad uses a photo to show an amusing situation–and to describe the kind of drivers who choose Land Rovers.

Emphasis

The volume of words and images we encounter daily is overwhelming, leaving us no choice but to look at them selectively. Writers and designers all want first to attract our attention and then to direct us to what they consider important. One way they focus our attention is by giving emphasis to certain material.

Writers have many tools for creating emphasis, including headings, boxes, callouts, typesizes, boldfacing, italics, and sentence structure. The placement of elements matters. Whatever comes at the beginning or end—whether it be of a book, a chapter, a paragraph, or a sentence—is most likely to be remembered.

In most images, emphasis can be created by composition, by choosing and arranging elements in order to direct the viewers' eyes to whatever the designer wants them to notice. The photograph of a Georgia convict on his day of release does not show his face but instead places his hands at the center, letting them suggest his nervousness. Size and color can also be critical, as the example from *World Tour* magazine illustrates.

▶ *John, Day of Release, Georgia.* Photo by Michael Stipe. This picture emphasizes the inmate's hands, focusing our attention on his nervousness on the day of his release from prison.

▶ Pages from *World Tour* Magazine. These pages show emphasis in different ways—with type so large it almost doesn't fit on the page, with headings that are sized differently in a way that affects their meaning, and with a single line on a black page.

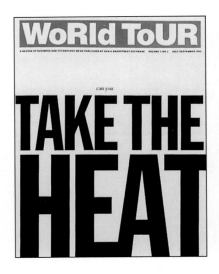

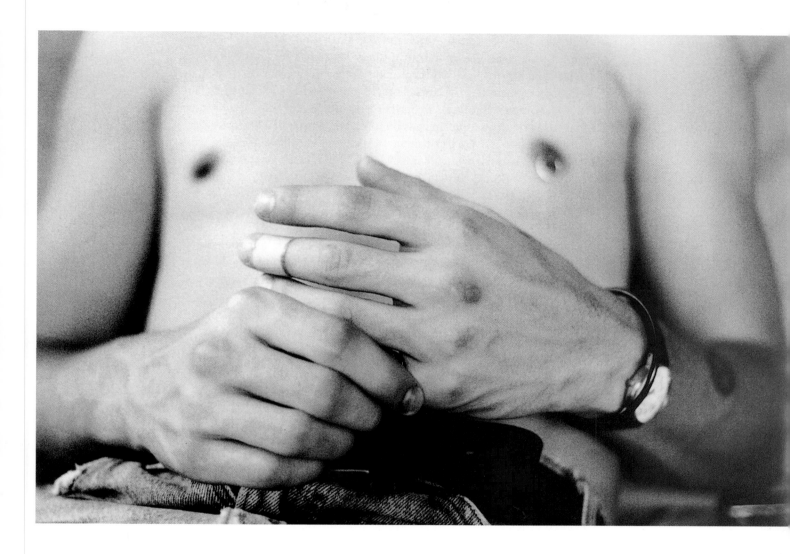

"Friends, Romans, countrymen, lend me your ears," begins the famous speech from *Julius Caesar*. When we hear these familiar words, we do not think about their literal meaning unless we pause to consider that Mark Antony was not asking the crowd to remove their ears and pass them to him.

When you tell a friend "your barber is a butcher," you do not mean that the barber carves up animals on the side. Instead, you likely are teasing him or her about a bad haircut. A meaning associated with the word "butcher" is carried over to "barber." These are examples of metaphor, language that paints a picture in our minds, allowing us to "see" a comparison or analogy and thus to better understand it.

Metaphors can be made with images as well as with words. Often, visual metaphors use a familiar image in an unexpected way as a way of making a point—turning a cigarette into a smoking gun, for example, to show how dangerous smoking is. The fresher the metaphor, the more impact it is likely to have. Overly familiar metaphors lose impact over time until they become clichés.

Metaphors always bring additional associations to the literal meaning. The spoof Marlboro ad is metaphorical precisely because it isn't just an image of a Chinese man smoking.

▶ Spoof ad. The Great Wall of China replaces the OK corral in this parody of an old Marlboro ad. Note the name change, from Marlboro to Malboro, mal connoting "bad." Adbusters <*www.adbusters.com*>.

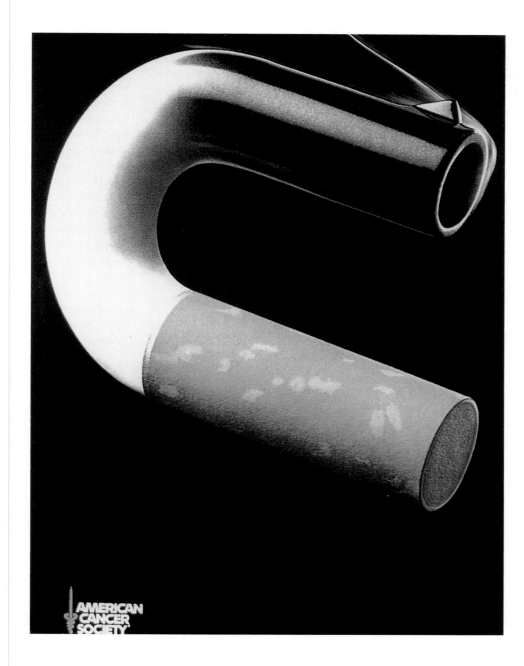

American Cancer Society ad. This ad against smoking uses a simple but effective metaphor: a cigarette as a smoking gun.

Narration

Narrative writing tells a story, "what happened." Language is well suited for narration. Children can tell about what they did at the playground because language, like events in time, flows in sequence. Although we often think of narratives as stories and novels, many other kinds of writing depend on narration. Histories and travel accounts are obviously narratives, but other common genres, such as instructions, lab reports, and minutes of meetings, also follow narrative patterns.

By contrast, images portray a specific moment in time and don't lend themselves as readily to narrative. Nevertheless, images can tell stories. We know something terrible has happened in this photograph of Mannheim, and the caption tells us that the city has been bombed. We do not have to see the planes overhead to understand the horror shown by an unknown photographer in Germany.

The invention of motion pictures made it possible to use many more images to tell a story. Yet, as with still images, movie and television narratives depend on our ability to fill in gaps, to follow abrupt cuts between scenes and to understand flashbacks. Similarly, we can look at a series of still images and create a story—imagining the action and events by connecting the frames.

▶ *Guernica*, by Pablo Picasso, 1937. This painting depicts the bombing of Guernica, Spain, during the Spanish Civil War. It shows a scene very similar to that in the Mannheim photo, even down to the architectural background, but renders it in a different manner. By overlapping multiple views of people and animals, Picasso creates a dynamic composition of twisted movement that echoes the anguish of his subjects.

▶ Street scene following the bombing of Mannheim, Germany, World War II. We understand instantly the story this photo tells, starting with the woman's face looking straight at us in shock and pain.

▶ Stills from an early
motion picture, 1902.

Pattern

▶ The Chinese symbol of Yin and Yang.

▶ Left: Wrangler ad, 1998. This ad literally reverses background and foreground by cutting a hole in a billboard in the shape of pants. The background (the trees) becomes the foreground as a pattern that we see on the pants.

Writers use patterns to make meaning. We recognize certain kinds of writing by the patterns they follow. For example, we depend on certain patterns to read a newspaper: the comics, the classified ads, the stock market report, the box score of a baseball game, and the kinds of headings that announce them.

One important design pattern is *notan*, a Japanese word that means dark and light. The idea of notan is expressed in the ancient Chinese symbol of Yin and Yang, in which light and dark revolve in equilibrium around a center. Often there is a clever reversal of foreground and background in a notan pattern as in the legs image on the facing page: focus on the dark and you see men's legs; focus on the light and you see women's legs.

But notan is not just an optical pattern; it is one way we see the world. We see it simultaneously as parts and as a whole. Think, for example, of how we see the individual trees in a forest. Do we see the trees, the light between them, or both? We can read the fashion photo here in a similar way—when we look at the white, we see gloves; when we look at the dark part of the image, we see something else. Our eyes move back and forth, between the white and the black; neither is foreground or background. The creators of the Wrangler ad have done this by actually cutting a pair of pants out of the white billboard, allowing the actual trees in the background to show through. When we look at the trees, we see pants; when we look at the white banner, we also see the shape of pants.

We rely on patterns both to communicate and to understand. Patterns lead us to read texts in certain ways. We expect cartoons to be funny and when they're not, we wonder why. The same is true of visual patterns.

▶ This image uses a black-and-white notan pattern—focus on the dark, and you will see men's legs; change focus to the light, and you'll see women's legs.

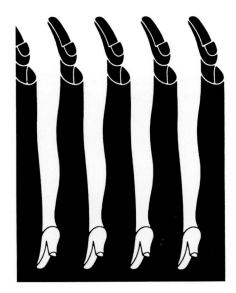

This fashion photo uses a light-dark pattern to direct our attention as our eyes dance from foreground to background and back again.

Point of View

Point of view refers to perspective. Writing can be in the first person singular "I" ("I have a dream") or the third person singular "he" or "she" ("Mrs. Dalloway said she would buy the flowers herself"). Ads frequently use the second person "you" ("You'll love what we have in store for you!"). It's also possible to write in the first person plural "we," as we often do in this book.

In images, point of view refers to the vantage point the designer provides. For example, a painter might show a person facing us or in profile, from above or below, close or distant. Writers, too, describe things from various vantage points—giving a close-up or distant point of view, moving from left to right, top to bottom, and so on.

We use our knowledge of perspective to understand space and depth in an image. We know that objects in the foreground tend to be larger than those in the background and that things in the front overlap things behind them. Colors fade with distance, disappearing into the haze of the atmosphere. Writers also foreground subjects, by describing them in detail while giving little mention to other possible subjects, causing them to fade into the background. With writing as with images, a subject becomes more or less prominent depending on how closely it is examined.

Designers sometimes exaggerate perspective to grab attention, as in the psychiatrist's ad on this page in which the shoes in the foreground are gigantic. We should be aware of point of view because it affects meaning. Advertisers use the second person to imply that there's something *you* need to have: the psychiatrist ad puts the reader in the shoes of someone who clearly needs to visit a psychiatrist.

Afghanistan. Photo by James Nachtwey, 1996. The vantage point of the photo accentuates the incongruity of two Afghan boys sitting on a cannon as if it were a teeter-totter and the nearby city that was presumably destroyed by such weapons.

At left, ad intended to show an advertising agency's ability to design attention-getting ads. The extreme camera angle and point of view result in an image that grabs our attention.

Proportion refers to the relationship of parts. The term is used much more in design than in writing, yet when we pick up a book printed in the nineteenth century and find a paragraph that runs for several pages, our modern sense of proportion tells us that the paragraph is too long. Likewise, when a writer makes a strong claim about a particular issue, we expect to find sufficient evidence and reasons to support the claim.

Proportion also refers to the relationship of one element to another within a whole piece. Since we tend to see the world in relation to ourselves, the scale of something in relation to the size of a human is generally used as the reference point in our minds. Scale that seems to be out of proportion usually grabs our attention, such as the girl who evidently has outgrown her playhouse. Frank Horvat's image of Paris manipulates size for striking effect, a technique commonly used in advertising.

▶ *Paris.* Photo by Frank Horvat, 1974. The proportion of the shoes in relation to the people and buildings in the distance focuses our eye on the shoes, the most important part of this fashion photo.

▶ *Katherine in the Playhouse.* Photo by Margaret Sartor, 1989. Proportionally, the child becomes a third column holding up the house.

All texts include various discrete parts: sentences, paragraphs, lists, headings, illustrations, colors, and so on. It's important for us as writers to create unity, a clear focus on a main idea or on some dominant impression. In writing, unity is achieved by consistency in subject matter and organization, including headings and titles. Topic sentences, consistent use of terms, and clear transitions from one point to another also help to articulate the point we are trying to make.

In art and design, the unifying structure may be apparent or it may be invisible. Methods to establish unity include the use of repetition or of an overall pattern. Unity is achieved in the photo below in several ways: the girls are dressed alike, are of similar age, and are facing each other. The viewer's eye is drawn to the center of the photo as we follow their gaze. In the Link photo, there's a unity of subject matter, forms of transportation: a field of cars, an airplane on the movie screen, a train roaring by.

Magazine designers rely on an invisible grid that underlies the headings, words, photos, and other elements and that creates unity between two facing pages. If the grid is simple, the variations are few. If the grid is complex—three or more columns, for instance—the variations are numerous. The grid provides a unity to the text by creating an underlying pattern the eye can recognize.

▶ *Hot Shot Eastbound, at the Iaeger Drive-In.* Photo by O. Winston Link, 1955. Three modes of transportation and the strange cinematic lighting unify this photograph.

▶ From *Other Pictures,* by Thomas Walther. The hair ribbons create a physical unity, as does the way the girls are all looking at one another, leading viewers to follow their gaze.

Images and graphics are especially common in certain kinds of writing. Even information that is easy to follow with words alone sometimes becomes much easier to *understand* with graphics. Take, for example, a set of facts about the composition of Earth's atmosphere. We can write that our atmosphere contains 78 percent nitrogen, 21 percent oxygen, and minor amounts of argon, neon, methane, ozone, carbon dioxide, carbon monoxide, and sulfur dioxide that total 1 percent. But see how much easier this information is to understand when presented visually. The fact that nitrogen is the predominant gas in our atmosphere is immediately visible in the PIE CHART—and therefore it is much easier to remember.

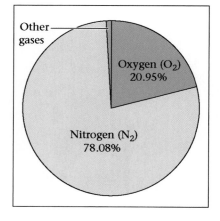

A pie chart is a way to show statistics when the proportion of the segments to the whole is important. This chart also uses color to differentiate one segment from another.

Some concepts are so difficult to understand through words alone that they almost demand a visual explanation. Our understanding of our planet as a complex, evolving system depends on the visualization of key concepts, even if they are presented in words. The examples in this section are from Stephen Marshak's *Earth: Portrait of a Planet*, an introductory geology textbook. Early in the book, Marshak explains the concept of air pressure.

The density of the atmosphere at a given elevation reflects the pressure caused by the weight of the overlying column of air; this overlying air decreases with increasing altitude, so pressure also decreases with increasing altitude. By definition, pressure is the "push" acting on a material (pressure = force per unit area); in this case it squeezes molecules in the air closer together. At sea level, air pressure on average is 1 atmosphere (atm; 1 atm = 1.03 kilograms per square centimeter = 14.7 pounds per square inch; and 1 atm = 1.01 bars, another unit of pressure); at an elevation of 5.6 km, air pressure is 0.5 atm (50 percent of the air lies below 5.6 km); while at the peak of Mt. Everest, 8.85 km high, air pressure is only 0.3 atm.

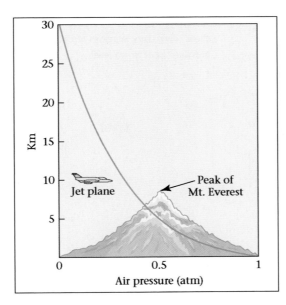

A graph displaying the variation of air pressure with elevation is enhanced by the use of images, which graphically illustrate altitude.

The statistics that Marshak describes are in a continuous relationship. Such relationships can be visually depicted as a graph, such as the one above displaying the variation in air pressure according to altitude. The atmospheric pressure 30 kilometers above sea level is only 1 percent of the pressure at sea level. The image of the jet plane flying at 10 kilometers above Earth and the peak of Mt. Everest at 8.85 kilometers provides visual indicators of altitude.

Visual presentations do more than simply convey information; they can illustrate powerful analogies. The reason why the atmosphere is denser near sea level is because the weight of the upper atmosphere presses down on the molecules in the lower atmosphere. That's easy enough to say with words, but see how much easier it is to comprehend when shown visually.

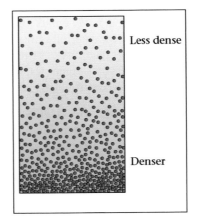

A graphic depiction of atmospheric density makes the concept easy to see.

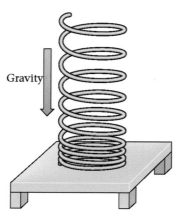

▶ A drawing that serves as a visual analogy to show how gravity increases atmospheric pressure closer to sea level.

Gravity

This principle can also be illustrated with the visual analogy of a spring, showing how the weight of gravity in the upper portion of the spring squeezes together the coils on the lower part. Again, the visual explanation is easier to understand than the verbal explanation.

Readers often need words to interpret an image—as the captions here demonstrate. Some images require other images. See the photo here of an island surrounded by a lagoon and a coral reef. Stephen Marshak explains what constitutes a lagoon and reef:

> In shallow-marine settings where relatively little clastic sediment (sand and mud) enters the water, and where the water is fairly warm, clear, and full of nutrients, most sediment is made up of the shells of organisms. . . . Beaches collect sand composed of shell fragments, lagoons (quiet water) are sites where lime mud accumulates, and reefs consist of coral and coral debris.

The photo helps us see what the words say. But a more effective way of explaining how a lagoon and reef form around an island is with a drawing *and* words. The drawing shows how they build up over time; the words label the key elements of the image. Together, photo and drawing—and captions—help us understand how lagoons and coral reefs are formed.

▶ (a) A coral reef and adjacent lagoon surrounding an island in the South Pacific. (b) The different carbonate environments associated with a reef. The photo and drawing show two different points of view, aerial and underwater, the process and the result.

(a)

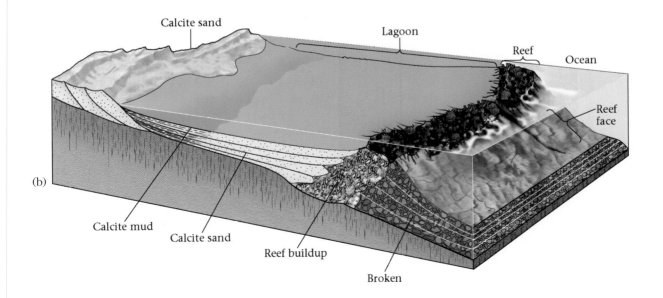

(b)

Calcite sand

Lagoon

Reef

Ocean

Reef face

Calcite mud

Calcite sand

Reef buildup

Broken

Some visual texts require no explanation—we can tell just by looking at them what they are or what they say. Some visuals, however, need to be explained with words. Sometimes parts of a visual might be labeled with words, as some of the charts in the preceding section are. But usually images or charts that need to be explained are accompanied by captions. Whatever else they do, captions affect and even direct what we see. We see the photo of the dog shown here one way with a caption telling us that his name is Finny—but we would see him differently if the caption told us he had recently bitten a child, or that he was in need of a new home.

Captions generally identify the visual and give any necessary information about the visual—title, author, date, any source information if it's taken from another source. In addition, they might include any information necessary to explain the visual—what it demonstrates, why it's important, and so on.

▶ *Finny surveys winter in New York from the warmth of John's overcoat.* Photo by Michael Ian. This caption focuses our attention on the dog. But imagine the same photograph used in a fashion magazine in an article about winter coats. The caption might then tell us that the coat is a wool-cashmere blend, is made by Canali, and can be found at Saks Fifth Avenue. In each case, the caption directs the way we read the photo.

WHAT WE SEE WHEN LOOKING AT A TEXT

What we see when looking at a text affects the way we understand it. The process of seeing a visual text is different from reading words. Words can be highlighted, boldfaced, capitalized, or italicized to draw a reader's attention or to add emphasis where desired. And readers typically follow a predictable path, starting at the beginning and reading to the end. With visual texts, a reader's eye is more free to go where it will. The reader of a visual text will read the many details of the entire image simultaneously in an instant. Then almost immediately, the eyes begin to wander around the image, caught and directed by the details that attract them.

The word "seeing" brings to mind the way we use our eyes to perceive patterns of light and dark and shapes and such. But seeing is as much about memory and experience as it is about perception. We imagine that we see things as they "are"—that a photo of a person on the beach with a deep suntan might strike us as healthy, but a dermatologist might see the same person as having damaged skin and at risk of cancer.

Seeing is learned. It is as much about making sense of what we see as it is about using our eyes to recognize patterns. As children, we learn to perceive light and shadow as light and shadow and not as tangible forms because when we reach out to touch them we cannot physically feel them. We also learn to perceive distance so that when we see a tiny figure in the distance, we recognize it as such and not as a miniature man within arm's reach. As we develop, we incorporate more and more of our own personal experiences and knowledge into our understanding of what we see. When we walk alongside of a railroad track, it does not become narrower the farther we walk even though we might see it that way initially due to perspective. When we use visuals as a form of communication, we count on broader cultural and historical contexts—we know, for example, that a red octagon means stop in the United States sometimes even without the word "STOP" on it.

▶ This image shows us a classic photography trick, playing with changes in scale due to distance. By lining up one figure with another, the photographer creates the illusion that the small figure is a miniature. We learn as children to understand perception and can therefore translate this optical trick in our minds and recognize it as a trick and not as "real." Photo by Sam Mapp.

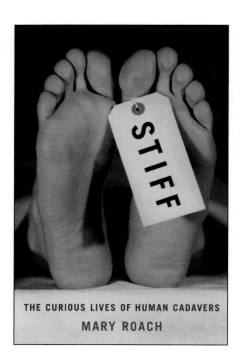

THE CURIOUS LIVES OF HUMAN CADAVERS

MARY ROACH

▶ This book cover design uses a disturbing image—of a cadaver—to grab our attention and to tell us what the book is about. Together, the title and the design make the book noticeable and memorable. Design by Keenan; photo by Marc Atkins/ Panoptika, 2003.

image conscious

The images on this page are cropped in a way that leaves out certain details. What is the effect of this cropping—how does it affect the statement each book cover makes? Examine some of the other photos in this chapter to see what is left out of each image, and how that affects the "meaning" of the image.

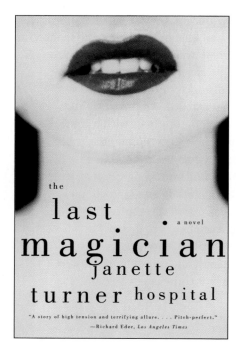

the
last
• a novel
magician
janette
turner hospital

"A story of high tension and terrifying allure. . . . Pitch-perfect."
—Richard Eder, Los Angeles Times

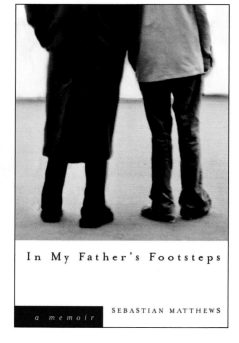

In My Father's Footsteps

SEBASTIAN MATTHEWS

a memoir

▶ The covers on the right use soft focus and unusual cropping to convey meaning in a simple and direct way.

What we see depends on what gets our attention, on what details we observe, and on our own experience and memory. Usually the more important, extreme, unexpected, or disturbing something is, the quicker it catches our eye and also the more memorable it is. But often we do not see well, for many different reasons—we're distracted, or not looking carefully; or personal biases cause us to see something a certain way—or not to see it at all. If we don't understand what we are looking at, we may not even recognize that it exists. If we don't understand the concept of "mockery," for instance, we cannot recognize a mocking expression on someone's face nor can we fully understand what it means.

snapshot

A snapshot is a photo casually taken, generally by an amateur. Snapshots are glued into family photo albums or carried around to show off kids or new babies or emailed to friends and family. Unlike photos in newspapers or magazines, snapshots don't routinely include captions. Or do they? When Dad shows off a family photo, he generally tells us about it. Photo albums usually say when and where photos were taken—Cancun, Grandma's sixty-fifth birthday party, and so on. Emailed photos are rarely sent all alone; they come embedded in a message made up of words. Whatever form the words take, they function much like captions.

Find a snapshot you've taken or received and write a caption for it. You'll need to have a particular audience in mind and a purpose—to tell someone about a friend or family member, to record an important event as a keepsake in a photo album, or even just to write about a photo for your writing teacher.

The goal of this brief assignment is to think about what you can do with words and images. What can you communicate with a photo alone? with words alone? What can you do with a caption—What kind of information is appropriate? What's not appropriate? Write a short paragraph exploring these questions.

By Means of the Visible

MITCHELL STEPHENS

Mitchell Stephens (b. 1949) is a professor of journalism and mass communication at New York University. This essay is a chapter from his book *The Rise of the Image, the Fall of the Word* (1998). As the title indicates, the book examines the general criticism made by educators and cultural critics that electronic media have eroded national consciousness. You've no doubt heard charges that the average American reads less often and writes less well than once was the case. A more sweeping claim alleges that the saturation of images we experience daily makes us think less profoundly. Stephens answers these criticisms by first placing them in a historical perspective. He acknowledges that words often embody ideas better than images, but at the same time he argues that we should better understand the possibilities of image communication.

Painting is much more eloquent than speech, and often penetrates more deeply into one's heart.
—ERASMUS

Ask the creators of the wilder, more interesting-looking new television commercials, promotional announcements, news videos and even feature films where they found their inspiration, and their answer, more often than not, will contain the same three letters. Director Oliver Stone, when citing the antecedents of the jangled, fast-cut style he used in the movie *Natural Born Killers*, mentioned "commercials and MTV." Don Schneider is senior creative director of the BBDO advertising agency, which has produced some groundbreaking Pepsi commercials, including [the] attack on the artichoke chef and the old TV.[1] He made a more sweeping confession: "Ninety percent of this has to do with MTV." ABC News took more than ideas from MTV: It hired one of the youth network's talented young producers, David Berrent.

MTV's influence begins, of course, with the music videos themselves—which "might be the only new popular art form in American life," Norman Mailer has suggested. But many of the network's innovations appeared as more substantive

supplements to those dizzying collages of guitar strummers and visual metaphors for lust. ABC wooed Berrent after executives saw his documentary *Decade*, a historical look, MTV-style, at the 1980s.

Decade includes a thirty-three-second segment on former President Ronald Reagan's planned "Star Wars" defense system. I make no claims for it journalistically, but in technique and style it is intriguing. An excerpt from a Reagan speech on national security is shown, along with an attack on Star Wars by the late rock musician Frank Zappa. These are sound-bites—the same (except for the use of Zappa as an expert) as might be seen in a traditional news story. But in between, Berrent placed a kind of rock video: While the phrase "guns in the sky" is sung over and over, and Zappa begins to talk, computer simulations of lasers attacking rockets are shown on screen. Those scenes, in turn, are interrupted by flashing, static images: a dollar sign, the symbol warning of possible nuclear contamination, the skull-and-crossbones symbol for danger.

Neither the word *danger* nor its synonyms is vocalized. Berrent clearly is relying on these flashing images not just to illustrate what is being said

---

1. A TV commercial in which a dull, old-fashioned ad explodes into a fast-cutting dance montage.

but to communicate their own meanings. In the introduction to [an] ABC documentary on churches, [director] Roberta Goldberg, who learned from Berrent, does the same with the shot of three candles being extinguished. These images, the point is, are intended to take the place of words.

Many of the images that decorate our world have similar aspirations. Among the most interesting are the icons that increasingly crowd the edges of computer screens. Small drawings—of a file folder, for instance—first began to replace lines of text on computer displays at a research center run by the Xerox Corporation in the 1970s. The driving force behind this work was Alan Kay, a Ph.D. in computer science, whose dreams for the future of the computer, inspired in part by Marshall McLuhan, included a major role for images.[2] Each icon used on the screen, Kay suspected, was worth not just a word but a whole sentence.

A group of Apple Computer executives and engineers made an expedition to the Xerox center in 1979. They returned with many ideas and then added some of their own. In 1983 Apple released a slow, expensive, unsuccessful, "graphics-oriented" computer named Lisa and then, the next year, a faster, relatively inexpensive, hugely successful computer, using a similar operating system, named Macintosh. The indomitable Microsoft Corporation noticed the idea (Apple suggested, in court, a different verb), and with the success of the Windows operating system in 1990, sets of icons began to appear on most computer screens.

Similar images currently express meanings on traffic signs, rest room doors, Olympic venues and biceps. Armies continue to march under images; the devout of many faiths continue to pray to them. The Pioneer 10 spacecraft, now embarked on a long journey toward the star Aldebaran, is equipped with a plaque designed to satisfy the curiosity of any aliens encountered along the way—a plaque covered not with words but with images (sketches of a naked man and woman, our solar system, the position of our sun, the hydrogen atom).

Some meanings clearly are better communicated pictorially than verbally, as David Berrent, Alan Kay and most of the world's painters and sculptors have recognized. We live, however, in a culture that, despite the proliferation of images, not only has little faith in their ability but has at times been actively antagonistic toward them.

The Old Testament, characteristically, does not mince words: "Thou shalt not make unto thee any graven image, or any likeness of any thing that is in heaven above, or that is in the earth beneath"—a commandment second only to the demand that no other gods be worshiped before the source of these commandments. An antagonism toward images first appeared here at the beginning of Western culture. It appeared, too, after the development of the alphabet in Greece: Among Plato's targets in the *Republic* is the painter, whom he dismissed as "a magician and imitator." A similar scorn surfaced among Muslims: Muhammed is said to have proclaimed that "the angels will not enter a temple where there are images."

This fury was unleashed, always, by partisans of the word—written or (for Plato) spoken. Behind it was a multifaceted fear: fear, to begin with, *for* the word. Images—easy to understand, fun to look at—inevitably threatened to turn the populace away from the deeper, more cerebral rewards of sacred writings or philosophic discourse.

---

2. Marshall McLuhan (1911–1980), media culture theorist.

There was fear too of the magic that seems to lurk in images. They steal likenesses. They do what only gods should be able to do: They recreate the living and preserve the dead. It is hard not to see this as black magic. Images allow us actually to look in on (not just hear about) the familiar from another perspective, an external perspective, often a disorienting perspective—to see ourselves, for example. They are, in this way, inherently unnatural—further evidence of magic.

Then there is the persistent "reality" issue. Images look real but are fake. They pretend to be what they are not. They lie. The portrait is a mute, lifeless substitute for the person; the idol, a primitive and superficial knockoff of the god. But that idol is also attractive and easy to see. It can distract from the more profound but more amorphous glories of the god. A painter, Plato warned, can deceive "children and fools" with mere "imitation of appearance," instead of "truth" or "real things." Images can entrance.

Worse, in imitating "real things," images tend to devalue them. This is what the French theorist Jean Baudrillard called "the murderous capacity of images." Once we begin to lose ourselves in this world of illusions, it can begin to seem as if "truth" and "reality" are just further illusions (deserving of quotation marks). Images, on this level, are, as Baudrillard put it, "murderers of the real, murderers of their own model." The person is now seen as if posing for a portrait. The god is perceived as if just another idol.

"Cursed be the man who makes a graven or molten image," the Old Testament proclaims. We have reconciled ourselves to painting and sculpture by now; nevertheless, echoes of that curse can still be heard in many of the jeremiads launched by television's critics—most of whom retain an almost biblical allegiance to the word. The fear behind that curse undoubtedly was also present in some of the admonitions I heard from my parents: "You've had that thing on all evening!" "You look like you're in some kind of trance!" I'm sure it is present too in some my children have heard from me.

For television also has been judged too easy to watch: not sufficiently challenging, cerebral or deep. It displays a similarly suspect magic: It too captures appearances. Television too is accused of being "unreal," of duping children and fools. And television too has seemed to make the world it portrays—the social and political world—less "real." It has helped fill it with "pseudo-events," to use Daniel Boorstin's often-repeated term. "The shadow has become the substance," Boorstin, with deference to Plato, warned.

Here is a prejudice even Thoth did not face.[3] Video is not only suspiciously new and immature; it is tainted by its reliance upon facile, shallow, unreal, cursed images.

*   *   *

Oddly, it was a group of thinkers not only steeped in biblical values but influenced by Platonic (or, more precisely, neo-Platonic) values who began to question this fear and scorn. "We do no harm," Pope Gregory I wrote in a letter in 599, "in wishing to show the invisible by means of the visible." In the thirteenth century, Thomas Aquinas outlined an argument in support of "the institution of images in the Church."

The power of the visible has been disparaged and then rediscovered many times since: with the development of painting in the Renaissance (including the use of perspective), with the woodcut and the mechanical reproduction of illustrations, with

—————
3. Thoth, Egyptian god of wisdom.

the arrival of photography. Over the centuries, those prepared to defend images have produced various calculations of the comparative "worth" of pictures and words. They often seem silly. However, an investigation of the potential of video must begin by confronting the lingering prejudice against images and acknowledging that there *are* some things images do better than words.

Images, to begin with, are marvelously (though never perfectly) accessible. Aquinas explained that the "unlettered" might learn from pictures "as if from books." (Christians were not prepared to ignore the needs of the uneducated, of children or of fools.) We take advantage of the accessibility of images to aid those who may not understand a particular language—visitors to the Olympics, perhaps, or any space aliens who happen upon Pioneer 10.

Another strength of images is their concision— a significant advantage for drivers speeding by or on a crowded computer screen. A native American rock drawing found near a precipitous trail in New Mexico, for example, shows a goat who is climbing but a man on a horse who has fallen. It is difficult to imagine a sign made for the "lettered" that could communicate this warning more efficiently. David Berrent and the others who have begun flashing images on our screens are attempting to exploit this efficiency in their efforts to say a lot in a short time.

Images also can wield great power—religious, tribal, romantic, pedagogic. One of David Berrent's productions for ABC was a public-service announcement on behalf, of all things, of PLUS: Project Literacy U.S. In its thirty seconds, five or six fathers are shown reading to or reading with their children, with scenes from children's books and newspapers gently superimposed on top of them. The fathers explain why this activity is important,

but the public-service announcement's power comes not from their words but from the images Berrent has placed before us—images of togetherness, of caring, of warmth.

Aquinas suggested that images can be used to "excite the emotions, which are more effectively aroused by things seen than by things heard." That is why we find images in houses of worship, in military emblems and in tattoos, as well as in public-service announcements. "If the poet can kindle love in man, more so . . . the painter, as he can place the true image of the beloved before the lover," observed Leonardo da Vinci.

There are also understandings, sometimes deep understandings, that can be put into images—accessibly, concisely, powerfully—but are difficult to put into words. The study of botany, zoology, anatomy, geography and astronomy were all advanced during or after the Renaissance by more precise depictions, models, representations and diagrams. "Primates are visual animals," Stephen Jay Gould, the scientist and science writer, has asserted, "and we think best in pictorial or geometric terms. Words are an evolutionary afterthought."

* * *

Bill McKibben was appearing on TV. This was an event akin to the Unabomber going on-line or Ralph Nader driving a Porsche. For McKibben, a distinguished environmental writer, had just published an ardent attack on television: a book, *The Age of Missing Information*, based on his experience in watching every program that had appeared on a ninety-three-channel Virginia cable television system during one twenty-four-hour period. McKibben wrote of his concern not only with what TV offers but with what it does not offer: highs, lows, perspective, consciousness of the body, an awareness of death, of the seasons, of nature and of what happens "behind a face." "We use TV as we use tranquilizers," he concluded. But now here McKibben was on the *Charlie Rose Show*, himself part of the dose.

Among those savoring the irony was the *New Republic*'s Robert Wright, who admitted that McKibben looked more "earnest and thoughtful" than he had expected from reading reviews of his book. "TV has won for his cause one small battle that his book alone couldn't have won," Wright observed, "both because I don't have time to read it and because it is missing some kinds of information. (Some very 'natural' kinds of information, like how a person looks when saying what he believes. The written word, we sometimes forget, was invented as a crude if useful substitute for the real thing.)"

That last thought is worth freeing from parentheses. No one, as Wright noted, has been earnest enough to read through, say, all the publications to be found one day on one newsstand (an exercise likely as dispiriting as McKibben's). But we can still come to some conclusions about what the printed word lacks.

Writing's great limitation grows out of its great strength: its abstractness. It is a system of representation, or code, that represents another system of representation, another code: spoken language. The written word *face*—to oversimplify a bit—calls to mind the sound "fās." It is, therefore, two steps removed from that expressive skin sculpture itself. These steps back needed to be taken and have been hugely productive. Still, it is important to keep in mind the price paid for that abstraction. Printed words may take us, metaphorically at least, "behind a face"; they can help us see what we might not ordinarily see in a face; but they must work hard to tell us what a glance could about the expression on that face. In interpreting the code we make little use of our natural ability to observe: letters don't smile warmly or look intently.

This code, writing, also ignores our ability to find spatial and temporal connections between objects in the world. When we speak with each other, we can point: "That belongs over there." We can demonstrate: "Then she did this with her hair." We can indicate: "You want to give them control over this?" And we can gesture—with a look, a shrug, a grimace. All this information could alternatively be put into words; it could be written down. But in reading it, rather than seeing it, we sacrifice our ability to quickly and intuitively spot relationships—between here and there, this and that, words and gestures, ideas and expressions. We sacrifice our ability to judge earnestness and thoughtfulness, say, by observing people's faces as they speak.

Comparing what he saw on those ninety-three channels to what his senses can pick up in nature or at a circus, McKibben moaned that we are "starved on television's visual Pritikin regimen." This is a point I am anxious to debate. But for the moment it is sufficient to note that, if the measure is *direct* stimulation to our senses, a page of print makes a few moments of television look like a five-course French meal.

Printed prose is "an act of extraordinary stylization, of remarkable, expressive self-denial," stated Richard A. Lanham, who writes on Renaissance rhetoric and contemporary computers. Our eyes were selected over millions of years of primate evolution for their ability to notice, search, compare, connect and evaluate. Increasingly, in the five thousand years since the development of writing, they have been reduced to staring at letters of identical size and color, arranged in lines of identical length, on pages of identical size and color. Readers, in a sense, are no longer asked to *see*; they are simply asked to interpret the code.

Written words, as Aquinas realized but we tend to forget, are hardly a perfect form of communication. No such thing exists. I don't want to overstate the case for images—at least still images—either. Certainly, as the Bible seems to suggest, but for centuries most Europeans tended to forget, nonmoving images have great difficulty conveying certain kinds of meaning. There are limits to what the Dutch humanist Erasmus called their eloquence.

Alan Kay ended up dissatisfied with his experiments in the use of images on computer screens. He had understood, from having read educational theory, that icons were good at helping people "recognize, compare, configure." The success of the Macintosh and Windows operating systems has proven that his understanding was correct. But Kay had a grander ambition: He dreamed of using images to express abstract thought. Kay envisioned a kind of language of images.

That is an old dream. It was long surmised that the mysterious hieroglyphs that could be seen on the Egyptian obelisks that had been dragged to Rome represented such a language of images. "The wise of Egypt . . . left aside . . . words and sentences," wrote Plotinus, the third-century neo-Platonist, "and drew pictures instead." As late as the eighteenth century, the historian Vico assumed that "all the first nations spoke in hieroglyphs."

Behind this notion was the belief, still held by many today, that nature is a "book" with a divine author. If each tree, each ox, has a spiritual message for us, then that message might also be "read" in paintings or even iconic representations of trees or oxen. An image language would be closer to that original divine language. Over the centuries many Europeans attempted to craft such a language. They produced various occult codes, systems of gestures, systems of concepts, guides to memory and tools for international understanding.

These various image languages all had something [35] in common: To the extent that they tried to communicate meaning effectively without depending on words, they failed. The conviction that the Egyptians had succeeded in this also crumbled. In 1799 one of Napoleon's soldiers in Egypt happened upon an old stone that included an inscription written both in Egyptian hieroglyphic and in Greek. With the "Rosetta stone" Europe finally was able to piece together accurate translations of those mysterious Egyptian writings, and it became clear that not even hieroglyphic had escaped the dominance of language. Instead, like all other successful writing systems, these icons were directly connected to words: For example, they made heavy use, as in King Narmer's name, of phonetic indicators, of homonyms.

Alan Kay's efforts to produce abstract thought from systems of icons on the computer screen failed, too. "All I can say," Kay wrote, "is that we and others came up with many interesting approaches over the years but none have successfully crossed the threshold to the end user." The problem: "In most iconic languages it is much easier to write the patterns than it is to read them," Kay explained.

Here, for example, is the series of hand signals one Renaissance experimenter, the Abbé de l'Epée, used in his language of gestures to indicate the concept "I believe":

> I begin by making the sign of the first person singular, pointing the index finger of my right hand towards my chest. I then put my finger on my forehead, on the concave part in which is supposed to reside my spirit, that

is to say, my capacity for thought, and I make the sign for *yes*. I then make the same sign on that part of the body which, usually, is considered as the seat of what is called the heart in its spiritual sense. . . . I then make the same sign *yes* on my mouth while moving my lips. . . . Finally, I place my hand on my eyes, and, making the sign for *no*, show that I do not see.

All that is quite clever, even poetic. It must have been great fun to devise but almost impossible for "end users"—those who were watching the abbé's energetic performance—to decipher. That undoubtedly explains why at the conclusion of his elaborate pantomime de l'Epée felt called upon to add one more action: "All I need to do," he stated, "is . . . to write *I believe*."

If images cannot form languages without a reliance upon words, it is in part because they have a great deal of difficulty escaping the affirmative, the past or present indicative. De l'Epée was able at least to shake his head to put something in the negative; in some traffic signs we use a red diagonal line to say the same thing; but most still pictures must strain to say something as simple as "no" or to ask "why?" or to wonder what might be. They state much more effectively than they negate or interrogate or speculate. Pictures are better, similarly, with the concrete than the abstract, better with the particular than the general. These are significant handicaps.

The other great obstacle to images forming a language of their own stems not from their muteness but from the fact that they tend to say too much. For example, Michelangelo's awe-inspiring depiction at the summit of the Sistine Chapel of God giving life to man through the touch of his finger also can be seen as showing a father-son relationship and perhaps a lover-beloved relationship; it can be seen as showing caring, effort, joy, and undoubtedly numerous other emotions. This richness of meaning is testament to the artist's genius. But if we did not receive some verbal explanation, how could we be expected to "read" this scene as we might read a piece of writing?

Knowing the genre helps. The location of this [40] great fresco tells us that we should search for a religious interpretation in it. But which one? The older man could be saving the younger man; he could be calling him to heaven; he could be giving or taking his soul. To know for sure, we must be directed to a story, to Genesis. Were this scene asked to serve as part of a language without the aid of such a story, how could we pinpoint specific meanings in it? "The image is freedom, words are prison," wrote the film director Jean-Luc Godard, never one to shy from controversy, in 1980. "How are laws decreed today? They are written. When your passport is stamped 'entry to Russia forbidden,' it is not done with an image." True, but neither the Bill of Rights nor the Declaration of the Rights of Man was composed in images either. The freedom images provide comes at a price.

"The ability of a visual language to express more than one meaning at once," contended Umberto Eco, "is also . . . its limitation." Eco, whose academic speciality is semiotics, the study of systems of signs, called this excess of meaning "the fatal polysemy of . . . images." Aquinas recognized the problem: "One thing may have similitude to many," he wrote. "For instance the lion may mean the Lord because of one similitude and the Devil because of another." How can we develop a lexicon of images if we have no way of determining which of the many possible interpretations of an image is correct? (The perplexing graphics that are supposed to explain to speakers of different languages how to operate European appliances provide another example of this problem.)

To use images more precisely without captions, explanations or instructions—without words—it is necessary to rely on the most obvious of images, on clichés: a skull and crossbones, for instance, or a father snuggled up with a book and a child. France's expert on semiotics, Roland Barthes, gave the example of the use of a bookcase in the background of a photograph to show that a person is an intellectual. As a result, as images that try to convey meaning without the use of words become less ambiguous, they also become less interesting, less challenging, and vice versa.

"I don't want there to be three or four thousand possibilities of interpreting my canvas," Pablo Picasso once insisted. "I want there to be only one." However, the artist in his more thoughtful moments undoubtedly realized what anyone who has stood before one of his canvases has likely realized: That is impossible.

Words also can say too much, of course. *Man*, *woman*, or *god*, for example, have no shortage of potential meanings. Dictionaries contain lists of them; occasionally we concoct our own. Writers can never be sure that their words have only one possible interpretation. As our literary theorists have spent a third of a century pointing out, readers bring different experiences and interests to the sentences they read and therefore take different meanings from them.

While working on this book, I reread *Madame* 45 *Bovary* and, wouldn't you know, began to uncover in Flaubert's novel a series of lessons about images and words. Did he intend for me to read his book this way? Probably not. Nonetheless, Flaubert's problem with me and probably most of his other readers is much less acute than that faced by the authors of potential image languages. With the help (alas) of a translator I was able to get the gist of Flaubert's words. I followed his narrative. I was not so preoccupied with my own concerns that I missed the fact that he had many things to say that are not communications-related.

Our strategies for reading words are fairly well understood. We can, at least, make use of those dictionaries, with their limited lists of meanings. And the problem of comprehending words is further eased, if never entirely eliminated, by syntax. Using a grammar, the basic structure of which seems built into our genes, we modify the form of our words to signify their relation to their fellows in sentences. And then we narrow their potential meanings further by surrounding them not only with various qualifiers but with prepositions and articles. There are few equivalents for such parts of speech in the realm of the image.

In spoken and written languages, word builds upon word, sentence upon sentence, idea upon idea. The ambiguity of images, on the other hand, is increased by what Alan Kay called their "unsortedness." Painters may have mastered some tricks for guiding our eyes across canvases. But we are not born with, nor have we created, any particularly sophisticated systems for organizing still images to specify or build meanings. "Unlike paragraphs and lists of words, images have no *a priori* order in which they should be understood," Kay noted. "This means that someone coming onto an image from the outside has no strategy for solving it."

This chapter might be helped by a depiction of Thomas Aquinas, Bill McKibben or Alan Kay. It would be useful actually to see how the Abbé de l'Epée looked when he made "the sign of the first person singular." But such concepts as "efficiency," "abstract thought" or "by means of the visible" would be difficult to communicate through still images. And how might an argument composed of such images be organized? Left to right? Up and down? In a kind of circle? Unless, following de l'Epée's lead, such pictures were appended to a written version of the chapter itself, an observer would not know what "strategy" to employ in understanding them.

David Berrent and others of the most interesting workers in video—MTV alumni or MTV watchers—aim a barrage of images at us. Those images can do some things better than words; once we move beyond the scorn and the fears of word lovers, that becomes clear. Certain pictures can put most sentences to shame. But this is as far as I'm willing to go in making the case for still images.

The truth is that I am not one of those folks ₅₀ who spend an inordinate amount of time staring at dew-covered fields, wizened faces, cloud formations, or paintings thereof. It took some decades, and the guidance of a photographer friend, before I learned to notice light, not just the things upon which it shines. I'm good for a few hours in major museums, not a few days. Which is to say that while this is a book that gets rather excited about the potential of image communication, it is not based on a particularly romantic view of images or our visual sense in general.

Some continue to argue that pictures are more honest and profound than words, that they can claim some direct, mystical path to a higher reality. You won't find that argument here. In fact, I've tried to make clear in this chapter that still images operate under severe handicaps when attempting to embody ideas. For certain important purposes, a picture may actually be worth *less* than a single, relatively narrow, well-placed word. I agree with Umberto Eco that some of the most complex uses of images must "still depend (parasitically) on the semantic universe of the verbal language." This, perhaps, is the true "curse" upon those who attempt to communicate through such images, graven or otherwise.

However, Eco did allow for one possible exception to his rule about the limitations of images—an exception even someone who won't pull the car over to gape at a sunset can accept: Eco suggested, with some reservations, that "the images of cinema and television" might escape those limitations.

There is a sense in which David Berrent and his colleagues and successors in video seem better positioned than Michelangelo, Picasso and computer guru Alan Kay might have been to communicate abstract thought unambiguously through images—for motion, sound and computer editing have indeed begun to solve the image's intelligibility problems. And at MTV speeds, in ten or fifteen minutes it is now possible to present *a thousand pictures*.

focus.

1. Stephens begins by discussing commercials and MTV, both of which represent what some critics think is especially wrong with television— flashing images and sound bites with no substance. He quickly turns to the long history of complaints about the power of images to misrepresent, distort, or devalue reality, beginning with criticism in the Hebrew Bible, or Old Testament. As you read, underline each specific complaint about images. Which ones are similar to today's complaints about the general effects that television, videos, and computer images are having on our society?

2. Stephens makes his living by the word. He is a professor, book author, and frequent contributor to the *New York Times*, *Washington Post*, and *Los Angeles Times*. Yet he celebrates the power of the image, especially in digital media, over the word. Do you think he grants too much power to new media? Could he have made the same points in his chapter as effectively on video as he does in print? Why or why not? Think of examples where the same points are made in more than one medium. How does the difference in medium affect the message?

respond.

1. A complaint about images is that the ease of reproducing them on a mass scale diminishes their meaning. This charge is made especially about fine art. For example, you many never have been to the Louvre in Paris, but you recognize images of the Mona Lisa in advertisements, on greeting cards— even on the side of barns! A Web site even gives examples of the Mona Lisa reproduced on socks, puzzles, T-shirts, cookie jars, gift wrap, wrist watches, and other products, along with parodies of the painting—Mona Lisa in hair curlers, Mona Lisa in braces, and so on. Have a look at the site <www.studiolo. org/Mona/MONASV13.htm#LIST>. Do you think that these images help us see the Mona Lisa in new ways or do these uses trivialize the power of a famous painting? Write an essay taking a position on this question, citing Stephens as part of the support for your response.

2. The miniaturization of computers and advances in wireless digital technologies now make it possible for a person to have continuous access to the Internet. As these technologies become less expensive, the decision not to have 24/7 access to the Internet will become more a matter of choice. If continuous access to the Internet becomes part of our daily lives, what changes do you foresee happening? Write an essay imagining your life ten years from now.

3. Elsewhere in *The Rise of the Image, the Fall of the Word*, Stephens argues that video has the potential to give us new perspectives on the world, the way writing and printing once did. Stephens has attempted to demonstrate this claim by composing a series of short travel videos, which you can view at <www.nyu.edu/classes/stephens/Road_Video_Page.htm>. In a short essay, argue for or against Stephens's claim that video can offer new perspectives and ways of thinking, citing examples from his Web videos as evidence for your position.

4. Do you find it surprising that an essay called "By Means of the Visible" consists entirely of words? Imagine you were Stephens's editor. What illustrations would you suggest?

Scott McCloud (b. 1960) is an award-winning writer and illustrator of comics, whose work has appeared in *Wired, Nickelodeon,* and *Computer Gaming World*. His own books include *Zot!* (1984–91), *Destroy!!* (1986), and two books about comics, *Understanding Comics* (1993) and *Reinventing Comics* (2000), from which "Through the Door: Digital Production" is taken. He studied illustration at Syracuse University and then worked at DC Comics until he began publishing his own comics. You can read more about McCloud at <www.scottmccloud.com>, where you will find a timeline of his life thus far, links to his online comics, and the following advice to young artists: (1) Learn from everyone; (2) follow no one; (3) watch for patterns; (4) work like hell.

Through the Door: Digital Production

SCOTT McCLOUD

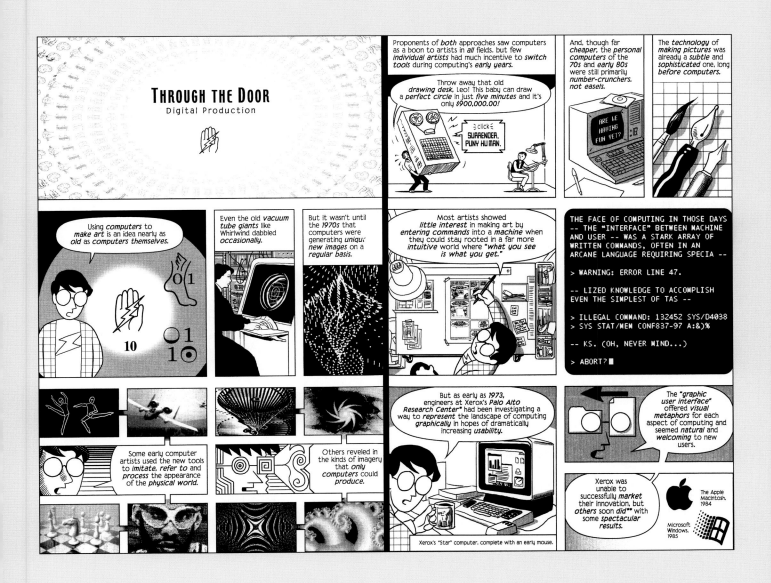

THROUGH THE DOOR
Digital Production

Proponents of *both* approaches saw computers as a boon to artists in *all* fields. but few *individual artists* had much incentive to *switch tools* during computing's *early years.*

Throw away that old *drawing desk,* Leo! This baby can draw a *perfect circle* in just *five minutes* and it's only $900,000.00!

≥ click ≥
SURRENDER, PUNY HUMAN.

And, though far *cheaper,* the *personal computers* of the *70s* and *early 80s* were still primarily *number-crunchers. not easels.*

ARE WE HAVING FUN YET?

The *technology* of *making pictures* was already a *subtle* and *sophisticated* one, long *before computers.*

Using *computers* to *make art* is an idea nearly as *old* as *computers themselves.*

0 1
10
1 ⊙

Even the old *vacuum tube giants* like Whirlwind dabbled *occasionally.*

But it wasn't until the *1970s* that computers were generating *unique new images* on a *regular basis.*

Most artists showed *little interest* in making art by *entering commands* into a *machine* when they could stay rooted in a far more *intuitive* world where *"what you see is what you get."*

THE FACE OF COMPUTING IN THOSE DAYS -- THE "INTERFACE" BETWEEN MACHINE AND USER -- WAS A STARK ARRAY OF WRITTEN COMMANDS, OFTEN IN AN ARCANE LANGUAGE REQUIRING SPECIA --

> WARNING: ERROR LINE 47.

-- LIZED KNOWLEDGE TO ACCOMPLISH EVEN THE SIMPLEST OF TAS --

> ILLEGAL COMMAND: 132452 SYS/D4038
> SYS STAT/MEM CONF837-97 A:&)%

-- KS. (OH, NEVER MIND...)

> ABORT?█

Some early computer artists used the new tools to *imitate, refer to* and *process* the appearance of the *physical world.*

Others reveled in the kinds of imagery that *only* computers could *produce.*

But as early as *1973,* engineers at Xerox's *Palo Alto Research Center** had been investigating a way to *represent* the landscape of computing *graphically* in hopes of dramatically increasing *usability.*

Xerox's "Star" computer, complete with an early mouse.

The *"graphic user interface"* offered *visual metaphors* for each aspect of computing and seemed *natural* and *welcoming* to new users.

Xerox was unable to successfully *market* their innovation, but *others* soon *did** with some *spectacular results.*

 The Apple Macintosh, 1984

Microsoft Windows, 1985

Unfortunately, in the *80s*, the G.U.I.'s impressive toolbox was hampered by a lack of *speed* and *power*.

The adage that *"a picture is worth a thousand words"* proved an *understatement* when a single *print-quality image* could be composed of up to *100,000,000 pixels.***

Thus, the first *digitally-produced* comics** in the mid-80's were necessarily *raw* and required *enormous investments* of *time* and *expense*.

Later, more *elaborate* digital comics art often allied itself with *safe, familiar* genres.

Art from *Batman: Digital Justice* by Pepe Moreno.

As the technology has *matured*, a few have used computers in the service of a distinctly *natural media* sensibility.

Art from *Mr. Punch* by Neil Gaiman and Dave McKean.

And a few, *very* few, have put the most *exotic* aspects of computer generated imagery *front* and *center* in hopes of presenting something unmistakably *new*.

Art from *Blue Loco* by Mark Landman

Meanwhile, *behind the scenes*, computers are becoming ubiquitous in the *finishing* of comic book art for publication.

As of this writing, the *lettering* and *coloring* of pen-and-ink *mainstream titles* is rapidly being commandeered by *digital* systems, with surprisingly *understated* results in many cases.

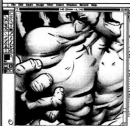

Many in the profession use the computer as merely a *tool* to accomplish more *efficiently* tasks that were already being done in the years when *color separation* was up to a team of *old ladies* in Bridgeport with *Exacto Knives*.

Such *conservatism* is a small example of the *broad tendency* we all have to interpret *new media* through the *filter* of the *old*.*

Early *written language* was filled with artifacts of the *oral tradition* --

-- early *radio* was steeped in *print* --

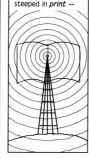

-- early *television* was bred of radio and the movies.

It's not surprising, then, that the sensibility derived from ink *line art* and *mechanical reproduction* would dominate the *early days* of *computer-generated comics*.

Naturally, a sensibility of ink drawing will always be relevant to works *reproduced* in ink --

-- and even art destined for the *screen* can benefit from the study of *old masters* --

-- but to choose computers as one's *primary* art-making tool is to choose an almost *superhuman* palette of *options* --

-- and to devote it to merely *imitating* their predecessors is a bit like hunting *rabbits* with a *battleship*.

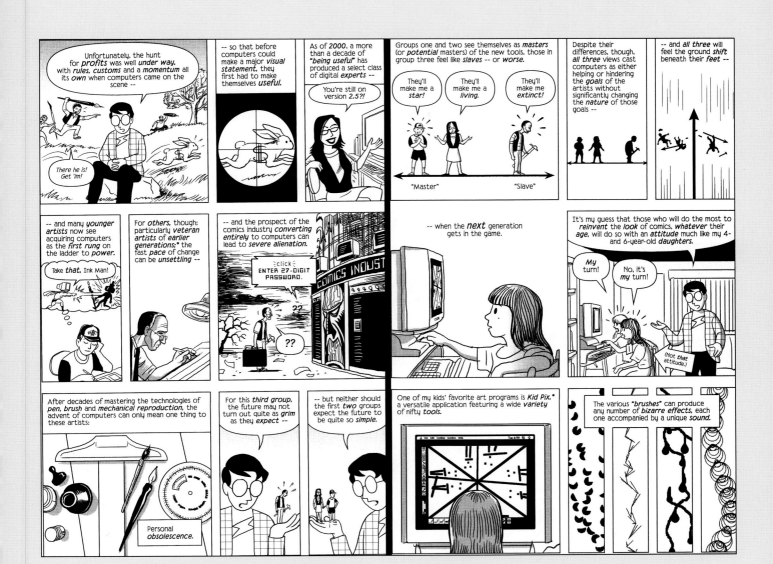

Each item on the *tools palette* has a vast *sub-palette* of *variations*, and even our *youngest* has *explored* them thoroughly.

One of the "*eraser*" variations is a little stick of *dynamite.* If you select it and *click* on your picture --

-- there'll be a *loud boom*, some spreading *concentric circles* --

-- and the picture will *disappear.*

This ability to *play* with the new tools, to learn them from the *inside*, is our best hope of *understanding* them.

Kids don't have a *monopoly* on the ability to play. This phenomenon is as much about *attitude* as about *age.*

But for many artists *my age* and up, a certain amount of "*un-learning*" may be in order.

That's what it's *for.* But that's not all my kids *use* it for.

It seems if you click on the dynamite *again*, before the circles are *gone*, you'll find that they *stay in place* --

-- and can then be *combined* with *other* such patterns by repeating the process in a *different spot.*

Now just try telling my kids that's *not* what an eraser is *supposed* to do!

Sometimes, when I look at my kids' art, it reminds me of a certain afternoon in *1994...*

I was getting my first look at some of the year's best *CD-ROMs* when our friend *Carol* and her *14-year-old* son *Brad* came over.

Brad *sat down* and started *playing* with one of the disks, and within *minutes*, he looked up and said: "Hey, Scott --

"-- did you go through the door marked '*Do Not Enter*'?"

My kids don't see their *relationship* with the computer as either master *Or* slave.

MASTER   SLAVE

To them, the computer is an *environment* to *explore*, an *extension* of their *whims* --

-- and a place where things "happen" *first* and are understood *later.*

Needless to say, I *hadn't*; and I've since become aware of how *many* artists like me have failed to open *any number* of doors that could have led to *new possibilities*, simply because it wasn't their *job.*

Do Not Enter   Do Not Enter   Do Not Enter   Do Not Enter   Do Not Enter   Enter   Do Not Enter   Do Not Enter

It rarely *starts* that way. *Beginners* in digital media often *revel* in their *newfound abilities*, flinging open *door* after *door.*

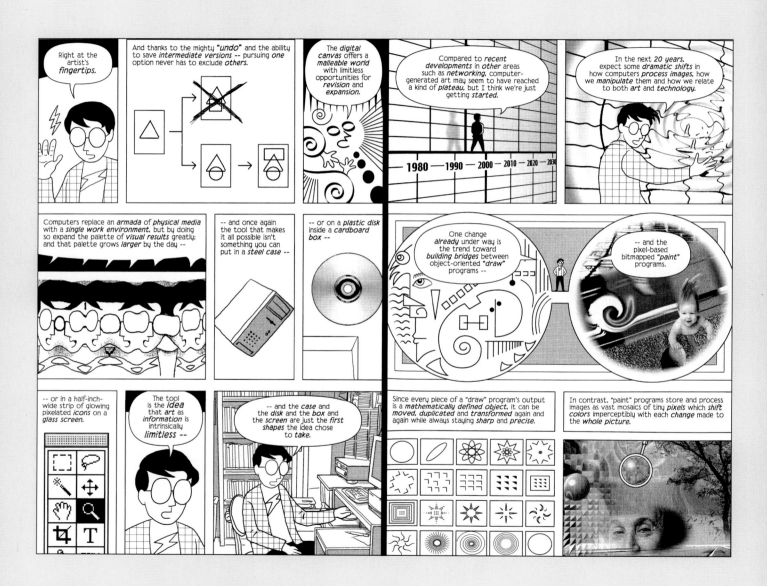

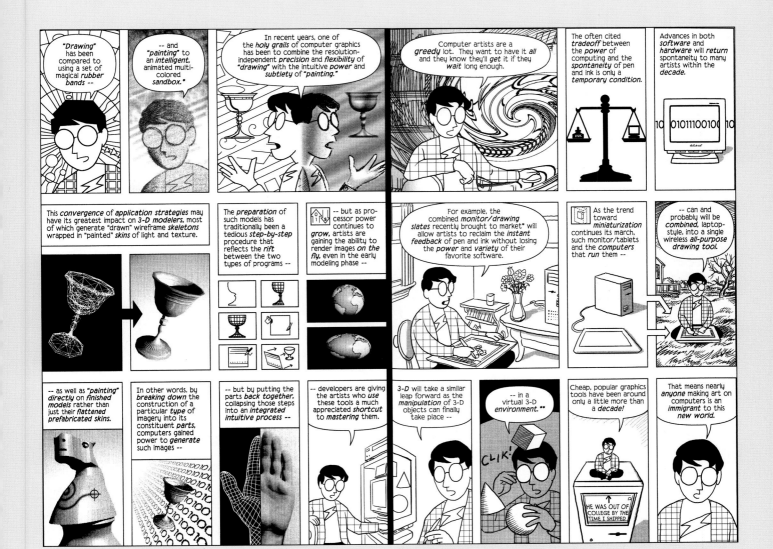

Expect the *native-born* to speak the language far more *fluently* --

-- and to go through *door* after *door* as if they *didn't exist.*

DO NOT ENTER

There is *one door,* however, that even my *daughters'* generation may *hesitate* to *enter:* the door beyond which the *human artist* ceases to matter --

As I write this, despite *plummeting prices,* getting *started* in computer graphics is still far from *cheap** --

COMPUTER ?

-- and may seem to contravene the spirit of at least one of our *earlier* revolutions which often revolves around *economically disadvantaged* artists.

? =

Still, *traditional art* was never without its *expenses* --

-- and the computer *itself* becomes the *"artist."*

The *absolute* version of this scenario is a bit beyond the scope of this chapter.*

Transitionally, though, as computers do take on a more *"creative"* role (such as in the software that generated this *landscape*) an interesting *shift* in *perception* occurs --

-- and *Moore's Law* isn't done with us *yet!*

Within a *decade,* anyone with *modest means* and *sufficient desire* will be ready and able to *reinvent* the *look* of comics *forever* --

-- *if* they can find a way to *reach* their potential *audiences.*

-- as our consensual *definitions* of art retreat to dwell only in the *part* of the work --

-- that only *humans* do!

10100111001
1110010001
11010101100
10110001001
01001101100
10100011001
11100100101
10110001001
01001101100
11100011001
11010101100
10110001001

Humans are hardly in *danger* of being *replaced* just *yet* --

PANT! PANT

-- but survival as a *species* doesn't necessarily guarantee survival on the *job,* and artists *without* computer experience may have *good cause* to fear *"replacement"* in at least *some* areas.

Unfortunately, as we've seen, that kind of connection is hardly *guaranteed* in today's market.

And this brings us to *another idea* hinted at in the Whirlwind project 50 years ago, which became a *modest reality* in *1969* and which *exploded* into *public consciousness* just a few short years ago.

And it's an idea that *won't* be *going away* anytime *soon.*

focus.

1. Like Mitchell Stephens, who argues that digital technologies foster new perspectives on the world (see the preceding essay, "By Means of the Visible"), McCloud claims that for children "the computer is an environment to explore, an extension of their whims, and a place where things 'happen' first and are understood later." But isn't what McCloud claims true for children in general—that unless they are made to fear the world, they will explore first and understand later? What specific evidence does McCloud give that computers change their (and our) perspectives?

2. What difference would it make if McCloud made his argument only in words rather than in words and images? What, if anything, would be lost?

respond.

1. The image tools on compluters have become extraordinarily powerful, as McCloud shows. Perhaps you've tried out some of these tools on image editors such as Adobe Photoshop or Macromedia Fireworks. If you do not own one of these programs, you likely can find them in a campus computer lab or you can download them from the manufacturer's Web site for a thirty-day free trial.

Open a digital image in an image editor and try the effects of the filters McCloud mentions as well as those that he doesn't. McCloud asks how we would react, for example, to a cartoon that was entirely embossed. Begin to answer that question by writing a paragraph about the effects each filter has on the image you have selected.

2. Select one of your favorite comic strips and try to convey the same information using words alone. What is different when the images are missing? Is there anything you can convey in words that the images cannot?

3. McCloud asks what the potential is for comics made out of clip art. His question is interesting because not all of us have the ability to draw, but we might be able to assemble comics out of clip art. Your word-processing software probably has a clip art file, which enables you to drag and drop images into a document. If not, you can access large collections of clip art on the Web (type "clip art" in the search window at <www.yahoo.com> to find collections). Your word-processing software and presentation software (such as PowerPoint) will also allow you to add balloon captions to images.

Use clip art to tell a story or to explain a process without using words. When you finish, pass the file to a student or a friend. Ask that person to write out the story or the explanation. How close does he or she come to matching in words what you intended to say? If there are gaps, what are they? What conclusions can you draw about the limitations of each medium?

Original photo

Photo with "twirl"

Photo with "edges"

Photo with "emboss"

M&Co (1979–93) was a design firm known for offbeat, often controversial, conceptual designs, ranging from album covers for the band Talking Heads to the redevelopment of Times Square. It was founded by Tibor Kalman (see p. 000) and then closed by him when he founded *Colors,* a magazine published by Benetton. M&Co was one of the first design firms to use vernacular and unsophisticated art at a time when commercial graphics favored slick images. The text here is from the advertising campaign M&Co created for Restaurant Florent, which opened in New York City in 1986. We have included some of the print components of the campaign along with a discussion among the members of the design team and the owner of the restaurant about the ideas they were trying to convey.

The Restaurant Florent
Ad Campaign

M&CO

A diner for the debonair and the dispossessed, Restaurant Florent opened in 1986 with most of the features of its previous life as an old luncheonette left intact, and enhanced by a minimal but memorable graphic identity by M&Co. The icon postcard, matches and neon sign played a subtle semantic game, providing a new image for the old diner while hinting that they had been sitting there at the front window for decades. It was the start of a seven year barter, design services in exchange for food, that brought M&Co to the public eye and helped spawn a love affair between the design profession and the vernacular work of its unsung forebears.

The postcard was printed on the crude paperboard used to stiffen shirts. The design came out of the idea that a French client with a no-frills restaurant, no money and a sense of humor was entitled to some grandeur.

TIBOR KALMAN: "At first we went to Florent with six heraldic symbols taken from military medals, but he said no to that; he had come from a country where decoration had been rejected in the name of modernism. So then we started to think about using icons for the copy."

ALEXANDER ISLEY (designer): "That's when a cheap, readily accessible source of illustration came to mind: the Yellow Pages."

MICHAEL BIERUT (designer): "The impact was stupendous. M&Co had never had pieces in *Communication Arts* magazine, which was the usual route to fame. They had been producing these complicated vernacular ideas that no one understood, or were ugly, until they came up with something that people could rip off. It caught the zeitgeist. Designers recognized the postcard icons were from the Yellow Pages and realized that ugly could also be pretty, especially if they had the wit to make these juxtapositions."

ALEXANDER ISLEY: "The whole idea of the architec-ture was to make it look like a diner that had already been there, where things didn't really line up. For the neon sign, we didn't want to be the graphic designers picking a nice typeface so we drew it out, and gave it to the neon sign company, who showed up with a plug-in briefcase of different lights. We picked a color and they made the sign."

ADVERTISING FLORENT

The restaurant's print campaign began on an unforthcoming note.

KALMAN: "The first pieces we did for Florent were only advertised in *Paper* magazine. We wanted it to be the cool restaurant, so we designed the ads with no address, no telephone number, no American Express cards. If you didn't know somebody who knew, you were out of it."

PUBLICIZING FLORENT

Proof that gastronomy is the mother of invention. The cup and glass postcard was produced using transfer lettering and photographic prowess. Others celebrated the dining and digesting process.

FLORENT MORELLET (owner): "I loved the table and type card; the female has the napkin on her lap, the male is a slob as usual and has his on the floor. He's wearing loafers, she's wearing pumps, he's eating meat (of course) and she's eating fish. She giggles, she's flirting, there's mirth, there are maps on the wall, she's drinking from a glass of wine. But my favorite is the stomach card. It's so sick. I like things to be a little shocking."

MARLENE MCCARTY (designer): "The table card was one of those ideas that happens where you're taking a shower or brushing your teeth. By today's standards, it's really traditional typography, but I actually like things you can read."

On facing page,
print ad for
Restaurant Florent

Postcard using
typography as a
description of the
dining experience.

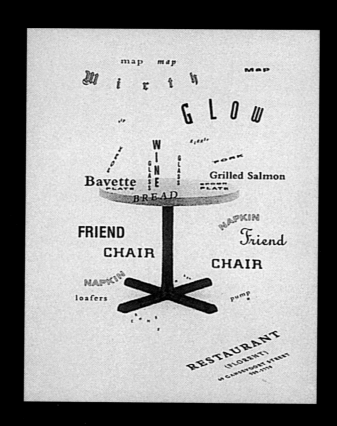

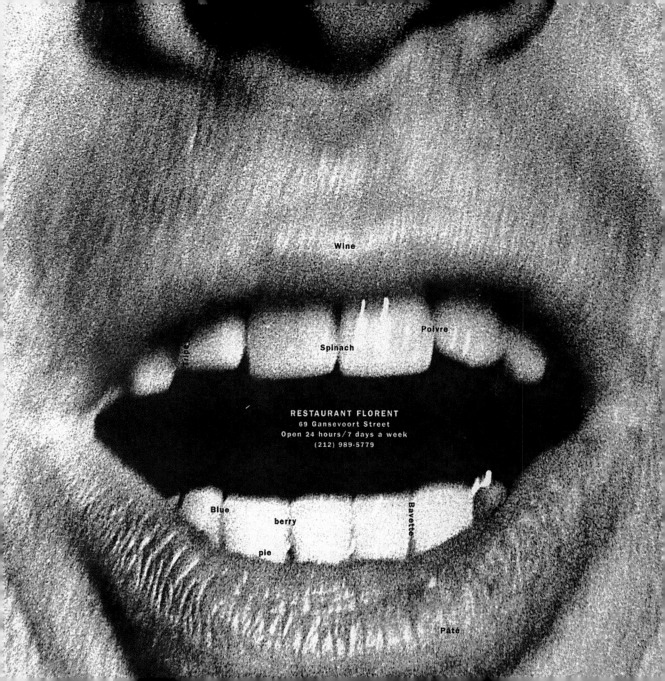

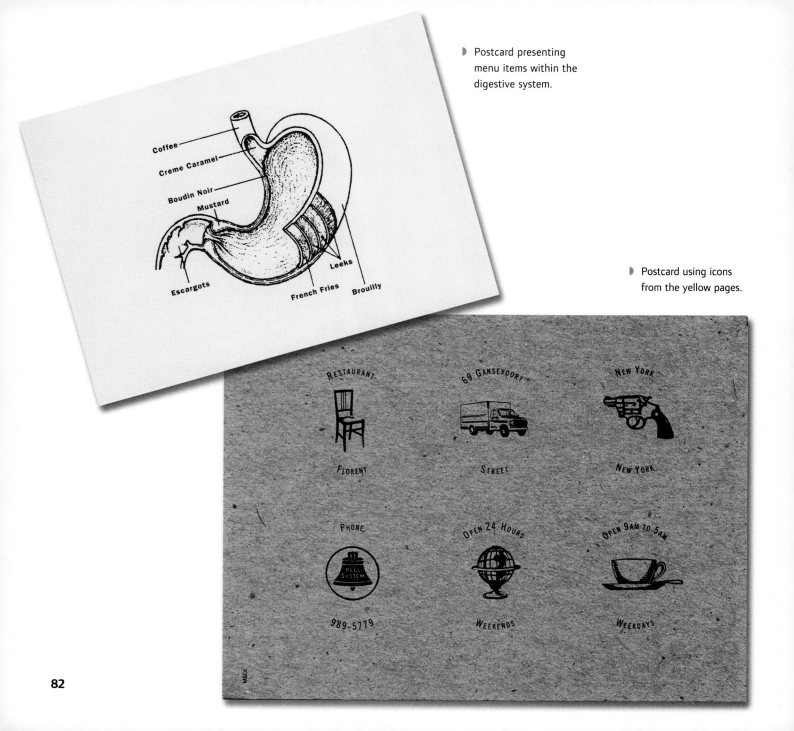

▎ Postcard presenting menu items within the digestive system.

▎ Postcard using icons from the yellow pages.

focus.

1. The advertising for Restaurant Florent emphasizes the things we don't think about when we go to a restaurant—that we can spill food on ourselves, that the food goes to our stomachs, and that food is part of an environmental cycle. Although these ideas are presented humorously, they might appear to be exactly what a restaurant would not want to advertise. Why do you think M&Co decided to test the boundary of conventional restaurant advertising?

2. M&Co used images from the Yellow Pages and stock photography rather than creating new images for this ad campaign. The strategy must have worked, for Restaurant Florent soon became extraordinarily popular. Why do you think the strategy was so successful? Would it have worked in your hometown?

3. What narratives do the Florent ads suggest?

respond.

1. In a 1997 interview in *Print* magazine, Tibor Kalman questioned the role of designers in our society:

   "Isn't that what most design is about—making something seem different from what it truly is? That's the point at which I began to worry about what we designers, who are very skillful and have powerful tools at our disposal, are doing in the world—what role we are playing—making the filthy oil company look 'clean,' making the car brochure higher-quality than the car, making the spaghetti sauce look like it's been put up by grandma, making the junky condo look hip. Is all that okay, or just the level to which design and many other professions have sunk?"

   His concern repeats the old accusation that images don't always tell the truth about reality. Read Michell Stephens's essay, "By Means of the Visible," earlier in this chapter. Then write a response to Kalman from Stephens's point of view.

2. M&Co was ahead of its time in creating ads that do not present their subjects in expected ways or even in ways that are necessarily appealing. Beer ads, for example, now sometimes present beer drinkers as not very bright people. Find examples of print, Web, and television ads that use potentially negative associations. Write an essay that analyzes why they work—or why they don't work.

Jessica Helfand (b. 1960) is a Web designer who writes frequently about technology and design and teaches design at Yale University. Her design credits include the *New York Times* Web site, and her written works include *Looking Closer 3* (1999) and *Screen: Essays on Graphic Design, New Media, and Visual Culture* (2001). Although she is best known as a graphic designer, Helfand publishes regularly on a wide range of subjects, from talking Barbies to scratchy typography to chicken nuggets. The following essay comes from *Eye* maga-zine (Autumn 2001), an international review of graphic design.

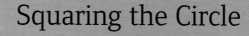

Squaring the Circle

JESSICA HELFAND

The circle has no beginning and no ending. It is unbiased, solid and unwavering in its geometric simplicity, denoting unity and eternity, totality and infinity. It represents the cosmos, the cycle of the seasons, the life of man and the orbits of planets around the sun. In astronomy it indicates a full moon; in meteorology, a clear sky; in cartography it represents a village, town or community. Over time and across many cultures, the circle has come to represent an ideal of unsurpassable perfection, yet it eludes mathematical exactness. It is thus the essence of all that is natural, primordial and inescapably human.

The circle's sustained presence throughout the Middle Ages and the Renaissance is evident from thirteenth-century wheel windows to sixteenth-century condos, from studies on human proportion to treatises on architectural construction. The circle draws its rich symbolism from such sources as Christian theology (St Augustine described God as a circle whose centre was everywhere, and whose circumference nowhere), Babylonian legend (it is said that the ancient Babylonians developed the 360-degree circle as well as the 60-minute hour), Buddhist mandalas (a picture-tool for contemplation and meditation) and Byzantine rotundas (like halos in the Renaissance, a celebration of geometric purity gesturing upward to the heavens).

The circle is present in hieroglyphs and ideograms dating as far back as 3000 B.C. Its shape has formed the basis for numerous astronomical instruments, including the armillary sphere (used in the seventeenth century to teach the concepts of spherical astronomy) and the astrolabe (an ancient astronomical "computer" for solving problems relating to time and the position of the sun and stars in the sky); the orrery (an eighteenth-century mechanical model of the solar system in which the planets rotate about the sun at correct scale speeds) and the observatory (a circular, dome-like structure typically positioned at high altitude for maximum star and sky visibility). In the south of England, the circle has informed the design not only of the massive monuments at Stonehenge, but also of the "crop circles" that have appeared in cornfields each summer for the past 21 years. In more practical terms, the circle has also defined the urban plans of such cities as Washington DC, designed by Pierre L'Enfant in 1791 according to the radial arrangement of Paris, where streets stretch from a common centre like the spokes of a wheel.

Conceptually, the circle has intrigued thinkers from Plato to Pythagoras, Husserl to Hobbes, Einstein to Emerson. ("The eye," wrote Emerson, "is the first circle.") Philosophers ponder something called a "hermeneutic" circle, which refers to the inherent circularity of all understanding. Indeed, the idea of the circle as a self-fulfilling loop—a trap, or a set of recurring, cyclical limitations—presents a darker side of its hitherto pristine character. In literature, the circle is frequently seen as threatening or intractable. Dante's *Inferno* invokes seven circles to depict the inescapable nature of hell. Alexander Solzhenitsyn's *The First Circle* (1968) adapts the circle as a metaphor for government repression and crimes against humanity. In *La Ronde* (1900), Arthur Schnitzler portrays a circular pattern of sexual deceit in turn-of-the-century Vienna, while William

▶ *The Kitchenette Wheel.* Roman Press Publishers New York, 1940s. From "Creamed Oysters with Celery" to "Schnitzel Holstein." users can concoct recipes by ("dialling" the ingredients. This early example of an interactive kitchen tool offers a progressive search option flow to create menus by combining what you already have at home) through a simple rotary interface. Its culinary content betrays its age: most recipes are unusually saucy, nutritionally questionable, or both.

Somerset Maugham's 1921 satire *The Circle* illuminates the vicissitudes of bourgeois life between the wars. Across cultures, disciplines and multiple media the circle has endured, from a symbol for cosmic revelation to a model of human behaviour, a captivating emblem at once mystical, metaphorical and moral.

And mathematical. Older graphic designers may recall the proportional wheel, designed to determine the sizing of photographs for reproduction. While circular calculation devices were first introduced in the mid-seventeenth century it was not until the nineteenth century that advances in scientific thinking combined with discoveries in technology to produce what are, in retrospect, some of our earliest computers. Circular form is strikingly evident in their design: Charles Babbage's steam-powered Analytical Engine of 1833, widely considered the first computer, was based on circular logarithmic tables. Early calculation machines were sometimes called "arithmometers" and "comptometers" and, like Babbage's, were predicated on a data-entry system that used punch cards. By the end of the nineteenth century, calculation devices were designed to facilitate everything from data tabulation and physical measurement to the mechanical representation of logic. Many relied on concentric wheels: even father-of-hypertext Vannevar Bush's first automatic computer of 1933 (he called it a "differential analyser") gave its initial solutions in the form of curves.

Circular design conceits thus have ample precedent in the technologies of the last two centuries, yet in contemporary culture we expect our information to be framed by rectangular, Cartesian co-ordinates. We digest our data in bytes and bits via squared-up monitors and drill/pull-down menus in a tyranny of rigorous alignment that mirrors the rational substrate of modern civilisation where text squares up, buildings stand up and the world, by and large, follows an orderly, axial progression of straight lines and right angles. Conversely, the notion of the circle-meets-technology instantly conjures images of the most archaic of appliances: oversized television sets and cumbersome radio consoles, telephone switchboards and analogue synthesizers, all "navigated" by clumsy dials and knobs. It is hardly the stuff of modern convenience, let alone a model for progressive interaction design.

The process of mediating the tension between rational (square) and rotational (circle)—that of imposed order versus natural order—is hardly new. One of the earliest problems in Greek mathematics was something called "squaring the circle"—the attempt to construct geometrically a square equal in area to a given circle. But does "squaring" the circle also reflect our subconscious attempt to impose upon it a forced logic? If roundness is "the suitable shape for objects that belong nowhere and everywhere," as Rudolph Arnheim put it, then what better working metaphor for the digital denizens of the Internet, whose "everywhere and nowhere" peregrinations so perfectly characterise the nomadic nature of modern telecommunications—wireless, global and intangible? According to this view, circular form presents an intriguing case study: it is a vessel at once adaptable, flexible and pure, simple and streamlined, culturally and categorically neutral.

The images of wheel charts that accompany this piece show circles in use not only as conduits of information but, more importantly, as two-dimensional precursors to interface design. At their core they are all about eye/hand co-ordination, much as we navigate on screen through the delicate balancing act of eye/hand and mouse/cursor. In formal terms they subdivide the circle's circumference into segments that address complex yet navigable details—some numerical, some informational, some trivial. Included here are data-discs and fact-finders, at-a-glance charts and quiz wheels, trouble shooters, mileage converters and geographic locators. There are wheels to preview weather patterns, to predict nuclear fallout and to plan the period of gestation; there are perrigraphs (diving planners), planispheres (star maps) and wheels that quantify some of the finer statistical points of presidential trivia. Yet while these specimens of paper ephemera represent a broad categorical sweep of social history, they are radical in their articulation of space, time and user-driven functionality. Consider, too, their graphic complexity—not to mention the pre-desktop publishing manual labour required to achieve it—and the function they perform: turn, point, find; a paper version of "point and click."

▶ *The Wheel of Life,*
Natural Foods Institute,
Olmsted Falls, Ohio,
1941. Here is a perfect
example of the two
basic compositional
concerns in wheel chart
design: the outer wheel
displays its content
through a periphoral
plan (data organized
along the outer edge,
leading horizontally)
while the inner wheel
displays its content
through a radial plan
(data organized from
the center point, read-
ing vertically). In this
example, the major
food groups, including
meats, seafood, cereals,
and vegetables are list-
ed on the outer wheel,
while the vitamins (A,
B, C, D, E, and G) and
minerals (including
sodium, potassium,
magnesium, and iron)
are listed on the inner
wheel. The back fea-
tures a health chart
with recommended
food combinations.

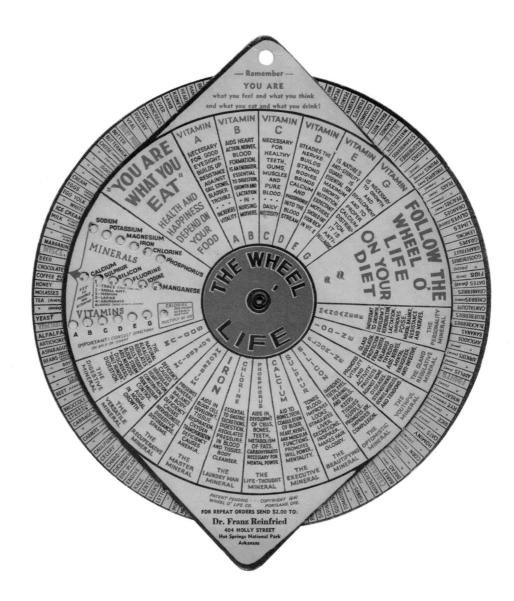

1. Circles are used by many of the world's major religions—including Buddhism, Hinduism, and Christianity—as objects of contemplation. Based on Helfand's essay, why do you think the circle is favored in so many diverse traditions? Is it because a circle conveys the concept of unity?

2. The difference between a digital clock or watch and a traditional clock or watch with hands is a classic example of Helfand's distinction between the rational (square) and the rotational (circle). Which do you prefer—the digital clock or the traditional clock? Why? Cite the reading to defend your choice.

1. For one day, keep a log of circles you find in design. Make copies, take photographs, and take screen shots from the Web. Classify the circles you find according to subject matter. What subjects are most likely to be represented with circles?

2. This essay is heavily influenced by the thinking of theorist Rudolph Arnheim, who believes that every work of visual art has a spatial organization, from shapes on a canvas to parts of a building in space. He maintains that spatial organization is made up of two dynamics: *centricity*, in which things come out of or are pulled toward a center, and *eccentricity*, in which there is not true center but rather a grid of horizontal and vertical relationships. Look at a selection of famous paintings on a Web site of a major art museum (for example, the Art Institute of Chicago, the Metropolitan Museum of Art, the Louvre). Find two or three paintings that illustrate centricity and two or three that show eccentricity.

In July 1942, seven months after the United States entered World War II, over 500 U.S. magazines displayed the American flag on their covers. The simultaneous publishing of flag images was not an accident. Magazine publishers were concerned that civilian publications might be restricted during wartime, and they wanted to demonstrate the importance of magazines to civilian morale. The National Museum of American History in Washington, D.C., displayed over a hundred of these covers in a 2002 exhibition; below is a selection published in *Smithsonian* **magazine** (March 2002).

The motto of the wartime magazine campaign, "United We Stand," originated in a 1768 patriotic ballad and has been used as a rallying cry since the American Revolution, most recently following the terrorist attacks of September 11, 2001.

Covered in Glory

SMITHSONIAN MAGAZINE

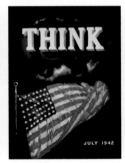

focus.

1. Each cover displays an American flag, but the particular themes are different. From the twenty examples, what different themes can you classify?

2. How did individual magazines retain their identities while displaying images of the flag? (For example, *Silver Screen* has an image of a uniformed usher saluting the flag.)

DON'T BUY IT.

WAR IS NOT THE ANSWER

Download this poster free at www.anotherposterforpeace.com

respond.

1. When the president and other elected officials refer to the American flag, they usually speak of the flag representing justice, freedom, and equal opportunity for all. How, then, do we account for the use of the flag to sell products, from the huge flags that fly over car lots and strip malls to the tiny flags on jewelry and clothing labels? Why is the image of the flag stuck on so many ordinary products? Write an analysis of what the flag signifies on various products and locations. (See Chapter 2 for guidelines on analyzing texts.)

2. Keep a list of all the American flags and images of the flag you see in one day. You might also try to find as many flags as you can inside your room, apartment, or house. If you look hard, they will turn up in unexpected places. If possible, take pictures. Then, beside each entry on your list, note why you think the flag or flag image appears in that place or on that object.

3. *Smithsonian* editor Edwards Park says of our love of the flag: "We Americans don't have a king or queen. We have a flag" ("Our Flag Was Still There," *Smithsonian* [July 2000]: 22). What does Park mean by this statement? Write an essay in which you examine the meaning the flag has to people in the United States. Many people would say that the flag is an expression of patriotism; however, the flag also is displayed on many commercial products and in locations that seem to have nothing to do with patriotism. Use the list in the preceding exercise to get started. You should be able to group particular uses of the flag.

4. What if you were assigned to *revise* the U.S. flag. How would you change it? Try your hand at redoing the U.S. flag, and then write a paragraph explaining your changes.

Write about someplace you know and like: your family home, your dorm room, a local café, a favorite spot on campus, somewhere you visited on vacation. Write a paragraph or two describing the place to someone who's never been there. You'll want to describe what it looks like, what goes on there, and of course why you like it.

Next, try to describe the same place using visual texts: photos, drawings, clip art, images you photocopy or cut out of magazines, anything visual. You'll probably need to label the visuals with captions, but be brief—this text should be more visual than verbal.

Now, combine the verbal and visual texts. Put them together however you wish—you could use the visuals as illustrations of the verbal, or you could weave them together.

Finally, take a few minutes to consider the differences between verbal and visual texts. Did you use them differently? Did you, for example, use visual texts for descriptive purposes and verbal texts for more narrative purposes? Which do you think works better to describe a place? Given a choice, would you use verbal, visual, or both elements?

АВИА

CWA
MR. AND MRS. A.A
111 EAST KELLOGG
ST. PAUL, MINNES
U.S.A.

ГОСТИНИЦА
АНГАРА

ИРКУТСК, ул.СУХЭ БА

АВИА — PARAVION

26 JUNE 1974
MOSCOW

DEAR GRANDMA AND GRANPPA,
                            HAPPY 55 YEARS TO YOU! A SMALL
PARCEL WILL SOON BE EN ROUTE TO YOU, TO EAT IN GOOD HEALTH. I WAS
HAPPY TO GET YOUR LETTER— MOSCOW HAS BEEN DELIGHTFUL, ITS
BEAUTY AND LIFE ALWAYS GOOD (BUT QUITE ENHANCED BY 6 MONTHS
ON A TROPICAL ISLAND). I'VE BEEN RUNNING IN CIRCLES, FROM
BOLSHOI BALLET TO MOSCOW CIRCUS TO OPERATIC RECITAL BY LA SCALA
TO BOLSHOI OPERA. THE CITY HAS REALLY MODERNIZED IN 3 YRS —
BUT I'M PLEASED TO SAY THE PEOPLE ARE AS 18TH CENTURY AS EVER,
SO THERE'S NOW A GROCERY STORE, BUT IT'S RUN EXACTLY LIKE A
BACKWOODS FRUITSTAND! AND SOMEOF THE CASH REGISTERS LOOK TO
BE COMPUTERIZED, BUT THE CLERKS STILL CHECK THE COMPUTATIONS
ON AN ABACUS.
                          SIBERIA WAS QUITE SIMPLY THE
GREATEST TRIP I'VE EVER EXPERIENCED, AND CENTRAL ASIA
GORGEOUS. BUT WAS IT SOMETHING, GOING FROM SNOW AT LAKE
BAIKAL TO 113° AT BUKHARA! DETAILS TO COME IN A LETTER TO
MOM.
            HOPE ALL'S WELL. LOVE, MARE

2 | looking closer

Of the many press images following the September 11, 2001, attack on New York City's World Trade Center, Thomas Franklin's photo of three firefighters raising the American flag against a backdrop of gray dust and twisted steel may be the best known. Many compared it to Joseph Rosenthal's 1945 Pulitzer-Prize–winning picture of American marines raising the U.S. flag on Mount Suribachi, Iwo Jima. In the days and weeks following the Trade Center attack, those two photos appeared side by side in newspapers and magazines, on posters, Web sites, and office walls. To some, the photos together represented hope in the face of disaster. For others, the two images identified that moment in 2001 as a declaration of war and New York City firefighters as new soldiers in that war. Still others saw the comparison as a distortion of the events of September 11.

Even if it had not been placed next to Rosenthal's photo, the image of the firefighters very likely would have become central to what the U.S. press called the "nation's mood" following September 11. Franklin has said that he knew he had an important shot even as he was taking it. How one picture can make such an impact—how an image carries and conveys meaning—is the subject of this chapter.

U.S. Marines raising the flag on Mount Surabachi, Iwo Jima. News photo by Joseph Rosenthal, 1945.

Firefighters raising the American flag at the World Trade Center, September 11. Digital news photo by Thomas Franklin, 2001.

As we read a message, most of us don't think much about how it was put together. This is especially true of visual messages. They seem to communicate naturally, even simply. Yet, as we have seen in Chapter 1, visual messages have much in common with verbal ones. They consist of a complex of elements, including how and why the image was made, who made it, how an audience reads it, and where it appears. We call these elements the immediate and the broader contexts; they influence the creation of a message and how audiences receive it.

Immediate Context

The IMMEDIATE CONTEXT is anyone or anything that has an immediate role in forming the message. As with verbal texts, visual texts have an author (or authors), an audience, a subject, and a purpose. Whoever made the image had to decide what technology to use (medium) and what kind of image it would be (genre). Visual messages, also like verbal ones, present a point of view and involve a conscious selection of materials, as well as decisions about what to emphasize or focus on and how to arrange or organize the information.

Broader Context

The BROADER CONTEXT includes larger questions about the cultural, economic, social, and historic circumstances in which the image was produced and, later, read.

Most of us don't separate the immediate from the broader context when we read. If you are to understand how images communicate meaning, however, you will want to look closer—think about both. Notice how such an analysis might work with the two photos that open this chapter.

WHO IS THE AUTHOR?   For some images, this question is a simple one. For example, Thomas Franklin took the photo of firefighters raising the flag at the World Trade Center site. At the time, Franklin was a photographer for New Jersey's *Bergen County Record*. Joseph Rosenthal, who took the photo at Iwo Jima, was a World War II war correspondent. As photojournalists, each was looking for newsworthy images. For both Franklin and Rosenthal, then, the photos began as events related to their work.

Other images are not as easily identified with an individual author or a particular event. Billboards, postcards, stamps, logos, book covers, and product labels are images we see and read every day. We rarely know who created them, but even when we cannot name the individual responsible for a text, we can identify something about that author. We can guess, for example, that a CD cover was probably created by a graphic designer, a digital artist, or a team of designers hired by the recording company to make a message that will attract attention and suggest the type of music on the CD.

In many cases, it matters less whether or not we can actually name an individual author than whether we can identify purpose and point of view. For example, most readers don't think much about an individual author when they look at a commercial for ESPN, but everyone knows that it is an advertisement for a sports network told from the point of view of that network. A commercial for PBS is likely to have a very different look because it has a different point of view and targets a different audience.

WHAT IS THE PURPOSE? Asking about purpose might also seem like a straightforward question, but you will quickly discover that most communication has more than one purpose and that the purpose shifts as a text is placed in different contexts. It is obvious, for example, that the Franklin and Rosenthal photos were initially taken as visual representations of news events. It is the job of photojournalists to report the news through pictures.

However, once the firefighters photo is reproduced on a T-shirt by a designer, for example, the purpose shifts. It becomes a kind of memorial, a way of identifying loyalties, and even a fashion statement. That same photo is presented in this textbook as an example of a familiar and complex piece of visual communication. It is the same image, but it takes on additional meaning as its purpose changes with use and reuse.

The same can be said of the Iwo Jima photo. Almost immediately after it was first published, it was being used for a number of different purposes. Only five months after the picture first appeared in newspapers, the U.S. Post Office issued a stamp featuring it. By 1995, when a second

image conscious

Look around and note down all the images that surround you—calendars, photographs, posters, screen savers. To what extent can you identify an author for these texts? Even if you cannot name a person or design team, what could you say about the author's point of view and purpose?

▶ Two U.S. commemorative stamps, based on the Iwo Jima photo. The vertical stamp was issued in 1945; the horizontal stamp, in 1995. Notice how the shape of the stamp affects the arrangement, and the emphasis: the vertical stamp emphasizes the flag, whereas the horizontal one emphasizes the soldiers struggling to raise the flag. See also how the horizontal cropping did not accommodate the original flag, and a new larger flag was inserted.

version of the stamp appeared, even those Americans who knew nothing about the image had probably seen it in countless versions, including the memorial statue that now stands in Washington, D.C.

In 1945, the stamp was produced as a memorial representing courage under fire. In 1995, it was a piece of history. For stamp collectors, the image is an artifact. A postage stamp itself is simply a proof of purchase, but an individual stamp design either survives—becomes popular—or not, depending on how many people decide to buy it.

The Iwo Jima photo remained a familiar image throughout the twentieth century, even showing up in folk art, such as this cigarette machine triptych purchased in South Carolina in 2000.

▶ Folk art triptych juxtaposing the Iwo Jima photo with various other iconic images— Dana Carvey as Garth in *Wayne's World*, The Rock, among others, 2000.

Whatever else the artist had in mind in placing Rosenthal's photo in this particular triptych, it is certain that reporting the news is no longer the purpose the photo serves in this context.

WHAT ARE THE MEDIUM AND GENRE?　The way a message is created as well as what kind of message it is affects the way we read. For example, a letter seems different depending on whether it is received as an email message or a note in a greeting card, whether it is handwritten on delicate stationary or typed as a formal memo with a company logo printed at the top. Each of these involves a different medium, set in a different genre.

When we use the term MEDIUM, we are talking about the technology used to create and communicate a text. Movies, television, film photography, digital photography, watercolor painting, and charcoal drawing are all examples of different visual MEDIA. They all use different technologies. The Franklin and Rosenthal images, though both photographs, were produced using different media. Franklin's photo is digital; Rosenthal's is film. Both, however, are the same genre (or type) of photo: news photos.

The meaning we take from an image has as much to do with its GENRE—what *kind* of an image it is—as with the technology used to make it. News photos, for example, are typically read as objective records (whether they are or not), whereas paintings are considered interpretations. A film or television drama is a fiction, an interpretation of reality—though it might look very realistic. An advertisement is selling you something. Knowing the genre helps readers identify what the message is supposed to be. For example, not many readers would look at an ad for toothpaste and mistake it for a scientific report, but the advertiser tries to give it as much truth value as possible, perhaps using some of the conventions of the genre of scientific reports (charts and graphs, for example), so that readers think about the science in the ad more than its commercial purpose.

WHAT IS THE SUBJECT?　Look again at the Iwo Jima photo. Two days after its publication, Congress already was talking about it as a model for a memorial statue. Somehow, in addition to recording a single moment in time, the photo also carries a symbolic and emotional message. The same is true of Franklin's firefighter photo. Within months after it had appeared, the photo was being talked of as a model for a future memorial. Its symbolic significance was obvious to everyone who saw it.

How is that possible? To begin with, the subject of both photos was newsworthy. The public wanted to see the real people, places, and events depicted. Many news photos are significant solely on the basis of what they depict and the context in which they depict it. As press photos, then, both simply showed people at the actual scenes of events of international significance.

In addition, the subjects of these photos carried a powerful emotional impact. Both depicted a moment of triumph after devastating defeat. The 1945 battle that ended with a marine victory on Mount Suribachi had gone on for four days in some of the fiercest fighting of World War II. By the time Rosenthal took his picture, 40 percent of the company engaged in this battle had been killed. Similarly, the firefighter photo was taken on the evening of September 11, 2001, at the end of a day of national tragedy. In Franklin's words, the photo "had drama, spirit, and courage in the face of disaster."

So, the subject depicted by each photo and the significance of that subject are key elements we need to consider as we read these images.

Both photos carry strong symbolic meaning. The U.S. flag, an easily recognized SYMBOL of U.S. patriotism and nationhood, is at the top and is the focus of both images. The individuals in each photo also carry symbolic significance: marines and firefighters are historically associated with courage and self-sacrifice.

Not everyone who sees these images will have positive associations with patriotism, the flag, or marines and firefighters, however. That is why it is very important to consider the audience when you think about how an image communicates meaning.

WHO IS THE AUDIENCE? You can sometimes identify the intended audience for an image very precisely, but that is not always the case, and it might not be necessary. It is necessary, however, to think about how an author might expect an audience to receive the work. A photojournalist expects the audience to be readers of the news publication in which the photo

image conscious

Cover the flag in the Rosenthal and the Franklin photos (p. 99) so that you can see only the men. Once you eliminate the flag, how does each photo change? Without the flag, what is the subject? What is each photo's new symbolic significance?

appears. Ideally, that audience will accept the photo as a piece of news—a faithful reproduction of something that actually happened. The news photo allows readers to witness an event they would not be able to see for themselves.

Of course, no designer or author can control audience response. The best you can do is know something about the audience you are aiming for and make choices based on what you know. That is what happened when the Franklin and Rosenthal pictures were placed side by side on posters after the World Trade Center attack. These posters were designed for an audience that would see the two moments (1945 and 2001) as corresponding—not just in the way the photos looked but in their reference to war and tragedy and triumph. Those who did not see the correspondence or who did not agree that the September 11 attack was analogous to World War II very likely dismissed the message of the poster as overly simple— even manipulative.

HOW IS IT ARRANGED? When we talk about ARRANGEMENT, or COMPOSITION, we mean the way an image is organized within its frame or visual space. In the case of these two photos, the arrangement is a classic and stable triangle, with the flag forming the apex and the figures below forming the base. Like verbal composition, visual composition is a process of selection and emphasis—what is included in the space and what is left out, what is placed in the foreground (at the front of the picture) and what is relegated to the background. In other words, the way a text is arranged or organized suggests what the author believes is important about the subject and influences the way the audience reads the text.

Designers and visual artists must choose between a closed or open form when they compose an image. With a CLOSED FORM the entire image is inside the visual frame and the viewer's attention is focused within the picture. The Rosenthal and Franklin photos are arranged in very similar ways and both are closed forms. As you can see in this diagram of the Rosenthal photo, the men at the base seem to be moving in a mass toward the flag, which then forms the top of the closed triangular form. A similar form is made in the composition of the Franklin photo on page 99. An OPEN FORM is one that suggests that there's something more outside the visual

▶ Diagram of closed form in Rosenthal photograph.

frame. The image might be cut off at the edges, or a person in the image might be looking at something outside the image—even at the camera, making it seem as though the viewer is a part of the world of the image. We see this kind of composition quite often in contemporary advertising such as this Nike ad, in which the model is literally stretching out of the frame. We know he is moving. He isn't looking at the camera but concentrating on what's ahead—and outside—of the frame.

Billboard, New York City, 2002. The runner's arm extending off the frame, along with the half-missing *swoosh*, creates a sense of movement.

An open form suggests that the image is not completely self-contained, that there is something more beyond the visual space that viewers should be thinking about. Even a memorial statue, like the one shown here, can be arranged in an open form, when it directs our attention forward, beyond the artwork itself.

Advertisers are very careful about how they compose their visual texts because they need to make sure their message comes across. In the Nike ad, for example, the most important part of the message is the suggestion that wearing Nike products gives us energy, speed, and a great body. Readers of ads generally know that they are dealing with a message that is carefully constructed in order to put the product in the best light.

Most readers don't think of news photographs as carefully arranged. News photos are assumed to be moments in time captured just as events happened, with little thought about composition beyond the quick decisions a skilled photographer might make while looking through the viewfinder. And yet even here composition is rarely a matter of chance.

The Iwo Jima photo, for example, was cropped from its original longer shot, which had much more sky and landscape, making a tighter, more closed composition—and a greater visual impact.

WHAT IS THE HISTORICAL CONTEXT? All texts are created at a time, in a place, and sometimes in response to specific events or feelings. Visual texts, like all others, derive their meaning partially from their historic context. We have already seen some of that in our discussion of two photographs. To read either the Franklin or Rosenthal photograph, it helps to understand events in history, but, again, the historic context will not guarantee a single reading of these photos.

On the one hand, many Americans know that the Iwo Jima photo was taken during World War II. However, because most of us do not know the details of the event depicted, the image has come to be understood as a generalized reference to Americans at war, perhaps to heroism or to the horrors of war. The firefighter photo, on the other hand, is still current. Most of us know some details of the events of that day, and that knowledge affects the way we read the image.

▶ On the left, the original Iwo Jima photo, by Joseph Rosenthal, 1945. On the right, the final cropping of the photo, by Rosenthal. Notice that the soldiers are now centered in the image, giving them greater emphasis.

Not all images have such an easily defined historic context, but all are created at a particular historical moment and all are read at particular moments in time. The way readers understand an image will depend on when they read it, when it was made, and what was happening in the world at the time.

WHAT ARE THE CULTURAL AND SOCIAL CONTEXTS? In addition to having historical contexts, images take on meaning within certain cultural and social contexts. Our two photos are good examples. Firefighters have traditionally been considered heroes in U.S. culture, which is why television producers and filmmakers often position them at the center of the action willing to sacrifice themselves to save others. In that way they are like soldiers—or, at least, like the idealized soldiers of movies and novels.

Moreover, the firefighter photo takes on much of its meaning because it reminds viewers—especially once it is compared to the Iwo Jima photo—of World War II and other battles that Americans have fought. Once the reference to World War II—a war some have called America's last "good war"—is made, the image evokes some of the pride that Americans felt at winning the war with Hitler. The meaning of the photo, then, begins to shift from an inspiring moment at the end of a long day of catastrophe to what the press quickly began to call "America's New War." All of the films and photos and novels that we have seen and read about World War II and especially about Iwo Jima influence how we understand this new image. It might even bring to mind John Wayne in the 1950s film *The Sands of Iwo Jima*. Of course, if you are not familiar with the Rosenthal photo or have never thought of World War II or of any war as a "good" war, or if you are from a different culture entirely, the meaning you take from the firefighter image will differ. You will still very likely see it as a patriotic image, but patriotism in this form might not appeal to you.

Considering cultural and social contexts is especially important in analyzing advertisements. Beauty products, for example, often focus on ideal male and female forms. One way to read the image shown here would be to consider how ads often distort female beauty or promise the impossible, featuring close-ups of models airbrushed to conform to cultural ideals of perfection.

WHAT IS THE ECONOMIC CONTEXT? Thinking about the economic context can help you more fully read a text. Consider, for example, how powerful news photos help to sell newspapers. That is one reason the two photos we have focused on here have been reprinted so often. A photo with wide distribution can affect the way that the public sees or understands an event—something we need to keep in mind when thinking about what such an image *means*.

The economics of advertising seems obvious: advertisers spend money to influence our purchases. But what if an advertiser doesn't *seem* to be selling us something? What if an advertiser seems to be presenting a message about hunger or human rights or violence in the streets? United Colors of Benetton has become famous for "message" ads such as the one reprinted below featuring dying AIDS activist David Kirby. This image is shocking; it forces readers to think about what is going on in the picture and perhaps even to become more aware of issues surrounding AIDS. In fact, this particular ad is part of the United Colors of Benetton's institutional campaign, not their product campaign. Yet it is still an ad by a company that sells clothing. If we think of them as a socially responsible company, will we think it socially responsible to buy their clothes?

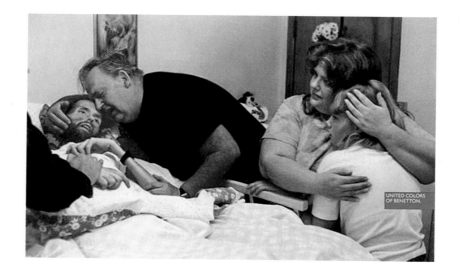

▶ United Colors of Benetton's "Faces of AIDS" campaign, 1992.

Not all texts are as richly complex as the two we have focused on in this chapter, but they all can be understood in terms of author; purpose; audience; composition; medium; genre; social, cultural, historical, and economic contexts; and so on. When you analyze a visual text, you will likely begin with your personal response and then consider the text's immediate and broader contexts.

WHAT IS YOUR PERSONAL RESPONSE?   Images often evoke memories or quick reactions. Take a moment to write about your response to Franklin's photo and then compare your response with fellow students. Although there are likely to be many similar responses to a photo such as this one, there will also be responses that differ significantly from yours. The fact that people have different reactions should not be surprising given that the way we read or react to a text depends on what we bring to it. For example, if you live in New York City, if you are a firefighter, or if you lost friends or family in the September 11 attack, your response is likely to be very different from the response of someone who does not have your experience.

Think, as well, of your response to the Iwo Jima photo. Is it the same as your response to the firefighter photo? If you were to ask a World War II veteran for a response to Rosenthal's image—which, of course, you could do—how would his or her reaction differ from yours? Very likely, the veteran would know a lot about the Iwo Jima photo—and would, of course, have different memories and thus a different response to the photo than you do.

Most of us have some response to everything we see—even if that response is indifference. We are not likely to know immediately how an image evokes that response, however. In order to account for how an image conveys a message or evokes a response, you will need to understand how different elements come together as a visual language. Some of those elements are embodied in the image itself, whereas others come from outside the image.

HOW DOES THE TEXT WORK?   To read any text, a reader pulls meaning from a system of signs: letters, words, sentences, paragraphs, shapes, colors, pictures. In verbal texts, even the typeface and page design contribute to meaning, but here we will focus mostly on visual texts—photographs, postcards, advertisements, and so on. When we examine how a sign carries and conveys meaning, we are engaging in analysis. Visual analysis, like any analysis, begins with a single question: How does it work?

Take, for example, our analysis of the firefighter photo (on p. 99). As we wrote about that image, we noted its subject matter: three firefighters raising the American flag at the wreckage of the World Trade Center on the evening of September 11, 2001. We noticed the composition, how the arrangement of the men and flag contributed to the photo's meaning. We could also consider the medium by which it was produced (digital photography) and the fact that digital imaging can be easily manipulated and so does not carry as much truth value as film photography traditionally has.

▶ The same high school student shown in a candid photograph and a formal studio photograph.

We made a point to identify the genre as a news photo. Genre is important in this case because a news photo carries more authority than an art photo or a studio portrait. Think, for example, about your high school yearbook photo. If you had your senior picture taken at a studio, you were posed in clothes you chose for the occasion. You were prepared to be photographed so that your parents could send the picture to friends and put it up on the wall. The photo might have been airbrushed to remove any blemishes. That is a very different kind of photo from one that a friend might have taken of you at a party later that same day. You are the same person in both photos, but the two are read differently—the first as an ideal portrait of you, the second as a candid snapshot.

As a news photo, the Franklin image promises to show us the truth about an event. We don't expect it to be posed or retouched. We count on photojournalists to show us "the real story." But, put the photo on a T-shirt or in a textbook, and it takes on additional cultural meaning as a national icon, a piece of history, and a photo significant enough to reprint in a school book. Each time the photo shifts from one medium and genre to another—and especially when it is reproduced thousands of times—it takes on additional meaning.

**WRITING UP
AN ANALYSIS**

The list of questions on the following pages provides a good start for a written analysis. You may wish to make notes in response to them. But remember that notes are just the beginning of your work. To complete your analysis, you will have to go back through your notes, decide what to focus on for your analysis, and choose the information and ideas that will support your conclusions.

When you write up an analysis, you won't be able to pay attention to all of these elements for every image, but you can focus on several of them to explain how an image works—how it conveys meaning, or how it is possible for you and your friends to have different responses to the same image, or why some images are easy to read while others take more time and seem difficult to understand.

snapshot

Social, cultural, historical, and economic context help shape the way we read all visual texts, even the most casual family snapshots. Locate old photos of family or friends or just ones that you can find in magazines like *Look* or the *Saturday Evening Post* in your local library. Notice how details in the photos "date" them or suggest a certain level of income or a particular event (like graduation or prom or a family picnic). Then, take your own snapshot of family members or friends. In a one-page discussion of the photo, point out what details in your snapshot will, eventually, "date" it.

SOME QUESTIONS FOR ANALYZING IMAGES

- What is your first response?

- What is the subject or content?

- What is the primary purpose? Are there additional purposes you need to consider?

- How is the image arranged in the visual space? Can you diagram its overall composition? What effect does this arrangement have on the way you read this image?

- What strikes you as important, interesting, or emotionally moving in the image? Can you identify elements of the image that could be seen as symbolic?

- What is the medium and what do you normally expect from images in this medium?

- What is the genre? Does the image conform to the conventions of that genre or does it break from the expectations? (We expect something different from a museum painting for example, than from a cartoon. And we expect cartoons on the comics page to be different from those on the editorial page.)

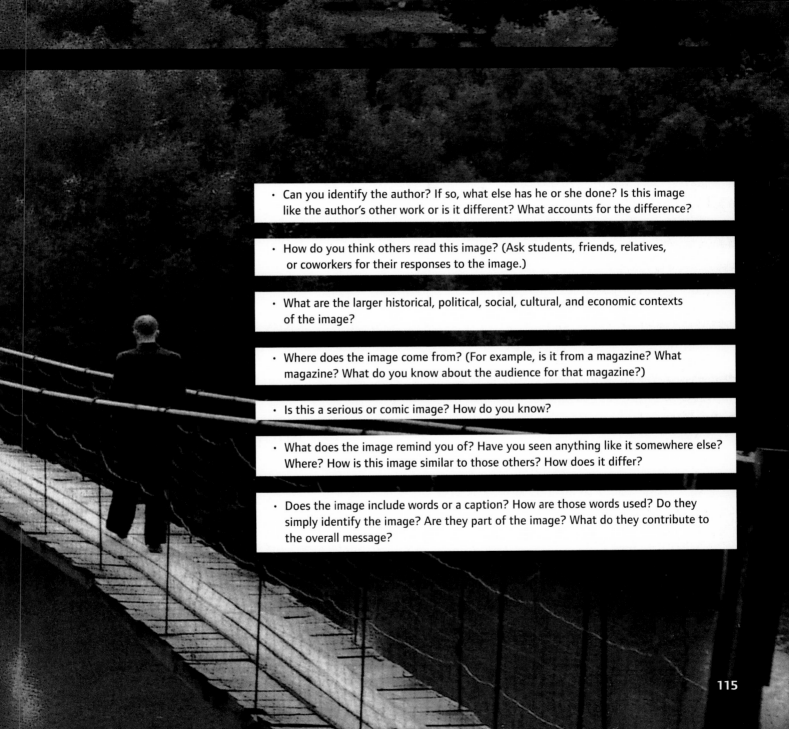

- Can you identify the author? If so, what else has he or she done? Is this image like the author's other work or is it different? What accounts for the difference?

- How do you think others read this image? (Ask students, friends, relatives, or coworkers for their responses to the image.)

- What are the larger historical, political, social, cultural, and economic contexts of the image?

- Where does the image come from? (For example, is it from a magazine? What magazine? What do you know about the audience for that magazine?)

- Is this a serious or comic image? How do you know?

- What does the image remind you of? Have you seen anything like it somewhere else? Where? How is this image similar to those others? How does it differ?

- Does the image include words or a caption? How are those words used? Do they simply identify the image? Are they part of the image? What do they contribute to the overall message?

115

Edward Hopper (1882–1967) has been called one of America's most important twentieth-century realist painters. His subjects were ordinary people in cities, towns, and rural communities across America. *Nighthawks, 1942* is one of Hopper's most famous paintings. It depicts a late-night diner in downtown Chicago.

We present here Hopper's painting along with an essay and a poem written in response to it. The first reaction most of us have to an image is a personal response. That response can take many forms. Some people react by thinking about how much they like or dislike an image. Others find that the image reminds them of something else—a person, an event, maybe another image. Some are moved to make an image of their own or to write a story prompted by what they see. The accompanying pieces illustrate two ways personal response might find expression.

Nighthawks, *1942*

EDWARD HOPPER

Hopper

MARK STRAND

Mark Strand (b. 1934), a former U.S. poet laureate, is the author of numerous books of poetry including *Blizzard of One*, which was awarded a Pulitzer Prize in 1999. He has also published many stories and essays, including the collection *Hopper* (1994), in which this essay first appeared. Strand begins by explaining why he has always felt a personal connection to the scenes Hopper painted. Notice that, though Strand begins with personal recollections of watching the world from the backseat of his parents' car, he moves quickly to analysis, examining the geometric patterns in the painting and the subject (which, he says, suggest there is a story to be told) and using that analysis to come to his conclusion that it is the little, seemingly insignificant details in a painting that keep viewers looking and wanting to know more.

I

I often feel that the scenes in Edward Hopper paintings are scenes from my own past. It may be because I was a child in the 1940s and the world I saw was pretty much the one I see when I look at Hopper's today. It may be because the adult world that surrounded me seemed as remote as the one that flourishes in his work. But whatever the reasons, the fact remains that looking at Hopper is inextricably bound with what I saw in those days. The clothes, the houses, the streets and storefronts are the same. When I was a child what I saw of the world beyond my immediate neighborhood I saw from the backseat of my parents' car. It was a world glimpsed in passing. It was still. It had its own life and did not know or care that I happened by at a particular time. Like the world of Hopper's paintings, it did not return my gaze.

The observations that follow are not a nostalgic look at Hopper's work. They do, however, recognize the importance for him of roads and tracks, of passageways and temporary stopping places, or to put it generally, of travel. They recognize as well the repeated use of certain geometrical figures that bear directly on what the viewer's response is likely to be. And they recognize that the invitation to construct a narrative for each painting is also part of the experience of looking at Hopper. And this, inasmuch as it demands an involvement in particular paintings, indicates a resistance to having the viewer move on. These two imperatives—the one that urges us to continue and the other that compels us to stay—create a tension that is constant in Hopper's work.

II

In *Nighthawks*, three people are sitting in what must be an all-night diner. The diner is situated on a corner and is harshly lit. Though engaged in a task, an employee, dressed in white, looks up toward one of the customers. The customer, who is sitting next to a distracted woman, looks at the employee. Another customer, whose back is to us, looks in the general direction of the man and the woman. It is a scene one might have encountered forty or fifty years ago, walking late at night through New York City's Greenwich Village or, perhaps, through the heart of any city in the northeastern United States. There is nothing menacing about it, nothing that suggests danger is waiting around the corner. The diner's coolly lit interior sheds overlapping densities of light on the adjacent sidewalk, giving it an aesthetic character. It is as if the light were a cleansing agent, for nowhere are there signs of urban filth. The city, as in most Hoppers, asserts itself formally rather than realistically. The dominant feature of the scene is the long window through which we see the diner. It covers two-thirds of the canvas, forming the geometrical shape of an isosceles trapezoid, which establishes the directional pull of the painting, toward a vanishing point that cannot be witnessed, but must be imagined. Our eye travels along the face of the glass, moving from right to left, urged on by the converging sides of the trapezoid, the green tile, the counter, the row of round stools that mimic our footsteps, and the yellow-white neon glare along the top. We are not drawn into the diner but are led alongside it. Like so many scenes we register in passing, its sudden, immediate clarity absorbs us, momentarily isolating us from everything else, and then releases us to continue on our way. In *Nighthawks*, however, we are not easily released. The long sides of the trapezoid slant toward each other but never join, leaving the viewer midway in their trajectory. The vanishing point, like the end of the viewer's journey or walk, is in an unreal and unrealizable place, somewhere off the canvas, out of the picture. The diner is an island of light distracting whoever might be walking by—in this case, ourselves—from journey's end. This distraction might be construed as salvation. For a vanishing point is not just where converging lines meet, it is also where we cease to be, the end of each of our individual journeys. Looking at *Nighthawks*, we are suspended between contradictory imperatives—one, governed by the trapezoid, that urges us forward, and the other, governed by the image of a light place in a dark city, that urges us to stay.

Here, as in other Hopper paintings where streets and roads play an important part, no cars are shown. No one is there to share what we see, and no one has come before us. What we experience will be entirely ours. The exclusions of travel, along with our own sense of loss and our passing absence, will flourish.

Joyce Carol Oates (b. 1938) is a poet, essayist, and fiction writer, and one of America's most prolific authors. Among her many honors, she has won a National Book Award and the O. Henry Award for Continued Achievement in the Short Story. The poem reprinted here was included in the 1991 *Best American Poetry* anthology. In it, Oates imagines who the people in the painting are, why they are there, and what they must be thinking. Her poem fills in the blanks for her, detailing characters and motivations and circumstances from the scene suggested in Hopper's painting.

On Edward Hopper's
Nighthawks, 1942

JOYCE CAROL OATES

The three men are fully clothed, long sleeves,
even hats, though it's indoors, and brightly lit,
and there's a woman. The woman is wearing
a short-sleeved red dress cut to expose her arms,
a curve of her creamy chest; she's contemplating
a cigarette in her right hand, thinking that
her companion has finally left his wife but
can she trust him? Her heavy-lidded eyes,
pouty lipsticked mouth, she has the redhead's
true pallor like skim milk, damned good-looking
and she guesses she knows it but what exactly
has it gotten her so far, and where?—he'll start
to feel guilty in a few days, she knows
the signs, an actual smell, sweaty, rancid, like
dirty socks; he'll slip away to make telephone calls
and she swears she isn't going to go through that
again, isn't going to break down crying or begging
nor is she going to scream at him, she's finished
with all that. And he's silent beside her,
not the kind to talk much but he's thinking
thank God he made the right move at last,
he's a little dazed like a man in a dream—
is this a dream?—so much that's wide, still,
mute, horizontal, and the counterman in white,
stooped as he is and unmoving, and the man
on the other stool unmoving except to sip
his coffee; but he's feeling pretty good,
it's primarily relief, this time he's sure
as hell going to make it work, he owes it to her
and to himself, Christ's sake. And she's thinking

the light in this place is too bright, probably
not very flattering, she hates it when her lipstick
wears off and her makeup gets caked, she'd like
to use a ladies' room but there isn't one here
and Jesus how long before a gas station opens?—
it's the middle of the night and she has a feeling
time is never going to budge. This time
though she isn't going to demean herself—
he starts in about his wife, his kids, how
he let them down, they trusted him and he let
them down, she'll slam out of the goddamned room
and if he calls her *Sugar* or *Baby* in that voice,
running his hands over her like he has the right,
she'll slap his face hard, *You know I hate that: Stop!*
And he'll stop. He'd better. The angrier
she gets the stiller she is, hasn't said a word
for the past ten minutes, not a strand
of her hair stirs, and it smells a little like ashes
or like the henna she uses to brighten it, but
the smell is faint or anyway, crazy for her
like he is, he doesn't notice, or mind—
burying his hot face in her neck, between her cool
breasts, or her legs—wherever she'll have him,
and whenever. She's still contemplating
the cigarette burning in her hand,
the counterman is still stooped gaping
at her, and he doesn't mind that, why not,
as long as she doesn't look back, in fact
he's thinking he's the luckiest man in the world
so why isn't he happier?

focus.

1. Although Strand and Oates use different genres to respond to Hopper's painting, they both see the potential for story in the image. With a group of your classmates, identify the features of this painting that might lead someone to tell a story based on it.

2. What is the story in the painting according to Oates's poem? What are the relationships she imagines among the people in the painting?

3. Strand writes that he relates easily to Hopper's paintings because they are about a world he recognizes. He grew up in America during the period when Hopper was painting, and the places and people from those paintings look to Strand like places and people in his life. How might someone who did not grow up in a world that looks like Hopper's respond to a painting like this one? Very likely, you did not grow up in the same world. How does your response differ from Strand's? How is it similar?

▶ *Doing Hair.* Photo by Roland Charles.

respond.

1. Show Hopper's painting to 3–5 people of different ages and backgrounds and see how they respond to it. You will probably find it necessary to prompt a response by asking specific questions. For example, do they find the painting appealing? Does it remind them of anything? What do they think is happening in the painting? When you have gathered several responses, write a response that, like Strand's, accounts for what you and others see in this painting.

2. Look at the photo below and take notes on your first responses. With a partner or a group, identify details in the photo that might lead someone to want to create a story from it. What is happening in the photo? How is the setting important? How would you characterize the people? Consider also any elements of composition that you think are important in your response (the frame around the mirror image, for example). How do these elements contribute to the way you see the image? What seems to be the most important part of the picture? What is left out? Where was the photographer standing? Where do you seem to be

standing when you look at the people in the picture?

Next, write a one-page analysis of the details of the image that prompted your responses. What memories (if any) did this photo evoke for you, and what other knowledge do you think was important for the way you responded? What details in the photo suggest that there is a story to tell?

3. Below is the complete text of a story written in response to the photo at the right. Study the photo and read the story (written by Ethan Canin, a critically acclaimed fiction writer who teaches at the Iowa Writers Workshop). Talk with classmates about what Canin saw in this photo and what prompted the story he wrote in response. Then find a photo yourself that brings out the storyteller or poet in you. Write a memoir, story, or poem in response. Include the photo with what you write.

Vivian, Fort Barnwell
by Ethan Canin

I tell my wife, I'll always remember this photograph of my mother. She's out in back, hanging the blankets to dry on our backyard lines after one of our picnics, and she looks so young, the way I remember her before we moved to California. I was ten, I think. We used to have picnics out there under the

water tower when my father got home from work, out in back on the grass on a set of big gray movers' blankets. My father and the man next door had built a pool from a truck tire set in concrete, and they filled it with water for my brother and me to splash in. I remember the day this picture was taken, because my mother had to hang the blankets to dry after we'd soaked them from the pool. My father was mad but she wasn't. She was never mad at us. I haven't seen that picture in years, I tell my wife. But I remember it.

And then one day for no reason I can fathom, my wife is looking through the old cardboard-sided valise where my mother had kept her pictures, and she says, Here? Is this the one you're always talking about? And I say, Yes, I can't believe you found it. And she says, Those aren't movers' blankets, those are some kind of leaves up in the foreground. They look like something tropical, maybe rubber leaves. She's not

hanging laundry at all. I say, Wait a minute— let me see. And I laugh and say, You're right. How can that be? My whole life I've remembered that picture of her hanging those blankets after we'd soaked them. I can even remember the picnic. She says, That's funny, isn't it? I say, My mother was so beautiful.

Our own children are out back in our own yard. It's too cool here for a pool, but I've built them a swingset from redwood, and I take a look out the window at them climbing it the way I've told them not to.

And then a few minutes later my wife says, Look at this, and she hands me the picture again, turned over. On the back it says, Vivian, Fort Barnwell, 1951. That's not your mother at all, she says. That's your grandmother. I say, Let me see that. I say, My God, you're right. How could that have happened?

Joel Sternfeld (b. 1944) is an internationally known photographer who has exhibited his work at such museums as New York's Museum of Modern Art, the Getty, the Chicago Art Institute, and the San Francisco Museum of Modern Art. He is the recipient of two Guggenheim Fellowships and a Prix de Rome. He has taught in the Harvard Visual and Environmental Studies Program and now teaches photography at Sarah Lawrence College.

Sternfeld is known for beautiful landscape photography that is often characterized by an unexpected sense of drama. The photo here is of a pumpkin patch in Virginia—but that's not all. As you look at the picture, think about how the details of the image are arranged in the visual space and consider different ways of framing the image. What is included in the picture? What is left out? What is in the foreground? What is in the background? Does one part of the image contradict or enhance another part?

McLean, Virginia, December 1978

JOEL STERNFELD

focus.

1. Write a brief description of Sternfeld's photograph. In your description, note what you see the first time you look at the image and what details emerge as you spend more time looking at it. How does your response to the image change as you examine the details more carefully?

2. The farm stand in the foreground of this photograph seems to be totally unrelated to the activity in the background. Notice, for example, the person who seems to be shopping for a pumpkin, completely unaware of the fire raging nearby. How would this image change if the man were standing beside the market and watching the firefighters?

3. Traditionally, landscape photography focuses on the beauty, power, or tranquility of a place. Sternfeld's landscapes, like this one, break with that tradition. When Sternfeld photographs a landscape, he looks for surprise or contradiction. In that way, he complicates the viewer's notion of what is beautiful and what is appropriate for landscape. You might notice in this photo, for example, that the colors of the house and fire closely match the colors of the market stand and the pumpkins. With a group of students, consider this photo as a landscape image. How does the photo convey the beauty of the landscape? In what ways does Sternfeld complicate that beauty?

respond.

1. For this assignment, begin by making a viewfinder, following the instructions below.

   a. Cut two identical right angles out of cardboard or paper as shown. You can make a viewfinder as large or small as you want. For viewing the Sternfeld photo, make each side of the right angle aproximately 4 inches in length.

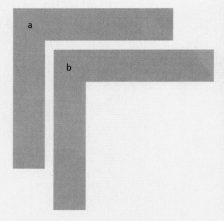

   b. Flip one of the right angles over.

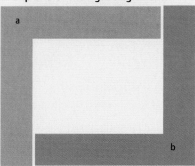

c. Adjust the right angles, moving them together and apart to view different sections of the photograph. When you move them together you "crop tightly" around a small section of the image. Moving them apart allows more of the image to appear.

Use the viewfinder to reframe Sternfeld's image several times by moving it over the photograph, isolating portions of the photo to make new images.

As you move the viewfinder around, notice how the image changes. Even the subject of the image changes depending on what you select and what you leave out.

Once you have isolated (or composed) several different images from this one photo, use your experiment as the basis for a written analysis of how composition, selection, and emphasis contribute to the way an audience reads an image. You can begin by describing the original photo as it appears here, and then explain how your viewfinder experiment changed the photo. To illustrate your analysis, you can either photocopy your individual selections and include them with your analysis, photocopy the entire image and draw squares indicating which views you isolated, or sketch your selections.

2. On first glance, the Sternfeld photograph—with its country market and pumpkins all around—might seem like the kind of image a greeting card company would choose for Thanksgiving or Halloween. In this photo, however, the house on fire in the background stands in sharp contrast to the country charm in the foreground. Make a greeting card using this image. Take advantage of the elements of contradiction and surprise in Sternfeld's photo to create an unconventional greeting.

John Szarkowski (b. 1925) is Director Emeritus of the Department of Photography at the Museum of Modern Art in New York City. In *Looking at Photographs: 100 Pictures from the Collection of the Museum of Modern Art,* from which this postcard and the accompanying description are taken, Szarkowski provides a tour of the museum's photography collection.

The postcard reproduced here seems to have been chosen for the museum's collection not because of its beauty alone but also because of the sender's written response to the photograph. The juxtaposition of postcard image and handwritten message evokes both the person who chose this card and "Miss Annie" who received the postcard. Here we have an entire relationship in a very ordinary message. Of course, we don't know the nature of that relationship. Miss Annie could be a fiancée, a family friend, a former teacher. We only know that John A. thought she would appreciate those apples.

Sometimes, just the act of making an image from the most ordinary objects can give those objects special significance. When we consider how an image communicates a message, then, it can be helpful to bear in mind the subject of the image (apples), how that subject is handled by the designer, the medium through which it is produced (photography), its genre (postcard), and what use is made of the image (originally surface mail, now art object and historical document).

On *Apples Grown by Irrigation at Artesia, New Mexico*

JOHN SZARKOWSKI

Among the characteristics to be noted about traditional painting are that it was slow, difficult, rare, and expensive, and was therefore used only to record things of great importance, such as religious sacrifices, kings and condottieri, ancient myths, and the rich. (The Dutch, especially, also painted good things to eat, but generally along with good silver and good linen, making the subject a subcategory under *the rich.*)

Photography, on the other hand, was quick, easy, ubiquitous, and cheap, and was used to record everything, most of which seemed, by painters' standards, evanescent and trivial. It is true: Most of what photography recorded *was* trivial. Nevertheless, once the pictures were made a curious thing happened: By the very fact of being transfixed these trivial things were somehow elevated, and became part of formal history and tradition. Many of these odd, scrubby pictures finally came to rest on the walls of painters' studios, where their strangely compelling qualities might be contemplated and abstracted.

The postcard reproduced here was postmarked 7 P.M., July 27, 1907, Artesia, New Mexico. It was sent by Jim A. to Annie Schrock of Toyah, Texas. The picture itself would, in retrospect, be moving, memorializing as clearly as it does the triumph of a dead, unheralded pomologist and the sincere and simple construction of an anonymous provincial photographer. But it is better still by virtue of Jim A.'s beautiful line: "Miss Annie How are these for apples?"

1. Go to your school's bookstore or someplace that sells local postcards and look through them to get a sense of how your school or town is represented in the photographs on these cards. Note the kinds of photos, whether they represent the way you see the school or the town, and which cards you would send if you wanted to tell someone about this place who has never been there. If you can, bring 3–5 cards with you to class for your discussion of this reading.

2. According to Szarkowski, most of the subjects of early photographs were trivial, but they became "somehow elevated" by the fact of being photographed. If you studied some postcards in the preceding question, how does his observation apply to those images? What do those (or other) postcards say about the place they represent?

3. Szarkowski claims that this picture, even without John A.'s question, would be "moving, memorializing as clearly as it does the triumph of a dead, unheralded pomologist and the sincere and simple construction of an anonymous provincial photographer." What do you think Szarkowski sees in this photograph that causes him to make that claim?

1. Write an analysis in which you examine the several meanings or messages the apples postcard conveys depending on how it is used. Begin by making a chart listing the ways the image might be described—postcard, art object, early twentieth-century American photograph, textbook illustration, and so on. Next to each of these, explain how the meaning or significance of this image changes with each use and what it retains from other uses. Compare notes with several students and add any uses you had not considered. Use your notes as a basis for your analysis of how the image changes depending on how it is used.

2. The arrangement or composition of an image can affect how we see it or what meaning we take from it. In a 1–2 page analysis, explain how the composition of these apples contributes to the way Szarkowski reads the image as an art photo. It might be helpful if you make a sketch of the photograph's composition. You can do this by placing a thin piece of paper over the photo and drawing lines to indicate the basic structure of the image. Refer to the way we diagrammed the Rosenthal photo on page 105. Remember that a closed composition emphasizes the importance of the subject within the frame or visual space, whereas an open composition suggests that there is also something important outside the visual space.

3. Experiment with composition yourself. Take eleven large apples and a ruler and arrange them in a number of positions. Take notes, make sketches, or take photographs of your arrangements, paying attention to which seem more like art images and which seem random, nontraditional, or just messy. If you aren't sure what constitutes an "art image," you can find examples of still lifes in any art history book. A still life is a painting or photograph of ordinary objects, often (though not always) food. Some contemporary still-life imagery includes such common objects as ketchup and mustard bottles on a diner counter. Use your notes and your research on still life painting and photography as the basis for your analysis.

Bruce Grierson, writer and cofounder of
Canada's *Adbusters* magazine, argues that so many
of us have become cynical about advertising that the
ad industry has resorted to shock tactics in order to
get our attention. We know what an advertiser wants
us to do—buy the product—and we have been
surrounded by advertising our entire lives. Grierson's
article places advertising into the broader context
discussed in this chapter, showing it in terms of
cultural, economic, and other contexts. In an age of
media overload, Grierson argues, the aims of
advertisers haven't changed, but their tactics have
had to adjust.

Shock's Next Wave

BRUCE GRIERSON

In the late 1950s and early 1960s, dozens of psychiatric patients at the Allan Memorial Institute in Montreal fell under the care of Dr. Ewen Cameron, a man with some radical ideas about how the human mind is wired, and how it might be therapeutically rewired by a skilled psychiatrist such as himself. Cameron believed the roots of mental illness lay in faulty thought patterns patients developed over time. He reckoned patients could be "depatterned" through the ceaseless repetition of a key word or phrase—a technique he called "psychic driving." Confining the patients to "sleep rooms" in the Institute, Cameron "implanted" a carefully chosen "driving message" (usually a negative message, followed much later by an affirming message) into their heads via speakers or earphones. Each message—for example, "You have no confidence in yourself. You are weak and inadequate"—was broadcast continuously for 15 hours a day, seven days a week, for up to two months.

Not surprisingly, "psychic driving" quickly became a torturous ordeal for the subjects. Indeed, Cameron's depatterning work suggested the mind-control experiments being carried out in North Korea, where Communist soldiers were allegedly turning captured POWs into robotically programmed acolytes. (The CIA, eager to know more about brainwashing, and to develop countervailing techniques of its own, funded Cameron's work for three years under a project code-named MKULTRA.) To "break down their resistance" to the incoming messages, Cameron tranquilized his subjects with electroshocks, LSD, hypnosis, or sleeping pills that kept them in unconscious suspension for up to 22 hours a day as the driving messages played on.

If you don't recall Ewen Cameron's famous brainwashing experiments, don't feel too bad—neither do his patients. Upon their release, most had no memory of receiving treatment. In some cases, patients who had listened to hundreds of thousands of repetitions of their driving message could not repeat that message back even once. Rip Van Winkle–like, these people were simply missing a chunk of their lives.

But something profound had clearly happened to them. Immediately following the deprogramming trials, they appeared stunned and disorganized. Many could not remember their own names, or how to eat, or in fact much of anything that had gone on in their lives. Even today, Cameron's former patients report such symptoms as violent mood swings and the inability to concentrate enough to read.

The Allan Institute experiments ceased in the late 1960s. Nine patients would later launch million-dollar suits against the CIA, which settled out of court with them for a much smaller sum, in 1988.

In a broader sense, though, Ewen Cameron's work never really stopped. Under new stewards and another guise, the "electric lobotomies" continue apace. The subject pool has expanded from a few dozen people to a couple of billion. The driving messages have become more sophisticated: cryptic, alluring, alarming. There are no longer called implants. They are called ads.

Today's advertisers operate under far tighter constraints than Ewen Cameron did. Ethically (or practically), they cannot "break down" their subjects' resistance with thorazine or acid. They cannot paralyze them with curare poison. They can and do use a kind of hypnosis—the seductive glow and flicker of television light—but for the most part, their tools are simply the ads themselves, which must be sharp enough to puncture a subject's consciousness and arresting enough to keep said subject from squirming as the payload is delivered.

("You have no confidence in yourself. You are weak and inadequate. Try these jeans.") You might think of modern advertising as broad-spectrum depatterning: a cocktail of thousands of different repeating messages, their aggregate effect no better understood than the effect of those messages implanted in Cameron's patients 40 years ago. What does advertising do to human beings over the long run? We don't know.

All we know is that year by year, as the commercial messages come faster and more obliquely, the modern media consumer is growing hard to impress. She's no longer the alert student sitting quietly front-and-centre. She's slumped, snoozing, in the back, or else trying to climb out a window. The old-school of admaking—establishing the product's "unique selling position" and carefully building brand loyalty—is dead. Traditional agencies like Leo Burnett and J. Walter Thompson are hemorrhaging business to smaller, balls-out agencies like Fallon McElligott and Wieden & Kennedy, who understand that you can't play chess with an attention-deficit-disordered kid: he'll walk away from the board. It's got to be strip chess now, or chess for money. Or you've got to pelt the kid with the pieces.

All of which explains the rise, in recent years, of so-called "shock" advertising. For ads to work, the industry is conceding, they have to be rare and juicy and in your face. They have to offer back-of-the-cabinet images few of us have ever seen—like a black horse humping a white one, or a supermodel taking a dump, or a woman aiming a jet of breast milk into another woman's cup of coffee.

Advertisers will tell you that shock boils down to truth. Drop a truth-teller into a dinner-party full of genteel liars and shock ensues. The current level of candor in tampon commercials would make Cathy "I think it's perfectly natural" Rigby blush, but mopping up a cafeteria spill with a Kotex is really just life as it's lived by real people, no?

Epater les bourgeois. Shock middle-class values. Art, it is said, has no interest in morality. Which may be where art and advertising—at least shock advertising—differ. Shock ads are all about morality. They usually involve sniffing out, simply for the sake of provocation, the ripest cultural taboo. In Germany, that probably means Nazi imagery; in Italy, the Catholic church; in North America, sex. What's left of this particular topic to explore? Incest? Pedophilla? Defecatiovoyeurism? (Those Jenny-McCarthy-on-the-throne print ads turned a few people on, a few people off, and purportedly boosted sales of Candies shoes by 19%). Shock advertisers tend to measure success by the controversy their campaigns generate. If you can't shock the middle class, shock William Bennett and Newt Gingrich. Piss off the powerful jackleg Republicans. Earn some salty reprobations on the Congressional record. Shock Jesse Helms. Conservatives are about the only people you can still get a rise out of these days. That's why shock advertisers love them. They *need* them.

The rest of us, not wanting to be mistaken for anyone liable to revoke arts grants or suppress free expression, adopt an open position of blanket permissiveness. Two horses fucking shocks you? Hey, you don't get out much, do you, friend? I'll bet you found *A Clockwork Orange* troubling, too.

And so we've learned not to be fazed by anything. Even as advertisers mine the most sacred parts of ourselves for distribution and resale, we sit passively by, pretending not to care and ultimately not caring. Baby, we are Teflon-coated, like those skillets from France. The media can't touch us because we are cynics.

But could it be that we are cynics because the media has already touched us? Touched us *there*?

The almost banal truth is, it's very hard to [15] shock us now. So advertisers are giving up trying to shock in the conventional way, and are working on a kind of silent electromagnetic pulse aimed to inflict grave, undefinable damage on any circuitry it hits.

I'm going to argue that there are now three levels of shock in advertising: visceral shock, intellectual shock and, for lack of a better term, "soul" shock.

Let's assume I'm an advertiser whose aim is to shock you at the gut level. I want to bypass your brain, evoke an involuntary response. I want to scare you or sicken you or, especially, turn you on. Twenty years ago, that might have meant showing a woman in a bra. Ten years ago, it might have meant showing a woman out of a bra. We're in Calvin Klein's bailiwick here, of course. Klein shot to the top with a succession of increasingly provocative icons: Brooke Shields in her unzipped jeans: Jeff Aquilon, hung like a grizzly bear, posing in his y-fronts; Kate Moss naked on the couch. Things have gotten really quite skanky of late: young girls deep-throating bananas, inflatable sex dolls looming from highway billboards, semi-naked kids lounging like chickenhawk-porn actors in crummy wood-paneled rumpus rooms. The fashion retailer French Connection recently discovered that while you cannot use the word "fuck" in a mainstream magazine, the word "fcuk" is just fine. You can produce commercials that say "fcuk fashion" and "fcuk advertising"—thus smuggling the king of the seven taboo words past the border guards and into print, because everyone reading the word "fcuk" on the page is saying "fuck" in their head.

But visceral shock is getting harder to deliver in a culture wallpapered with surreal and violent and erotic imagery. This may be why a current trend in advertising is to go not for the gut but for the head. What I call "intellectual shock" really just means advertisers upsetting the expectations of readers and viewers. We see it, most commonly, when an advertiser apparently "comes clean" and is honest with us—a fairly shocking thing for an advertiser to do.

Thirty-five years after the birth of irony in advertising, and 15 years after the birth of reflexive irony in advertising, we may be seeing the dawn of a new core form—beyond irony, closer to a kind of hyper-calculated faux-naïvete. Yes, advertisers seem to be saying, the jig's up, you're on to our game.

Call them anti-ads: actually commercials that [20] look very much like the kind of parodic "subvertisements" magazines like the one you're holding pioneered. Ads that not only undersell the product, but often send up advertising itself. Advertisers today must feel like punk rockers in the mid-1970s, when the punk movement began unexpectedly to find the mainstream. To survive, true punkers understood, punk had to "reject itself." Most advertisers realize that advertising, too, must reject itself if it hopes for any credibility with a cynical public.

Consider the TBWA/Chiat Day spots for ABC TV. "Who among us hasn't spent an entire weekend on the couch, bathed in the cool glow of a Sony Trinitron, only to return to work recuperated and completely refreshed?" The campaign acknowledges, candidly—if tongue-in-cheekily—that the thing being sold is bad for you. (This may not be as risky as it sounds: it worked pretty well for "Death Cigarettes.")

Or the Amstel beer ads featuring the fictitious activist Garrison Boyd, who calls for a serious boycott of Amstel beer. The campaign began with conventional ads for Amstel that ran for a couple of weeks. Then into the picture rode Boyd, loaded for bear, papering over the Amstel ads with anti-Amstel stickers. Finally, the campaign devolved (or evolved) into Boyd's anti-Amstel screeds: "Avoid these Amstels at all costs!"

Or Sprite's recent campaign wherein two schmucks watch TV ads for a pretend soda called "Jooky," until it dawns on them that drinking Jooky isn't going to improve their sex lives anytime soon. The unspoken message: neither will Sprite.

Other examples abound. In recent Fosters beer and Simple running shoe campaigns, we're given a behind-the-scenes look at the genesis of the ads themselves—for example, briefings from the creative director to the copywriter on how the pitches can move product. Such ads follow in the tradition of the famous Isuzu ads where David Leisure played a congenitally lying car salesman, and Nike's Bo Jackson spots, where the preposterousness of shoe ads is held up to the light. But they take Isuzu and Nike a step farther, inviting the readers to laugh along at the whole shallow business of admaking from the inside.

Selling to a generation of cynics requires real 25 finesse. Advertisers must acknowledge their own naked calculatedness, acknowledge that the customer is wise to that naked calculatedness, and then still try to make the sale. "The thing to remember about popular culture," precocious cartoon kid Calvin tells his tiger pal Hobbes, "is that today's TV-reared audience is hip and sophisticated. This stuff doesn't affect us. We can separate fact from fiction. We understand satire and irony. We're detached and jaded viewers who aren't influenced by what we watch." Then Calvin takes a break from his sermon to inflate his basketball shoes. Calvin is the postmodern consumer.

Why do faux-naif ads work? One reason is that the advertiser is trafficking in paradox. The consumer gets two conflicting messages. One is, Since advertising itself is bogus, you should be deeply suspicious of the worth of any product you see advertised these days. The other is, We've been so honest with you about everything; would we lie to you about the worth of this product?

In effect: Don't trust us. Trust us.

Something very strange happens when people receive a mixed message. They are temporarily paralyzed. Let me illustrate this point. A friend of a friend of mine, a small guy who frequents nightclubs where things routinely get out of hand, has learned to use the mixed-message to great effect. When goaded by a bigger, tougher guy, he will step right into the aggressor's face and say, "I don't want to fight, do you?" The big guy always takes a second or two to process this—here's an openly aggressive gesture coupled with a declaration of peace—which is long enough for my friend to a) disengage, or b) land the two punches that will end the fight before it can begin.

The shock of the faux-naif ads is the shock of subverted expectations. Imagine the job applicant you're interviewing suddenly saying, "Don't hire me. I'm stupid and I'll skim from the till." Or your date opening with "Hi, I'm Kelly. I have manic-depression and genital warts." This shock is the shock of getting the last thing you thought you were going to get. Briefly, your belief systems are shaken. Most 14-year-olds experience a similar disorienting moment when they realize their parents are using "reverse psychology" on them. ("Son, I rolled you a couple of joints for the Everclear concert. And take my car—here are the keys.") It catches the kid off guard, reduces him to a single reflexive response: You are fucking with my head.

Intellectually shocking ads, then, are not high- 30 voltage electrodes applied at the scalp and the

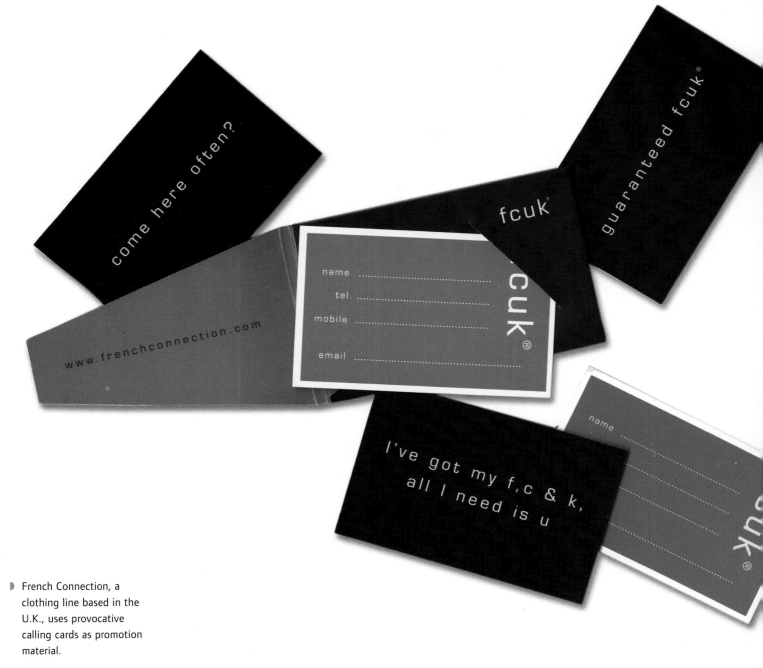

come here often?

guaranteed fcuk®

fcuk

fcuk®

www.frenchconnection.com

name ....
tel. ....
mobile ....

email ....

I've got my f, c & k,
all I need is u

name

cuk®

▶ French Connection, a
clothing line based in the
U.K., uses provocative
calling cards as promotion
material.

ankle, but a dilute concentration of nerve gas sent through the air ducts. Over time they can break down your confidence in your opinions, judgments, values. It becomes very confusing to consumers when antagonists (advertisers and subvertisers) start using the same language. When identical words are used, as situationist Guy Debord might have put it, to create the spectacle and to attack it, the consumer does not know whom to trust, if anyone.

For advertisers, this is a delicate game. It's as if, by parodying themselves, stealing the subvertisers' thunder, they are challenging subvertisers to make a counter-move—to jam the negative with a positive. What's a magazine like *Adbusters* to do? Run ads straight-facedly promoting Amstel beer or Marlboro cigarettes or Nike sneakers, on the assumption that the public is so suspicious of ads, any ads, that their response is to reject the message out of hand?

Which brings us, in a convoluted way, to the third and final new kind of shock. "Soul shock" goes beyond titillation, beyond headgames. These ads aren't clever, or coy, so much as deeply unsettling. *Advertising Age* columnist Bob Garfield calls them "advertrocities." Examples? Benetton's dying AIDS patients and dead Bosnian soldiers. Calvin Klein models drowsing in shooting galleries with hunted, heroin-hollowed eyes. Recently the Italian jeans-maker Diesel launched an extremely disturbing print campaign. The company's cryptic ads-within-ads, set in North Korea, feature images of, for example, skinny models on the side of a bus packed with (presumably) starving, suffering locals. "There's no limit to how thin you can get," says the ad on the bus.

These strike me as some of the most complex shock ads ever made. They appear to be operating on a deeper level than even the advertisers themselves know or understand. Many have one foot in the "intellectual shock" camp. Diesel Jeans' North Korea ads, for example, deflate fashion ad conventions. But unlike, say, the ABC TV spots, they aren't very funny.

If intellectual shock rocks our belief systems, "soul shock" targets our values. There's probably something immoral about ads that inure people to the suffering of other people. The way shock encourages malaise reminds me of what David Korten called the "cycle of alienation," to which today's jaded consumers are somehow intuitively wise. [Basically, we move through four stations: (1) Advertisers assure us their products will make us whole. (2) Buying their product requires money. (3) The quest for money widens the gap between ourselves, family and community. (4) Deepening alienation creates a sense of social and spiritual emptiness, which can only be assuaged by . . . see (1).] The first time you see a starving child on late-night TV, you're appalled. You send money. But as these images become more familiar, your compassion fades. These ads start to repulse you. You never want to see a starving kid again. Cynical consumers understand what's being done to them. They just don't really care.

This idea of the deepening spiral of consumer 35 cynicism is nothing terribly new. And yet it can, I think, explain whole lives. It provides a credible answer for why mood disorders have risen 50% in North America in the last 20 years. (More credible, at least, than the theories that point to the additives in our food or the volume of information we must now contend with or the wash of electromagnetic radiation millions of times greater than our ancestors experienced). The repetition of unsettling messages may be having, must be having, some effect, however unquantifiable, on the deeper strata of our minds, the primitive parts, the limbic regions where sexual and creative impulses live.

Never in history have advertisers so specifically isolated their targets. Who has disposable income? Increasingly, it's the young. (America, a current vein of wisdom holds, is basically run by teenaged girls.) So the agencies crank out shock ads, anti-ads, "advertrocities" for their compassion-fatigued, hard-to-impress young clientele. It's as if 75% of us are being forced to listen to the soundtrack of the world way louder than is comfortable for us because the volume has been calibrated to the damaged eardrums of the other 25%. Over time, this creates not just tension but anger. Eventually, the 75% start hunting down the other 25% with torches.

What shocks us now? Maybe nothing. We can be titillated, still, we can be amused, but perhaps we can never really be shocked. To be shocked requires a measure of innocence you rarely find these days in people over five. More than we care to admit, maybe we have already been depatterned, like Ewen Cameron's psychiatric patients. Maybe we are the Manchurian Candidates of the consumer village, wandering through malls with our heads full of messages driving our behavior ("You have no confidence in yourself. You are weak and inadequate."), messages we cannot repeat back even once.

focus.

1. Grierson begins his article with a story of brainwashing experiments in the 1950s and 1960s, comparing those experiments to the advertising industry's attempts to influence our actions. Do you think the comparison is justified? What, in his discussion of mind control and advertising, do you recognize in ads you see every day? Are some ads more skillful at this than others? How?

2. Grierson writes that advertising uses three levels of shock: visceral, intellectual, and "soul" shock. How would you distinguish among the three? Find examples of ads that rely on each.

3. Who would you say is the primary audience for shock ads? Are these ads equally effective with all audiences? with your parents? your grandparents? your friends? you? Why? Why not?

respond.

1. Find some ads like the ones Grierson describes. In what ways do they draw on current styles or current events? Choose one or more for an analysis in which you examine their value as shock ads.

2. Grierson writes that shock ads target our values. Examine his discussion of how such ads work. Find a current ad campaign that relies on shock tactics. Benetton is one company whose ads have done that for several years, and you can find Benetton ads on the Internet, but other companies rely on similar tactics. You could look for the French Connection ads or some of the others mentioned in the article. Next, write an analysis in which you set your chosen campaign in its broader context. What values does the campaign assume you have as an audience? Does it draw upon current issues to make its impact? Are there historical references that are crucial to the campaign? Does it draw on youth culture?

3. Grierson asks, "What shocks us now?" and then answers his own question: "Maybe nothing." What do you think? Write a response to Grierson in which you address the question of what shocks us now, especially in advertising.

picture this

looking closer

Several years ago, a group of Michigan Technological University students created the postcard reproduced here. They were inspired by an old joke—that you had to go to the end of the earth to get to MTU. They constructed their own highway sign, went out to US 41, took a photograph, and reproduced it as a postcard. Their postcard has since become immensely popular with residents and visitors alike on Michigan's Upper Peninsula. The postcard joke works because it uses familiar visual elements: We expect a highway sign to tell us place names and the distance we have to drive before we get there. The fog and the empty highway going straight into what looks like nothing reinforce the joke.

Because these students took what looks like a normal tourist picture, the humor of the photo comes through only when the reader realizes what the highway sign actually says. In other words, the image relies on our familiarity with postcard photos and our expectations for a photograph like this one to convey the message. The photo is, in effect, a parody of tourist postcards.

Make your own postcard of your school, your hometown, or of a place you know well. Draw on common knowledge of the place and of expectations for postcard art for your production.

Next, in a follow-up essay, explain what you were trying to accomplish in your image, what you have drawn on to make your statement, and how you hope your audience will receive your message. To do that, you will have to explain your purpose, what audience you are aiming for, what message you are sending about the area, and how your composition of the image contributes to that message. Be sure to point to specific elements in the image to support your explanation.

gallery
of
images

looking closer

① *The Human Condition,*
painting by René
Magritte, 1933.
René Magritte was
a surrealist painter
from Belgium. His work
often employs visual
puns that question our
assumptions about
what we see and what
we think we see.

2 *World Trade Center Mural,* Austin, Texas, 2001. This
mural appeared on the side of an Austin laundromat
after September 11, incorporating the events of
that day with angels and the Virgin of Guadalupe,
to whom many miracles have been atrributed.

③ *Chicago 1959/61,* photo
by Yasuhiro Ishimoto.
Ishimoto lives in both
Japan and the United
States, and his work
reflects both sensibilities.
In this photo, the young
man's hand looks to be
holding a mask. Looking
closer, however, we see
that this is an illusion.

④ *Untitled (Jasper County,
Iowa),* photo by John
Vachon, 1940. This
documentary photograph
has a closed form that
focuses our attention on
the women's faces—that
makes us look closer.

⑤ *Trailer Light,*
by Warren Wheeler. By
capturing the shadows
on the side of the trailer,
the photographer allows
us to see a part of the
lives of those who live
inside.

⑥ *Untitled #5,* photo by Anna Gaskell, 1996. Gaskell's photos use
posed figures, artificial lighting, unusual camera angles, and
close-up cropping to suggest an ambiguity between reality and
fiction, what we see and what we imagine. This photo is from her
"Wonder" series, in which she explores issues of girlhood through
allusions to *Alice in Wonderland.*

 making lives visible

remember when you were applying to colleges and you had to write an essay about yourself for the admissions committee—your life, your goals, your accomplishments, the reasons you wanted to attend college?

What did you say about yourself? How did you describe who you were? What stories did you tell to illustrate your experiences or your opinions? How did you describe your personality? How, in other words, did you use written language to make your life "visible"?

Now imagine that you have a similar task today—writing something about yourself for an unknown audience. This time, however, you are invited to include *visual* as well as *verbal* information. What visual texts would you send? What visual media would you use—photography? print? video? drawing? animation? What would you choose to show—your childhood? more recent interactions, with friends or family? your involvement in some activity or sport that you enjoy? your room? your dog or cat? video footage from high school graduation? a performance you were in? Would you refer readers to your Web page? Would you add explanatory captions? How would you organize the visuals you chose?

What additional information could you convey with visual texts that you could not with words alone? What new things do these texts reveal to you about yourself? What different purposes could they help you achieve as a writer? What additional stylistic or design choices would you then have to make?

This chapter focuses on familiar genres we use to write about our experiences and how they help us to understand the world and our place in it, to make meaning from personal observations, and to communicate what we learn to others. In particular, we'll look at various kinds of autobiographical narratives and how people compose these narratives as a way of making their lives visible.

The first stories most of us encounter are bedtime stories told to us by our parents or other family members. Soon we begin to make our own observations of the world, and we structure these observations into stories that we tell about ourselves, about what we see, discover, and accomplish during the day. We tell these stories to exchange information, to explain how we see the world, to express who we are and who we want to be. In this sense, we start to become part of the stories we tell. But it isn't only our own stories that help us understand who we are. As we grow up and expand our personal range—exploring our street, our neighborhood, our schools, our hometown—we meet new people, both like ourselves and different, who have their own stories, ones that may come to involve us. It is within the language of all these stories that we start to see ourselves, that our identity starts to take shape.

Our lives are saturated with stories. We hear stories in religious communities and at school, from friends and relatives. We read stories in magazines and newspapers, in novels and textbooks, in email and letters, in scrapbooks and photo albums, on billboards and Web sites. Because we live in a world saturated with images, the stories we read, as well as the ones we compose, frequently include both words and images. Both communicate information, and both are formulated around conventions that reflect cultural values and have roots in historical forms of social exchange.

Consider, for example, the diary entry on this page. Written in 1897 by Alexander Goodall, a working man in Australia, it provides a glimpse into life there during the last decade of the nineteenth century. Like many people who

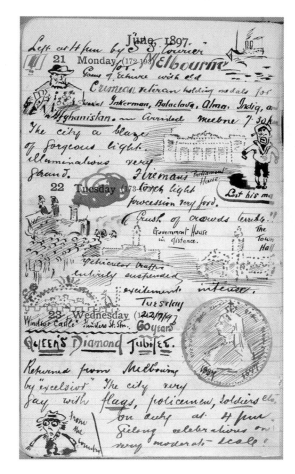

A page from *Diaries of a Working Man*, by Alexander Goodall, 1897. These diaries can be read online at <www.slv.vic.gov.au/slv/exhibitions/diaries/index.html>.

keep diaries, Goodall provided a day-by-day account of his activities. Diarists often enjoy the habit of personal reflection, and many also like the idea of creating a record of their days that they can look back on later in life. Few diaries are intended for public consumption, although many of them make fascinating reading, as you know if you have read Anne Frank's *Diary of a Young Girl*, Charles Darwin's *Beagle Diary*, or John Ransom's *Andersonville Diary*.

Goodall tells the story of his trip to Melbourne to attend the Diamond Jubilee celebration for Queen Victoria, recording his arrival in the city, the crush of the crowds, the spectacle of the torchlight procession, the parade, the flags. His sketches provide additional details—a commemorative coin with Queen Victoria's profile, a young boy in a sailor suit crying because he lost his mother, a drawing of the town hall. Because they are included in his diary and juxtaposed with his written explanations—the text flows around and surrounds the images—these small sketches read as an integral part of the story he tells.

Both the images and the writing on this diary page contain information coded by the cultures of the day, and both need to be read in the context of the history of Australia. For instance, the distinctive profile of Queen Victoria and the elaborately written "Queen's Diamond Jubilee" take on additional meaning if we understand that Australia was then a British colony. Similarly, the sketch of the young boy means more if we recognize his clothes as a child-sized version of the sailor suit worn by the British Royal Navy. Together, the visual and linguistic components add texture to Goodall's account of the Jubilee celebration and what it must have been like for a working man. Goodall's narrative also gives us a sense of his personality and the world he lives in: the kinds of people and sights he notices, the events he attends, the stories he tells.

In this chapter, we explore some of the narrative forms that people use to write about their lives and to make their experiences meaningful—and visible—to others. We will begin with some familiar genres—scrapbooks, memoirs, letters, diaries, and other autobiographical texts—that are linked most directly to personal experience and to writers' efforts to tell something about their lives.

From cave paintings to carvings, drawings to cartoons, photographs to animations, humans have always used visual elements in the narratives we write about our lives. We do so because visual components can convey information and stories in more compressed ways than language alone.

Consider, for example, the relief shown below, a stone carving from 2040 B.C.E. celebrating the life of Egyptian princess Kauit of Deir el Bahri, from the walls of her tomb. Although the primary purpose of the images and the accompanying hieroglyphics is to depict the princess as an individual, the visual nature of this narrative gives us additional information. It reveals, for instance, a number of details about the Egyptian culture in which Princess Kauit lived: the ways in which privileged women arranged their hair and ate breakfast, the kinds of furniture such women had in their homes, how they decorated their houses, and the kinds of dishes they used.

This personal story also reveals information about the values of Egyptian society, showing, for instance, how the members of the royal family

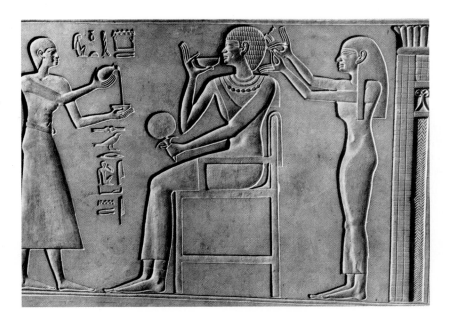

▶ A stone carving showing the Egyptian princess Kauit of Deir el Bahri, from the walls of her tomb, 2040 B.C.E. National Museum, Cairo, Egypt.

were treated and the kinds of relationships they had with their servants. The carving also tells us something about Egypt's technological development (consider, for instance, the mirror, the bowl, the pitcher, the system of hieroglyphic writing) and about Egyptian society's practices of personal adornment and the relation of such practices to social class (consider the princess's clothes, her necklace, and her ankle bracelet—and compare these to the lack of adornment of the woman who is arranging her hair).

The personal forms of storytelling that we will focus on in this chapter frequently contain similar kinds of richly coded visual elements.

To take another example, look at the pages shown here. This multimedia text, "a year in letters," tells a traditional family story in a less-than-traditional digital medium; it was created by designer Cheryl Ball for her grandparents, who met and married as World War II threatened Europe.

These letters and images together provide a richly textured narrative that spans one year in the lives of Ball's grandparents, Ruby Lemmond and Robert Moore, focusing on the historic events in which they were caught up in 1941 during the bombing of Pearl Harbor. The materials themselves—letters, envelopes, telegrams, snapshots—are evocative of a period when written correspondence by post was a major form of exchange and when families stored their photographs in shoe boxes and cardboard albums.

image conscious

Find a current image or advertisement that reveals details about life in the United States in the twenty-first century. Write a paragraph explaining what it shows and why.

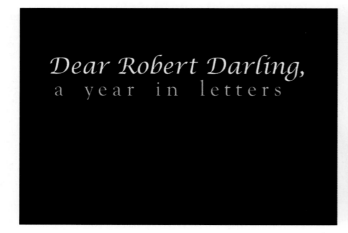

Considered in isolation or as a transcription, the text of these letters would convey only part of the story that Ball wanted to tell. When we see the images of the actual handwritten letters and the envelopes they came in, along with the old stamps and the postmarks from military bases, we get more dimensions of their correspondence—that it took place in an era when long exchanges were not instantaneous, and when letters sent by U.S. mail were the only realistic way of corresponding in depth. And when the letters are read along with the photographs and the telegram saying "Am safe don't worry," we *see* as well as read about what Ruby's and Robert's lives were like: what she worried about on a daily basis ("everything is being censured"), what Hawaii was like just after Pearl Harbor had been bombed ("all our radio stations have closed"), and what patriotism meant to citizens of the United States as they prepared to enter World War II ("Try your dead level best not to let your own feelings get the best of you"). With letters and photographs side by side, we can imagine what Robert saw from the deck of the U.S.S. *Enterprise* and understand how Ruby felt as she sat in a bomb shelter and worried about her husband's safety. The combination of elements in a digital medium creates a text that exceeds conventional boundaries and lets us experience a conversation in a way that plain words or pictures alone seldom do.

▶ Pages from *Dear Robert Darling: A Year in Letters,* a multimedia memory book by Cheryl Ball that collects the 1941 correspondence of Ball's grandparents. You can read the entire book online at <www.hu.mtu.edu/~ceball/eworks/1941.html>.

Ruby holding a friend's daughter. They shared a bomb shelter in Hawaii.

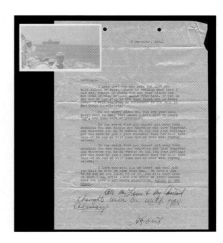

AUTOBIOGRAPHICAL GENRES

There is nothing more personal than the stories we compose about ourselves. Autobiographical texts focus on experiences important to the author and are generally characterized by a strong personal voice. Such texts communicate who we are and who we want to be; they convey something about the significance we see in our own lives and actions. Although these texts focus on us as individuals, they also reveal a great deal about the times and places in which we live, the belief systems that order our lives, the cultures that shape our values, the ways we relate to friends and family. Given these characteristics, autobiographical texts are valuable not only for what they can tell us about a person's insights but also for what they can *show* us of specific times and places and events.

Autobiographical texts can also be fun to read—they come from the heart, they employ a strong authorial voice, and they provide glimpses of other people's daily lives. Some genres are especially engaging visually. We'll look here at several kinds of autobiographical writing—scrapbooks, memory books, diaries, journals, letters, memoirs, and full autobiographies.

Although early forms of SCRAPBOOKS and MEMORY BOOKS were compiled in the seventeenth century, these collections were generally limited to handwritten entries. It was not until the eighteenth century that interest in scrapbooks really began to build, as mass-produced magazines and newspapers provided ideal sources of short pieces that individuals could clip and collect. In the nineteenth century, when printing and photography became less expensive, scrapbooks and memory books assumed their modern form, telling stories about our lives not only through bits of writing but also with the physical evidence of photographs, drawings, doodlings, poems, letters, menus, posters, ticket stubs, cash register receipts, and so on.

These texts, assembled over long periods of time and often around a theme, can be as much collage as writing. In the eclectic nature of their contents, scrapbooks represent the layers of our lives and the colliding bits of personal experience that help formulate our identities. Look, for instance, at two pages from an online scrapbook by Eric Rodenbeck, a designer of interactive digital books that are filled with "physical traces of the world": snapshots, ads, notes, biblical passages, and more.

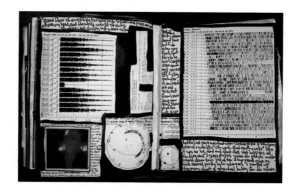

▶ Two pages from an online scrapbook by Eric Rodenbeck. More of Rodenbeck's work can be accessed at <book.stamen.com/books/index.html>.

As collections of material artifacts, scrapbooks demonstrate a kind of respect for small things, ephemeral items that together convey personal meaning.

DIARIES, JOURNALS, and LETTERS are autobiographical works that usually follow the rhythms of our days, as we report on what we do, how we feel, what we see, whom we meet. Diaries and journals, written generally for the author's own eyes, provide a record of life as experienced by a single individual. Some writers, however, seem willing to imagine a wider circle of readers, as indicated in this poem from the 1798 travel journal of Richard Champney, a British citizen who traveled in the United States in the eighteenth century.

> Reader! for goodness sake, forbear
> To change one word that's written here,
> Bless'd be the man that spares my scribbling,
> But curs'd be he that would be nibbling.

> In hopes that they may be read with some indulgence, & that my
>   Fellow Beings may not only find amusement, but some good
>   hints & morals useful to themselves . . .

> Truth has & shall be the Polar Star, by which I shall shape the
>   course of my Adventures; I consider it my duty to report as I
>   find: my motto is, "Nothing extenuate, nor set down ought in
>   malice."

Champney, of course, did not know his journals would one day be published on a Web site at the University of Delaware <www.lib.udel.edu/ud/spec/exhibits/selfwork/>.

Letters can also function as autobiographical writing spaces, perhaps because composing can be easier when we have a trusted audience in

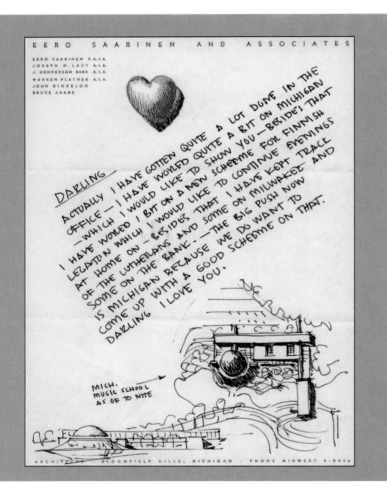

mind. Most of us have written and received letters that contain only words. Here are three letters that combine images and words. These are created by artists, but they include the kinds of stories that most personal letters tell—Eero Saarinen describes his work on the architectural plan for the University of Michigan in a 1953 letter to his wife; R. Lortac describes

image conscious

Find an email you have sent and try illustrating it. You can drag in clip art or images from the Web or scan in photos or other visuals—you can even print out your email and illustrate it by hand.

Letters by Eero Saarinen, R. Lortac, and Moses Soyer. Archives of American Art. <archivesofamericanart. si.edu/exhibits/sketch bk/sketchbk.htm>.

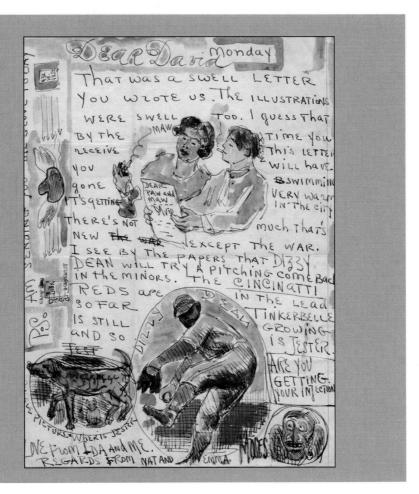

Brittany to a friend looking for a vacation rental; Moses Soyer sends news from home to his son at summer camp. The drawings allow the authors to show as well as tell their stories—and let readers *see* what they're up to in a way that we might not with plain words.

Diaries and journals also often include both verbal and visual components, such as drawings, doodles, diagrams, and other graphic details. Look, for instance, at the pages from the pocket diaries of artist F. Luis Mora, describing with both words and images letters Mora received, fish he caught, and paintings on which he was working.

▶ Pages from the diary of F. Luis Mora, 1913. Archives of American Art.<archivesof americanart.si.edu/ exhibits/sketchbk/ sketchbk.htm>.

See also Joseph Squier's *Urban Diary*, a hypertext diary. Squier teaches in the narrative media program at the University of Illinois; his diary is a kind of narrative constructed out of the details of his day—photos, the weather, bills to be paid, books he wants to read. Diaries, journals, and letters can be collected and arranged to tell stories that stretch over a period of time; they can also be enjoyed in small doses, one at a time.

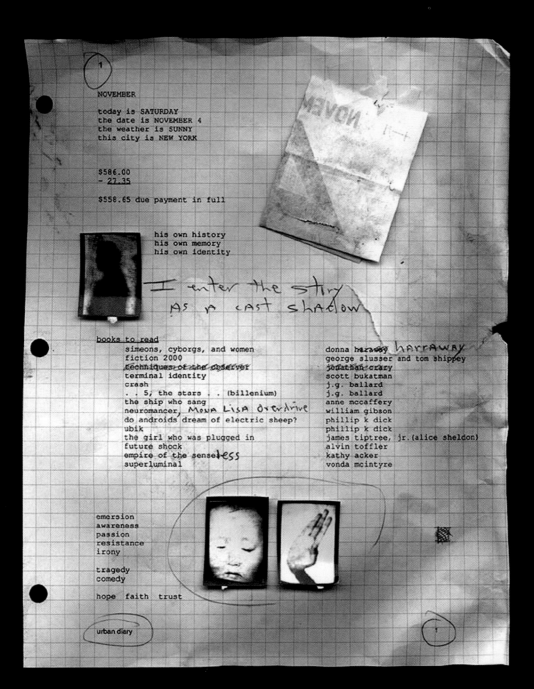

Page from *Urban Diary,* by Joseph Squier, 1995. <theplace.walkerart.org/place.html>.

Memoirs and autobiographies tell longer stories about people's lives, often drawing on letters, memory books, diaries and journals, photographs, and personal records. Composed in retrospect, these texts provide a systematic look back. Memoirs generally examine a significant event or period in a person's life, whereas a full autobiography looks at a whole lifetime.

Memoirs have long been an essayistic genre without many (or any) illustrations. See how the following excerpt from essayist Annie Dillard's memoirs describes with words a scene from her childhood. Consider how this text might be different had she written it for an online environment, where visual elements are expected and more easily incorporated.

When I was five, growing up in Pittsburgh in 1950, I would not go to bed willingly because something came into my room. This was a private matter between me and it. If I spoke of it, it would kill me.

Who could breathe as this thing searched for me over the very corners of the room? Who could ever breathe freely again? I lay in the dark.

My sister Amy, two years old, was asleep in the other bed. What did she know? She was innocent of evil. Even at two she composed herself attractively for sleep. She folded the top sheet tidily under her prettily outstretched arm; she laid her perfect head lightly on an unwrinkled pillow, where her thick curls spread evenly in rays like petals. All night long she slept smoothly in a series of pleasant and serene, if artificial-looking, positions, a faint smile on her closed lips, as if she were posing for an ad for sheets. There was no messiness in her, no roughness for things to cling to, only a charming and charmed innocence that seemed then to protect her, an innocence I needed but couldn't muster. Since Amy was asleep, furthermore, and since when I needed someone most I was afraid to stir enough to wake her, she was useless.

—ANNIE DILLARD,
An American Childhood

As we crossed the Mexican border the border patrol would

ask me my citizenship. I would reply, "AMERICAN"

because my parents taught me to say that.

But in California, people

would ask me "WHAT ARE YOU?"

I guess because they didn't

quite know how to ask

"ARE YOU AMERICAN ?"

I would proudly reply,

"MEXICAN".

I always wished I had dark skin
and dark hair like my mother.

The text above shows a screen shot from *Glass Houses*, a digital memoir composed by Jacalyn Lopez Garcia, a multimedia artist who teaches at the University of California at Riverside. Her memoir tells the story of her family's efforts to assimilate into American life after moving from Mexico to the United States. The site is structured using the metaphor of a house that readers are invited to explore (the author has left virtual keys under the virtual doormat). Though the excerpt here looks relatively old-fashioned, the site includes music and a message board to which readers are invited to add their voices—elements no print memoir could have.

Memoirs and autobiographies provide more cohesive, coherent personal stories than texts such as diaries and journals that are compiled on a daily basis, perhaps because authors are more conscious of selecting stories and memories that are germane to a particular focus or of setting their individual lives within the context of a particular time and place.

▶ Screen shot from *Glass Houses*, a digital memoir by Jacalyn Lopez Garcia. <www.cmp.ucr.edu/students/glasshouses/default.html>.

Whenever we make a life "visible", we are never simply recounting information we have taken in. Our own acts of seeing always mean that something else is unseen. In looking *at* something, we must look *away* from something else; in choosing to focus on one event, we let another event pass out of our line of vision. It would be impossible, then, for two individuals to "see" the same event in exactly the same way. Not only do we all have different perceptual and intellectual abilities, but our perceptions are filtered through very different educations, personal experiences, family values, and cultural understandings. Moreover, in telling stories about our observations and experiences, we never relate every detail. Instead—in the interest of time, efficiency, or effectiveness, and given the limitations of memory, eyesight, and understanding—we *select* which details to include and, in doing so, we *represent* a story, choosing to include some elements and to leave out others.

The two YEARBOOK pages shown here provide good examples of this kind of selection. In each case, the students had one page on which to picture something about their lives. It is commonplace for students to include things like photos of family and friends, favorite quotations, messages thanking people who've been kind or important to them, and so on. Whatever words and images they use create a narrative, one that tells—and shows—something about their lives. Of course they must choose, including photos of some people and not of others, deciding whom to quote and whom to thank. In the examples here, Bowen Zunino decided to include only photos, of her immediate family and best friends. Carolina Arellano included both images and words (in English and Spanish), quoting favorite lyrics, thanking her parents and others, showing pictures of her family and friends. Both pages represent a selection of details that make each of their lives visible.

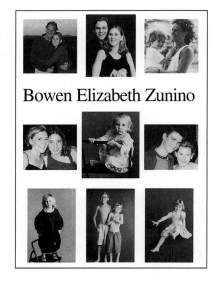

The process of making our lives visible, of selecting details for the stories we tell about ourselves, is not always done consciously. When we compose narratives about ourselves, we may consciously or unconsciously model them on archetypal stories we have seen or read or heard before—stories about heroes who undergo trials and succeed because they are brave, adventurous, or quick-thinking; dutiful children who are eventually rewarded for their attentiveness; parents who protect their children with their lives; tricksters who use their wits to overcome adversaries; evil enemies who attack and are vanquished; friends who are loyal; couples who love one another and refuse to be parted. The outlines of these stories are familiar because they come to us from so many sources: movies, folk tales, religious texts, literary works, family gatherings. Because we are told them again and again, in different versions and at different times of our lives, the narratives and the values contained within them become deeply sedimented in our minds, inscribed in cultural patterns that we come to see as normal, as "common sense."

These archetypal narratives influence the way we live, and they also serve as patterns that structure the stories we ourselves come to tell. For this reason, the personal narratives we write often reveal as much about the way we believe the world *should* be as they do about the real world in which we live, as much about the ideal daughter and the ideal parents as about any real daughter or real parents. The family stories we hear, for instance, are repeated so often because they convey a message—a life lesson—about such ideals: the right way to behave toward your parents, the best kind of marriage, the ideal relationship between brothers. Even the negative stories told in families help constitute such ideals by serving as a contrast to ideal narratives. To compose these "ideal" stories, as Michelle Citron notes in her essay about home movies later in this chapter, we often leave out squabbles and disagreements, disappointments and tensions, in order to more closely follow the lines of the archetypal narratives we love so much.

The ways in which a culture codes a particular medium of storytelling can also add to the effects of selecting and structuring a story. Since the invention of the still camera in the nineteenth century and the movie camera in the twentieth century, for instance, we have associated photographs and documentary films with the cultural codes of realism and science when photographs were employed as a means of identifying criminals and movie cameras were used for aerial reconnaissance in wartime situations. Hence, when we see documentary movies or photographs of people, we are prone to believe that what we are seeing is what exists in reality. But as Citron reminds us, even home movies tell only part of any story. That which is *untold*, that which remains unseen in the visual narrative of a photograph or home movie, often as not lurks just outside the frame of the camera.

As careful and thoughtful readers, we need to seek the outlines of untold elements in a narrative and to ask questions: Why has the writer focused on one particular scene rather than on the other scenes? What details have been left out and why? How have the interests of the writer affected the narrative? Why were certain photos included—and which ones were not? As bell hooks explains later in this chapter, the processes of looking closely, of reading attentively and skeptically, can lead to the testing of tired conventions and well-worn perspectives and to the insights we gain as we compose texts that make our lives visible.

---

snapshot

Yearbooks, birthdays, weddings, proms: these are just some of the events that many of us see as photo ops, occasions to take pictures of friends and family. In Japan, November 15 is one such day. It is a holiday known as shichi-go-san, 3-5-7 day, when parents take 3-, 5-, and 7-year-old children to Shinto shrines to pray for their happiness and good health. The children are dressed up in their best clothes and generally photographed at the shrine. What are some similar photo ops from your life, and what kinds of stories do they tell about you? The picture shown here from Tokyo is clearly being "composed," the father carefully arranging the little girl for the photo. In your experience, how have such photos been composed? How does the composition affect the statements such images make?

Nancy Carpenter (b. 1939) is a retired auditor whose memoir about shopping for hats in Winston-Salem, North Carolina, appeared in *Crowns: Portraits of Black Women in Church Hats* (2000), by Michael Cunningham and Craig Mayberry. The book features photographic portraits along with written reflections of fifty-four women about their Sunday hats. The book is about more than hats, however: the stories the women tell about their hats reveal details about their lives, their personalities, and their spiritualities.

The selection here by Nancy Carpenter, for instance, sets the story about her hats in the context of the American Civil Rights movement. Carpenter's narrative—about the otherwise mundane activity of shopping—is imbued with special significance when it is understood as part of the history of African Americans in the segregated South.

And My Hats Were Prettier

NANCY CARPENTER

Back when I got my first hat, blacks could shop only in certain stores. Those were some different times. We didn't have shopping centers yet in Winston-Salem, so every Saturday we would go downtown. We'd go to Mother and Daughter, Anchor, and Davis, and all the other stores blacks could go to. Back then, you could get a nice hat for ten dollars, and you got a really good hat.

I married young, when I was eighteen. I bought my first hat right after that. The hat made me feel a little older, a little more mature. I didn't make a lot of money. Most blacks didn't have real good jobs. But I could use the layaway plan. Stores didn't have thirty-day layaway back then. You just paid until you could get it out. You could lay away a hat for a dollar and pay a little bit along, a dollar a week if you wanted.

One of the stores black people couldn't shop in was Montaldo's. It was "Whites Only." I saw quite a few hats in their window that I liked, but you just didn't go in. Being reared the way you were at that time, you didn't push.

Looking back on it, Montaldo's hats weren't any prettier. They didn't have anything so nice that we couldn't afford it. I guess it was just the thought that you couldn't go in there that made you want to go in. It wasn't a good feeling.

I'd walk by with my head in the air like, "I'd like 5 to shop in here. But it doesn't bother me that I can't." I stuck with that attitude. "My money's green, too. If you don't want it, so be it."

In the sixties, we were finally allowed to go in Montaldo's. The first time I went in, it made me feel good to show them that I could shop there. I got all dressed up. I said to myself, *If I don't have but just enough to buy one hat, they'll never know it.*

I strutted in, playing the part just like I had money. I was going to get the prettiest hat I could afford. I'd pick one up, turn it around, take a look at the tag quickly, and put it back if it was too much.

When I went up to the counter with a hat, the lady said, "May I help you?" But she was looking down her nose like she was thinking, *I know she's not going to buy that hat.* That made me even more determined. If it took all the money I had at that time, I was going to purchase that hat.

I opened my purse. She said, "Will that be layaway?" I pulled out all these crisp bills and smiled. The lady looked shocked. I bought that hat, took my bag, and strutted out just like I strutted in.

Montaldo's closed down a few years ago. Some 10 people might say they deserved to close because of the way they used to be. But being a Christian, you have to forgive. You just have to say that they didn't know any better. Funny thing was, by the time they closed, I owned about a hundred hats—more than they had in the whole store. And mine were prettier.

focus.

1. This reading comes from a book called *Crowns*. Why do you think the editors chose this title? What are some other possible titles?

2. Look at the photograph of Nancy Carpenter. What does this picture suggest about her as a person? How might you read her story differently if it did not include the picture?

respond.

1. Think about how you dress and what your style conveys about you. Look up the word "style" in a dictionary. How does a style trend start? Why do different generations adopt different styles?

2. Think of some clothing or style that is popular among friends of yours—tattoos, baseball caps, piercings, sneakers, twinsets, Nomination bracelets, and so on. Interview a friend who wears the item and photograph him or her, focusing on both the item and the person wearing it. Make sure that your photographs are respectful of the style and the person. Write a 1-page essay exploring the significance of the item and what it reveals about the generation that values it.

3. Alternatively, do the same task as in the preceding question with your parents or someone of their generation. What clothing or styles do they favor, and why? What does it say about them and their generation?

4. Select an article of clothing or jewelry or body adornment that you like or dislike. Write an essay about what you think about it and what significance it has for you—where you got it, why it matters to you, where you usually wear it, what if any memorable events it evokes. Try to do what Nancy Carpenter does—to write about the item in a way that tells readers something about *you*. Include a picture of the item you write about.

Sabrina Ward Harrison (b. 1977) was born in Canada and attended the California School of Arts and Crafts in Berkeley. She began keeping a journal while she was enrolled in a life stories class and later collected some of her journal entries in *Spilling Open: The Art of Becoming Yourself* (2000). In a bold mixture of words, colors, shapes, hand-drawn images, diagrams and maps, prose and poetry, Harrison makes her life visible, once describing that book as "my life in progress." In 2001, she published a second book, *Brave on the Rocks: If You Don't Go, You Don't See*. You can read more about her at <www.sabrinawardharrison.com>. We include here one of the entries from her earlier collection, a very short narrative about advice her grandmother once gave her.

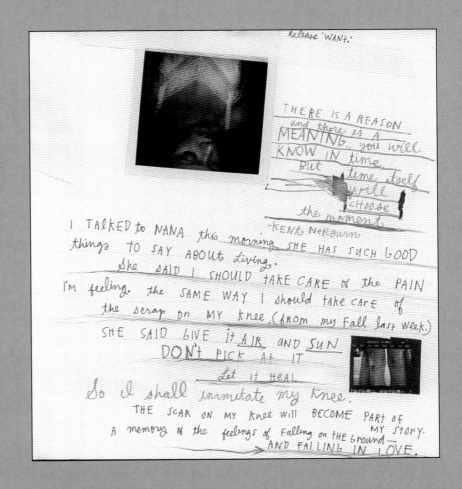

I Talked to Nana This Morning

SABRINA WARD HARRISON

focus.

1. Pay attention to the arrangement of the words and images on the page. Do you read the verbal text differently than you do the visual? If so, in what way? Which do you read first—and why?

2. What do you think is the significance of Harrison's use of capitalization? Is there any rhyme or reason for what's written in all caps and what's not?

respond.

1. Choose someone from your immediate family who has been influential in your life and write a 1–2 paragraph narrative about an interaction you had with him or her. Your goal is to tell about the person, recalling things he or she said and did, and to indicate his or her significance to you. Try to include a photograph of this person with your narrative—if possible, one taken around the time your story is set.

2. Create a scrapbook page about someone who has been important to you. Put your page on paper, on the Web, or in a PowerPoint presentation. You could include poetry, snapshots, letters or email, stories he or she often told, sayings or small mementos that remind you of him or her.

   You might want to mention some important day of that person's life—a birthday, the day you first met, the last time you saw each other. Following are some Web sites that might inspire you:

   Today in History
   <www.thehistorynet.com>
   Any Day <www.scopesys.com/anyday/>
   Those Were the Days
   <www.440.com/twtd/today.html>

3. Write a 1-page memoir about the subject of your scrapbook page in the preceding question, this time with words alone. Study your scrapbook page carefully to see what story it tells about the person, and try to tell a similar story with words. Then compare the two texts. What conclusions do you draw about the differences between words and images?

bell hooks (b. 1952) is a cultural critic whose work focuses on the intersections of race, gender, and class as these social formations affect the lives of Americans. She was born Gloria Jean Watkins but took the name bell hooks to honor her grandmother. Her work has great resonance, in part because of the stories she tells—about herself, her family, and people she has known—and what they say about the significance of her life and the lives of other black Americans.

The following essay starts with a single snapshot of her father and proceeds to explore the importance of photography as a means of representing black identity in America. This piece was first published in a collection entitled *Art on My Mind: Visual Politics* (1995). In the introduction to this volume, hooks argues that people should be "critically aware of visual politics—the way race, gender, and class shape art practices (who makes art, how it sells, who values it, who writes about it)."

Becoming critically aware of the practices involved in artistic representation can be a highly political act that acknowledges the "transformative power of art," according to hooks. As you read this text, consider, in particular, the relationship between the essay and the photograph. What information does the essay convey? the photograph? What information do they convey in tandem? How do you read the text of the essay? How do you read the text of the photograph?

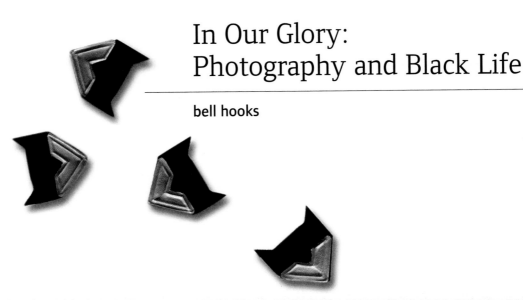

In Our Glory:
Photography and Black Life

bell hooks

▶ Snapshot of Veodis
Watkins, 1949.
Courtesy of bell hooks.
Photographer
unknown.

Always a daddy's girl. I was not surprised that my sister V. became a lesbian, or that her lovers were always white women. Her worship of Daddy and her passion for whiteness appeared to affirm a movement away from black womanhood and, of course, away from that image of the woman we did not want to become—our mother. The only family photograph V. displays in her house is a picture of our dad, looking young with a mustache. His dark skin mingling with the shadows in the photograph. All of which is highlighted by the white T-shirt he wears.

In this snapshot he is standing by a pool table. The look on his face is confident, seductive, cool— a look we rarely saw growing up. I have no idea who took the picture, only that it pleases me to imagine that he cared for the person—deeply. There is such boldness, such fierce openness in the way he faces the camera. This snapshot was taken before marriage, before us, his seven children, before our presence in his life forced him to leave behind the carefree masculine identity this pose conveys.

The fact that my sister V. possesses this image of our dad, one that I had never seen before, merely affirms their romance, the bond between the two of them. They had the dreamed-about closeness between father and daughter, or so it seemed. Her possession of the snapshot confirms this, is an acknowledgment that she is allowed to know—yes, even to possess—that private life he always kept to himself. When we were children, he refused to answer our questions about who he was, how he acted, what he did and felt before us. It was as though he did not want to remember or share that part of himself, as though remembering hurt. Standing before this snapshot, I come closer to the cold, distant, dark man who is my father, closer than I can ever come in real life. Not always able to love him there, I am sure I can love this version of him, the snapshot. I gave it a title: "in his glory."

Before leaving my sister's place, I plead with her to make a copy of this picture for my birthday. She says she will, but it never comes. For Christmas, then. It's on the way. I surmise that my passion for it surprises her, makes her hesitate. My rival in childhood—she always winning, the possessor of Dad's affection—she wonders whether to give that up, whether she is ready to share. She hesitates to give me the man in the snapshot. After all, had he wanted me to see him this way, "in his glory," he would have given me the picture.

My younger sister G. calls. For Christmas, V. has sent her a "horrible photograph" of Dad. There is outrage in her voice as she says, "It's disgusting. He's not even wearing a shirt, just an old white undershirt." G. keeps repeating, "I don't know why she has sent this picture to me." She has no difficulty promising to give me her copy if mine does not arrive. Her lack of interest in the photograph saddens me. When she was the age our dad is in the picture, she looked just like him. She had his beauty then, the same shine of glory and pride. Is this the face of herself that she has forgotten, does not want to be reminded of, because time has taken such glory away? Unable to fathom how she cannot be drawn to this picture, I ponder what this image suggests to her that she cannot tolerate: a grown black man having a good time, playing a game, having a drink maybe, enjoying himself without the company of women.

Although my sisters and I look at this snapshot and see the same man, we do not see him in the same way. Our "reading" and experience of this image is shaped by our relationship with him, with the world of childhood and the images that make our lives what they are now. I want to rescue and preserve this image of our father, not let it be forgotten. It allows me to understand him, provides a way for me to know him that makes it possible to love him again, despite all the other images, the ones that stand in the way of love.

Such is the power of the photograph, of the image, that it can give back and take away, that it can bind. This snapshot of Veodis Watkins, our father, sometimes called Ned or Leakey in his younger days, gives me a space for intimacy between the image and myself, between me and Dad. I am captivated, seduced by it, the way other images have caught and held me, embraced me like arms that would not let go.

Struggling in childhood with the image of myself as unworthy of love, I could not see myself beyond all the received images, which simply reinforced my sense of unworthiness. Those ways of seeing myself came from voices of authority. The place where I could see myself, beyond imposed images, was in the realm of the snapshot. I am most real to myself in snapshots—there I see an image I can love.

My favorite childhood snapshot, then and now, showed me in costume, masquerading. Long after it had disappeared, I continued to long for it, and to grieve. I loved this snapshot of myself because it was the only image available to me that gave me a sense of presence, of girlhood beauty and capacity for pleasure. It was an image of myself I could genuinely like. At that stage of my life I was crazy about Westerns, about cowboys and Indians. The camera captured me in my cowgirl outfit, white ruffled blouse, vest, fringed skirt, my one gun and my boots. In this image I became all that I wanted to be in my imagination.

For a moment, suspended in this image: I am a 10 cowgirl. There is a look of heavenly joy on my face.

I grew up needing this image, cherishing it—my one reminder that there was a precious little girl inside me able to know and express joy. I took this photograph with me on a visit to the house of my father's cousin Schuyler.

His was a home where art and the image mattered. No wonder, then, that I wanted to share my "best" image. Making my first real journey away from home, from a small town to my first big city, I needed the security of this image. I packed it carefully. I wanted Lovie, cousin Schuyler's wife, to see me "in my glory." I remember giving her the snapshot for safekeeping: only, when it was time for me to return home, it could not be found. This was for me a terrible loss, an irreconcilable grief. Gone was the image of myself I could love. Losing that snapshot, I lost the proof of my worthiness—that I had ever been a bright-eyed child capable of wonder—the proof that there was a "me of me."

The image in this snapshot has lingered in my mind's eye for years. It has lingered there to remind me of the power of snapshots, of the image. As I slowly complete a book of essays titled *Art on My Mind*, I think about the place of art in black life, connections between the social construction of black identity, the impact of race and class, and the presence in black life of an inarticulate but ever-present visual aesthetic governing our relationship to image, to the process of image making. I return to the snapshot as a starting point to consider the place of the visual in black life—the importance of photography.

Cameras gave to black folks, irrespective of class, a means by which we could participate fully in the production of images. Hence it is essential that any theoretical discussion of the relationship of black life to the visual, to art making, make photography central. Access and mass appeal have historically made photography a powerful location for the construction of an oppositional black aesthetic. Before racial integration there was a constant struggle on the part of black folks to create a counterhegemonic world of images that would stand as visual resistance, challenging racist images. All colonized and subjugated people who, by way of resistance, create an oppositional subculture within the framework of domination recognize that the field of representation (how we see ourselves, how others see us) is a site of ongoing struggle.

The history of black liberation movements in the United States could be characterized as a struggle over images as much as it has also been a struggle for rights, for equal access. To many reformist black civil rights activists, who believed that desegregation would offer the humanizing context that would challenge and change white supremacy, the issue of representation—control over images—was never as important as equal access. As time has progressed and the face of white supremacy has not changed, reformist and radical blacks would likely agree that the field of representation remains a crucial realm of struggle, as important as the question of equal access, if not more important. Roger Wilkins emphasizes this point in his recent essay "White Out."

> In those innocent days, before desegregation had really been tried, before the New Frontier and the Great Society, many of us blacks had lovely, naive hopes for integration . . . In our naiveté, we believed that the power to segregate was the greatest power that had been wielded against us. It turned out that our expectations were wrong. The greatest power turned out to be what it had always been: the power to define reality where blacks are concerned and to manage perceptions and therefore arrange politics and culture to reinforce those definitions.

Though our politics differ, Wilkins's observations echo my insistence, in the opening essay of *Black Looks: Race and Representation*, that black people have made few, if any, revolutionary interventions in the arena of representation.

In part, racial desegregation—equal access—offered a vision of racial progress that, however limited, led many black people to be less vigilant about the question of representation. Concurrently, contemporary commodification of blackness creates a market context wherein conventional, even stereotypical, modes of representing blackness may receive the greatest reward. This leads to a cultural context in which images that would subvert the status quo are harder to produce. There is no "perceived market" for them. Nor should it surprise us that the erosion of oppositional black subcultures (many of which have been destroyed in the desegregation process) has deprived us of those sites of radical resistance where we have had primary control over representation. Significantly, nationalist black freedom movements were often concerned only with questions of "good" and "bad" imagery and did not promote a more expansive cultural understanding of the *politics* of representation. Instead they promoted notions of essence and identity that ultimately restricted and confined black image production.

No wonder, then, that racial integration has created a crisis in black life, signaled by the utter loss of critical vigilance in the arena of image making—by our being stuck in endless debate over good and bad imagery. The aftermath of this crisis has been devastating in that it has led to a relinquishment of collective black interest in the production of images. Photography began to have less significance in black life as a means—private or public—by which an oppositional standpoint could be asserted, a mode of seeing different from that of the dominant culture. Everyday black folks began to see themselves as not having a major role to play in the production of images.

To reverse this trend we must begin to talk about the significance of black image production in daily life prior to racial integration. When we concentrate on photography, then, we make it possible to see the walls of photographs in black homes as a critical intervention, a disruption of white control over black images.

Most Southern black folks grew up in a context where snapshots and the more stylized photographs taken by professional photographers were the easiest images to produce. Displaying these images in everyday life was as central as making them. The walls of images in Southern black homes were sites of resistance. They constituted private, black-owned and operated gallery space where images could be displayed, shown to friends and strangers. These walls were a space where, in the midst of segregation, the hardship of apartheid, dehumanization could be countered. Images could be critically considered, subjects positioned according to individual desire.

Growing up inside these walls, many of us did not, at the time, regard them as important or valuable. Increasingly, as black folks live in a world so technologically advanced that it is possible for images to be produced and reproduced instantly, it is even harder for some of us to emotionally contextualize the significance of the camera in black life during the years of racial apartheid. The sites of contestation were not *out there*, in the world of white power, they were *within* segregated black life. Since no "white" galleries displayed images of black people created by black folks, spaces had to be made within diverse black communities. Across class boundaries black folks struggled with the issue of representation. This issue was linked with the issue of documentation; hence the importance of photography. The camera was the central instrument by which blacks could disprove representations of us created by white folks. The degrading images of blackness that emerged from racist white imagination and that were circulated widely in the dominant culture (on salt shakers, cookie jars, pancake boxes) could be countered by "true-to-life" images. When the psychohistory of a people is marked by ongoing loss, when entire histories are denied, hidden, erased, documentation can become an obsession. The camera must have seemed a magical instrument to many of the displaced and marginalized groups trying to carve out new destinies for themselves in the Americas. More than any other image-making tool, the camera offered African-Americans, disempowered in white culture, a way to empower ourselves through representation. For black folks, the camera provided a means to document a reality that could, if necessary, be packed, stored, moved from place to place. It was documentation that could be shared, passed around. And, ultimately, these images, the world they recorded, could be hidden, to be discovered at another time. Had the camera been there when slavery ended, it could have provided images that would have helped folks searching for lost kin and loved ones. It would have been a powerful tool of cultural recovery. Half a century later, the generations of black folks emerging from a history of loss became passionately obsessed with the camera. Elderly black people developed a cultural passion for the camera, for the images it produced, because it offered a way to contain memories, to overcome loss, to keep history.

Though rarely articulated as such, the camera became in black life a political instrument, a way to resist misrepresentation as well as a means by which alternative images could be produced. Photography was more fascinating to masses of black folks than other forms of image making because it offered the possibility of immediate intervention, useful in the production of counterhegemonic representations even as it was also an instrument of pleasure. The camera allowed black folks to combine image making, resistance struggle, and pleasure. Taking pictures was fun!

Growing up in the 1950s, I was somewhat awed and at times frightened by our extended family's emphasis on picture taking. From the images of the dead as they lay serene, beautiful, and still in open caskets to the endless portraits of newborns, every wall and corner of my grandparents' (and most everybody else's) home was lined with photographs. When I was young I never linked this obsession with self-representation to our history as a domestically colonized and subjugated people.

My perspective on picture taking was also informed by the way the process was tied to patriarchy in our household. Our father was definitely the "picture-takin' man." For a long time cameras remained mysterious and off limits to the rest of us. As the only one in the family who had access to the equipment, who could learn how to make the process work, my father exerted control over our images. In charge of capturing our family history with the camera, he called and took the shots. We were constantly being lined up for picture taking, and it was years before our household could experience this as an enjoyable activity, before any of the rest of us could be behind the camera. Until then, picture taking was serious business. I hated it. I hated posing. I hated cameras. I hated the images that cameras produced. When I stopped living at home, I refused to be captured by anyone's camera. I did not wish to document my life, the changes, the presence of different places, people, and so on. I

wanted to leave no trace. I wanted there to be no walls in my life that would, like gigantic maps, chart my journey. I wanted to stand outside history.

That was twenty years ago. Now that I am passionately involved with thinking critically about black people and representation, I can confess that those walls of photographs empowered me, and that I feel their absence in my life. Right now I long for those walls, those curatorial spaces in the home that express our will to make and display images.

Sarah Oldham, my mother's mother, was a keeper [25] of walls. Throughout my childhood, visits to her house were like trips to a gallery or museum—experiences we did not have because of racial segregation. We would stand before the walls of images and learn the importance of the arrangement, why a certain photograph was placed here and not there. The walls were fundamentally different from photo albums. Rather than shutting images away, where they could be seen only upon request, the walls were a public announcement of the primacy of the image, the joy of image making. To enter black homes in my childhood was to enter a world that valued the visual, that asserted our collective will to participate in a noninstitutionalized curatorial process.

For black folks constructing our identities within the culture of apartheid, these walls were essential to the process of decolonization. In opposition to colonizing socialization, internalized racism, these walls announced our visual complexity. We saw ourselves represented in these images not as caricatures, cartoonlike figures; we were there in full diversity of body, being, and expression, multidimensional. Reflecting the way black folks looked at themselves in those private spaces, where those ways of looking were not being overseen by a white colonizing eye, a white-supremacist gaze, these images created ruptures in our experience of the visual. They challenged both white perceptions of blackness and that realm of black-produced image making that reflected internalized racism. Many of these images demanded that we look at ourselves with new eyes, that we create oppositional standards of evaluation. As we looked at black skin in snapshots, the techniques for lightening skin that professional photographers often used when shooting black images were suddenly exposed as a colonizing aesthetic. Photographs taken in everyday life, snapshots in particular, rebelled against all those photographic practices that reinscribed colonial ways of looking and capturing the images of the black "other." Shot spontaneously, without any notion of remaking black bodies in the image of whiteness, snapshots posed a challenge to black viewers. Unlike photographs constructed so that black images would appear as the embodiment of colonizing fantasies, snapshots gave us a way to see ourselves, a sense of how we looked when we were not "wearing the mask," when we were not attempting to perfect the image for a white-supremacist gaze.

Although most black folks did not articulate their desire to look at images of themselves that did not resemble or please white folks' ideas about us, or that did not frame us within an image of racial hierarchies, that desire was expressed through our passionate engagement with informal photographic practices. Creating pictorial genealogies was the means by which one could ensure against the losses of the past. Such genealogies were a way to sustain ties. As children, we learned who our ancestors were by listening to endless narratives as we stood in front of these pictures.

In many black homes, photographs—especially snapshots—were also central to the creation of "altars." These commemorative places paid homage to absent loved ones. Snapshots or professional portraits were placed in specific settings so that a relationship with the dead could be continued. Poignantly describing this use of the image in her novel *Jazz*, Toni Morrison writes:

> . . . a dead girl's face has become a necessary thing for their nights. They each take turns to throw off the bedcovers, rise up from the sagging mattress and tiptoe over cold linoleum into the parlor to gaze at what seems like the only living presence in the house: the photograph of a bold, unsmiling girl staring from the mantelpiece. If the tiptoer is Joe Trace, driven by loneliness from his wife's side, then the face stares at him without hope or regret and it is the absence of accusation that wakes him from his sleep hungry for her company. No finger points. Her lips don't turn down in judgment. Her face is calm, generous and sweet. But if the tiptoer is Violet, the photograph is not that at all. The girl's face looks greedy, haughty and very lazy. The cream-at-the-top-of-the-milkpail face of someone who will never work for anything, someone who picks up things lying on other people's dressers and is not embarrassed when found out. It is the face of a sneak who glides over to your sink to rinse the fork you have laid by your place. An inward face—whatever it sees is its own self. You are there, it says, because I am looking at you.

I quote this passage at length because it attests to a kind of connection to photographic images that has not been acknowledged in critical discussions of black folks' relationship to the visual. When I first read these sentences, I was reminded of the passionate way we related to photographs when I was a child. Fictively dramatizing the extent to which a photograph can have a "living presence," Morrison describes the way that many black folks rooted in Southern tradition once used, and still use, pictures.

They were and remain a mediation between the living and the dead.

To create a palimpsest of black folks' relation to the visual in segregated black life, we need to follow each trace, not fall into the trap of thinking that if something was not openly discussed, or only talked about and not recorded, it lacks significance and meaning. Those pictorial genealogies that Sarah Oldham, my mother's mother, constructed on her walls were essential to our sense of self and identity as a family. They provided a necessary narrative, a way for us to enter history without words. When words entered, they did so in order to make the images live. Many older black folks who cherished pictures were not literate. The images were crucial documentation, there to sustain and affirm memory. This was true for my grandmother, who did not read or write. I focus especially on her walls because I know that, as an artist (she was an excellent quiltmaker), she positioned the photos with the same care that she laid out her quilts.

The walls of pictures were indeed maps guiding us through diverse journeys. Seeking to recover strands of oppositional worldviews that were a part of black folks' historical relationship to the visual, to the process of image making, many black folks are once again looking to photography to make the connection. The contemporary African-American artist Emma Amos maps our journeys when she mixes photographs with painting, making connections between past and present. Amos uses snapshots inherited from an uncle who once took pictures for a living. In one piece, Amos paints a map of the United States and identifies diasporic African presences, as well as particular Native American communities with black kin, marking each spot with a family image.

Drawing from the past, from those walls of images I grew up with, I gather snapshots and lay them out to see what narratives the images tell, what they say without words. I search these images to see if there are imprints waiting to be seen, recognized, and read. Together, a black male friend and I lay out the snapshots of his boyhood to see when he began to lose a certain openness, to discern at what age he began to shut down, to close himself away. Through these images, my friend hopes to find a way back to the self he once was. We are awed by what our snapshots reveal, what they enable us to remember.

The word *remember* (*re-member*) evokes the coming together of severed parts, fragments becoming a whole. Photography has been, and is, central to that aspect of decolonization that calls us back to the past and offers a way to reclaim and renew life-affirming bonds. Using images, we connect ourselves to a recuperative, redemptive memory that enables us to construct radical identities, images of ourselves that transcend the limits of the colonizing eye.

focus.

1. Look closely at the photograph of Veodis Watkins (on p. 176). What kind of person do you see in this picture? Compare your response to bell hooks's description of the picture and to that of her sisters. What makes a particular photograph a favorite one?

2. Think about the role that snapshots have played in your family. Is there one photograph that captures an important moment in your life, one you would like to have in your home always?

3. How does your family display photographs? Is there a wall of photographs in your house? a collection on a shelf or a mantel? an album? Try to remember what pictures are included. What individual images you remember? What do you remember about the group of pictures as a whole? What did you think about these pictures when you were growing up? Why?

respond.

1. Get a copy of a favorite family photograph, or choose another photograph that you like a lot. We like the one shown here because of the way it focuses on our friend's red shoes and striped socks. (She, by the way, says that reflects more about us than about her!) Take a few minutes and write about why certain pictures become favorites. Why do we like these pictures? Does the subject have to be smiling? caught unaware? part of a group? someone you're close to? What do these favorite pictures convey that other similar snapshots do not? What do they hide, *not* show? What do they tell about the subject? Why do such pictures assume an important place in our lives?

Write a 1–2 page essay reflecting on your photo and what it says about favorite pictures. Use specific references to the photograph to support your argument. Address your essay to people 100 years from now to read as they look at the photograph. They will, of course, not have known the person pictured.

2. Find a collection of photographs on campus: of past presidents, members of the board of trustees (often in the main administrative building or the student union), sport teams or cheerleaders (usually in the sports arena), members of the student body (in a yearbook), winners of various awards. Choose one coherent grouping of these pictures—from one era, perhaps, or of a certain kind of team, or from one page of a yearbook.

Observe the group carefully, jotting down notes: Who is portrayed? Where are they portrayed and what is included? What characteristics do the individuals have in common? What is the photographer trying to communicate about them? How does the photographer convey this message? What are the individuals themselves trying to say, and how do they do so? What if anything leaks through all these intentions, and how does this happen? What elements in each picture are emphasized? How? What techniques does the photographer use to create unity in the composition?

Next, consider the relationships between the photographs and you as a student. How are you similar to the people in the pictures? different from them? Why? What do these similarities and differences say about your experience as a student at this campus?

3. The above picture might be called *Empty Frames Begging for a Story*. Using snapshots from your life, compose a visual story by pasting pictures or parts of pictures into the frames. Your purpose in composing this story is to create a meaningful gift for a friend—one that expresses something about you or your friendship. Write a personal letter to accompany this visual gift, explaining why you chose these pictures and what you hope it says to your friend.

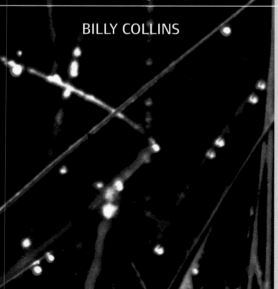

Billy Collins (b.1941) was the U.S. Poet Laureate from 2001 to 2003. He lives in New York and is a professor of English at Lehmann College of the City University of New York. Critically acclaimed and widely accessible, his poems are often about ordinary things—forgetfulness, pin-up calendars, nostalgia—and are known for a deft mix of humor and insight. The poem here, first published in *Nine Horses* (2002), uses a series of metaphorical comparisons to make visible the relationship between and personalities of two people. This poem, like many of Collins's works, is characterized by highly visual language that plays on what the author calls the "plentiful imagery of the world."

Litany

BILLY COLLINS

> You are the bread and the knife,
> the crystal goblet and the wine.
> – JACQUES CRICKILLON

You are the bread and the knife,
the crystal goblet and the wine.
You are the dew on the morning grass,
and the burning wheel of the sun.
You are the white apron of the baker
and the marsh birds suddenly in flight.

However, you are not the wind in the orchard,
the plums on the counter,
or the house of cards.
And you are certainly not the pine-scented air.
There is no way you are the pine-scented air.

It is possible that you are the fish under the bridge,
maybe even the pigeon on the general's head,
but you are not even close
to being the field of cornflowers at dusk.

And a quick look in the mirror will show
that you are neither the boots in the corner
nor the boat asleep in its boathouse.

It might interest you to know,
speaking of the plentiful imagery of the world,
that I am the sound of rain on the roof.

I also happen to be the shooting star,
the evening paper blowing down an alley,
and the basket of chestnuts on the kitchen table.

I am also the moon in the trees
and the blind woman's teacup.
But don't worry, I am not the bread and the knife.
You are still the bread and the knife.
You will always be the bread and the knife,
not to mention the crystal goblet and—somehow—the wine.

1. Read the two lines by Jacques Crickillon that serve as the introduction to the poem. What do they lead you to expect from the poem? Why?

2. The illustration next to the poem was chosen by the editors of this book, not by Billy Collins. Does it affect the way you read the poem—and if so, how?

3. John Updike once said that Billy Collins's poetry is "consistently startling." What if anything in "Litany" supports this statement?

1. Thinking in terms of metaphorical images like those Collins uses, what things—what images—would you "happen to be"? Write a stanza or two of a poem about yourself, patterning it on the fifth and sixth stanzas of Collins's poem.

2. Try illustrating Collins's poem with drawings or photographs or other images. How do the illustrations change the way you read the poem? Do you like it more with or without the illustrations—and why?

3. Compose a rendition of this poem that is made *entirely* of visual images, one that includes no words. If you have access to a simple digital movie-production program (such as iMovie), try creating a digital rendition.

Barbara Kruger (b.1945) was born in New Jersey and studied art at Syracuse University and the Parsons School of Design in New York City. She started out as a magazine designer (for *Mademoiselle* and *House & Garden*), but she is now best known for her poster-style red, white, and black photographs overlaid with words that often read like slogans—"memory is your image of perfection," "I shop therefore I am," "when I hear the word culture I take out my checkbook". Her work is often displayed on billboards and bus stops, as well as in museums and galleries worldwide.

Kruger created the text here in 1982. It shows an X-ray of a woman, almost like one we would see in a doctor's office—but with jewelry, high-heeled shoes, and a message that leads us to question our assumptions about gender, the nature of memory and of perfection, and perhaps the image we have of ourselves.

Memory Is Your Image of Perfection

BARBARA KRUGER

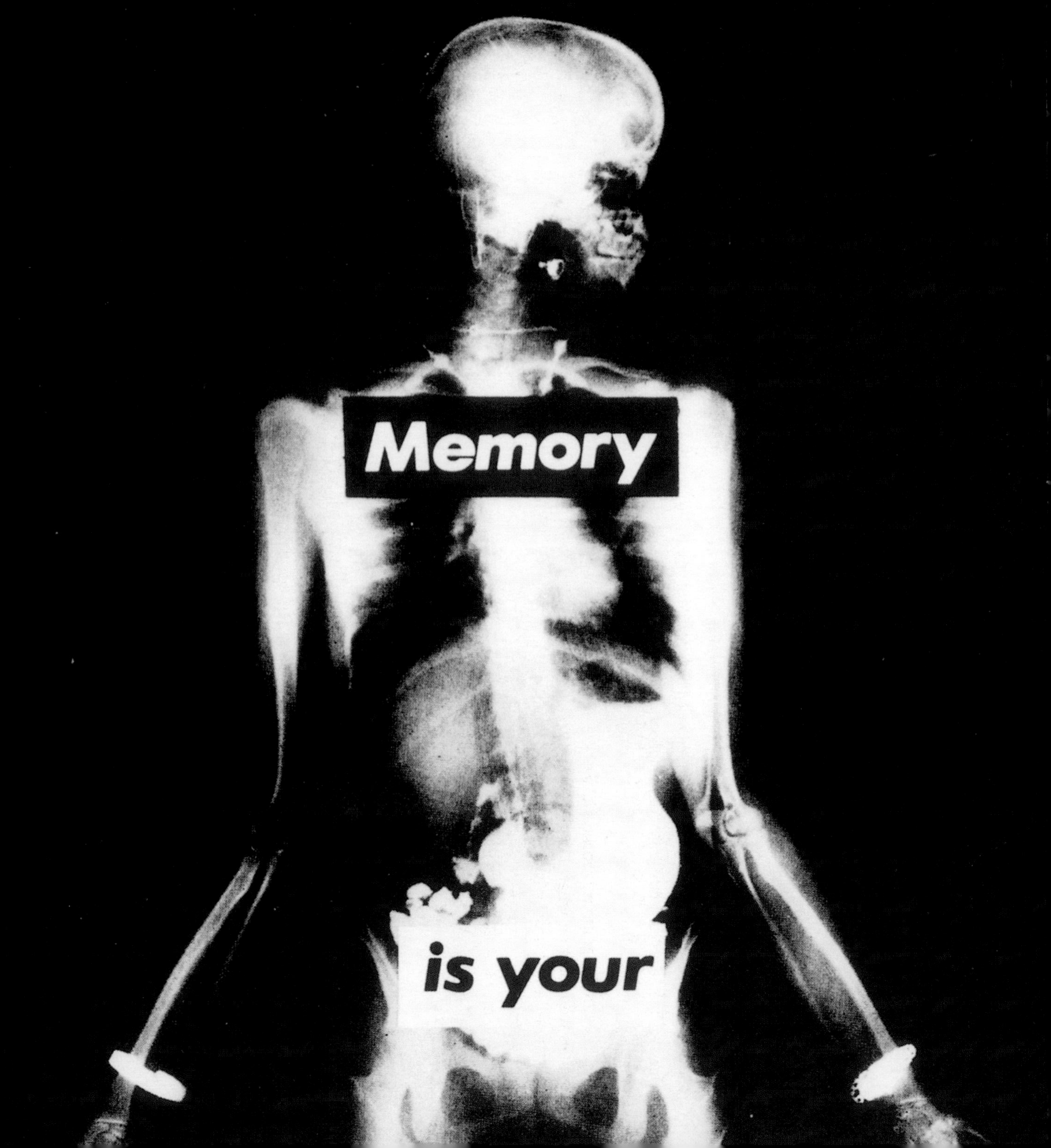
Memory
is your

1. What effect do the jewelry and the high heels have on your interpretation of this text? How would it be different without them?

2. To whom does the word "your" refer? Why do you think so? How would the text's meaning change if it said "our" instead?

3. How would the text differ if Kruger had used a different typeface? Imagine the words in Comic Sans or *Edwardian Script*. How does Kruger's choice of typeface affect her message?

1. Compare the Planned Parenthood postcard of the women holding signs with the Chose Life billboard. What messages about reproductive rights do each of these texts articulate? Choose one of the images and write a short commentary explaining the message your chosen text conveys. Be sure your explanation takes into account both the verbal and visual components. Imagine that this commentary will go into the catalog for an exhibit of similar texts at the headquarters of Planned Parenthood or of the organization of St. John's Respect Life Society.

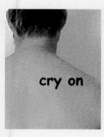 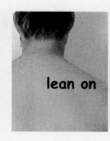 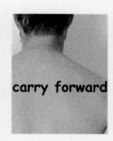 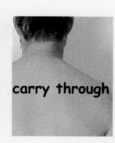

cry on   lean on   carry forward   carry through

2. Compose a text along the lines of Barbara Kruger's or Lorna Simpson's (see p. 227). Start by studying the text on this page by Cynthia and Richard Selfe, which was inspired by their work. What story does this text tell? Try reordering the words—How does the message change? Consider the type—How would the tone be different if the type were much larger? if it were a different typeface (*garamond italic*, for example)?

Now think of a story *you* want to tell or a message you want to convey. Take a picture or cut one out of a magazine and photocopy your chosen image several times. Consider using a picture that shows only *part* of something—but make sure that the part you choose has some connection to your message. Write out the words you want to use to tell your story and combine them with the images in some way. You can produce words on a computer or a typewriter or from letters cut out of a magazine. Ask two or three other students to look at your text and to write a short summary of the story it tells. Compare their summaries with the narrative you hoped to tell.

3. Create a postcard articulating a message that you believe in and want to communicate to others. Consider, for instance, attaching words to images of desks, plants, cars, computers, houses, shoes, tools—whatever objects are appropriate to your message. Make sure the words and images work in tandem to articulate your message. You could create this postcard for a favorite charity or organization: Habitat for Humanity, the Red Cross, Big Brothers Big Sisters, the Salvation Army, and so on.

Michelle Citron is an independent filmmaker and a film professor who teaches at Northwestern University. The following selection comes from *Home Movies and Other Necessary Fictions* (1999). What you will read is part of the first chapter, "What's Wrong with This Picture?"

This selection is presented here as it was in the original — on facing pages. On the left-hand pages, under the first part of the title, "What's Wrong," Citron describes her family's habit of making and watching home movies, which she says were "powerful and necessary fictions that allowed us to see and explore truths that could only be looked at obliquely. . . . Home movies were our memory, anchoring us in time and perpetuating the fictions we needed to believe about ourselves." On the facing right-hand pages, under the second part of the title, "with This Picture," Citron juxtaposes a sequence of frames from the home movies her father made and a thoughtful exploration of the kind of information captured by family photographs and home movies—how we construct image-based stories according to our own desires, hopes, and expectations; why we consider such narratives both true and "authentic"; and how the images actually reveal what is outside the frame of the snapshot or the movie.

As you read this selection, pay attention to the relationship between the words and the images. Do they tell the same story or different stories? to the same audience, or different audiences? How are they related? How do we read each? How are the images organized? the words?

What's Wrong with This Picture?

MICHELLE CITRON

I WATCH A HOME-MOVIE snippet shot by my father in 1956. It is a living moment, more than forty years old, fixed onto a slender thread of film: My mother holds my sister's and my hand as we walk away from and then toward the camera.

We move away, turn, then come closer to the viewer. In this one aspect only, it is the women of the family, and not my cameraman father, who are active. This sequence is actually made up of two shots: my father has chosen to stop the camera briefly when we turn around in the distance. Perhaps this moment does not interest him. More likely, he wanted to save film. This sequence is the next to the last one on the reel; he knew the film was running out. It is ten seconds long and was shot using a regular 8mm camera with a normal prime lens.[1]

We parade up and down the sidewalk, for my father and the camera, in front of the apartment building where we lived. It is now expensive real estate. Forty years ago it was a waystop for working-class Jews fleeing from the poverty of inner-city Boston neighborhoods toward the suburbs of ranch houses and open lawns. My family never quite reached its middle-class goal, although this failure is inscribed in my memory and not in the image. What the image reveals is a mother and her two daughters, stylishly dressed in what I know were the clothes we wore to shul[2] on the High Holy Days of fall. These clothes say more about a time and place (fifties America, special occasion) than class; clothes for women can conceal economic status.

---

1. A lens of a fixed focal length that provides a high level of picture clarity on film.
2. School (Yiddish).

THE PROMENADE

In 1888 a little camera called the Kodak allowed us to realize personal memories both inside the mind's eye and visible to the eyes of others. These memories were moments frozen in time, never-changing images of ourselves that we could revisit and show to our friends. Then in the twentieth century personal photographic memory began to move and flow: first with home movies and more recently with home video.

No matter how distinctive the technologies of still photography, motion pictures, and video may be—adding color, motion, sound, instantaneity—the images captured have remained surprisingly the same. As visual anthropologist Richard Chalfen has pointed out, changes in technology did not significantly change the images themselves; home moviemakers generally photographed the same things that snapshooters did.

We take billions of photographs and millions of hours of video yearly. Our lives are steeped in home images. These images spill out of photo albums, shoeboxes, wallets, desk tops, and bookshelves, reflecting our memories back to us; who we were, who we knew, what lives we lived.

The desire to capture these home images is, to a great extent, shaped by commerce.

My sister and I sport matching pink outfits in the New Look: the full skirts and swinging A-line jackets of the prosperous postwar years. Dressed in these beautiful clothes made by my mother, we wear her optimism about the future on our backs. My mother herself hasn't quite made the transition out of the scarcity of the depression and the war. Her dark blue suit (also homemade) is a straight skirt number with a shoulder-padded jacket pinched at the waist. There is as yet no extravagant use of fabric in her clothes. Only her shoes—the impossibly high, pointed-toe heels of the fifties—hint at a different longing.

In my memory, my mother is overweight and often depressed, my sister is beautiful, and I am plain, if not ugly. The image, however, challenges this memory. My mother is beautiful, with the womanly figure fashionable at the time. My sister and I are both cute, if not downright pretty. But beyond surface appearance, there is an animated physicality, an energy, between us that brightens the screen. These people seem nice, warm, alive.

This ten-second image shimmers with the delight of possession: my mother of the clothes she made and the children who wore them, my father of his wife and daughters, the entire family of the camera that has occasioned this promenade.

As we walk toward the camera, my mother silently chats first to my sister, then to me. Forty years later I imagine her saying, "Stand up straight," or perhaps, "Smile." My sister doesn't quite understand the home-movie ritual and is more interested in my mother and her own feet. As we walk forward, my mother shakes my sister's hand for emphasis and nods toward the camera. My sister, so prompted, looks up and waves. "Bye-bye," she mouths.

I need no such coaching. In fact, I instruct. I coax my sister, point at the camera, and perform with assurance. I lean into the lens, pulling my mother and sister into close-up. I already understand the camera and have my own relationship to it. I am already a director. Only my mother's firm grip on my hand reigns in my energy. But my bobbing head, swinging arms, and bouncy steps suggest that she can't quite contain me.

When *America's Funniest Home Videos* was first broadcast, camcorders, donated by manufacturers to ABC affiliates, were made available to viewers for test shoots. This stimulated home videomaking, thereby providing programming for the show. People were further encouraged by the $10,000 prize awarded each week for the audience's favorite tape. Not surprisingly, in its second year of broadcasting *America's Funniest Home Videos* received two thousand tapes daily. At the same time, camcorder sales were up noticeably. An increased desire for home videos was created, selling cameras to consumers and audiences to advertisers.

This has always been the case. We became a nation of home-movie makers in the first place because of a massive marketing initiative. When Kodak developed 16mm motion picture film in 1921, they asked Marion Norris Gleason, a neighbor of one of the film's inventors, to write a short film to be used to publicize the new technology. The original home movie, *Picnic Party*, was of her son Charles's first birthday celebration. This film promoted the possibilities of the new technology to both company executives and the potential home market.

By 1927 the United States had about half a million amateur moviemakers. This technology was expensive. In 1932 Kodak's cheapest motion-picture camera, a spring-wound 16mm with one prime lens, cost what an average hourly worker earned in two weeks. Three minutes of film and processing

There is another way to interpret our actions. My three-year-old sister is still connected to the Mother. I am already moving toward the Father. Am I posing for the camera with my mugging and waving, or is it my father I'm smiling for? Does this image represent how I want to be seen, or how my father chose to see me? Is my attraction to my particular father, or to the power of the Father, expressed through my real father's ability to conduct this walk? By growing up to be a filmmaker, do I become the Father and thus ascend to a kind of power? Or do I want to become him simply because I desire to stand outside the scene—in the space of safety behind the glass wall of the lens, where I can't be touched?

One side of our faces is brightly lit, the other side lies deep in shadow: the sharp low-key lighting of either early morning or late day, the light of melodrama and film noir, the dark side of both soul and culture. This lighting is intensified by the film stock itself. The highly saturated Kodachrome reds and yellows have faded, leaving behind only shadowy, cool blues and greens. Ironically, and certainly unintentionally, this lighting hints at my remembered, as opposed to my photographed, family.

The year this image was filmed was a difficult one for me, though you can't see that in the moving image. In 1956, at age eight, I wanted so desperately to die that all I could think about was ways to kill myself: drink the bottle of cough syrup, chew up all the aspirin in the jar, run in front of a moving car. But paralyzed by an overwhelming fear of death and screams of terror in the night, I didn't do any of these things. Instead I became ill and was hospitalized on and off for a good part of the year. All of this is banished from the space of the image. The low-key lighting is due to the vagrancies of the available light; the dark colors are the result of the natural chemical deterioration of the film.

In my family, home movies were powerful and necessary fictions that allowed us to see and explore truths that could only be looked at obliquely. We'd gather in front of the large flickering images projected onto the living-room wall because to look directly at the tiny frames of the film would reveal nothing. We'd stare at these grainy and subdued images,

cost a day's labor. But in that same year regular 8mm film was introduced. It cost half as much as 16mm and made home movies financially accessible to working-class families.

Further technical accessibility came in 1965 with the introduction of Super 8. With its slip-in cartridge, battery-operated motor, zoom lens, and built-in light meter, Super 8 was a consumer-friendly camera that anyone could run. Now we have fully automatic video camcorders, around sixteen million in the United States, or about one for every six households.

We are bombarded with print advertisements and television commercials telling us to capture our memories on film and tape. Supermarkets sell film at the checkout counter, nudging you to buy that extra roll. Hotel lobbies, souvenir stores, and airport newsstands display throwaway cameras, just in case you've forgotten yours at home. Is it any surprise that vacationers take 70 percent of all photographs shot worldwide?

Advertisements for film, camera manuals, and even photo shop displays of the various enlargement sizes provide us with examples of what the "good" memory looks like: having fun on vacation, children with animals, families that play or celebrate together. From the glossy surface of these home images slides the story of the happy family.

For the family is central to the images shown: the birth of a baby is one of the primary motivations for purchasing a

looking for their secrets, because to turn and peer into the lens of the projector would blind us. Home movies were our memory, anchoring us in time and perpetuating the fictions we needed to believe about ourselves.

Home moviemaking began in my family in 1947 when my father borrowed a regular 8mm camera to take with him on his honeymoon. Soon after, my father bought his own camera, which he continued to take movies with during the twenty-seven years of my parents' marriage, the first twenty-six years of my life.

In my family there were always home movies: shooting them and watching them. My father filmed birthday parties, holiday dinners, barbecues, Girl Scout picnics, couples' club outings. These, like our promenade for the camera, were public moments of family pride. My father, quite interestingly, also filmed many private and banal domestic events: my sister and I cleaning house, washing dishes, mending clothes, making the beds.

An integral part of the movies was their exhibition. Every few months, when we had nothing to do or had relatives visiting, the small reels came out of the shoeboxes, the screen and projector were set up, and an evening was spent watching ourselves. We all provided the live sound track.

Picture this. It's Sunday night, sometime in the early sixties. We've all just settled down to watch our home movies, adults on the sofa, children cross-legged on the floor. The lights are dimmed. The grainy and scratched image of an earlier time flickers on the wall:

The Birthday Party
INT. LIVING ROOM DAY. 1952

The decor is a working-class fantasy of upper-class life: heavy, ornate furniture, gold-painted mirrors, porcelain figurines of chubby cherubs and court ladies. The room is packed with family—children, parents, grandparents, cousins, aunts—and playmates. At the center of all this activity, dressed in matching pink organdy dresses, are the two daughters—Michelle and her younger Sister, ages four and one.

camera. On *America's Funniest Home Videos* we see families everywhere: families on picnics, families on vacation, families at little league games, families at the mall. And kids are the heart of the family: in bathtubs, in kitchens, in backyards; scrubbing, eating, playing, splashing, spilling, slipping. On the surface everything is wholesome and cute, but a dark shadow of power bleeds through.

Susan Sontag writes in *On Photography* that "to photograph is to appropriate the thing photographed. It means putting oneself into a certain relation to the world that feels like knowledge—and, therefore, like power." Many of the tapes shown on *America's Funniest Home Videos* reveal that power by capturing the small humiliations of childhood: falling into your food, being caught on the toilet, dropping your pants. The embarrassments are even manufactured to create a more competitive video.

A mother, unable to stop her three-year-old daughter from interrupting her in the bath, threatens to disappear down the drain if her daughter won't behave. The mother sets up the camcorder, hides behind the shower curtain, and in a high, squeaky voice pretends to have been sucked down the drain. Predictably the child, panicked, cries into the drain, "I don't know what to do! Mommy, come out!" The audience laughs and applauds; the child is publicly disciplined. Though we all probably have at least one embarrassing childhood moment hidden away on a home-movie reel, in my imagination these moments have multiplied

As the image plays on the wall, WE HEAR OFF SCREEN the voice of the family in 1962—Mother, Grandmother, Grandfather, Michelle, Sister, and Dad—watching, commenting.

The CAMERA sweeps the room. Children crowd the table, the mothers and fathers hover behind them, making sure cake meets mouth. The CAMERA comes to rest on the birthday girl, the younger Sister. She puckers and blows out the candles.

DAD (V.O.): You were such a cute baby.

SISTER (V.O.): Dad!

The shaky CAMERA PANS up to Mom, cutting the cake.

MOTHER (V.O.): God, I've put on weight.

GRANDMOTHER (V.O.): No, you haven't.

MOTHER (V.O.): Look at me there.

The image suddenly shifts. Another birthday party. Michelle, the older daughter, holds up a cellophane-wrapped doll.

MOTHER (V.O.): Remember that toy?

Michelle grunts. The mother ignores her daughter's adolescent surliness.

MOTHER (V.O.): It was your favorite doll until the arms fell off. (*To no one in particular*) Who gave it to her?

GRANDMOTHER (V.O.): Cousin Ruth.

The CAMERA PANS the adults, clustered in the corner, smoking, schmoozing. At the center is the Grandmother.

MOTHER (V.O.): You look so young there.

Michelle, the birthday girl, wanders by. An adult reaches down and adjusts her party hat.

GRANDMOTHER (V.O.): You were always such a happy baby. Look, there's Sadie! She's dead now, *keyn eyn-ore*. God, she could make me laugh till I peed in my pants.

There is giggling as all remember.

Flicker. Change. The image of Michelle kissing her cousin fills the wall.

MOTHER (V.O.): You always loved your cousin.

THE PARTY

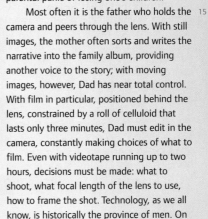

a thousandfold as people scramble for the show's prize. The visual memory of childhood is thus sold to the highest bidder.

Photographs are usually taken by parents of children. They represent the parents' memories, not the child's. Later the "children are offered a 'memory' of their own childhood, made up of images constructed entirely by others . . . one version of family history, which represses much lived experience."

The camera freezes the child's life, which can then be stored for safekeeping in an album or a box or a tape. In home images the child never grows up, gets drunk, sleeps around, or breaks your heart. Deterioration and death are stopped, but so is the process of development and independence. At a deep-down level, these images may betray a parental panic of losing one's children.

Most often it is the father who holds the camera and peers through the lens. With still images, the mother often sorts and writes the narrative into the family album, providing another voice to the story; with moving images, however, Dad has near total control. With film in particular, positioned behind the lens, constrained by a roll of celluloid that lasts only three minutes, Dad must edit in the camera, constantly making choices of what to film. Even with videotape running up to two hours, decisions must be made: what to shoot, what focal length of the lens to use, how to frame the shot. Technology, as we all know, is historically the province of men. On *America's Funniest Home Videos*, the $10,000

15

GRANDFATHER (V.O.): (teasing) Yeah, kissing cousins.

The reel runs out, the wall flickers white. Silence . . .

Watching home movies together, providing live commentary, gave my family a sense of history of themselves as a unit and a way to position themselves in the past, where everyone was younger, thinner, healthier, happier, and together. This of course was not a real past, for only the younger part was true. We needed to believe that the visual "evidence" was honest (seeing is believing). We took the surface image as a sign for the whole lived experience. We wanted to believe that the piece was, in fact, the whole.

By watching the home movies in this way, retelling our story, my family created yet another level of necessary fiction, a fiction that could help us cope with older, deteriorating bodies in a less-than-ideal and fractured present. The home-movie images allowed us to believe that the sunny side of life did exist, if only in the past, and thus they gave meaning to otherwise difficult lives.

I like the silence of the home movies (unlike video, which 20 has unceasing sound). There were moments in my childhood when I would lean against my grandmother's body, my head rising and falling with her breath, the warm smell of popcorn in the room, a salty taste on my tongue . . . and just listen. As I drifted in and out of sleep, adults filled up the silent space of the images with memories evoked: the joy of a moment well lived, the desolate pain of a death. The past tense of the images mingled with the present tense of the storytelling. For this brief space of timelessness I felt a part of something larger than myself; I was safe.

It is 1997. I thread up the projector: the 8mm reel of "The Birthday Party" filmed by my father in 1952. But times have changed. I'm watching it alone, my family members either scattered or dead. It is my turn to give the movies a present tense.

Now I can say that I see a large and happy Jewish family of the early fifties. It is a family where the children seem special. They are the center of attention. It is their birthday. The adults are always watching, primping, holding, giving, and

prize winner is announced and the program's host, Bob Saget, approaches the family sitting in the audience. He kneels down and sticks the microphone in Dad's face. "You were [the one] videotaping?" asks Bob. "I was, yes," says Dad. "Taking a guess here," says Bob with a shake of his head and a knowing smile.

Family home movies are filled with images of the girls—the mother, wife, or daughters—parading as objects in front of the father's gaze through the camera's eye. There are, of course, the occasional acts of rebellion: the mother sticks out her tongue, covers the lens with her hand, runs out of the frame. She attempts to resist the father's total control. In a filmic sense, this is a moment of the subject's power. The mother returns the gaze of the symbolic Father and defies it. But her action is playful and tame. We all know families have such tension; these moments do not threaten the real balance of power.

In home movies we often connect directly to the person behind the lens, a relationship found in portrait photography but rarely in commercial narrative film. Home movies represent how the person behind the camera chooses to film the way the person in front of the camera presents his or her "self." As cultural theorist Roland Barthes has written about the photographic image, "In front of the lens, I am at the same time: the one I think I am, the one I want others to think I am, the one the photographer thinks I am, and the one he makes use of to exhibit his art." With parents and children, husbands

the camera itself spends most of its time looking at them. Children are the family's pride and joy. There is love and safe harbor in the constant intermingling of generations, as seen, for example, in the image of my grandmother with her young grandson and granddaughter (my cousins) leaning contentedly against her body. There is a lot of smiling. There is a lot of action: talking, eating, touching, playing. The birthday party looks busy and chaotic; this family is not quiet or repressed.

There is also gender differentiation. The little boys wear ties and look like men, while the little girls wear frilly, pastel dresses with round collars and full organdy skirts, presenting the innocence of girlie perfection. Everyone is dressed in his or her best, suggesting a distinction between work and leisure, public and private. And, there is the showing off of material gain. Hence how we look—what we wear, eat, carry, buy—is important. The adults pictured grew up in the depression, after all. The camera records plenty: plenty of food, plenty of decorations—special hats, plates, cups— plenty of gifts. As in the home movie of "The Promenade," these people seem proud of their possessions. The home movies offer a fiction of the family that reinforces what they want to know about themselves and sanctions a public view of a most private space: the home.

But I must add, when I've read my home movies with this ethnographic eye, it has always provided distance and protection for me: from the images themselves, the feelings they elicit, and the family they represent. By focusing on the social and deemphasizing the psychological, I have made the home movies safe.

When I asked my father for the home movies, my request was motivated less by ethnographic interest or sentimental longings and more by my anger about the absences: the grim fights over money (there was never enough), suffocating intrusiveness, emotional manipulations, and the rage, always the rage, I had felt as a child. These absences invalidated my memory and thus my feelings about my childhood, family, and self. I could not tolerate the conflict between the image truth and the memory truth.

25

and wives, the image often reproduces the power dynamic existing outside the frame. The ubiquity of these home images, each resembling another, makes what they record seem natural. By providing the "good" memory, home movies show us an ideal image of the family with everyone in his or her proper place: parents in charge, men in control, families together.

Sometimes, however, the ideal family memory is used ironically. The film *Philadelphia* (1993) ends with a montage of romanticized home-movie images: a boy-child plays baseball, carries a Halloween pumpkin, builds sandcastles on the beach. These images of Andrew Becker (Tom Hanks) as a young child are seen on a television placed in the midst of the memorial gathering of his friends and family following his death from AIDS. These images evoke a more innocent time, not only for the character, but for a pre-AIDS, more sexually liberated America.

The home movies represent family warmth and normality for the boy-character who grows up gay and sympathetic in a film marketed for mainstream America. Going on a picnic, playing on the beach—these images look like the home movies we all have of our childhoods. We see that Andrew Becker was a child just as we were children; Becker is like us, we are like Becker. Our identification with the character, through the homogeneity of home-movie images, breaks down the otherness of homosexuality.

I watched my family's home movies over and over, trying to understand why they didn't show what I remembered; why I felt a lie. This family seemed so nice, loving, normal. I was disturbed. I was obsessed. I kept trying to figure out why the images I saw flickering on the wall had no correspondence to the memories flickering in my mind. Sister, friends, strangers came over to my house for dinner. Little did they know there was a price to pay. For after dinner I would sit them down in the darkened living room and make them watch the home movies. What do you see? Does this seem like a happy family to you? Do you think all is as it seems to be? I badgered them with questions. I'm sure they thought me meshuggeneh,[3] as my mother would say. But I had to understand the split between what I saw and what I remembered. This is why I made *Daughter Rite*, my fifth film: to reread the image of my family's home movies. To unpack the pictures, exposing the meaning I knew lay just beneath the surface appearance.

Daughter Rite is a faux documentary film of two adult sisters, Stephanie and Maggie, who have returned to their mother's home while she lies ill in the hospital. This "cinema verité" narrative thread, of the sisters talking about their relationship to their mother, is interwoven with a second family's story: that of an unnamed Narrator and her relationship with her sister and her mother. The Narrator speaks over home movies that have been optically printed to manipulate the images, often repeating a movement over and over again. The documentary footage is staged, scripted, and acted; the home-movie images have been processed with techniques developed by avant-garde filmmakers in the early seventies. Thus the film's aesthetic blurs the boundaries between documentary, narrative fiction, and experimental filmmaking. By doing so, it brings into relief yet another fiction: the separation between documentary, experimental, and narrative fiction film.

Daughter Rite is a movie of my family's home that incorporates my family's home movies, expressing what I *felt* when I watched them. Let me illustrate with two scenes from

---

3. Crazy (Yiddish)

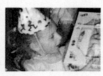

The point is driven home by our belief in the authenticity of these images, or at least a belief that what we see in the photograph must exist, or have existed, in order to be photographed. As Roland Barthes has written, with the photograph, "the power of authentication exceeds the power of representation." Or, in the words of one of anthropologist Richard Chalfen's home-movie informants, "It's real if you've got a picture of it."

This is the intent behind the use of home-movie-like images in political commercials. Mark McKinnon, the media consultant who created 8mm political spots for Clair Sargent, the Democratic Senate nominee from Arizona in 1992, says he created false home movies designed to look like the real thing to "communicate a sense of reality and humanity about the candidate." Despite their phoniness, the Sargent home movies signify, like all home movies, "authenticity": an objective recording of an actual event captured by the home-movie camera.

Film historian Patricia Erens analyzed the use of faux home-movie images in conventional narrative commercial films. Looking at such films as *Raging Bull*, *Peeping Tom*, *Unsuitable Job for a Woman*, *The Falcon and the Snowman*, and *Paris, Texas*, she found that the home-movie scenes were "coded as documentaries, images which . . . don't lie." Even in experimental films, such as the work of avant-garde filmmakers Stan Brakhage, Ken Jacobs, and Jonas Mekas, the visual style of

the film. One is a sequence where the Narrator relates a dream in which she was forced to take an injection she did not want. The second scene follows sequentially in the film. In this scene, Stephanie, one of the "documentary" sisters, looks directly into the lens of the camera and tells the story of being raped by her stepfather.

The dream sequence uses eight of the original forty shots filmed by my father in the home movie of "The Birthday Party." I've selected the most disturbing moments and refilmed them to investigate and present their implicit, rather than explicit, meanings.

Slowed down and repeated, the images reveal another film that had been obscured at the normal speed. Under the scrutiny of slow motion, my mother repinning my hair becomes an agonizingly intrusive and possessive gesture; her helping me with a spoon becomes an invasion of my boundaries; her reaching for a gift blots me out. I am obviously very angry with my mother and see her as the source of my disturbed childhood. It is in this shadow film of the home movies that I believe my real family exists. It is in the nonverbal communication revealed through the image manipulation that a deeper meaning lay for me: a more profound family that cannot be hidden from the camera despite my father's focus.

In the second sequence, Stephanie's story of her rape, my film characters are talking heads, not whole bodies. Although Stephanie tells a traumatic body story, it is expressed through language and faces only. It's as if the bodies are too dangerous or shameful to be seen. She tells the moment; we do not see it. If the home movies are about behaviors, these "documentary" sequences of the film are about words. If the home movies are about moving, acting bodies, these "documentary" scenes are literally talking heads. Much of *Daughter Rite* uses talking heads, not bodies, as though the images of bodies cannot be trusted.

Daughter Rite strikes a chord with many women. I'm not sure why. At the time it came out I suspected it spoke to a dark secret that lay in many a daughter's heart: the anger we felt toward our mothers. An anger that needed to be seen

30

THE KISS

home movies is used to express the spontaneous, untampered nature of their own films. But what exactly is real?

We are not naive. We know these images are staged. We've all been asked to pose in front of a famous landmark or file past the camera, waving as we look directly into the lens. With their moments of family members mugging at the lens and children's birthday parties that seem to exist only for the camera to record, home movies teeter at the edge of both documentary and fiction. Herein lies a paradox: spontaneous *and* directed, authentic *and* constructed, documentary *and* fiction. This paradox is revealed every time we look at an image with which we have a personal relationship.

Kodak might have taught us how to film a vacation, but it is still *our* particular family's vacation that father shoots. On the surface of the home image, one family looks like any other: roughhousing on the beach, having a picnic, visiting the Statue of Liberty. Yet each of us has knowledge that cracks the smooth surface of our home images: a pending divorce, an alcoholic parent, an unemployed father, a depressed child. This information outside the frame is a constant reminder that home movies are highly selective in what they show.

We film Christmas dinner with family and friends, not the meal eaten alone; birthday parties, not the emergency room visits; baby's first step, not fighting with the adolescent; vacation, not work; wedding

25

in the larger patriarchal context I only alluded to in *Daughter Rite*. I screened the film in museums and festivals around the world: the Museum of Modern Art, the Whitney, the Walker, New York, Berlin, London, Edinburgh. I was not afraid of public presentation. But my mother was another story.

After I made *Daughter Rite*, I didn't show it to my mother for almost two years. When she finally saw it I cheated. I sliced out two scenes. I believed she would hate me if she saw those scenes, but I wasn't sure why. The scenes I cut were stories told to me by two of the thirty-five women I had interviewed in preparing the film. One was Stephanie's rape story. The other was a brief scene near the beginning of the film in which the Narrator-daughter speaks of her mother's denial about her own (the mother's) debilitating depression. Neither scene was autobiographical. But I was overwhelmed with guilt and anxiety about the secret the film spoke—a daughter's anger—and somehow I thought that without these two scenes I could fool my mother about the depth of my rage. I was so emotionally overwrought when my mother saw even this edited version that I burst into tears before the opening credits. Being a good mother, she stroked my hand and told me everything was going to be fine. I had conveniently shifted the emphasis of the viewing from her reactions and feelings to mine.

Daughter Rite was a story I constructed but could not read. But my mother could and did. Here is what eventually happened. Two years after I showed my mother the abridged edition, I was invited to show *Daughter Rite* at the art museum in the city where she lived. She was excited. She planned a party for me afterward and invited all her friends. I was, of course, terrified. The day of the screening I ate almost two pounds of crystallized fruit—pure sugar—and proceeded to get very sick. This was uncharacteristic. I stood outside my body and watched myself abuse it. I was astounded. I knew my behavior was a sign of a deep disturbance, but I couldn't name it, nor could I stop myself.

The day after the screening my mother and I went for a walk. She said she wanted to tell me something disturbing, but she knew I could handle it. The sun was shining. The hibiscus swayed in the trade-wind breezes. I smiled at her, nodding my

35

parties, not divorce proceedings, births, not funerals. Through our selective filming, the "sunny side of life" is preserved and the dark side of life is cast out. We record the noteworthy, the celebrated, the remarkable, and the extraordinary. Or perhaps their memorialization on film codifies these events as such.

In presenting the image of an ideal selective past, home movies announce what is absent. They stand in for what is there *and* what is not there. In their ambivalence they both confess and hide. The home movies are simultaneously acts of self-revelation, self-deception, and self-conception.

I receive a Christmas photo card from a friend. The image shows him, his partner, and their four children, dressed in matching outfits—black trousers or black skirts with bright red turtleneck sweaters—posed for the camera. The card is like many I receive, except that both parents are male. This image startles. Shot in a studio, floating against a white backdrop, my friend's "family," unlike the families in the other Christmas photographs I'm sent, is disconnected from the environment in which they live. The card at once parodies the suburban nuclear family they are outside of *and* calls it forth to legitimize themselves and their children. Being both gay and a parent is an experience that allows my friend to appropriate the typical Kodak family Christmas image when he creates his own.

I agree with art critic John Berger when he writes in *About Looking* that "photo-head with encouragement. Inside I was silently screaming, "No, shut up! I don't want to know!" But I kept smiling and nodding and so my mother told me: how she was sexually abused by her brother from the time she was eight until she was twelve. How he would sneak into her room at night, tie her to the bed, and rape her. As he left he would say, "If you ever tell anyone about this, I'll kill you. Even when you're grown up I'll come after you and get you." I am the first person my mother ever told this secret to; she was sixty-four years old when she told me, the day after seeing *Daughter Rite*. I think she believed that if I could make *Daughter Rite*, I could hear her secret. And she was right.

This moment of secret sharing changed forever my relationship to my mother: I understand the enigma of my childhood and my rage, misdirected in its exclusivity toward her. This moment changed forever my relationship to myself: my mother's telling me about her incest broke apart my own life and forced me to finally come to terms with my own experience of incest with my grandfather. This moment changed forever the meaning of the home movies. I had read my family's narrative in the home movies. I had appropriated the medium that was complicit in preserving the idyllic vision of the family, though I was unconscious of what I was doing at the time. And my mother had read my film back to me. As a family, we finally remembered and started to understand and speak our secrets.

In home movies we look directly into the lens, a filmic moment rare, even for documentaries. In home movies the gaze of the subject meets the gaze of the spectator. When I look at my family's home movies, my forty-eight-year-old self and my eight-year-old self meet each other's gaze across the gap of decades. I wonder what she will speak.

I go back to the home movies. I sift through the images, looking for evidence of my abuse. A clue. A visual symptom. Freud said the repressed always returns. Trauma always leaves a trail, if only you know how to read the markings. I want to find evidence of the incest secreted in the behaviors I see on the screen.

There is a sequence that arrests me. By the time this bit of film was shot, I was already experiencing ongoing sexual

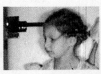

graphs . . . [and I would include home movies] in themselves do not narrate. . . . The private photograph . . . remains surrounded by the meaning from which it was severed . . . a memento from a life being lived."

Personal home images are fetishes. In the Freudian sense of the term, the home movie is counterphobic : a device that avows and disavows in the same sequence. The home movie opens a potential space where we can enter either its affirmations or its silences. What we experience in this ambiguity is determined at the moment of reading.

Parents express their displeasure at errant children by taking their high school portraits off the wall. People vent their anger at divorced spouses by slashing their images out of the frames. Out of sight, out of mind. Gone. A grandiose power over life and death.

When a friends's house was threatened by fire, all she took was two suitcases: one filled with clean clothes and toiletries, the other jammed tight with photographs of her recently deceased brother. She felt deeply about these images: their iconic nature made them sacred.

When someone dies and fades from memory, you can look at a photograph and lived moments with that person burst into your mind: a secret shared, a heart-stopping betrayal, a mysteriously intimate moment. Perhaps that is why it was once fashionable among immigrant families to have a photograph of the deceased enameled onto the

abuse. I am six years old, my sister is three. We are in our pajamas: frilly baby dolls that make us look like baby Lolitas, curlers that bestow a poignant vulnerability.

I pull my sister toward me, place her arms around my neck, and hold her tight against my body as I kiss her. Repeatedly, I kiss her long and hard on the mouth. I don't know how she reacts in this first shot because the camera discreetly, or so it seems to me, tilts down to give us privacy. There is an ellipsis. In the second shot I scoop my sister into a bear hug. She tries to pull away. I reach down and grab her ass and hold her to me. She struggles and squirms out of my grip. She beats her little fists against my chest, her face scrunched up with tears. I react by jumping up and down while I laugh at the camera. My parents, or at least my father, who was looking through the lens of the camera, watched me manhandle my sister and saw nothing of what I see now. He kept filming, so he probably thought we were being cute.

I find my behavior aggressive, dominating, and disturbingly sexual. And though hints of this type of behavior exist in earlier home-movie clips, this strip of film is the first moment where they coalesce into an obscene parody of male dominance. I want to attribute this filmic moment to the incest: an acting out on my sister of the sins of my grandfather, a displaced sexual aggression forced onto a child younger, smaller, and more helpless than myself. I am mean and corrupted and I laugh. I seem thrilled by the coupling of sexuality and power. In the harsh, flat glare of the camera's floodlights, the film is profoundly disturbing. This image breaks my heart.

If in the home-movie clip of "The Promenade" I want to identify with the Father behind the camera, in this fragment of film my desire is fulfilled. I become the Father in all his grotesqueness. I did not know for what I wished.

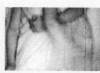
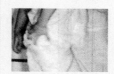

gravestone, a device both literal and symbolic, profane and sacred.

Historian Michael Lesy writes that snapshots (and I would include all home images) "are primarily psychological documents. They may be understood aesthetically, anthropologically, and historically as well. But . . . because they are personally and privately made images whose information is graphic, tacit, factual, and allusive, they must first be deciphered as if they were dreams." Like all dreams they hold the promise of both insight and terror. In the image, we confront what we both long for and deny.

The meaning of home images is in constant flux. This is due, in part, to the fact that we provide a second track, either stories or memories, at the moment of viewing. By doing so we fuse the present tense of viewing to the past tense of recording. Time folds back on itself. Two places on the time line of our life meet. In this moment of superimposition, a space is created from which insight can arise. This is the latent hope in all home movies.

In my family, my mother expressed her defiance by sticking out her tongue at my father's camera eye. She expressed her anger toward the institution of the Father by pulling her own father's photographs off the wall and hiding them. I grew up, formed by feminist politics and the study of film, to take the means of producing the visual memory of the family away from the Father. If I had daughters, I am sure, they would tell a different tale.

focus.

1. Why do you think Citron juxtaposes the home-movie frames with her discussion? What effects did this arrangement have on your reading of the text? What information do the movie frames add? When you look at a page of her text, what do you notice first—and why?

2. Try reading Citron's words *without* reading the images (or the reverse). Does the meaning change—and if so, how?

3. What is your understanding of an ideal family? How is it similar to or different from Citron's understanding?

respond.

1. Find a few snapshots of you or someone you know. Choose one or more pictures and write a brief 1–2 page essay describing what ideal narrative you think they are meant to tell. Consider in your discussion what facts or stories remain outside the frames of the pictures and why they might have been left out.

2. Look in several magazines to see how families are represented visually in advertisements. Select two or three and write an essay about the story these images tell about family. How is family represented? Who is included? Who is left out? What characteristics do these ads suggest most families share? How are the individual family members portrayed? Are any family members represented more prominently than others? less prominently? How is this accomplished? What information about family do any words convey? How do these representations of family compare to your own experiences and understanding of family? Don't try to answer all of these questions—focus on one or two. Be sure to provide specific examples from the ads and from your personal experience as support for your argument.

3. Imagine that you have an opportunity to make a home movie about a day in your life, a movie you could show to your family. Create a sequence of storyboards for a single scene within that home movie, as follows:

Start by dividing a piece of paper into twelve small frames arranged horizontally, four frames each in three rows, leaving room for captions. Create several sheets of paper with this format. Next, using the frames, draw a rough sketch of how the action or events will unfold in your imaginary scene. Use a separate frame for each action, event, or camera shot in the scene. Provide a caption for each frame.

To see what a storyboard looks like, go to <www.ecst.csuchico.edu/~vertolli/spring97/storyboard/index.htm> or <www.wabash.edu/depart/theater/thar4/story.htm>.

Write a brief analysis of your movie scene. What story did you want it to tell? How did you select which shots to include and which to leave out?

Between 1994 and 2001, the endowment at Harvard University almost tripled, going from $7 billion to $20 billion. During that same period, the wages of its lowest-paid workers were cut, with janitors, security guards, and food-service workers forced to accept lower wages and diminished benefits. In 1998, a group of students began a campaign to guarantee living wages for those who work at Harvard (a campaign that soon spread to many other college campuses). Three years later, and after a week-long sit-in, Harvard granted a one-time wage increase, to $11.35 an hour, for all the lowest-paid workers on campus. It was an increase of more than 40 percent for some workers.

Greg Halpern was one of the student organizers. He spent several years since then photographing and interviewing many of the workers, and has just published a collection of the photos and narratives in *Harvard Works Because We Do* (2003), from which the following texts were taken. **Frank Morley** is a custodian who works at the Littauer Center for Public Administration at Harvard. We include his narrative, along with photographs of several other workers, in part because they are splendid examples of texts that make lives visible—and also because they say something about invisibility, about what it's like to feel as if no one even notices you are there.

The Man Didn't Even Know I Was There

GREG HALPERN AND FRANK MORLEY

FRANK MORLEY

Custodian,
Littauer Center

I recently had to go into an office and the professor was in there, and he's got the problem written on the board, and he's sitting there studying that thing, and I'm standing there fixing the file cabinet. The drawers were jamming, and the man didn't even flinch. I swear, the man didn't even know I was there. About twenty minutes later, he asked me if I fixed his cabinet yet. I told him I finished it twenty minutes ago. You might initially think it's a class thing, but it's not that at all. It's just they're so busy, and in a way, I've always admired a person who can sit down and be totally riveted right on whatever they're doing.

I'm the only one who cleans this building during the day and I got ninety-four rooms here. Once, between my two jobs I worked thirty-five days straight without a day off. I can usually pull that off, but this week, for example, I'm starting to catch a cold. A lot of us are tired. Tired of watching every dime, too. But it's like everyone's afraid to speak up. Most of the people who work for UNICCO come from other countries, primarily Spanish-speaking countries, because they're here on a green card there's intimidation going on. You hear stories that managers threaten to call the immigration office if they ask for a raise or if they ask for their vacation time. And if you lose your job with a green card, you have thirty days to get a new job or you're out of the country. One guy didn't get paid time and a half for his overtime, but the guy was so scared he wouldn't say anything. Once I requested a vacation and forty-five minutes later two supervisors came over and said, "What do you mean, you're taking a vacation?" See, UNICCO advertises that you get vacation, but in reality it's a little different. All that, and we have a union, Local Two-fifty-four of SEIU—the Service Employees' International Union.

My alarm goes off at four in the morning. That morning time is the only real time I have to myself. I shower, I shave, I listen to the news. Out the door by five-thirty. Get to the station by five-fifty. Catch the train at five fifty-five. Get to work at seven fifteen. All told it's an hour and forty-five minutes from Mansfield. I finish working for Harvard at four P.M., get on the train, grab a cup of coffee, throw down a doughnut, get off the train, and walk—twenty minutes from the station to the supermarket. I bag and stock until ten-thirty P.M., walk back to the train, take it home, get in the door around eleven-thirty. In bed around midnight—usually I hit the pillow and I'm out. Up again by four A.M. I've been on that schedule for a little over two years now.

There are a lot of days when you're walking around in a fog. But you don't think on it too much—you just go. There was a time when I was working Monday to Friday and four hours

Saturday and four hours Sunday. I stopped that, but for a while after that I was still waking up early Saturday mornings, thinking I was going to work, getting dressed, until halfway through it I realized I didn't have to. Now, Saturdays I'll clean up at home, grocery-shop, do laundry. Sundays I sit down and watch football. Time is precious—at least at age sixty-one it is.

Right now I'm using the retirement money to pay back the money I borrowed from the bank. So I still got some money in the retirement fund, but that'll be gone soon. Still, I'd like to go out and indulge a little, you know? Sit down at a place and eat. I do that now when I get the tax refund. Nowadays, I tend to eat at work when I can. After the luncheons, we get a shot at the leftovers. So you save money where you can.

You've got to remember with a cleaning company that their primary purpose is to make a profit. Managers always try to cut expenses, and they see wages as expenses. They forget that it's people—it's a person they're talking about who's trying to live on that. For example, they'll keep your hours down below seventeen a week so they don't have to pay you benefits. That's part of their cost control. It's just that I'm tired up here, in the head, and I'm tired physically. Things bug me that normally don't. Sometimes I just need to back off and cool down a little.

I've been wearing a custodial uniform now going on twenty years. And I think by now they figure they own me like a piece of equipment, like a barrel or a buffing machine. Plus, people figure if I had any brains, I'd be doing something else. But it's really got nothing to do with being lazy or not having the smarts. I work hard, and I did a few years for a while at Roxbury College. I got an associate's degree in management, and I was going for the bachelor's. I was going to start my own business. That's when my father was diagnosed with cancer. My mother too, eight months later, so I hung up the school.

We recently got a raise, though, after three years of the Living Wage Campaign, the sit-in, and then finally after nine of us went so far as to get arrested at a rally. That was big news. It was pretty soon after that that we won our contract. So now I'll go from ten dollars to about eleven-fifty. That buck-fifty adds up to twelve dollars a day, sixty dollars a week, which may not sound like a lot to some people, but in my case you don't sneeze at it. Ever since the sixties, we always looked to the college students to get the action going. They'd get out there and do the work and get people to get out on the streets. The students have the knowledge to do the organizing. And they don't have jobs to lose and families to feed, so they can take the risks, they can get out there when we can't.

5

focus.

1. Greg Halpern took these photographs to make the Harvard workers more visible. How do the composition and arrangements of the photos help to do this?

2. The organizers of the Harvard Living Wage Campaign distributed written narratives, including the one by Frank Morley reproduced here, as one way to win support for their cause. What kind of appeal can such narratives make that posters, newspaper articles, editorials, letters to the editor, speeches, and other texts do less well?

respond.

1. In his book about the Harvard workers, Greg Halpern says he hopes that the photographs will "affect the way we see." How do the several examples shown here affect the way you see workers at your school? Write an essay exploring this question. You might want to include some images in your own text.

2. Halpern makes the lives of his subjects visible by focusing on them, by paying attention. Try doing the same. Pay attention to someone you don't normally notice and compose a text that makes that person visible. Try to interview your subject, and to include images and words, as Halpern does.

Sochea Uel, dishwasher, Winthrop House. On pages 212–213, Carol-Ann Malatesta, cleaning lady, Phoenix Men's Club; and Angel Hernandez, waiter, Faculty Club.

Judith Wilde teaches design at the City University of New York, Kingsboro Community College, and **Richard Wilde** is the chair of the graphic design and advertising departments at the School of Visual Arts in New York City. The business cards here were created in response to a design assignment in a course on visual literacy. We found these cards in *Visual Literacy: A Conceptual Approach to Graphic Problem Solving*, published by the Wildes in 1991. Each card features part or all of the designer's name in a prominent place and tells something about a specific personality trait (one assigned by the teachers) through the typography.

A business card is one way that we make our lives visible (a résumé is another— both are visual and typographic presentations of our selves to a larger world). Like a photographic portrait, a business card can describe attributes of our personality and uses emphasis and composition to create a personal representation. Both portraits and cards leave an impression. The following cards by **Sharon Harel** describe personality traits typographically. Are they memorable, in your opinion? why? Try reading these cards as if they were narratives. What stories do they tell? Pay close attention to the color, weight, juxtaposition, arrangement, size, repetition, pattern, and shape of the letters. Why do the Wildes call these cards "typographic portraits"?

Typographic Portraits

JUDITH WILDE, RICHARD WILDE, AND SHARON HAREL

My name is

SIARONHAREL

and I'm a chameleon

My name is

SHARON

and I'm an acrobat

My name is

Sharon

and I'm an amphibian

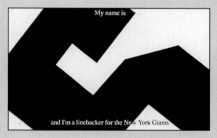

My name is

and I'm a linebacker for the New York Giants

My name is

sha**HAREL**ron

and I'm a taxi driver

My name is

sharon harel

and I'm a T.V. Evangelist

My name is

and I have an allergy

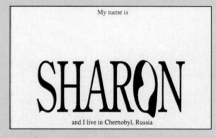

My name is

SHARON

and I live in Chernobyl, Russia

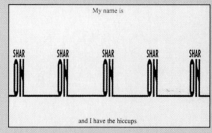

My name is

SHAR ON SHAR ON SHAR ON SHAR ON SHAR ON

and I have the hiccups

My name is

and I'm an accident prone

My name is

sharon

and I'm a magician

My name is

s**HA**ron**HA**rel

and I'm funny

217

focus.

1. Which of these business cards is your favorite? Why? Which do you think expresses the most information about the designer's personality? Which seems the most creative? Why?

2. Each of these typographic portraits conveys information about the designer, just as Rembrandt's or van Gogh's paintings tell us something about them. What can we learn about a type designer from his or her work? What can we learn about painters or photographers from their work?

respond.

1. Design a business card for yourself. Choose a typeface and other graphics that convey an aspect of your personality. Make sure your name is featured prominently on the card as part of the design and add a caption to the card if you wish.

2. Design a business card for a club, team, dorm, or other organization you belong to. The card should provide information about the group and its typeface and other visual elements should reveal something about the group's character. Your purpose is to project a positive image of the group as well as to inform the viewer about its mission or purpose.

3. Collect some business cards from friends and businesses. Try to get cards of different typefaces, sizes, shapes, and designs. Choose your favorite card and take notes about the message it conveys. Consider the use of color, the selection and arrangement of logos or other graphics, the typography (typeface, font, size), and the paper on which it is printed. Consider what elements on the card are emphasized and how, how the various elements are arranged on the card, and how the designer has unified these various elements (or has failed to do so).

Then, write a paragraph or two about the card analyzing what the card says to you about the person or business it represents and how it gives that impression. Your audience for this analysis is the owner of the card. Your purpose in writing is to inform him or her about the message the card conveys. If possible, when you are finished, show your paragraphs to the person.

picture this

making lives visible

Work with a small group to create a scrapbook about the students at your school. Assume that this will be displayed on campus for prospective students. The purpose of this book is to tell students about the school and to give them a glimpse of the opportunities they'll find there.

This assignment calls upon you to make some student lives visible. Because it focuses in part on your own life as a student, it is partially autobiographical in nature. It challenges you to tell compelling stories about your experiences as a student—the joys and the challenges—to an audience that's interested in the school you attend. You will have to be a keen observer, and you may have to do some research. The scrapbook might include excerpts from any of the genres covered in this chapter—diaries, memoirs, letters, photographs, and other mementos—calling for you to use both words and images.

1. Each of you should collect details about your experiences. Keep a diary for a few days about your life as a student—what you do, whom you spend time with, what you learn, how you study—and that says something about you—the things important to you, your goals and ambitions, hopes and fears.

Try to compose at least one entry a day. If you prefer, you could write daily letters rather than a journal. Whatever method you choose, your purpose is the same: to make your life visible.

Illustrate your writing with drawings, sketches, or photos and save some small mementos that document the stories you tell: tickets or scorecards; tests and quizzes; assignments; lecture notes; stories or headlines from newspapers; posters for campus events; pages from your daily planner; photos of your room, your friends, the campus.

2. As a group, look through the materials you each create and collect. Think about the purpose that this book is meant to fulfill and the audience who will read it. Consider which information you should include and how to organize the book. Should you compose separate sections focusing on academic classes, extracurricular activities, and living arrangements? Do you need to include an introduction, perhaps in the form of a letter from the group? Should you add a table of contents to help readers make their way through your text?

3. You will need to consider the overall length of your book and how each page will be arranged. You'll probably want to limit each group member to two or three pages. If you layer the materials, you'll need to plan what is more and less visible on the page. Remember that the visual and verbal elements on each page should relate. Think about whether you need to provide captions.

4. Finally, you will want to consider the overall unity and look of your book. How will you tie the various pages together visually? How will you make the book a unified whole rather than a random collection of unrelated pages? You can use some common graphic elements—lines, headings, icons, the school mascot—to create visual unity among pages. Or you can lay out each page around a common grid.

gallery
of
images

making lives visible

① *Three Self-Portraits*, by Art Paul, mixed media, 1993–97. Art Paul was the original art director for *Playboy* magazine and the creator of the *Playboy* bunny logo. For over a year, he created a self-portrait a day in his studio. These daily portraits combine image and words to convey his witty and poignant reflections on life. "When doing a self-portrait, I sometimes feel the need to write down my thoughts on the art to consider it finished," says Paul. "In my mind, the writing is as much a picture of me as the drawing itself, and the combination turns the work into a conversation between me and the viewer."

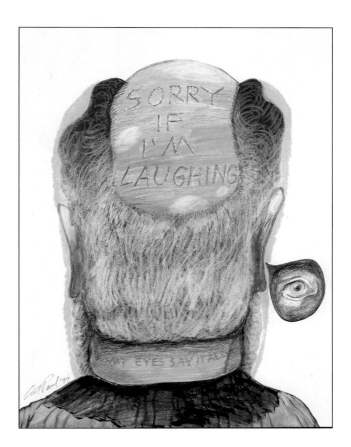

② *American Farm Family on Porch.* Photo by Jack Leigh. Leigh's work records the people, the environment, and the lifestyles of the contemporary American South. His photographs are characterized by a cool candidness; there are no obvious photographic tricks and we are unaware of the photographer's presence. In many family portraits, conscious posing and staging takes place, but Leigh allows the natural family dynamic to emerge on its own.

③ *Men in Park, Peoria, Illinois.* Photo by Arthur Rothstein, 1938. This photo of two dozing men in a park was obviously taken without their knowledge. The photographer had the time to compose his image and crop it so that it emphasized the relaxed state of his subjects. Note the many curves in this image and how they direct the viewer's eyes.

④ *Japanese Protestors.* Photo by Agence France—Presse. Just as we are concerned about privacy issues when our lives are made visible, so too are we concerned when our individual lives are made invisible by categorization and government standardization. On August 5, 2002, Japan put into operation a national computerized registry of its citizens. Under the mandatory system, each citizen has an 11 digit number for online identification by the government. In protesting the new system, these young men used various visual cues to convey their argument—prison stripes, bar codes, a figure from *The Scream,* the painting by Edward Munch, numbers along with words: "we are not numbers."

⑤ *Home Girl #1*. Painting by Daniel Galvez, 1983. Lowriders are cut-down, dressed up cars, usually from the 1950s. Their owners are also known as lowriders and as such the bond between driver and automobile is made clear. This portrait of a woman lowrider modifies the photographic convention of a man standing in front of his car by placing the car on the woman's chest.

⑥ *Daguerreotype and Commissioned Drawing of Emily Dickinson.* 1893, 1897. Asked at age thirty-one to supply a photograph of herself, the poet Emily Dickinson replied, "Could you believe me—without? I had no portrait, now, but am small, like the Wren, my hair is bold, like the Chestnut Bur—and my eyes, like the sherry in the glass, that the guest leaves—would this do just as well?" Shying from public view, Dickinson chose to represent herself in words rather than in image. She left behind only an oil portrait, a silhouette, and a daguerreotype made before the age of 20. Her family found these images inadequate and commissioned several modified versions which softened the hair, enlarged the eyes, and in some cases added lace trim to the dress, all in order to create a "less severe" image of the poet.

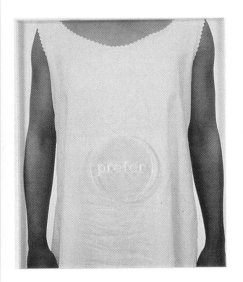 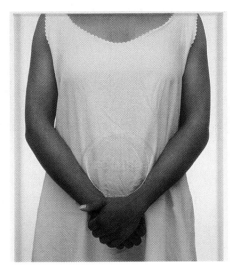 

(7) *Untitled (Prefer, Refuse, Decide),* by Lorna Simpson. Simpson's work combines words and photographs to create visual narratives that are both literal and suggestive. She is most interested in issues of race and gender, and the notion of "invisibility." She uses her own body as the model, but crops out her facial features or faces away from the camera in order to move away from making an auto-biographical statement. By repeating images and words and by then breaking the pattern, she conveys specific meanings.

4 | representing others

When you were a child, you probably drew a picture of your family. The drawing here was done by Quentin Petersen when he was six years old. Quentin probably didn't make many conscious decisions about how to represent his family. He did, however, make his father larger than other family members and gave him a beard, he gave his mom long hair, and he gave his brother what looks to be a brush cut. They're all smiling, perhaps reflecting something about the family's sense of humor.

▶ Six-year-old Quentin Petersen's drawing of his family.

As Quentin grew up, he learned additional methods of representing others—taking photographs, telling stories, and so on.

You've probably learned many of the same things. You've probably learned, in addition, to use various genres and media for writing about people—stories and essays, on paper and screen. You've learned to think carefully about what you say about others and to think consciously about the specific things to emphasize when you represent others—which characteristics to focus on and which ones to ignore, what to reveal and what to leave unmentioned.

We have many decisions to make when we write about or picture others, decisions involving our understanding of our subjects as well as of the broader contexts. If you are photographing a friend at an event—a graduation, a wedding, an athletic competition—you probably know enough about your subject's background, values, and hopes to have some sense of how that person would want to be seen or understood. You also probably know something about the broader context of the event to know how people there are supposed to be feeling, behaving, or looking. Your photographic representation will reflect all of this. In the case of the wedding snapshot here, the photographer no doubt knew something about weddings and certainly made a point of capturing the most joyous and memorable moments—bride and groom being showered with rice, for example—and would also have known which moments *not* to photograph.

These decisions are easier to make when you know the values, assumptions, and cultural traditions of the people you are representing as well as of those who will be seeing or reading what you do—your audience. Such decisions may be harder to make when you know very little about your subject or audience—especially when their backgrounds, cultures, and experiences differ from your own. No matter how much we know about people, the decisions we make about representing them are never the same as they would make themselves. We see them from our perspective, not theirs. Whether we are drawing, writing about, or photographing someone, our point of view is part of the mix. This chapter focuses on the challenges of writing about others, of representing individuals and groups who are different from ourselves.

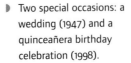 Two special occasions: a wedding (1947) and a quinceañera birthday celebration (1998).

The ability to recognize other people is a basic skill that we acquire very early in life. When we are babies, conscious only of what we need and want, one of the first distinctions we make is between ourselves and those people, usually parents, who fulfill our needs. Through this process of differentiation, we become aware of a world beyond ourselves—and of how others perceive and respond to us. Psychologists say that it is in this dialogue between ourselves and others that we form our identities as individuals. Without other people, we could not fully define ourselves.

This process of defining ourselves by defining others happens almost unconsciously. When you glance at family snapshots such as the ones here, you probably recognize things from your own childhood. Did you engage in similar activities? wear clothes like those pictured in the snapshots? pose for family photographs? By observing others and thinking about what you see, you consolidate your understanding of yourself, your identity, your experiences in relation to the experiences of others.

This process of defining our identities in relation to others continues throughout life. At school, on television, in the movies, we come in contact with people of different abilities and talents and interests. We encounter people of different sizes, ages, and races; we meet people with different experiences, home lives, and economic circumstances; we learn about the histories, habits, and accomplishments of people from different places.

▶ Kids and fish,
Minnesota, 1960.

When we are young, the first other people we notice are those closest to us, those who live with us and thus shape our lives in some way: mothers, fathers, stepparents, uncles, aunts, brothers, sisters, cousins, grandparents, and so on. Their attitudes and values, likes and dislikes, beliefs and biases shape our own, a fact often reflected in the stories and images we compose about family. Look at the photograph here of the small boy following the actions of his father.

▶ Father and son with wheelbarrow, New Jersey, 2002.

Visually, this photograph calls attention to the relationship that the boy and his father have and the traits they share. The composition of the snapshot establishes this emphasis, with the boy closely following the actions of his father. There is a clear pattern established through repetition, with both individuals working at the same physical task, with the same tools, in similar attire. The composition has unity, with the various elements in the photo cohering as a text, conveying the message that these two individuals are alike, sharing values and interests as well as a familial bond.

Now look at a more complex photograph of another family, taken by the award-winning photographer Gordon Parks. It uses some of the same strategies of visual composition to depict a woman feeding her grandchildren as her daughter looks on from another room. Notice that the photograph has been composed with two symmetrical parts—through the open door to the left we see the grandmother and children; on the other side of the door, in a mirror, we see the mother looking on, her gaze directing our own. Though we cannot actually know what was going on with the family, the photographer has given us a glimpse that arouses our curiosity.

▶ Ella Watson, a government charwoman, with her grandchildren and adopted daughter, Washington, D.C. Photo by Gordon Parks, 1942.

When we write about members of our family and take photos of them, the texts we create reflect the way we understand them. Even within our immediate family, others usually are not only similar to us; they are also different from us. As we grow up, we generally form an increasingly complex understanding of the people with whom we live—from seeing them, listening to them talk about their past, hearing the stories others

YOU DO NOT HAVE TO BE
YOUR MOTHER UNLESS SHE IS
WHO YOU WANT TO BE. YOU DO NOT HAVE
TO BE YOUR MOTHER'S MOTHER, OR YOUR
MOTHER'S MOTHER'S MOTHER, OR EVEN
YOUR GRANDMOTHER'S MOTHER ON YOUR
FATHER'S SIDE. YOU MAY INHERIT THEIR
CHINS OR THEIR HIPS OR THEIR EYES, BUT
YOU ARE NOT DESTINED TO BECOME THE
WOMEN WHO CAME BEFORE YOU. YOU ARE
NOT DESTINED TO LIVE THEIR LIVES. SO IF
YOU INHERIT SOMETHING, INHERIT THEIR
STRENGTH. IF YOU INHERIT SOMETHING, IN-
HERIT THEIR RESILIENCE. BECAUSE THE ONLY
PERSON YOU ARE DESTINED TO BECOME IS
THE PERSON YOU DECIDE TO BE.

tell about them. We can identify their strengths as well as their weak-nesses, their good and bad characteristics. We can portray them in multi-faceted ways. Within families, then, individuals are often able to develop a healthy understanding of others and to come to appreciate that the many differences among people are both necessary and desirable.

The Nike advertisement above reflects the complicated relationship children often have with their parents. The visual composition of the image emphasizes that the woman and the child are related, with similar hairstyles and facial expressions—but the words challenge readers to remember the differences that still exist: "You do not have to be your mother."

In this chapter are several texts about how people relate to—and rep-resent—their families. Joseph Bathanti's essay "Your Mum and Dad" gives a sense of how complex a child's relationship with his parents can be.

▶ Nike ad, 1991.
This ad makes use of comparison and contrast to make its point.

People do not always understand others in a positive light. Sometimes, the belief systems within which we grow up—those of family, religion, community, or culture—cause us to see other people's ways as unusual or even unacceptable. Most people learn to live with people who hold beliefs different from their own. Sometimes, however, people come to regard certain individuals or groups as *too* different from themselves—and to believe that those from a certain country or religion, or with a particular skin color or eye shape, or of a specific social status or lifestyle are fundamentally undesirable as a group. In the worst cases, those who base their understanding of others on stereotypes focus on a few simple traits as if they apply to everyone in a given group and are fixed for all time. Stereotypes are often based on race, gender, sexual orientation, class, nationality, geography, lifestyle, and other traits.

Stereotypes are often found in advertisements. Look at the IBM ad here, for instance, which reads, "With every incarnation, we hope to draw closer to Nirvana. But as each generation grows obsolete and dies, Sikander grows madder." Although this man is ostensibly a computer user, he is shown as a naïve inhabitant of an underdeveloped country, his Hindu reli-

▶ IBM ad.

gious beliefs linked to passing generations of computer hardware. The insulting stereotypes here are of course based on Western perspectives, just as they are designed for Western eyes.

▷ A gas station depicting the Aunt Jemima stereotype. Natchez, Mississippi, 1983.

Photographic images often portray stereotypes because even though they may capture one person or a single moment, they live on as people and moments frozen in time. The passage of time and history generally remains invisible within the frame of a single photograph. One photograph by itself cannot show how the people in it—their values, actions, and relations with others—might change over time. In this chapter, Helen Starkweather's "Crisis at Central High" tells the story behind an image that has typified many of the racial stereotypes from the civil rights movement in the 1950s and 1960s, explaining what was happening in the image and revealing what happened to the people in the photo after they passed out of the picture's frame. The photograph shows a moment of hatred frozen in time, but the words tell a more complete story of a relationship between two women that changes somewhat as time passes.

To understand how people end up thinking in stereotypes, it helps to consider how a larger set of historical circumstances can establish such thinking. Consider, for example, the genres of mug shots and wanted posters: How do we represent people as criminals in the twenty-first century? How do we define ourselves as "responsible citizens" and criminals as "others"? To understand how criminals have become stereotyped as "others" in mug shots and wanted posters, we must go back to the invention of photography in the nineteenth century.

In that century, scientists were making great strides in many disciplines, learning more about the world and about the natural phenomena that characterized it. Charles Darwin and other naturalists was cataloging the species of the natural world; Joseph Lister was identifying the causes of infection in the human body; Robert Peary and other explorers was *were* charting the geography of the earth; Sigmund Freud was studying the nature of the human mind.

When the new science of photography emerged in the middle of the nineteenth century as a way of producing images, it was understood within this context of scientific innovation as a way of recording data and documenting facts about the natural world. One area of scientific endeavor in particular—criminology—embraced photography almost immediately for its perceived impartiality and accuracy. The photo here shows a detail from a table that police used to identify the physical traits of those accused of crimes.

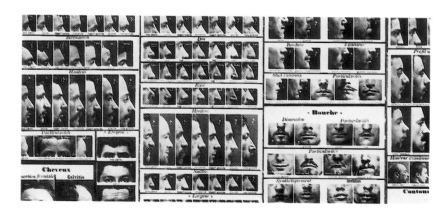

▶ Detail from the *Synoptic Table of Facial Expression for the Purpose of Systematic Identification.* From the Archives Historiques et Musée de la Prefecture de Police, Paris.

▶ Wanted poster, 1999.

▶ Mug shot of Cynthia Selfe, Houghton, Michigan, police department, 2002.

Police began to use standardized texts to represent people accused of crimes. These texts included photographs focused on the head and face—one facing front and one in profile. These photographs were designed to assist the police in identifying criminals. In such pictures, the subject was photographed unsmiling, standing against a plain background (sometimes with a grid indicating height), and identified by name and physical characteristics (height, weight, age, race, tattoos, and so on).

In relatively short order, such pictures became a recognizable photographic genre, a type of text associated with a specific purpose and context. It is a genre now associated with texts such as the ones shown here of FBI fugitive Donald Eugene Webb and Oklahoma City bomber Timothy McVeigh. The purpose of mug shots and wanted posters, we know from our collective historical experience, is to catch criminals. Given this widely accepted cultural understanding, such photographs have two effects: they establish a person's identity within a framework of scientific exactness (height, weight, build), and they characterize the subject as a criminal—often, even before a trial date has been set. Partly because such texts are displayed in post offices and on television and are associated with terrible crimes, and partly because of the history and purpose of this photographic genre, those pictured are often seen less as suspects than as criminals whose identity—and guilt—has already been established by the camera.

The history of photography and law enforcement, then, has shaped the manner in which we read such texts. Because we know something of the contexts in which they are commonly used, mug shots and wanted posters include all the cultural codings associated with crime and criminals. If, for instance, you saw the mug shot of Cynthia Selfe displayed at your local post office, would you be likely to hire her for a job at the bank where you keep your savings? trust her with sensitive information?

Your answers may help you understand the ways in which such photographic texts—both visual and verbal—can contribute to stereotyping. In this chapter, the reading "New Way to Insure Eyewitnesses Can ID the Right Bad Guy" describes some of these problems and the new measures now being taken to avoid them. Apparently, what we see in such pictures is less a matter of fact than of who we are and how the world is represented to us—especially in the ways we think about others.

▶ Mug shot of Timothy McVeigh, later convicted for the bombing of the Murrow Building in Oklahoma City, 1995.

Another context in which we often represent others in stereotypical ways is in our understanding of other cultures. The more different a culture is from our own and the less we know about the lives of its people, the more likely we are to "see" those people in terms of stereotypes. Such stereotyping is exacerbated, moreover, when we allow ourselves—or our texts—to focus only on the most exotic features, those aspects most foreign to us.

When Britain and the United States colonized China in the nineteenth and twentieth centuries, for example, Underwood & Underwood and other companies sent photographers to record their impressions. The snapshots these photographers took were transferred to stereoscope cards, which gave them a realistic three-dimensional look, leading American and British viewers to imagine themselves within the foreign landscapes. The photographs shown here, taken in 1901, rely on stereotypical representations, showing Manchu women dressed in exotic costumes. The use of the word "typical" in the caption—"A Group of Manchu Women, with typical head-dress"—implied to the American and English audience for these cards that all Manchu women dressed in this same fashion. Such oversimplified representations not only ignored the many regional, economic, and other differences that distinguished one Manchu woman from another, they also exaggerated the differences between the cultures of the viewers and the viewed.

▶ Manchu women in China. Because stereoscopic photos appear three-dimensional, those pictured in them look especially real. Stereoscopic photo by James Ricalton, Underwood & Underwood, New York and London, 1901.

We can still see such stereotyping today in magazines such as *National Geographic* and *Condé Nast Traveler* and in the photographs we take on our own travels. When we visit foreign countries, after all, we are probably most interested in things that are different, most unfamiliar to us. That, then, is what we photograph, and it is the way we represent the people we saw in our photo albums and in our memories. The photo here from Katmandu tells us something about the two women pictured and also about the perspective of the American tourist who took the photo.

▶ Women in doorway, Katmandu, 1974.

The problem is not necessarily with the images themselves; the problem is when they are used to represent an entire nation or culture without taking into account variation among the many members of the larger group. It may be more of a problem with images than with words, perhaps because we're more likely to use one or two images rather than many, and to select ones that are vivid or otherwise especially memorable to represent an entire culture or group of people.

But guidebooks and other travel writing can also describe people in ways that exoticize them or otherwise foster stereotypes. Consider this passage from the 1914 edition of Karl Baedeker's guidebook to Russia:

The GREAT RUSSIANS . . . are blond, blue-eyed, and vigorous, with broad shoulders and bull necks, often somewhat clumsy and with a strong tendency to obesity. Their character has been influenced not only by a long history of subjugation to feudal despotism, but also by the gloomy forests, the unresponsive soil, and the rigorous climate, and especially by the enforced inactivity of the long winters. In disposition they are melancholy and reserved, clinging obstinately to their traditions, and full of self-sacrificing devotion to Tzar, Church, and feudal superior. They are easily disciplined, and so make excellent soldiers, but have little power of independent thinking or initiation. . . . The important and fascinating literature of Russia reflects this dreamy and melancholy outlook on life, which is seen also in the national songs and music.

—Karl Baedeker,
*Russia: A Handbook
for Travelers* (1914)

The Baedeker book was published in 1914 by a German publisher, so it reflects a particular historical and cultural perspective of the Russian people. But travel books published today in the United States are not immune from relying on such stereotypes. *Let's Go USA*, for instance, tells us that "every April, San Antonians slip on their dancing shoes, call out the mariachis, and throw a ten-day party for anyone who wants to come," and it says that when visiting Corpus Christi, you should "shake the sand out of your toes, put on your boots, and dance up a storm" at a country-western dance hall that "fills up every night with restless cowboys looking to have a good time." *Let's Go* is a line of travel guides published for college students, written by Harvard students. Anybody who has ever lived in Texas would be able to tell these authors that not everybody in the state wears cowboy boots or listens to mariachi music.

Chances are that these descriptions of Texas were written by someone who did not grow up in that state—and who focused on things that he or she found most exotic. When visiting a new place, it is often tempting to describe the people and the details that we find most unusual, but it is always a good idea to stop and think about our observations and how they are shaped by our own culture. Have we chosen one person to represent an entire culture? Are we overgeneralizing? Are we ignoring the diversity present in the culture? Are we focusing on things that seem exotic to us while ignoring important details that are more familiar—and that might actually help us connect with others? Is this the way we ourselves would wish to be described?

Later in this chapter, see "Material World" and "The Cards We Choose to Send" for examples of how peoples and cultures are portrayed in photographs and on postcards.

▶ A poster for *Bend It like Beckham*, a film about the meeting of two very different cultures, 2003. The image is closely cropped to focus on the contrasting clothing styles of the two cultures.

image conscious

Imagine photos that visitors from other countries and cultures might take of you and your family and friends. What would they consider exotic, and why? What scene might they choose to represent you and your culture? What could you say to them to let them know that there are many different cultures and peoples in the United States?

Not all stereotypes are so serious or so destructive, of course. Cartoons and comic books often use stereotypes in self-conscious and ironic ways, to intentionally make fun of various groups. By using obvious and over-done stereotypes—mean bosses, obnoxious children, forgetful husbands, bossy wives—artists can poke fun and even call attention to the ways in which we all recognize and rely on such images.

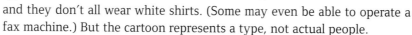
"My God, there's been a terrible accident in our Chicago office!"

The cartoon reproduced here, for example, shows three businessmen, all bald, all white, all in white dress shirts and neckties (two with stripes, one with dots) . . . and presumably none of them very good at using the fax machine. Without a doubt, these are stereotypical images—but do you think that they're read as such by everyone? This cartoon was published in the *New Yorker*, and it pokes fun at some familiar office styles and behaviors. But it makes fun as well of some familiar stereo-types—not all businessmen are bald or white, and they don't all wear white shirts. (Some may even be able to operate a fax machine.) But the cartoon represents a type, not actual people.

Comic books represent people in the same way, with stereotypical images. Superheroes and supervillains, for example, often possess exaggerated traits that appeal to youngsters and that are meant to represent a group of people. Although these characteristics are often based on stereotypes of race and gender, superheroes are usually meant to be read in a positive light, especially within specific historical and cultural contexts. In 1941, for instance, right before the United States entered World War II, Captain America was introduced by Marvel Comics to provide young men with a role model of a soldier willing and able to fight for a good cause and, presumably, to help the U.S. vanquish powerful enemies.

The stereotypical aspects of superheroes, however, often become less positive with the perspective of time and historical change. For example, a profile of Marvel's Jubilee (a part of which is shown on p. 246) tells us that she is a contemporary superhero and daughter of two prosperous Chinese

image conscious

Find a cartoon that includes both images and words that you think is especially funny. Think about what makes it funny. How much of the humor is due to the words, how much to the images? Is there any stereotyping—and if so, is it central to the humor? Who is likely to find the cartoon amusing, and is there anyone who would not?

CAPTAIN AMERICA

In 1940, as America prepared for war, a frail young man volunteered for an experiment that transformed him into the ultimate physical specimen: the American Super-Solider. Steve Rogers battled Nazis until a freak mishap placed him in suspended animation for decades. When he awakened, Rogers was truly a man out of time, though no less committed to fighting the evils of this perilous new era!

Real Name: Steven Grant Rogers
Occupation: Crimefighter
Group Affiliation: Avengers
Base of Operations: Avengers Mansion, New York City
First Appearance: Captain America Comics #1 (historical, 1941), Avengers (Vol. 1) #4 (modern, 1964)

Height: 6'2
Weight: 240 lbs.
Eye Color: Blue
Hair Color: Blond

Powers: Enhanced by the Super-Solider Serum, Captain America's agility, strength, endurance and reaction time are superior to those of an Olympic-level athlete. Also, Cap has mastered a number of fighting forms, including American-style boxing and judo. These abilities, combined with his indestructible shield, make him one of the finest human combatants Earth has ever known.

Weapons: Captain America's only weapon is his Vibranium shield, a concave disk 2 1/2 feet in diameter that weighs 12 pounds. The shield's exceptional aerodynamic properties enable it to slice through the air with minimal wind resistance and deflection of path. The disk's unparalleled overall durability, coupled with a natural concentric stiffness, allows it to rebound off solid objects with minimal loss of angular momentum.

Soldier

Soldier

Jubilee

Real Name: Jubilation Lee
Other Aliases: None
Identity: Secret
Occupation: (current) Student, adventurer, (former) Street performer
Legal Status: Citizen of the United States with no known criminal record, still a minor
Place of Birth: Beverly Hills, California

Marital Status: Single
Known Relatives: Dr. and Mrs. Lee (parents, deceased)
Base of Operations: (current) Professor Xavier's School for Gifted Youngsters, The Massachusetts Academy, Berkshire Mountains, Massachusetts, (former) Beverly Hills, California; Los Angeles County Juvenile Hall; Hollywood Mall, Hollywood, California; Professor Xavier's School for Gifted Youngsters, Salem Center, Westchester County, New York State

Group Affiliation: (current) Generation X, (former) X-Men
First Appearance: UNCANNY X-MEN #244

immigrants. She was educated at an exclusive high school in Beverly Hills, and her only other relatives live in Communist China. With mutant powers to match her "explosive personality," she hasn't been the same since she hooked up with the X-Men. Throughout the profile, Jubilee seems to reflect many stereotypical notions about Chinese immigrants, Southern California, and children who attend "exclusive schools." Clearly, Jubilee is a caricature, but does she poke fun at some things that not everyone finds amusing?

At the end of this chapter, you can see in "How to Draw Comic Book Heroes and Villains" how comic book artists go about creating such images.

Travel photography calls upon us to represent others. Whether we're taking pictures of people we know or don't know, we're representing them in a context that is meaningful to us. Choose a favorite snapshot of a person that you took on a trip or vacation. Jot down your thoughts about why you took the photo and why you like it. Try to recall the decisions you made composing the photo. Why did you choose to take this picture? Did you pick a specific moment? a certain pose or expression? a characteristic gesture? Why? Consider the place—were you trying to record a particular building or view? an event? If so, why? Consider context: What were you trying to show about the person and about the place? Try writing a caption that says in words what you meant the photo to convey. Consider, as well, how your experience and background shaped the photograph you took.

If you don't have a personal photo, find a picture book about a place you'd like to visit and choose a photo that contains a person. Look at how the photo is composed and think about what the photo says, both about the values of the photographer and about the values you might attribute to the person in the photograph. Compose a caption for this picture if it doesn't have one.

Try to imagine, as well, what kind of photograph the person in your picture might take of you. What caption would that person add to such a photograph? What would you want the picture and caption to convey?

What does this exercise demonstrate about the challenges associated with representing others?

CONSIDERING THE WAY YOU REPRESENT OTHERS

- What people or groups are represented, and how? If you're considering your own text, what are you trying to say or show about your subjects, and why?

- How are people represented visually, and what might those people think of the way they're being represented? How are they represented verbally—how are they described or quoted?

- Does the text overgeneralize or in any way suggest a stereotype? Is this intentional—and if so, for what purpose?

- What purpose(s) does the text have?

- Who is the intended audience? Who might like and appreciate this text? Who might dislike it?

- What is the point of view—critical? sympathetic? ironic? something else? What cultural or historical factors might account for the point of view?

Joseph Bathanti teaches creative writing at
Appalachian State University, in North Carolina. Born and
raised in Pittsburgh, he has also taught at Davidson
College and Mitchell Community College. He is the author
of *East Liberty,* a coming-of-age novel about growing up
in Pittsburgh in the 1950s and 1960s, and four volumes of
poetry, among them *Communion Partners* and *Feast of
All Saints*.

"Your Mum and Dad" was first published in 2002 in the
Sun, a journal of essays, fiction, poetry, and photography
published in Chapel Hill, North Carolina. In this essay,
Bathanti writes about his parents. As you read, pay
attention to how he represents them. Note what he
chooses to say and try imagining the things he does
not say.

Your Mum and Dad

JOSEPH BATHANTI

They fuck you up, your mum and dad.
They may not mean to, but they do.
They fill you with the faults they had
And add some extra just for you.

—PHILIP LARKIN

My parents hail from a generation who must arrive at least an hour before every engagement, for whom being on time is a divine mandate. Thus, we pull into the Charlotte airport *well* before the departure time for their return flight to Pittsburgh. They have been in North Carolina for two weeks: their annual spring visit, during which they exchange the routine of their household for the routine of ours. The key difference, of course—the rarifying element—is that our house has children, and my parents literally worship children, especially their grandchildren.

The apprehension that attends the arrival of my parents is like the buildup before a big game. Preparation is everything. The practices are long and grueling. My wife, Joan, is head coach and tactician. With her at the helm, we manage a year's worth of sprucing up and repairs in just a couple of weeks. My mother is legendary for the antiseptic cleanliness of her house, and it is apparently daunting for a wife to have such a mother-in-law.

Joan storms through the house like Vince Lombardi, and the boys and I have no choice but to do

250

251

her bidding. I console myself with the fact that these are things that have to be done anyway—that should have been done long ago. Closets and cabinets are cleaned out and rearranged, new towels hung from the bathroom rods, new sheets put on the guest bed. Garages and outbuildings are swept and tidied, grass mowed, shrubs and spring flowers edged and mulched, and a dogwood tree planted. There are numerous trips to the county landfill.

This year, I rented a pressure washer and used the lethal water jet to strip the old paint from the front porch. Then, wearing a surgeon's mask and dragging an extension cord with a caged light bulb, I put two coats of toxic-smelling barn red paint on it in the middle of the night. I also troweled on roofing cement around the chimney flashing, replaced the wooden steps on the back porch and coated them with a mold retardant, bought primer and aluminum paint and brushes for the outbuilding roofs, and pointed up the brickwork around the outside vents. But, mercifully, time ran out on me.

The final tasks prior to fetching my parents at 5 the airport were: rake out the fridge, clean the oven, scour the bathrooms and kitchen, put a vase of fresh flowers on the kitchen table and a pastel box of Kleenex in the guest bathroom, vacuum, and clean out the car, which had already been to the carwash. The house looked great: the new lamp in the living room, the new carpet in the dining room, the new bookshelves and carpets in the boys' rooms, the new tablecloth, the new throw rugs everywhere, the new hanging baskets on the front porch, the new items I didn't even know were new. As I nosed the car toward Charlotte, Joan admonished me not to let on—even remotely—to my mother that she'd gone to any fuss whatsoever. Then, having stayed up all night cleaning, she passed out.

My parents' visit went very well, despite a rough prelude: Shortly before they were to arrive, Uncle Dick, the last of my mother's brothers, had a heart attack. Early reports were encouraging, but "it destroyed his body," my mother said, and he died just days later. So, after spending two days at the hospital, three days at the funeral home, then the next day attending both the funeral *and* my niece's high-school graduation, my mother and father boarded a plane for North Carolina.

The second we had my parents buckled into our car at the Charlotte airport, they fell asleep. When we finally got home with them an hour later, we saw, parked in our front yard, a yellow bulldozer and a backhoe. This, of all days, was the day the county had chosen to bury new cable. Along the edge of our freshly clipped emerald green lawn, they'd gouged a ditch flanked by three-foot-high bunkers of red clay. Our yard looked like a construction site.

First order of business, as always, was to inventory the food my parents had hauled with them: salami, pepperoni, olives, fontinella, Jarlsberg, provolone, Pecorino Romano, pizzelles my mother had baked, and pizza shells and fresh loaves of Italian bread from Rimini's Bakery—which, my father pointed out, had still been warm when he'd fetched them at five o'clock that morning. We spread it all out on the kitchen table and sat down and ate, even though dinner was not far off. Whatever the kids wanted, we said yes to. Watching them eat gives my parents so much pleasure that it borders on the pathological. "God love their little hearts," my father said, gazing at his grandsons' bulging jaws.

As if in ecclesiastical response, my mother intoned, "God love them both," and dropped more cookies on their plates.

After eating, the kids came to our bedroom— 10 temporarily Grammy and Pap's room—for their presents: books, balls, Legos, clothes. There was another round of kisses and embraces. We all knew that this was really the best part of their stay, and we hung on to its perfection as long as we could.

Leaving my parents to settle in, I heard them talking behind the door to the bedroom. I couldn't make out any words, just the sound of their voices, pleasant and tired, the way they used to sound to me as a child, and for a moment I felt that same ineffable sense of well-being and safety. A little later, I tiptoed back in to get some jeans out of the closet and found them napping on top of the bedspread, lying on their sides like babies, their open suitcases resting side by side in a corner, their prescription bottles regimented on the dresser, my father's razor on a folded white washcloth next to a can of Right Guard. On the wall above my mother's head was her framed high-school-graduation portrait, taken in 1936. In it, she is indisputably beautiful. I looked down on her as she stirred, a handkerchief clutched in one hand.

At supper—the traditional first-night pizzas— we chatted a bit about Uncle Dick. I looked for signs of strain, but my mother seemed fine, if tired. I had to hand it to her: she's tough. A funeral and a commencement both in one day, and then a plane ride the very next morning.

Somehow, we got to talking about Jimmy Longo, a neighborhood character who used to pick up and deliver our dry cleaning back in Pittsburgh. We had a few laughs at his expense, and then I related a story he'd told me the last time I'd seen him: Jimmy was bowling, and he set his styrofoam cup of coffee down on a bench. A "great big black guy"—the fact that the guy was black being the coup de grâce for Jimmy—accidentally sat on it.

The story itself wasn't funny, but the way Jimmy related it, deadpan and with a little bitterness over the lost cup of coffee, was hilarious. I did my best to imitate his voice, the way he repeated phrases—"I mean, Jesus Christ, he sat right on the goddamn cup of coffee"—a hand flying up every few seconds to demonstrate his outrage.

As my mother laughed, something misfired in her circuitry. One eye closed. A silver asterisk fizzled in the other before that lid, too, fluttered and fell, and her head lolled back.

My mother is dying, I thought. I both knew this 15 to be true and was utterly detached and able to accept it: not scared, not frantic—though by now we were all calling her name, hailing her back from wherever she'd gone.

My father was slapping her hand. "Rose! Rose!" he barked, more scared than I'd ever seen him.

Part of me was already picking through the bones of what this would mean to me for the rest of my life: how I'd killed my mother, made her laugh until she died. I had pushed her to this, on such a night, in front of my family, my children. My childhood nightmare had come true, like some twisted fairy tale: the bad boy who killed his mother.

See, see, my mother was saying to me from beyond the grave, *I warned you. You've never known when to let up*.

I hope it was my voice that summoned her, my tenderly inflected, urgent "Mother" that brought her back to us. She opened her eyes and looked at me as if I'd awakened her from a spell. I was at her side, holding her hand, which I lifted and kissed quite unconsciously, the very image of the loving son.

By now, Joan had dialed 911, though my mother 20 was protesting that she was "fine" and didn't "need any 911." The rescue squad arrived in a hoopla of lights and sirens. The dogs went crazy. I waited for the EMTs at the door. Two of them turned out to be ex-students of mine, a benefit—and a hazard—of teaching at a small college in a small town. I introduced them to my mother, who eyed them imperiously. She was fine, as she had said more than once, and did not appreciate any of this. It was then that I finally thought to pry the traumatized, bug-eyed children from their seats and shoo them off to play.

Everything checked out, and my mother was pronounced OK. Probably hyperventilated was all, said the EMTs, but a little trip to the hospital wouldn't hurt, just to make sure.

My mother put up her hand—a gesture built into the family DNA, meaning that all discussion has ended—and said, "No."

Joan and I walked the EMTs to the door and thanked them. As I shook hands with one, he said, "I had the hardest time in your class. You don't give A's, do you?"

When we returned to the dinning room, my mother was clearing the table, and my father looked as if he had just lost an argument.

After the children were in bed, we ended the night in front of the television. My parents have been visiting now since 1976, and every year we go through the same discussion about what channels we do and do not get. Since my wife and I do not subscribe to cable and its smorgasbord of useless programming, we receive, alas, only the big-three networks, and our reception is rather tenuous as a result of our choice to live out in the country— another decision regarded as dubious by Mom and Dad. When we ask them what they would like to watch, they wistfully remark that we don't

get Channels 2, 4, and 11, the Pittsburgh channels. This is true, I say patiently, but we get the same network programs (though only one station actually produces a clear picture). We just have different numbers.

"We don't have to watch anything," my mother said, sounding disappointed.

"If you were home, what would you be watching?" Joan asked.

"You don't have to watch it just because of us," said my mother. "Do they, Joe?"

"Nah, nah, we don't care," my dad said.

"Sure," Joan said, "let's watch something."

We finally settled on one of the news magazine programs: *20/20*, I think. One segment was about a kid who'd been raped by his Little League coach, another was about genital mutilation, and the last was a little treatise on masturbation. My parents, as they fell asleep in their seats, tsked about what a horrible world we live in. Every few minutes my mother would snap out of her doze, find my father asleep on the couch beside her, and indignantly nudge him awake before nodding off again herself. But if we switched the TV off, it was as if the Angelus had been rung in their ears: *What happened to the TV?* In this absurdist manner, Joan and I were held hostage night after night while my parents slept through their favorite shows.

I've never seen the airport so crowded. My father and I muscle into the long baggage-check line while my wife, my two little sons, and my mother trail far behind. My mother is all but crippled by arthritis—spinal stenosis, to be precise. Even though she lives with constant pain, her inner domineering force, the source of which the rest of us can only guess at, will not allow her to admit it or accept others' help. When they catch up with us, however, I am astonished to hear that my wife has somehow convinced my mother to ride in a courtesy cart to the departure gate, nearly half a mile away.

I stay close to my dad, like a bodyguard. Just yesterday, my mother remarked to me that he is getting old. We were pulling up the driveway from her hair appointment, and my father, in T-shirt and shorts, was sitting in a chair in front of our open garage, smiling, my boys at his feet. I'd imagined him healthy and vigorous until my mother made her observation—very matter-of-fact, yet with a note of wonder and tenderness in her voice. After she said this, I'd swear she tailed off into a wistful internal monologue, replete with images of their genesis as lovers. But they are clearly not young lovers any longer, and I suspect my mother's pronouncement was commentary on her own mortality, as well. Still, she looks good, younger than her seventy-seven years. For her, looking younger is a great virtue, an accomplishment of intrinsic worth.

My dad, pushing eighty-one, looks good, too. Today he wears a cap, a plaid shirt, khakis, and a very stylish pair of Nikes. He chews gum and rattles his change. I'll be glad to look like him when I'm eighty-one. In the past few years, he has *walked* out of two surgeries—albeit on crutches—to repair a ruptured Achilles tendon and to reconstruct a knee. But my mother is right; he is getting old, and I stay close to him now at the airport because there is literally less of him. I am larger than my father: taller, broader, stronger, faster. This is, of course, inevitable, a fact of life, but this inversion of the old father-son paradigm requires some adjustments on my part. As I watch my father hand his tickets to the young baggage clerk, I am watching myself.

The clerk—a terribly official, pompadoured 35

sophisticate, well aware of the gravity of his position—asks to see a photo ID, which my father produces from the only wallet I've ever known him to own. He still carries in it his original Social Security card—from 1938. I see myself again in the photograph on his driver's license.

"Since you entered the airport, have you accepted anything from a stranger?" the clerk asks my father.

"No. I haven't."

The clerk stamps the tickets and returns them and the license to my father, who steps closer to the counter, smiles, and adds: "I never accept anything from strangers." The clerk attempts a smile in response, but has already started waiting on the next customer.

This type of friendly aside is my father's way of establishing communion with waiters and cabbies and cashiers. He feels his senior citizenship entitles him to a kind of ease with younger people, who have a lot to learn from him, and he wants to be liked—unlike my mother, who sees insularity as strength, familiarity somehow as capitulation. She chides him for these jaunty stabs at worldliness.

My father says to me, "They have to ask you 40 that *now*." *Now* as opposed to 1938. I nod and worry not so much about the harrowing world in which I must bring up my sons, but about whether they and I will find things to talk about when I'm an old man. The fact is, my father and I are a little too embarrassed to talk to each other about certain subjects. Over the years, we have remained, like Nick Carraway and his father in *The Great Gatsby*, "unusually communicative in a reserved way."

Once, when I was eight years old and playing Little League baseball, I had to fill in for our catcher, who was hurt. I was excited until my dad told me that I'd have to wear a cup. "For protection," he said. That was the sum of his explanation.

I was puzzled: What kind of cup? How did one wear it? And to protect what? I pictured an array of cups: coffee, tea, Dixie, demitasse. I couldn't quite equate any of these vessels with apparel, much less protection. I finally settled—don't ask me why—on a loving cup, the kind I had seen handed to jockeys on TV when their horses won the Kentucky Derby. I pictured myself behind the plate in mask, chest protector, and shin guards, with a golden trophy on its marble plinth standing guard before me.

Presented with the actual cup, I was confused and horrified. Beige plastic, its rim padded in rubber, it looked more than anything like the mask through which fighter pilots breathed oxygen. With it came a medicinal-smelling jockstrap with a marsupial-looking pouch, inside of which the thing was meant to be secured.

Faced with my look of utter incredulity, my father muttered, "For your pee-pee."

God, at that mortifying moment to have had a [45] good old-fashioned penis, and not a "pee-pee," or "privates," or a "weenie." But "pee-pees" are cute, harmless, and frequently powdered. A penis, on the other hand, is a hirsute sexual tool, and therefore the source of tension and terror.

The cup was as uncomfortable as it was embarrassing. After that first experience behind the plate, I never wore it again. I stashed it in a drawer, and eventually, like lots of things stashed in drawers, it disappeared. I have a vision of my mother spiriting it off to the backyard trash with ice tongs.

There can also be something very comforting, however, in my father's silence. My first forays into cheap wine as a teenager left me so besottedly drunk that I barely made it home; my guardian angel must have been a teetotaler. I ended up vom-

iting uproariously into the cold cellar toilet, as far from my parents' bedroom as I could get. When my dad showed up, I told him that I'd eaten one cheesesteak too many.

Despite the stench of regurgitated wine, my dad said nothing, just reached over, flushed the purple water, and asked me if I wanted some Brioski to settle my stomach. Then he walked me back to my bedroom. I stumbled up the two steep flights in what I was sure was stone-cold-sober fashion.

Another time, my father came home unexpectedly while I was trysting with a girl. I had time only to spirit her into my closet, hop back into bed, and feign an illness-induced nap. Dad marched right into my room and peered down at me. "I don't feel very good," I mumbled pitifully. When I opened my eyes, I saw behind him on my desk a pile of earrings, bracelets, necklaces, and hair barrettes. Clearly, these items did not belong to me. My father turned and looked down on them—I could see his face in the mirror above the desk—and then, without a word, he walked out, shutting the door behind him.

Maybe my dad didn't come through on the cup, [50] but more important to me, even now, is that he didn't devastate me on these and other occasions when he had every right to do so. Perhaps he held off because he thought, in those cases, it would be better for me. And maybe it was. I no longer vomit in the basement or secrete women in my bedroom. Or perhaps he was just trying to spare me and himself the embarrassment.

There is only one time I have seen my father embarrassed, and it is also on that occasion that he apologized to me for the first and only time. I was twelve, and he and I were cruising down Highland Avenue in our two-tone rose Rambler. My dad, always a cautious driver, had to brake and swerve to avoid a car that hurtled through the red light at the

Penn Avenue intersection. It would have plowed into us on my side. This was pre-seat-belt America. (Cars came equipped with them, but no one ever thought of using one.) So, in emergency stops, my dad would, rather roughly, throw his right arm across my chest to keep me from smacking the dashboard. As he did this, knocking the wind out of me, he shouted at the driver, "Where in the fuck are you going?"

Well! As if my breath hadn't already been snatched away by the sight of that speeding car bearing down on me and the big forearm across my chest. The sound of that taboo word—which I had only recently begun uttering among my pals—issuing from my dad's mouth all but made me lose consciousness. I wanted to fade away. Whatever came next, I did not wish to be present for it.

"Excuse my language" was all my father said, but it pained me terribly to hear him say it, because I knew he was ashamed.

Although we've extended advice to each other over the years, some things, it seems, we haven't needed to talk about, as if the transcendent bond between us is best expressed by silence, by the faith that everything will be OK if we just shut up. Maybe sometimes, as a parent, as a child, you have to play dumb.

My wife, my sons, and my mother are waiting for us in the courtesy cart. I walk with my arm around my dad. We get in and spin wildly off, the driver laying on the horn, which sounds like a police siren in a foreign film. Along the gleaming tiled concourse, people stream by us, going up and down escalators, in and out of restrooms, restaurants, bookstores, and boutiques. My mother calls out the name of each establishment as we buzz by. "We have those in Pittsburgh," she says, over and over.

There is not a lot of time before they board, and I am thankful for this. These leave-takings unnerve me. My mother, though not the weepy sort, invariably cries, filling me with regret. Trying to dilate this last moment, I hold her in my arms and tell her that it won't be long until we are all together again. I'd tell her anything to make her happy, since I know this life of silence—her way of loving—is breaking her heart.

I am working up the courage to tell my parents that I love them: to actually say, articulate, formalize my love in a sentence with a subject, verb, and direct object, then launch it out into the ozone, where it will forever orbit and echo. "I love you" simply was not something we said to one another in our family. Birthday, Christmas, and first Holy Communion cards were signed, "Love." Chiseled into tombstones was the word *love*. Occasionally, in a mood of maudlin bravado, one might say, "So-and-so sends love." But one would never look someone in the eye and say, "I love you." Not your mother, father, sister, or brother—and, I'd guess, not your wife or husband, either.

I don't think this silence hurt me. Each day of my life, my parents gave me dozens of examples of their love, though I wouldn't have conceived of them as such at the time. The children of immigrant parents, still in shock from the Depression and World War II, they selflessly donned half-century yokes—as a steelworker and a seamstress—that would have sent me and my rather pampered contemporaries to the existential ash pile, if not the cemetery, inside of a week. Fun and relaxation were absent from their lexicon. All they did was work and save and sacrifice so that they could provide for my sister and me. Though their love for us was manifest in every breath and action they took, they never *said*, "I love you."

But, of course, they didn't have books and talk shows and therapists to urge them to express their love, unlike my generation, which throws "I love you" around almost defensively, like confetti. My wife and I habitually, ad nauseam, tell our children that we love them. Certainly, we want them to know it, but maybe more than this, we are worried that they'll end up on the shrink's love seat if we don't tell them at least a hundred times a day how much we adore them.

For me, telling my parents I love them is self-absolution for all the times I didn't say or show it. I've got to get this off my chest, get it over with. Because I do love them, and what if they die and I haven't told them? So I say it:

"I love you, Mother. I love you, Dad."

They look at me as if I need to get a grip, then assure me that they love me, too; they love all of us. *Why would anyone need to say it? Was there any question?*

My wife hugs them. The kids shout goodbye, hold on to them, pet them, kiss their legs, their arms, wherever they can plant their lips. Like a rugby scrum, we huddle all the way to the door of the gate. My father is laughing. My mother is crying *and* laughing. "Goodbye," we croon. Around us, a blessed communion of travelers and their loved ones make similar spectacles of themselves.

My instinct, once my parents step across that symbolic threshold and out of sight, is to split, go home, begin to rewrite their visit into my own mythologized version.

"Let's leave," I blurt.

"Let's wait," Joan says.

Her policy—*our* policy—is to remain in the terminal until my parents plane is airborne. Of course, I know we should wait, but I'm still impatient to get out of here. In fact, I'm beginning to feel a kind of closed-in, otherworldly dread about being here.

We press against the terminal windows, amuse the kids by pointing out the various routines of the ground crew, the planes taxiing in. Finally, my parents' plane backs away from the terminal and heads for the turnaround. Awaiting its takeoff, we see, at the vanishing point of the runway, a serrated blade of lightning. It's far away. The sky overhead is not threatening. My parents' plane rolls leisurely into line behind the half dozen others also waiting to take off. Lightning again bisects the horizon. We hear the muffled rumble of thunder the window we are pressed against shimmies.

I want to escape so badly I'm able to deny the danger. *If they can just get up in the air and beat this storm*, I think. But it is obvious that their trajectory will take them right into the white band saw that reveals itself on the darkening horizon every thirty seconds or so. And there are several planes in front of them. Clearly, they will not be taking off anytime soon.

I ask the woman at the airline counter what's going on.

"They're just waiting for the weather to clear," she says, smiling.

I sit down and look out at the sky; black as a prayer book. My parents seem already gone. It's unbearably strange to think that they are just beyond this glass at the edge of the firmament. It looks like hell out there. I turn away. A boy with dyed-black hair and a girl with a pierced septum sit in the same chair and make out ferociously. An old man eating a hot dog ambles by and says loudly, "This is the worst hot dog I've ever eaten." A pilot, carrying his black box, walks by and, I swear, winks at my wife. "Just marry me," the boy with the ink black hair gurgles as he kisses the girl. I sneak another peek at the runway. It is nearly sliced in half by lightning.

It's been a half-hour since my parents' flight was due to leave. I get up and again ask the woman at the counter if she has any information. She gives me the same spiel about the weather, but she seems pensive. "They've turned off the air conditioning in the plane," she says.

I don't know why she tells me this, and I don't know what it could possibly mean, but I start to worry. I imagine my parents inside the plane, the stale air closing in, the sweaty cabin growing smaller, mothers wrestling with their crying babies, my mother getting worked up.

What's the matter? she says to my father. *Some-* 75 *thing must be the matter. I can't breathe.*

I want this sky to clear; I want this plane to take off. I want it to take off even if the sky doesn't clear. What I'm really afraid of, I realize, is that the flight will be scratched and the passengers returned to the terminal. My parents will have to come back home with us. Then there will be another endless round of goodbyes. "I love you" all over again. I don't have another goodbye in me. I want to go home.

Another twenty minutes goes by. The kids have started to go a little nuts, running and turning somersaults, giggling madly. An ambulance careens onto the tarmac with its lights flaring. It has been summoned for my mother, I'm sure. Sitting in that stifling cabin with the lightning threatening to knife her, she's had a heart attack or a stroke. I want to rush back to the counter and ask what an ambulance is doing out there, but I'm too embarrassed to show my face again. If she's dead, it'll be my fault—just as it would have been with the Jimmy Longo story. Subconsciously, I'm trying to kill her, to kill both of them. I want them to take off in dangerous weather because I don't love them enough to say goodbye again. It will be my fault if their plane crashes.

But the ambulance must be for someone else's parent, because suddenly the flight schedule lists my parents' flight as departed. The lightning has disappeared. In the ether, my mother and father are rooted once again in my fabrications of them.

"Let's go," I say.

Back home, delicate tendrils of neon green baby 80 grass push through the straw covering the scarred front yard. Inside, the house smells mysterious, the way it did when I first walked into it. Built in 1915, the year my father was born, it feels today like an empty church: solemn, silent, immaculate. Then I realize that this inscrutable hush enveloping the house is my parents' absence.

Wandering into our bedroom, where my parents have resided for the past two weeks, I find my father has left me his Right Guard (with a fifty under it), and my mother a bottle of Tylenol and the book she was reading. I wonder if I will ever see them again.

focus.

1. In what ways are Bathanti's mother and father like—and unlike—your parents? Imagine writing a piece like Bathanti's. How would you represent your parents? How would you describe them? What stories would you tell? Do you have a photo that would show them in a way you could not describe as well in words?

2. Think about the influence one of your parents has had on your life. How are you like him or her—physically or mentally, in your beliefs, values, attitudes, personality? How are you different? How has your attitude toward this parent changed over time? In what ways do you see him or her differently now than you did five or ten years ago?

3. Bathanti describes his parents in detail, but he does not actually *show* us what they look like. Do you wish he had included some photos? How would photos change the piece? Why do you think he did not include any?

respond.

1. Choose a photo of someone you're close to that you think represents that person well. Write a caption for the photo, adding with words things that the photo does not or cannot show.

2. Write an essay about a parent, grandparent, or other relative that focuses on a specific incident or trait. The incident or trait should provide a key for exploring something about that person and his or her experiences, beliefs, values, or personality. Illustrate your piece with a photo of the person, adding a caption that makes clear what you think the image shows about him or her.

Show the draft of your essay to another person. Ask whether the essay reads differently with the photograph. What does the image contribute to what you're trying to say about your subject, besides showing what he or she looks like?

3. Look at the representation on the facing page that Katherine Carlson did of her father and brothers (basing the idea from a Hewlett Packard advertisement). Using a photograph of your family and some photo manipulation software such as Photoshop, compose a similar study of one or more members of your family. Be sure the words and the type of font you choose work to achieve the goal of communication about your relationship with this person.

▶ Photo by Katherine Carlson, manipulation in Photoshop.

Dad
hunter
mechanic
loving,
stern, boy,
rough, sports,
disciplinarian,
retired, grandpa,
outdoorsman, son,
overprotective
opinionated, easy-
going, jokester
"three dogs"
husband,
fisher
strict

Clay,
prep,
slacker
cocky,
hockey,
cooking,
closest in age,
drafter, drinker,
single, boyish,
sloppy, lazy, guitar
computers, TV, sleeps
in, girl crazed, smelly
stranger, debator,
showoff, lives at
home, partier, no
school, likeable,
loud and
obnoxious!

Kirk:
crazy,
worker,
fire-
fighter,
husband, son,
hunter, fisher,
able, funny, short
temper, smile,
survivor,
loving,
giving

Erich
oldest
artist
husband,
daddy,
hunter,
fisher,
teacher, nuts,
navy seals,
"milo", chuck,
animal sounds,
wrestler, coach,
strong willed, fun,
gentle, patient, nice,
quiet, responsible, loving.

Richard:
middle,
daddy,
ADHD,
energetic,
impatient, hard-
working, fighter,
headstrong, story-teller
icefishing, little,
strong, shy, mouthy
construction, bric
layer, outdoors, kin
mature, no degree,
lively, fun, lost,
bunny hunter

Duane Michals (b. 1932) studied graphic design and once worked in the design department at Time, Inc., but his work as a photographer happened mostly by chance. In 1958, some tourist photos he took on a trip to the Soviet Union turned out to be uncommonly direct and simple and strong, so that he was invited to show them at a gallery in New York. He decided then to concentrate on photography as a career and was soon earning his living as a commercial photographer. He has taken photographs for *Vogue, Esquire, Scientific American,* and many other publications.

As an artist, Duane Michals uses all the tricks of camera and darkroom, including double exposure, blurred movement, and photomontage, to make his images more intense emotionally. He often adds written text to his photos, creating narratives about such life themes as desire, relationships, mortality, and memory. Much of his work stretches the definition of reality to encompass things felt or experienced rather than just seen. Combining written text with visual works toward that goal. With his childlike script, complete with cross-outs and mistakes, he creates an immediacy and intimacy in which he candidly expresses his views.

A Letter from My Father

DUANE MICHALS

A LETTER FROM MY FATHER

As long as I can remember, my father always said to me that one day
he would write me a very special letter. But he never told me
what the letter might be about. I used to try to guess what I might read
in the letter; what mystery, what intimacy we would at last share,
what family secret could now be revealed.
I know what I had hoped to read in the letter. I wanted him to tell me
where he had hidden his affections.
But then he died, and the letter never did arrive, and I never found that place
where he had hidden his love

focus.

1. If we read the photo without the written text, would the message be the same? What story is told by the facial expressions in this image? Who do you think is speaking, and what do you think he or she is saying?

2. Why do you think Michals chose a brick wall as the background?

3. How does the arrangement of the image—the direction each character faces, the use of light, and so on— affect what the whole text says?

4. What role does the mother play in this family tableau? How does her visual scale in the photo affect the way we perceive her role in the narrative?

respond.

1. Rewrite the caption on this photo from the perspective of the father or the mother. How does it change the way we see the image? Change the typeface to reflect the different voice. How does the different typeface affect the tone?

2. Find three or four photos that are somewhat related and make two photocopies. You could use photos you have, ones you find in a magazine, or the three shown here. Position them in a sequence, and write a brief narrative to go with them. Then change the sequence—put the images in a different order. How does the narrative then need to change? Pay attention to the placement and spacing of the images, and also to the typography of your narrative. What do these details do to the way we read the text?

Helen E. Starkweather (b. 1970) is an editor at *Smithsonian*, a magazine published by the Smithsonian Institution in Washington, D.C. She writes regularly about topics in the fine arts, photography, and American history. The article reprinted here crosses a couple of those categories, focusing on a famous photograph taken at an important moment in U.S. history.

This essay first appeared in the February 2002 issue of *Smithsonian*. It was written for the "Indelible Images" column, a regular feature of the magazine that looks at photography, and often at images that capture important moments in history or that give a sense of an era or event. The article included here does just that, focusing on a photograph from 1957, taken the day that the first African American students attempted to attend Central High School in Little Rock, Arkansas.

Crisis at Central High

HELEN E. STARKWEATHER

Photographer Will Counts had just begun working for the *Arkansas Democrat* when Arkansas governor Orval Faubus made a surprise televised announcement on the evening of Labor Day, September 2, 1957. In defiance of the federal government, Faubus had decided to dispatch more than 200 National Guardsmen to surround Little Rock's Central High School for September 3, the first day of classes. He claimed he was preventing violence as nine black students attempted to enroll in the all-white school as mandated by the landmark 1954 *Brown v. Board of Education* Supreme Court decision. In fact, the Guard prevented the "Little Rock Nine," as the students came to be called, from enrolling until the following day.

Counts, then 26, had himself graduated from Central, then called Little Rock High School, some few years before. Unlike the reporters in ties and jackets, some of whom were harassed as outsiders and arrested by the police, Counts wore an open-collared plaid shirt and blended in with the hostile crowd surrounding the school. On a reporter's tip, he slipped away from the media pack and went to another school entrance located near a street corner.

There, 15-year-old Elizabeth Eckford was approaching. "When I tried to squeeze past [a National Guardsman], he raised his rifle," Eckford, now 60 and a probation officer, recalls. "And the other guards moved in. I turned around and the crowd moved closer and closer." As she retreated, a dark-haired white student screamed "Nigger! Nigger! Nigger!" in Elizabeth's wake. Counts, who captured the scene on film, later wrote that "the courage and grace [Eckford] exhibited as she walked two blocks through the mob of school-integration dissidents became one of my most moving experiences." His image of Eckford taunted by the all-white crowd was a runner-up, along with other photographs he took during the crisis, for a 1957 Pulitzer Prize.

Over the decades Eckford rarely talked about that momentous day or of the many personal battles she and the other eight students fought that year. "My children never asked me about it because when they were little, they remembered reporters coming to the house [and] making Mommy cry." That reticence began to change in 1997. At a dedication of the Central High Visitor's Center and Museum, located across from the high school, Counts, then recently retired from Indiana University (where he taught photojournalism for 32 years), asked Eckford to pose for a 40th-anniversary photograph with Hazel Bryan Massery, the jeering girl in the picture. Although both women still lived in Little Rock, their paths had not crossed in 40 years (Massery, feeling, she says, like "the poster child of the hate generation," had

long since apologized to Eckford in a 1963 phone call). On her part, Eckford told Counts, "I have always wanted to meet her."

"It was like any meeting of two strangers," Vivian Counts, the photographer's wife, remembers, "a little awkward and a little strained." Soon, however, the two women were chatting about their children and mutual acquaintances.

Counts, greatly admired by both colleagues and students, died after a four-year battle with cancer at age 70 in Bloomington, Indiana, in October 2001. He "had a desire and passion to teach storytelling with photographs," says Scott Goldsmith, a former student who is now a photographer for *U.S. News and World Report*. Faubus served as governor of Arkansas until 1966. After that, he ran three times unsuccessfully for his former office and lost his last election to Bill Clinton in the 1986 Democratic primary. Faubus died of spinal cancer in 1994 at age 84.

▶ Forty years after the famous photograph was taken, Hazel Bryan Massery thanked Elizabeth Eckford for meeting with her. Eckford responded, "You are a very brave person to face the cameras again."

focus.

1. Look closely at the 1957 photograph and take notes on what you see. What details in this picture strike you as most important? Why? What details surprise you the most? Why?

2. Consider the composition of both photos. What formal elements of composition contribute to each picture's effect? How is each photo arranged, and what emphasis does the arrangement create? What do you see first, and why? What is the tone of each image?

3. The essay that accompanies the photographs explains some of the immediate and historical contexts of each picture. Make a list of questions the essay leaves unasked—and unanswered.

respond.

1. Part of the effectiveness of this selection resides in the dialogue established between the photograph, which shows a moment frozen in a specific historical context, and the essay, which tells some of the actual story behind and around that image.

Choose a photograph of yourself, your family, or your friends at some momentous time in your life. Write an essay that tells the story of the snapshot and the people depicted in it. Make sure that you select a photograph that is particularly striking or meaningful to you. In your essay, try to unfreeze the moment that the photograph captures by telling the story of what was happening at the time and why it was an important moment for you. Try also to tell about what happened *after* the photograph was taken.

Show the photograph to a classmate (without the essay) and ask that person to write down his or her reactions to the photo, to list the details he or she notices, and to describe the formal compositional elements of the photo that contribute to its effects. Then ask this person to read your essay and to respond to its effectiveness in telling the story of the photograph. Use this response to revise your essay.

2. Will Counts's original photograph was selected as a runner-up for a 1957 Pulitzer Prize—along with other photographs he took during the civil rights crisis at Central High—because it captured so accurately and vividly the tensions and emotions that characterized that time in history.

Go to your school library and look through some major newspapers or newsmagazines published during the last twelve months, or do the same online. Select a photograph that you think captures this year in history. Try to find a picture that provides some insight into the events of the year. Get a copy of this photograph.

Do some research about the particular event pictured in the photograph. Write an essay that tells the story of the image and what you think it reflects about the year.

An Indian from India

ANNU PALAKUNNATHU MATTHEW

Annu Palakunnathu Matthew was born in England and grew up in India. She teaches photography at the University of Rhode Island. Her work reflects her own struggle with identity, her relationship to the culture of her ancestors, her place of birth, and her current home.

The selections here are from a 2001 exhibit in which Matthew juxtaposed photos she took of herself and nineteenth-century photographic representations of Native Americans. India was a British colony from 1757 to 1947, during which time the British sent home photographs, including many highly exotic images of India's people. These photographs proved a popular—if extremely limited—means of becoming acquainted with those in distant lands.

Similar photos were taken in the United States during the nineteenth and early twentieth centuries, offering glimpses of Native American cultures. Often, the most exotic and stereotyped images—those that most recalled romantic visions of the Wild West—proved most popular. Photos by Edward Curtis, two of which are shown here, were especially celebrated as accurate depictions of Native American peoples—but it is now known that Curtis staged and even fabricated some of these images.

Matthew composed and fabricated her images to match the ethnographic tone of the nineteenth-century images; using similar color backgrounds, and even poses. Her photographs challenge us to think about the way "types" of people are stereotyped, and in particular about how photographers exoticize people whom they see as "different."

As an immigrant, I am often questioned about where I am "really from." When I say that I am Indian, I often have to clarify that I am an Indian from India. Not an American Indian, but rather an Indian American, South Asian Indian (never heard of that till I got here), or even an Indian Indian. It seems strange that all this confusion started because Christopher Columbus thought he had found India and labeled the native people of America collectively as Indians.

The more time that I spend in America, the more I learn about the injustices inflicted upon and stereotyping of Native Americans. I find similarities in how photographers at the time looked at what they called the primitive natives, similar to the colonial gaze of the nineteenth-century British photographers in India. It irks me that others call us primitive and exotic just because we are different.

In this portfolio I play on these stereotypes using photographs of Native Americans from the nineteenth century. I pair these with contemporary images of myself in clothes, poses, and environments that mimic these "older" images. I am challenging the viewer's assumption of then and now, us and them, exotic and local. Through this work I hope to question the way we all stereotype "types" of people.

▶ *The belle of the Yakimas*. Photo by E. S. Curtis.

▶ *The belle of the Deccan Plateau*. Photo by A. P. Matthew.

▶ *Navajo smile*. Photo by E. S. Curtis.

▶ *Malayalee smile*. Photo by A. P. Matthew.

▶ *Noble savage*. Photo by E. S. Curtis.

▶ *Savage noble*. Photo by A. P. Matthew.

focus.

1. Matthew says she is challenging viewers' assumptions of "then and now, us and them, exotic and local." What do you think she means by each of these six words?

2. As you look at these photographs, consider how your cultural background affects the way you see them. If the people pictured here were to exoticize you, how might they do so?

respond.

1. Compare Matthew's photos with the travel photos shown here. Why do you think the photographer chose the people she did? To take Matthew's phrase, what do you think these images say about "us and them"? Do they exoticize their subjects? If so, describe how. Write 1–2 pages about how to depict people different from you without exoticizing them.

2. Create a small exhibit of photographs of students from your school and from a school in another country. The audience

for this exhibit will consist of students at the two schools. Your purpose is to demonstrate photography's power as a medium for representing others.

Start by finding photographs of students from your school: you can find them in catalogs, "face" books, brochures, and on the school Web site.

Next, search for a foreign college's catalog and Web site. It's a good idea to choose a school in a country very different from your own. As you look through the photographs, identify a theme that allows you to juxtapose or compare the two sets of photographs.

Keeping your theme in mind, select five photographs of students from your school and five photographs of students from the other school, creating a bibliography to document the sources of all the photographs. Pair up the photos and title the exhibit.

Compose a one-page note explaining the purpose of the exhibit, the theme you've used to organize the photos, and something about the photographs you've included. You might want to use Matthew's introductory comment as an example.

Arrange your pictures and your notes on poster boards. Be creative—your goal is to design an exhibit that is informative, fresh, insightful, and carefully prepared and presented. Before you hand in your exhibit, show it to one or two students and ask them what message it conveys. Is your theme clear? Do the paired photographs make the point you intend?

Gina Kolata writes regularly on science for the *New York Times*. She
has received many awards for her writing and is the author of several
books, including *Clone: The Road to Dolly and the Path Ahead* (1999) and
Sex in America: A Definitive Survey (with Edward Laumann, John Gagnon,
and Robert Michaels; 1995).

Iver Peterson is a political columnist for the *New York Times*.

The piece here, a news story first published in 2001 in the *New York Times*,
focuses on the practice of using photographs to identify suspects in criminal
cases; it suggests that this technique is neither foolproof nor entirely accurate.
The reliability of human vision and memory—and their roles in establishing
truth—rests at the center of many controversies about criminal cases. A study
published in 1998 by the National Institute of Justice, a research arm of
the U.S. Justice Department, says that "eyewitness identification was the
strongest evidence in 28 convictions later overturned by DNA evidence."

New Way to Insure Eyewitnesses Can ID the Right Bad Guy

GINA KOLATA AND IVER PETERSON

Prompted by new insights into the psychology of eyewitnesses to crimes, New Jersey is changing the way it uses witnesses to identify suspects.

Starting in October, the state will become the first in the nation to give up the familiar books of mug shots and to adopt a simple new technique called a sequential photo lineup, said John J. Farmer Jr., New Jersey's attorney general. Sequential viewing of photographs has been shown to cut down on the number of false identifications by eyewitnesses without reducing the number of correct ones.

The difference between the old and new systems is subtle but highly significant, according to researchers who have studied the psychology of witness identification. At present, eyewitnesses browse through photographs of suspects, comparing, contrasting and re-studying them at will.

Under the new system, victims and other eyewitnesses would be shown pictures one after the other. They would not be allowed to browse. If they wanted a second look, they would have to view all the photos a second time, in a new sequence. Also, the pictures would usually be shown by a person who would not know who the real suspect was.

"It's just a reality that eyewitness identifications 5 are made under situations of incredible duress, when people are trying to recall what someone looked like, and they can be more or less accurate," Mr. Farmer said. "So what we're trying to do with these guidelines is to give law enforcement a way in which we think we can at least narrow the risk that a mistake will be made."

The new rules also change the way physical lineups, called showups, will be done, although the use of suspects and stand-ins is so rare in New Jersey these days that some prosecutors cannot remember the last time they were used. As in photo lineups, the new rules require that in showups, individuals must be presented to the witness one at a time, usually through a one-way mirror.

The New Jersey program, which is already being used in Camden and Hunterdon Counties, grows out of a quarter-century of psychological research and is supported by recommendations published two years ago by the United States Department of Justice for police forces nationally.

The federal recommendations followed a 1998 study by the National Institute of Justice, a research arm of the Justice Department, which asked police officials, defense lawyers, prosecutors and researchers to review 28 criminal convictions that had been overturned by DNA evidence. The study found that in most of the cases, the strongest evidence had been eyewitness identification.

The Justice Department published a guide titled *Convicted by Juries, Exonerated by Science* in 1999, summarizing its recommendations for change, saying, among other things, that sequential lineups were an acceptable option.

New Jersey, working with a pioneer in the field, 10 Gary Wells, a psychologist and researcher at Iowa State University, soon began drawing up its own guidelines.

New Jersey's program was developed by Debra L. Stone, deputy director of operations and chief of staff in the state's Division of Criminal Justice. Ms. Stone said that the plan elicited howls of protest when it was introduced to county prosecutors, and local police departments and prosecutors, who feared that the new procedures would make it harder to win convictions because fewer suspects would be identified.

They also expressed concerns that the procedures would impose additional burdens on the short-handed police departments.

"But we had a program for them where we had Professor Wells come in to tell them some of his horror stories about misidentifications, and about the way people's memories work, and in the end they were very supportive," Ms. Stone said.

Chief John Miliano of the Linden, N.J., Police Department said: "Every time you see something coming along that makes your job a little harder, you kind of cringe a little. It's going to take extra time and personnel, but if it's going to make a case a little more solid or if it's going to eliminate a bad identification or a situation where an officer may try to influence an identification, then it's beneficial."

Both Mr. Farmer and Mr. Wells said they believed that New Jersey will be the first state in the nation to use the new lineup techniques. 15

Over the years, researchers like Mr. Wells, and Rod Lindsay, a psychology professor at Queen's University in Kingston, Ontario, have demonstrated that sequential lineups made a huge difference.

Professor Lindsay would stage a mock crime—like a purse-snatching—in front of a group of people who had agreed to participate in a study. He would then show the witnesses a traditional lineup of suspects, like a group of photographs or a number of people standing in a row, but he would not put the "purse-snatcher" in the lineup. About 20 percent to 40 percent of the witnesses mistakenly identified someone as the criminal.

When the same suspects were put in a sequential lineup, and the eyewitnesses were shown photographs one at a time, and only once, the rate of false identifications dropped to less than 10 percent.

Other experiments showed that witnesses who did remember the criminal were just as likely to pick that person out of sequential lineups as they were from traditional simultaneous lineups.

The reason that sequential lineups work is rather simple. In simultaneous lineups, Professor Lindsay said, witnesses are able to compare individuals, choosing one from the group who looks the most like the person they think they saw commit the crime. But a sequential lineup limits the ability to compare. 20

The psychologists think that the chance of misidentification is reduced the most by allowing witnesses to view photos only once. New Jersey, however, plans to let witnesses see photos more than once, although the sequence would be changed between viewings. And even if witnesses declare a decision in midsequence, they are required to view the sequence through to the end, to assure that each picture has been seen the same number of times.

Harold Kasselman, deputy first assistant prosecutor in Camden County, which has been using the new system since December, said, "Our feeling is that if they request it, we shuffle all eight photographs again and show them again in random order." A witness who makes an identification is told to sign and date the chosen photo, and to initial the other seven. All eight photos become evidence in the case.

Another crucial innovation, the researchers found, was to be sure that a neutral third party conducted the lineup, in what is called a blind test. If the detective knows which person is the suspect, it could allow the detective, consciously or not, to guide the witness.

"Let's say you're the detective and you've got your person in position three" in the group of photographs, Professor Wells said. "You show this spread to the witness and the witness says, 'Well, No. 2.' A natural reaction is to say, 'Be sure you look at all the photos.' On the other hand, if the first words to come out of the witness's mouth are, 'No. 3,' then it's, 'Tell me about No 3.'

"It's just a natural human reaction," he said.

The studies also showed that witnesses can be just as certain about a mistaken identification as a true one. And being told that a false identification is correct makes witnesses even more certain.

"It is one thing to detect lying in court, but how do you figure out that one person made a mistake in identifying a suspect and the other didn't?" Professor Lindsay said. "Both are perfectly sincere in telling you the truth as they know it."

But even though the experts are confident that they have found a better way to conduct lineups, they have had a difficult time convincing law enforcement officials.

Attorney General Farmer said that New Jersey is unusual in that he has the power to order a change in lineup procedures statewide.

In New York's less centralized law enforcement network, however, officials say that a change to sequential lineups would most likely need to be spearheaded by district attorneys, but in cooperation with the police and the attorney general. District attorneys said that while they were interested in whether sequential lineups might improve identifications, the matter needed far more study and debate before a shift could be made.

George A. Grasso, the New York City Police Department's deputy commissioner in charge of legal affairs, said group lineups were based on long-established case law and could be particularly hard to change in New York's sprawling system.

New Jersey's new rules would allow an investigating officer to conduct the lineup in cases where no neutral officer is available because the police department is so small, or because it is so late at night.

Still, as Chief Miliano pointed out, detectives talk among themselves about their cases all the time, so even a fair-sized department like his might have a hard time finding an officer with no knowledge of a given case to conduct the lineup.

But as Richard P. Rodbart, deputy first assistant prosecutor for Union County, said, police officials know that once the new guidelines have fully gone into effect, any other approach will become a liability that defense lawyers will pounce on.

"I don't want an officer getting on a witness stand after he's used the old way and being asked, 'By the way, sir, are you familiar with the order from the attorney general that there has been a new way to do identifications?'" Mr. Rodbart said. "And then the officer says, 'Yeah, I heard something about that.' And then the defense attorney's voice rises, 'Did you follow that order?' and bang, he's on track to knock the case down."

focus.

1. What do you think about the procedures for the use of sequential photo lineups? Does the increased percentage of correct identifications convince you that these changes are necessary? What role should such statistics play in police procedures? Why? What other factors besides sequence might influence the way we read such texts?

2. Have you ever felt as if you were stereotyped as a particular kind of person? Under what conditions and circumstances? Think about that situation and reread this piece.

respond.

1. Compose a caption for the photo here. Then write a one-page essay explaining what in the photograph and in your own experience leads you to write the caption you did. Pretend, for the purposes of this essay, that you are teaching a group of high school students how to read a visual text carefully. Address your essay to this audience.

   Compare your captioned essay with those written by other students in your class. Consider what in each of your experiences caused you to write the captions you did.

2. Pretend that you are an ad designer for the American Council against Crime, a not-for-profit agency that creates ads for billboards, postcards, and T-shirts. Create an ad against crime that resists stereotyping. Your ad should focus on a visual image, but it can also have words in it. Aim this ad at a college-age audience.

   You can create your ad on a computer using editing or presentation software and images that you scan in or find on the Web, or you can work on paper using photographs or images cut out of magazines.

Peter Menzel is a professional photographer whose work has appeared in *National Geographic*, *Time*, and other magazines. He lives in Napa, California.

Charles Mann is a contributing editor to the *Atlantic Monthly*. He lives in New York City.

Material World offers a visual portrait of life in thirty nations through photographs of "statistically average" families, photographed in front of their homes and surrounded by all their material possessions. Along with each photo is a list of the objects pictured. The book's introduction suggests, "It is tempting to say that these photographs speak for themselves. Yes, they do, but only if the reader looks carefully and keenly at the wealth of detail. . . . [T]he real benefit of learning . . . depends upon going into the details, especially in a *comparative* basis." To allow for some comparison, we include portraits of two families, one from Japan and the other from the United States.

Material World: A Global Family Portrait

PETER MENZEL AND CHARLES MANN

UNITED STATES

The Skeen Family

6:30 A.M., AUGUST 4, 1993
PEARLAND, TEXAS, U.S.A.

KEY TO BIG PICTURE

1. Rick Skeen, father, 36
2. Pattie Skeen, mother, 34
3. Julie Skeen, daughter, 10
4. Michael Skeen, son, 7

OBJECTS IN PHOTO
(FOREGROUND)

- Family Bible
  (held by mother)

(LEFT TO RIGHT)
- Dog (Lucky, tied to real
  fire hydrant—souvenir of
  father's years as fireman)
- Sewing machine (antique,
  treadle-style)
- Easy chair
- Photo lights for shooting
  Big Picture (scattered
  throughout scene)
- End table with lamp
- Living room couch
- Coffee table (marble-
  topped with books)
- Storage cabinet
- Television (on cabinet)
- 2nd easy chair
- Stereo (on matching
  marble-topped table)

- Speakers (4, on either
  side of secretary)
- Dining table, chairs (6),
  place settings,
  bowl of fruit
- Curio cabinet (with china)
- Secretary (behind
  cabinet)
- Bicycles (behind
  secretary)
- Bookshelf (visible
  through window behind
  bicycles)
- Computer and computer
  storage unit (obscured by
  father's head)
- Motor vehicles (3, Ford
  F350 pickup, Ford
  Aerostar minivan, dune
  buggy)
- Storage shelving (in
  garage)
- Stuffed deer heads
  (2, above garage door)
- U.S. flag (between heads)

- Dressers (2)
- Dollhouse (on file
  cabinet)
- Cane-backed chair, 2nd
  end table, toys, U.S. map,
  globe
- Refrigerator
- Desk (with chair,
  toy train)
- 2nd TV (on table)
- Washer, range, dryer (with
  food processor, mixer,
  coffee maker, pots, etc.)
- Microwave (atop
  dishwasher)
- Beds (3, parents' with
  guitar)
- Ironing board and iron
- Piano and piano bench
- 2nd sewing machine
  (electric with table chair)
- Family portraits

JAPAN

The Ukita Family

4:30 P.M., DECEMBER 16, 1992
TOKYO, JAPAN

KEY TO BIG PICTURE

1. Kazuo Ukita, father, 45
2. Mio Ukita, daughter, 9
3. Sayo Ukita, mother, 43
4. Maya Ukita, daughter, 6

OBJECTS IN PHOTO
(SELECTED ITEMS, LEFT TO RIGHT)

- Unicycle, books, dolls, pogo stick, clock, miscellaneous toys
- Stacking basket for toys
- Clothes racks (2) with backpacks, hats
- Bookcases (3) with books, dolls
- Clothes (hanging on carport)
- Desk and chair (with stuffed animal, doll)
- Car (Toyota minivan)
- Suitcases (2, atop car)
- Dressers (2)
- Video-game player (on small dresser)
- Swimming trophies (2, on tall dresser)
- Electric piano and bench (with books)
- Crutches (behind piano)
- Shoes (28 pairs)

- Rubber rafts (2), ball, pool mask, snorkel, ice chest
- Refrigerator
- Coffee table (with Thermos, rice cooker, tomatoes)
- End table (with telephone, family portraits)
- Color television (with ceramic rooster)
- Pots and pans (on end table)
- China cabinet (with china, microwave oven, toaster oven, liquor bottles)
- Papier-mâché animal (on cabinet, school project)
- Bed (behind cabinet)
- Dressing table with mirror (behind bed)
- Umbrellas (by dressing table)
- Dining table (with family)

- Fire extinguisher (on wall)
- Dog house (on steps)
- Dog (named Izumaru)
- Bunk beds (with blankets, video cassettes, toys)
- Clothes rack (with woman's suit)
- Entrance gate (right half, black metal, with mail slot)
- Butcher block table (with cooking utensils)
- Food-storage unit (by washer)
- Electric washer/dryer
- Cleaning supplies (in basket, on plastic shelf unit)
- Tub toys (by bathmat)
- Skateboards (2, leaning on shelf)
- Bicycles (3, in far right background)
- Child's chair

focus.

1. What do these pictures tell you about people in Texas and Japan? What details in these pictures strike you as most important? Why? What details surprise you the most? Why?

2. Why do you think the authors of this book chose to represent the peoples of various countries by their material possessions and dwellings? What do you think their purpose is? Who is their audience? What is their point of view?

3. What do these pictures tell you about the cultures of the people depicted here?

respond.

1. Write a letter to one of the families in these pictures about what you read in the text of their picture. Mention specific details that you noticed in the photograph and think are important to your understanding of them and their circumstances. Ask questions and tell them something about yourself and your family, mentioning things you think you might have in common. Select a snapshot of your family that you could send with your letter.

2. Create a picture and an inventory like those in *Material World* of you and your possessions from your dorm room or bedroom. Your purpose in this assignment is to tell about yourself, your material possessions, and the room in which you spend much of your time. Your audience for this task is the same as that for *Material World*.

3. Write an essay about a key material possession you own. Choose a possession—or several possessions— that means a great deal to you and that reveals something about you and your life. Include a photo of the objects you write about, and try to make it show your relationship to material possessions. Choose the audience for this essay and write with this audience in mind. You could consider writing the essay for a family member who wants to know more about your life at school, for parents or grandparents who want to know more about you, or for a friend at another school.

▶ *Our Closet.* Photo-composite by Nora Mapp.

Tom Phillips (b. 1937) is an artist whose work spans various media—painting, essay writing, film, sculpture. He has long been a collector of postcards, writing about them and using them as source material for paintings and other projects. The postcards here come from his collection *The Postcard Century: 2000 Cards and Their Messages*. You can read more about Phillips and his work at <www.tomphillips.co.uk>.

The Postcard Century opens with an old postcard that depicts a young couple in a living room playing cards and thinking about their future together. The young man is drawing a playing card from the hand of the young woman, who is smiling up at him. The caption alludes to the possibilities inherent in their relationship: "The cards will tell the story."

The postcards here tell a story, too—each, in Phillips's words, is "a captive and witness of its time." In their pictures and often in the messages written on them, postcards reveal something about the ways in which we represent others.

The Cards We Choose to Send: Selections from *The Postcard Century*

TOM PHILLIPS

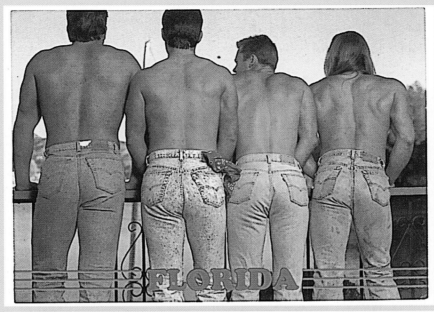

focus.

1. Choose two or three of the postcards and consider how each represents the people it pictures. What cultural and historical clues can you discern about the postcard's origin? What audiences might like and appreciate it? What audiences might dislike it? Does the card exoticize or suggest any stereotypes about its subject—and if so, how?

2. How does the photographer of each card use composition strategies such as emphasis, juxtaposition, balance, pattern, repetition, and unity? What point of view does the photographer take, and how does it influence the way you read the card?

3. Are there any words on or added to the image? If so, how do they contribute to the message of the text?

respond.

1. Choose one of the postcards and write a message as if you have visited the place and met people like those pictured. Write to someone you know who has *not* visited this place. Using the blank card that follows, write a note to this person and comment on those pictured in positive terms, keeping in mind your reader's experiences and knowledge of the card's subject. You might have to do a bit of research to write a convincing comment.

2. Create a postcard that portrays students at your school, using a picture you take yourself or an image from the school catalog or another official publication. Use both images and words. Your goal is to depict the students without stereotyping.

Next, draft a note to someone in your family for the back of this postcard. Tell your reader a bit about your life as a student and try to indicate how you see

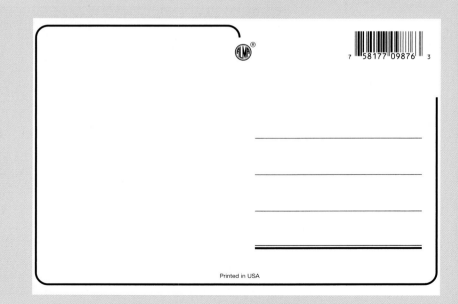

yourself in relation to the people depicted. Be imaginative in the way you design your note. Consider creating emphasis for key points in your message by using different colors, writing words in different sizes, adding small drawings, and so on.

When you are done, look carefully at your card and write a paragraph or two analyzing how the images, words, and design strategies you have used (such as balance, emphasis, juxtaposition, pattern, repetition) contribute to its overall unity of purpose.

3. Consider the way people and groups are represented in music—in lyrics as well as on CD covers and in videos. It should be easy to find stereotypes of gender or age or class or race or culture. Write a review for your school newspaper analyzing how a musical work (words and images) exoticizes or stereotypes, and explain what belief systems it depends on. You may need to cite specific lyrics and consider how they work in concert with the visual elements of the CD or video. Be sure to include a photocopy of the CD cover you use (in color, if possible) or—if you have this visual in digital form—import it directly into your review. Be sure to document thoroughly the sources of any visual images you use and any lyrics you quote.

This series of sketches is a preliminary, unfinished draft of a storybook for children aged 3-6. The author, Cynthia Selfe, wanted to see if very complex ideas—like appreciating the many differences among human beings—could be expressed in the language and images of a child's book in a way that would appeal to youngsters. Selfe wanted to keep the vocabulary of the story appropriate for young children and to use a type font that signaled a certain playfulness and informality. The illustrator, Marilyn Cooper, had the challenge of bringing the characters in the story to life in a way that would appeal to young children.

Cynthia Selfe and **Marilyn Cooper** are both English professors at Michigan Technological University.

Teo Gets a Brother: A Storybook in Progress

CYNTHIA SELFE AND MARILYN COOPER

Teo considered himself a very lucky boy.

He had a wonderful mother.

He loved his dog, Bosco.

And his three best friends—
Hui, Pooi, and Khai—
lived right next door,
in a brown house
with bright blue
windows and a
chimney.

Hui, Pooi, Khai, and Teo climbed trees together.

They hunted bugs together.

And they played together with Bosco down by the creek.

One day, Teo's mom told him
that he was going to have a new brother—
an adopted brother almost the same age
as Teo himself! Teo didn't know what
to say. He was surprised. So was Bosco!

When his new brother, Sam,
came home, Teo wasn't at all
sure he was the *right* brother
for his family.

Sam was *too different*!

Where Teo was brown and round,
Sam was pale and thin.

Where Teo's hair looked like a soft,
black brush that stuck up from his head,
Sam's hair was like silk and stuck close
to his head.

focus.

1. How do the images in this story work with the words to accomplish the author's purpose? Choose one page and examine its use of emphasis, balance, pattern, and unity. How does it use narration and description?

2. Go to a library or bookstore to examine some books for ages three to five. What is the ratio of words to images? the relationship of words to images? What materials are the books made of? What are their shapes? How are they constructed? Why? How do children's books use emphasis, balance, pattern, and unity to make their points?

respond.

1. Show "Teo Gets a Brother" to a few friends and see how they respond. Be sure they know its intended audience and purpose. Ask them what they think of it and if they have suggestions for revising the story. What is your own response? Write a brief review evaluating how successfully the story achieves its purpose.

2. Finish the story. You will need to pay attention to the level of vocabulary you use, the pictures you create, the way you lay out your pages. You will also need to pay attention to the length of the story and the depth of your discussion. Keep the audience of young children in mind as you make all of these decisions.

3. Revise the story for a different age group. Pay attention to the level of vocabulary, the font you use, the pictures you create or choose, and the depth of your discussion. Finally, decide on a new title for the story. Make all of these decisions appropriate for the audience you choose.

4. Revise and redesign the story for the same group of children, aged 3-6. Think of a different title; choose a different type font; arrange the pictures and the words in a different layout. You might even want to draw different pictures, or to replace them with photos or clip art. Make sure all of your decisions are appropriate for the audience you choose.

Christopher Hart is a professional artist
who draws comics for *Mad Magazine* and other
publications. The following pages from his books
How to Draw Comic Book Heroes and Villains (1995)
and *Comic Book Bad Guys and Gals* (1998) illustrate
how comic book artists use physical stereotypes to
create superheroes and supervillians—both men and
women—while also reflecting with some irony on the
limitations and the clichés associated with the traits
artists choose. Hart shows how comic books both
rely on stereotypes and remind us about the
foolishness of relying on them.

How to Draw
Comic Book Heroes
and Villains

CHRISTOPHER HART

THE CLASSIC "GOOD GIRL"

According to Morrow, "The 'Good Girl' is the gal next door: fresh, open, a pal. She's definitely sexy, but less obvious, and less affected, than her 'bad girl' sisters. She's exuberant, perky, sympathetic, pensive, and unsophisticated. The examples below are, of course, all stereotypes, presented as takeoff points or guidelines from which you can extrapolate your own."

BIG EYES, WIDE-EYED EXPRESSIONS, DIMPLES, CAREFREE OR TOUSLED HAIRSTYLES ALL HELP TO DEFINE THE "GOOD GIRL." ALSO, CHECK WITH THE WOMEN YOU KNOW FOR MAKE-UP AND FASHION TIPS. WOMEN'S MAGAZINES CAN BE A BIG HELP.

Only Bad Gals Have Face Tattoos

My rule of thumb is: Never date a girl who has a tattoo on her face or whose brother goes by the nickname Animal.

Here's a pretty normal looking gal. She's probably on the right side of the law. There's nothing to indicate otherwise.

With several earrings poked through the cartilage of her ear and a tattoo on her cheek, she looks more extreme and less likely to cuddle in front of a crackling fire while playing Scrabble.

Another good tattoo is tiger marks along the jawline.

The eye mask tattoo creates a crazed look.

Changing the hairstyle (and color) also makes a huge difference in a character's appearance. This head has the exact same facial structure and features as all of the others on this page, but it looks quite different because of the hair.

14

focus.

1. Examine the character of Captain America as represented in the image and profile (see p. 245). What characteristics seem stereotypical today? How might these characteristics be related to the historical context of the 1940s, when his character was conceived and drawn?

2. Can you think of any comic book characters who are not stereotypes? any comic book heroes or villains who do not follow the patterns shown in the examples here? How do they differ— and why?

respond.

1. Choose a favorite superhero or supervillain and write a profile of him or her for the Web site of the comic book's publisher. Your profile should provide a thumbnail sketch of the character and a detailed analysis of the physical characteristics (expression, posture, hands, costume, tattoos, and so on) that the artist uses to make this character look like a superhero or supervillain. The audience for your profile is adolescent fans. Include a page showing your character and refer to it in your profile to illustrate the specific points you make.

2. Draw and color your own superhero or supervillain and write a profile describing his or her physical characteristics and powers. Try to come up with at least one nonstereotypical characteristic that might appeal to adolescent readers. Your audience for this image and profile is the magazine editor who will decide whether to add your character to the company's roster. Your purpose is to convince the editor that your hero will appeal to a group of adolescents who will buy the comic.

Exchange your image and profile with a partner, who should take the role of a comic book editor who is interested in your character but wants you to revise your drawing and profile in some way. As the editor, he or she should write a letter telling you how to revise your character and profile. Revise your drawing and profile accordingly.

picture this

representing others

How is the student body represented at your school? Look at the school's Web site, view books used for recruiting, and other official publications. With a small group, investigate how these publications portray the student body as a whole and identify how various groups are portrayed. Then consider whether the portrayals represent students accurately.

1. Begin by compiling a profile of the student body. What races, ethnicities, and nationalities are represented? in what numbers or proportions? What age groups, and in what numbers or proportions? How many men and women? How many students with disabilities? Try to identify other groups that the institution tracks. You can get these figures from various administrative offices: admissions, international students, equal opportunity.

2. Next, see how these student populations are *visually* represented in two or three official campus publications. Count the numbers of students pictured who are of different races, nationalities, genders, ages, and disabilities. In pictures of large groups of students, count only those individuals whom you can clearly distinguish in a given group.

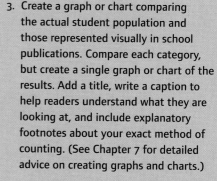

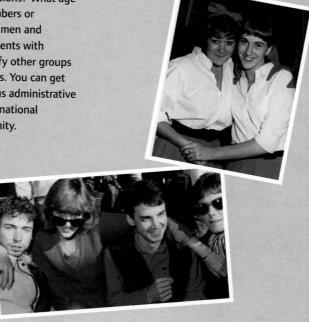

3. Create a graph or chart comparing the actual student population and those represented visually in school publications. Compare each category, but create a single graph or chart of the results. Add a title, write a caption to help readers understand what they are looking at, and include explanatory footnotes about your exact method of counting. (See Chapter 7 for detailed advice on creating graphs and charts.)

Summarize your findings in a paragraph, identifying any trends or patterns that you see in the two profiles. Do the official publications fairly represent the actual student body? Are there significant differences? If differences exist, what effect might they have on the impression given to readers unfamiliar with the campus?

4. Now examine the publications to see *how* various groups are represented.

- Are any groups shown only in certain activities, such as on sports teams? engaged in social activities? working with faculty? eating? receiving academic awards? graduating? reading a book? Are any groups consistently missing from certain activities?

- Are any groups shown only in certain places? in classrooms? in dorm rooms? walking to class? in sports venues? Are any groups consistently not shown in such places who should be?

- Are any groups absent from the official publications altogether?

- What kinds of students are shown in groups? individually?

- What students are shown close up? from a distance? mid-range?

- Are any groups consistently shown in active roles (writing on the board, using a microscope, passing a football)? in passive roles (listening, reading, taking notes)?

Analyze your findings to see whether any groups are consistently shown in ways that result in generalized representations.

5. Finally, write an investigative article for your school newspaper about how official publications represent the student body. Your article should tell *what* you found and *why* your findings matter. You should make some recommendations for change, if changes are warranted.

Include examples of photographs to illustrate your points, so that readers can judge for themselves whether or not the claims are well founded.

gallery
of
images

representing others

① *Woman Wrapped In Cloth.* Photo by Colin Anderson/Corbis. This photo presents a contemporary interpretation of the veiled woman.

2 *Mother Simeon Shooting Snooker, Tyburn Convent. Photo by Shannon Taggart, 1998.* This photo's charm and tension come from showing nuns as we don't usually think of them.

③ (overleaf) *India's Future Looks to Its Past.* Photo by Agence France-Presse. In Lucknow, India, 133 children dressed like Mohandas Gandhi to celebrate the anniversary of his birth. Gandhi was a spiritual leader who espoused nonviolent change. Compare this photo to the one of the child dressed like Elvis on this page.

④ *Elvis Day, 2002.* This photo of 2-year-old Madelyn Berzon was taken on Elvis Day at the childcare center she attends in Ellisville, Missouri. When the center sent home a color photo of Madelyn dressed up like Elvis, the background (a schoolroom) just didn't seem to be the right era, so Madelyn's mom digitally replaced it with this background of a diner and gas station. Since the new background was black and white, she then made the whole image black and white.

⑤ *Little Girls with Their Dolls and Buggies, Caldwell, Idaho.*
Photo by Russell Lee, 1941. Taken for the Farm Security
Administration.

6 *Pro-Choice Public Education Project.* Ad by the DeVito/Verdi Ad Agency. The format of this ad was inspired by the art of Barbara Kruger (see p. 189), who in fact looks to advertising for her inspiration.

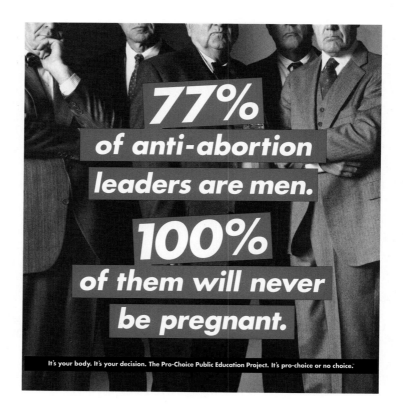

"IF IT IS A QUESTION OF THE SAFETY OF THE COUNTRY (AND) THE CONSTITUTION . . . WHY THE CONSTITUTION IS JUST A SCRAP OF PAPER TO ME."
JOHN J. McCLOY, ASSISTANT SECRETARY OF WAR, 1942

⑦ From *Postcards from Camp.* Painting by Ben Sakoguchi. This imagined picture postcard depicts life in the internment camps where Japanese Americans were sent during World War II (and where the artist spent his early childhood). The painting includes Sakoguchi's own family photos as well as archival images and quotations from government agencies. The words at the bottom were not written to be a caption for this image—and they affect the way we see the image.

8 *Harlem.* Photo by James VanDerZee. VanDerZee chronicled the Harlem Renaissance in New York City during the 1920s and 30s.

9 *Negro Women near Earle, Arkansas.* Photo by Dorothea Lange, 1936.

 constructing realities

In the 1958 live-action Disney film *White Wilderness*, there is a scene that shows migrating lemmings jumping off a cliff to their deaths in the icy river below. The images seem to confirm the common belief that overcrowded lemmings commit mass suicide by hurling themselves off cliffs. However, the images are not what they appear to be.

The cliff sequence was filmed in Calgary, far from the lemmings's natural home in the Arctic. The lemmings in the film were purchased from Inuit children, brought to Calgary, and placed on a large snow-covered turntable, which caused them to start running in the same direction. They were then taken to a cliff and pushed over the edge. The entire sequence was photographed using clever camera angles and editing to make the few dozen lemmings look like thousands in panic-stricken migration.

Today's filmmakers do not have to resort to such crude tactics. Computer-generated special effects now make possible almost anything that can be imagined—dinosaurs in *Jurassic Park*, android armies in *Star Wars: Episode I*, Forrest Gump meeting Richard Nixon during his presidency. Dangerous scenes that used to be performed by stunt doubles are now created on desktop computers. The scene in the action film *Blade 2* in which Wesley Snipes leaps off a three-story building, does a somersault, and lands on his feet ready to do battle was made on a computer in Berkeley, California.

▶ A still from the 1994 film *Forrest Gump* in which the fictional character Gump has been inserted into historical footage of Richard Nixon.

PICTURING REALITY

It's difficult to find a recent film or commercial that doesn't have computer-generated visual effects—even if it's only the clouds in the background. Many of the small details that make scenes *appear* real—hair blowing in the wind, dust rising when a helicopter lands, waves crashing over the bow of a ship—are digitally added. Computer-generated images have likewise changed the look of print media. Look at the sky in any magazine photograph. Have you ever seen an actual sky so blue?

We don't mind when films that are not documentaries alter reality; indeed, we've come to expect characters in action films to defy gravity. But the boundary between what purports to be real and what is actually fiction has become blurred. If you watch college and professional football on television, you've become accustomed to seeing the first-down line that is digitally inserted on the field. Did you know, however, that the advertisements on the wall behind the batter on televised baseball are often digital insertions? Fans at the ballpark do not see those ads.

Sports events are saturated with advertising, of course, but the ways video can be altered are not always so innocent. When Indian officials announced that they would alter their satellite imaging technology to disguise India's military bases, they had an understandable motive. But what if they were to insert images of Pakistani tanks massing on their border as evidence to justify a war? How would we know if the images were real? When U.S. Navy fighters shot down two Libyan planes over the Mediterranean in 1989, Libya claimed that its planes had been unarmed and flying a routine mission. The United States said that the Libyan planes *were* armed—and produced a blurry picture that appeared to show one with air-to-air missiles. Libya in turn accused the United States of fabricating the picture.

Beyond the political implications of whether or not the Libyan planes were armed, the incident demonstrates how much we depend on images for evidence. Most of us assume that photographs are accurate depictions of the world, even though we know digital images can be easily manipulated. In fact, even without the aid of a computer, images can be altered to present a particular point of view or to create a stronger or more extreme version of what is depicted. Professional photographers have long relied upon burning (overexposing) and dodging (underexposing) portions of photographs to artificially emphasize parts of an image. Even amateur photographers routinely select film and adjust light exposures to suit different purposes and create different effects.

Making autumn leaves a brighter yellow or a clear sky a deeper blue hardly seems dishonest. The question is, When does alteration become falsification? Some of the best-known examples of deliberate falsification come from the former Soviet Union; Joseph Stalin not only had his real and imagined enemies killed but subsequently had many of them disappear from the historical record—even from historical photographs. Long before digital imaging, Soviet workers displayed great skills in the darkroom, as the images on this page show.

▶ In the first photo, the man on the lower right is Abel Yenukidze, an Uzbek party official who was later eliminated in the purges of 1936–38 by one of Nikolai Yezhov's firing squads. The second image shows how the photo was then altered, eliminating Yenukidze and creating a suit for the man seated behind him.

▶ In 1940, Yezhov suffered the same fate as Yenukidze. The first photo shows him out for a stroll with Stalin; in the photo on the right, he has turned into water.

▶ A young Elvis look-alike moves seamlessly from childcare to a night on the town in this digitally altered image.

Stalin's brutality and distortion of history have been well documented, but if we did not have access to the original photographs, we might assume the falsified images were authentic. The techniques perfected in Stalin's darkrooms are in wide use today. For example, see the advertisement at <www.digital-restoration.com>: "Want to find a way to keep great pictures, without those people you would rather forget? Why not have us digitally remove those unwanted items from your photographs?" A flourishing market exists for making ex-partners and unwanted family members thus disappear.

Almost anyone can alter photographs today using the image editors that come with many computers and digital cameras. Changing photographs is not the same as murdering people or falsifying public records, but it is nevertheless changing history, even if it's just someone's personal history. Think of people who alter photographs to place themselves in exotic settings—on a beach in Tahiti or in front of the Blue Mosque. This kind of alteration may just be for fun. But what if someone claims to have been to Tahiti or Istanbul and uses the photograph as evidence? In such a case, the image then "proves" a lie.

To take an example closer to home, consider the case of the University of Wisconsin, which inserted the image of an African-American student into a photo of a crowd at a football game to make the crowd appear more diverse—and then put the photo on the cover of a brochure. Wisconsin is by no means the only school to alter photos to portray diversity; for several other examples, see "In Brochures, What You See Isn't Necessarily What You Get" on p. 340.

We expect certain kinds of photography to be unaltered, such as news photography and nature photography. Major newspapers do not allow news photographs to be altered. Disney's faked lemming images provoked outrage, though many nature films in those days were made in Hollywood studios rather than on "real" locations. But what if a picture is not literally faked but simply changed to make it look better? The work of Art Wolfe, a famous nature photographer, became controversial when it was discovered that he had digitally enhanced images of zebras, caribou, and other wildlife in his 1994 book *Migrations*—some animals he even digitally cloned. See "A Flock of Golden Retrievers" on p. 332 for more discussion on the ethics of altering nature photos.

▶ A colorized photo, originally black and white.

image conscious

Look at your school's Web site. Who's pictured, and who's not? Do the images reflect the reality of everyday student life?

All images are in some sense constructed, given that the photographer chose to take certain pictures and not others. Look in your family album. No doubt some family members are represented more often than others. Some may not be represented at all. If you have ever taken photographs of a gathering, it's likely you found afterward that you didn't get a good shot of some people and neglected to take a shot of others. You may not have meant to exclude them, but other people caught your attention. Then when you decided which photos to put in the album, you made further choices. Such choices contribute to the way we picture reality.

We make similar choices when we write. We mention some details and ignore others, describe things in a certain way, quote some people and don't quote others. Look, for instance, at the following text from a profile of actor Clint Eastwood. The paragraph describes the members of Eastwood's extended family as they gather one day in his kitchen.

> Eastwood's appearance in the kitchen, where Paco the parrot greeted him with repeated "I love you"s, didn't seem to slow down the lunch preparations that were under way. He introduced Dina, an ebullient, dark-haired woman. Morgan, a curly-haired miniature of her mother, was helping her make a huge salad. Dina's mother, a pretty, red-haired youngish woman, was cooking cheese quesadillas. Eastwood's sister, Jeanne, with her husband, was preparing a platter of rice and beans. His mother, Ruth, alert and trim in a gray warmup suit, was smiling benevolently at everybody. Additional husbands, some wearing pastel-colored pants with conservative, long-sleeved shirts, materialized. The dishes were placed, buffet style, on available countertops.
> — Lillian Ross, "Nothing Fancy"

Even if we assume that the writer has mentioned everyone who happened to be in the kitchen, the details chosen to describe them are clearly that — chosen. They reflect one writer's view; another writer would choose different words, and even different details.

INTERPRETING REALITY

We tend to assume that our personal view of reality is the truth. Much of that personal view is based on our sensory perceptions and especially on what we see: "I saw it with my own eyes," "Seeing is believing." We believe that our perceptions are accurate. However, research has shown that eyewitness accounts are often wrong. One reason why is that many of our visual perceptions are "photo-edited" in our mind's eye. What we see today is affected by what we've seen (or heard, or read about) in the past. We think something should look a certain way, so we "see" it that way. Preconceived notions about race, gender, beauty, and other things affect not only how we react to others but also how we see them. Images recorded in our brains can become altered during recall as they are filtered through our belief system, our own way of seeing the world. Our vision itself is somewhat limited: when we look at a flower, we see only those colors within the spectrum that humans are able to see. Certain insects, however, see the same flower with a range of colors that are invisible to the human eye.

We also must *learn* to make sense of what we see. People who gain sight after being blind their entire lives do not at first comprehend the images they see. For example, trees outside a window are perceived almost like a painting, as a series of flat patterns and light. The perception that the trees are some distance behind the window frame is, apparently, one that must be learned. And instead of perceiving a ball as three-dimensional, a newly sighted person will see it as a flat disk with a dark crescent shape on it—which to a "trained" eye becomes a sphere. Dimension is one more thing that is learned.

Our perception of reality is also affected by the images we are exposed to. Collectively and individually, we accumulate a visual vocabulary much as we build a vocabulary of words. This visual vocabulary contributes to our view of the world—and it affects *how* we see and understand the world. Think of travel images. If you've ever been to Scotland, you know that the men there do not all wear plaid kilts. Or if you've driven across Colorado, you know that two thirds of the state is flat. But we've all seen images of Scottish men in kilts and snow-capped peaks in Colorado, and those images become embedded into our minds. They affect what we see as "reality," and the way we understand what we see.

image conscious

Look at the cover of a magazine—one focusing on beauty, fitness, lifestyle, or a related topic. Considering both its words and its images, what reality does the cover project and how? How "realistic" do you think this image is?

To a large extent, then, we construct our realities as we learn to see, filtering information through our experience and memory. When we read a text, we understand it through our worldview, which is shaped by the cultural contexts in which we've lived. The same is true of all authors of texts—they are affected by particular social, political, economic, and cultural contexts. When we read an essay or look at a painting, we need to think about where the authors are coming from—their broader contexts and worldviews—and also where we ourselves "come from." Look back at the chart on p. 15 for a visual representation of the way these larger contexts surround all texts.

▶ Alabama school children saluting the flag, 1912. This is a startling image to us today, assuming as we do that Americans salute the flag hand over heart and that the straight arm salute shown here is a relic of Nazi Germany. Back in 1912, however, this really was the way Americans saluted the flag; it was thus reality, and would have been seen as such.

The beginning of modern science heightened the desire to see more than was possible with the unaided human eye. In 1609, Galileo Galilei heard of a Dutch invention that allowed distant objects to be seen as if they were near. Galileo used his skills as a mathematician and craftsman to improve on the Dutch spyglass, producing the first telescope capable of observing objects in the night sky. In 1610, he reported that the Milky Way is made up of millions of stars, that Jupiter has moons, and that Earth's moon has mountains.

The microscope was invented about the same time as the telescope. Many scholars credit Dutch inventors in the 1590s for developing the first compound microscope. In 1665, the miniature world was revealed in illustrations by British scientist Robert Hooke (1635–1703), who published *Micrographia* with images of a world heretofore unseen.

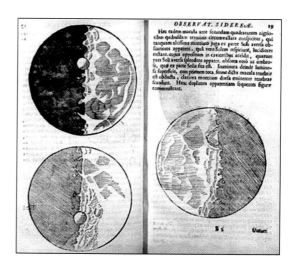

Galileo's drawings of the moon, in 1610, were based on his visual observations through a crude telescope.

Robert Hooke used a microscope to discover that plants are made up of cells. His 1665 drawing of cork cells is the first graphical statement of cell theory.

Even with telescopes and microscopes, however, human vision was limited to the light spectrum available to the human eye. Other kinds of light—heat, microwaves, ultraviolet light, radio waves, gamma rays and X rays—were "unseen" until 1895, when machines that could record X rays were invented. In the 1960s, computer-assisted graphics greatly expanded the potential and accuracy of images made possible by technology. In 1990, the Galileo spacecraft sent back images taken through violet and

infrared filters that described the surface composition of the moon. Our vision has been extended far beyond our solar system, and we now see Earth in new ways.

For over thirty years, scientists have been working to create machines with the ability to see. At present, their ability is not much more than a primitive insect's, but the goal of replicating human visual recognition may not be that far away. Future space missions will likely be assigned to robots with humanlike visual capabilities.

▶ Images of the moon sent back by spacecraft in 1990 reveal the composition of its surface. The blue regions are rich in titanium; the green, yellow, and orange regions are rich in iron and magnesium; the red regions are cratered highlands.

▶ Keanu Reeves dodging a bullet in the 1999 film *The Matrix*, along with a photo showing how this scene was filmed; 120 cameras took still images that were then put together to create the slow camera movement for which the movie is famous. The technology to create alternate worlds on film has long been a staple of Hollywood film-making, but *The Matrix* may be the first film to explicitly address the construction of reality as part of its story line.

CREATING REALITIES

▶ Left:
The Garden of Delights. By Hieronymous Bosch, late 15th century. At a time when art was becoming increasingly realistic, this Flemish painter chose to incorporate fantasy into his work. Here he mixes this world with the next and fantasy figures with real figures.

People have been constructing realities for as long as we have been creating images. The methods used to make these images have varied, usually determined by the available technology. In general, the images we make reflect the world we live in. But oftentimes we want to escape this world and to imagine alternative worlds.

In the 1999 film *The Matrix*, Keanu Reeves's character, Neo, is recruited by a cell of cyber-rebels to free humans from enslavement. The rebels have discovered that the "real world" as humans know it does not exist. In a previous war between humans and artificial intelligence, the machines won. They now hold humans in subjugation via the Matrix, a form of virtual reality designed to keep humans in suspended animation. "The Matrix is the wool that has been pulled over your eyes," the rebel leader tells Neo. Neo's escape from everyday appearances starts when he looks in the mirror—which cracks, and does not reflect his image. And when he touches the crack, the mirror merges with his finger. Neo's journey into a world beyond human-centered appearances is about to begin.

The opportunity to enter alternate worlds has been made possible by new digital technologies. Many people eagerly pull the wool over their own eyes to enter worlds where characters feel almost real, where they can have an athlete's or model's body, and where they choose the story of their life. These alternate worlds are called "games," but this word does not suggest their economic power. Video games generate many billions of dollars each year, far more than the movie industry. After Microsoft introduced their game system Xbox, Bill Gates observed in an interview on *60 Minutes II* that the key is "to bring that level of realism to a point where people forget they're playing a game."

In December 2002, the best-selling computer game of all time, *The Sims*™, introduced an online version in which each player can create a character and enter a virtual world that looks like an American suburb. As David Brooks describes in "Oversimulated Suburbia" (p. 366), there is no win or lose in *The Sims* (short for "simulation") world. Characters cope with the demands of jobs, family, housework, and personal hygiene. They can talk with other characters, live with them, and even marry them in a digital parallel universe that is sometimes not so different from their own. The creators of *The Sims Online*™, Will Wright and Chris Trottier, attribute their success to people's desire to be somebody else. Wright says, "You get amazingly immersed in this world. When you're sitting there in the house and having an interesting discussion with other players, you, you know, leave your body. I mean, you totally feel like you are in that environment." *The Sims* world is addictive: Wright claims that the average Sims player devotes twenty hours a week to the game.

Where is this technology headed? Some experts predict that people eventually will be able to plug into bioports that give the brain direct sensory input. With such technology, the alternative reality of *The Matrix* does not seem so implausible. The prospect of widely available virtual realities, however, is controversial. Is it a bad thing for people to escape into alternate worlds? Not necessarily.

People often feel more comfortable talking about personal issues in an anonymous online setting than they would face-to-face, even with close friends. Those who are self-conscious about their appearance find it easier to talk to others without their body attached. At another level, the mass experience of *The Sims* and similar games is a grand social experiment. The kinds of alternative social structures developed in the world of games might eventually change the ways we interact with others in daily experiences that are not computer-mediated. The goal of Sims players is to make their characters happy. It's not an unreasonable goal.

When people see photographs of themselves, they often say, "It doesn't look like me." On the one hand, they may find the images not as flattering as they would like. On the other hand, perhaps photographs do not capture the essence of a person. People who appear in photographs in the 1800s often appear frowning and posed, and we tend to assume that they were stiff people, forgetting they had to stay still because cameras of that era required long exposures. Today, nearly everyone smiles in snapshots, often appearing casual and fun loving. Yet many people rarely smile except when being photographed.

When tourists first visit the Alamo, their response is usually that it looks smaller than they imagined. Likewise, when people first experience Grand Canyon, they typically find it much more vast than they had imagined. No doubt their images of both landmarks were conditioned by words, photographs, and films. Words and images not only affect how we see, but they are additional means of seeing. It's not surprising that both the Alamo and Grand Canyon have IMAX theaters on site, providing visual stories that interpret the reality literally before the visitor's eyes. Having an IMAX theater on site confirms the importance of the site. We have become so accustomed to having reality explained in words and images that it often seems more real than what we see with our own eyes.

Kenneth Brower (b. 1944), the son of famed environmental activist and former director of the Sierra Club, David Brower, has been thinking about the relationship between conservation and photography from the age of twenty, when he first began editing nature books. Since then, Brower has traveled the world writing about environmental issues. He has written eleven books and has been a consistent contributor to magazines such as the *Atlantic Monthly*, where the following essay first appeared as the middle section of a work titled *Photography in the Age of Falsification*, in 1998. The title is a play on a well-known essay by Marxist critic Walter Benjamin called "Art in the Age of Mechanical Reproduction."

In the first part of the article, Brower recounts some of his early encounters with his father's colleagues, listening to them talk about what an older Brower dubs "photofakery." The portion here details a lesson on photographic ethics imparted by Galen Rowell, an internationally recognized photographer.

A Flock of Golden Retrievers

KENNETH BROWER

Among photographers, opinion on digital manipulation seems to fall into either of two schools, the principal spokesmen for which are Galen Rowell and Art Wolfe, who have both been collaborators of mine. These men are energetic in a force-of-nature way, tireless travelers, prodigiously productive. Neither is a photographer so much as a little but prolific photographic industry, producing books, prints, postcards, and advertising images.

Mountain Light Photography, Galen and Barbara Rowell's shop, is a converted warehouse in Emeryville, California, not far from the shore of San Francisco Bay. When I visited recently, I was greeted at the door by Khumbu, the Rowells' fifteen-year-old golden retriever. Khumbu wore a bandanna around his neck—a memento of a recent grooming visit to Dogs by Diane. The hair on his head and face had gone completely gray since I had seen him last. The bandanna and the salon pampering it symbolized seemed an indignity to an old outdoorsman like Khumbu, but he bore it cheerfully enough.

Mountain Light is bright and spacious inside, the white walls of the first-floor lobby museum-lit and hung with an ever changing gallery of Rowell's prints. Waiting for the photographer to appear, I made a circuit of his walls: *Sunset Over Machu Picchu. Last Light on Horsetail Falls. Polar Bear Resting Against Its Mother*. I lingered before Rowell's most famous photograph, *Rainbow Over the Potala Palace, Lhasa*. The rainbow strikes the palace dead center. This would put the pot of gold in the throne room or the pantry of the palace, formerly owned by Rowell's friend the Dalai Lama. On the evidence of this photo, Tibetan Buddhism is the answer. The rainbow seemed much brighter than in other prints of it I had seen. I gave it a hard look and then the benefit of the doubt. I moved on. At *Cuernos del Paine at Dawn, Lago Pehoe, Patagonia*, I paused again. For years I never quite believed this picture—the febrile radiance of the yellow-flowering shrubs in the foreground, the improbable aquamarine of the glacial lake in the middle distance, the sheer, phantasmagoric granite towers of the "Horns" of Paine in the sky. Then, last February, on an assignment to southern Chile, I found myself at dawn on the shore of this very lake, and I saw that it was all true. I crossed the room to *Alaska Brown Bear, Katmai National Park*. The bear is standing in the white torrent of a cascade, a salmon poised in mid-leap just inches from its open jaws. The shutter had arrested the fish forever in the instant before its demise.

Another brown bear was once on this wall, rearing to its full height and roaring directly into the camera. This bear was an actor named Bart, a grizzly everyman, the brown bear you see in all the movies and commercials requiring brown bears. When Bart was mounted here, roaring his signature roar, Mountain Light's visitors all gravitated to him. How in God's name, everyone asked Rowell, had he managed to take this photograph and survive? When Rowell explained that the bear was an acquaintance and a thespian, he saw a little light of admiration die in their eyes. It seemed to him that they now looked differently at all his pictures. He retired Bart from the wall.

Rowell, appearing at the head of the stairway, invited me up to his projection room. Khumbu followed at my heels. Khumbu was named for the Everest region of Nepal, one of his master's favorite hangouts. The dog was a climber once, but now his ascent of the stairway was labored and slow.

In the photography workshops Rowell teaches, he must, he believes, do more than impart technique. These days he needs to impart ethics as well. Even as images grow sharper with digital enhancement, the honest path grows murkier, and Rowell feels that students need guidance. Today's class was just Khumbu and me. Rowell loaded the carousel of his ethics lesson on the projector, closed the curtain at the door, and pressed the button. The first slide showed an Eadweard Muybridge sequence of running horses from 1872. This particular series had settled a $25,000 bet over whether all four hooves are ever off the ground at the same time. (They are.) The Muybridge was a relic of the day when the photograph was incontrovertible, prima facie evidence. The second slide showed a photograph doctored by Senator Joe McCarthy to juxtapose one of his targets with some Communist or fellow traveler. Guilt by association is a dubious proposition to begin with. This was *fake* guilt by association. The McCarthy represented the photograph as hoax. Rowell pressed the button again.

Elephants. A herd on the move, its subgroups tinted in several colors. "This picture is from Art Wolfe's book *Migrations*," Rowell said. "This is how it appeared in a story on digital manipulation in *The Denver Post*. They've color-coded the animals to show groups that are identical and have been cloned." He walked to the screen and began pointing. "This whole group of seven is this group of seven. Three of *these* seven, up here, are these three down here—which have been cloned yet again, right here. This one is this one is this one is this one. This pair is this pair, and this pair is this pair. Fifty-four elephants in a picture that originally had fifteen."

The Pyramids at Giza in the smoky light of evening. Three camels and their riders in the foreground. "The famous *National Geographic* cover," Rowell said. "The Pyramids were moved in relation to the camel riders to make room for the logo. Originally the cover was to be a picture of mine of a Tibetan boy. They kicked it off because the Chinese Embassy objected. The Chinese said they wouldn't let *National Geographic* writers and photographers

into Tibet again if they ran that picture on the cover. It was already at the printer's. When they decided to yank mine out, they needed an instant replacement. They chose this picture, which was a horizontal. In making it a vertical they reset the riders."

Zebras. A tapestry of stripes, the herd standing so close together that not a speck of ground or wildebeest or anything else non-zebraic shows in the frame. "This is a close-up of the cover of *Migrations*," Rowell said. He pointed to the face of a zebra just above the *t* in the book's title. Then he pointed to another zebra face just below the *e* in Art Wolfe's name. "Zebras have a 'fingerprint' in their patterns," he said. "These are different frames of the same zebra."

Cleft rock in silhouette against pale evening sky, [10] *with pink, ethereal cirrus above.* I recognized this photo as Rowell's own, one I had always admired: blackness versus brightness, earth versus sky, near versus far. Solidity of stone versus ethereality of vapor. "This picture was digitally altered on the cover of my book *Mountain Light*," Rowell said. "In order to make it fit the cover, they did two things— with my permission. They 'chopped and channeled' it, like an old hot-rod. They took a section of sky out, which moved the cloud down so they wouldn't have to crop it so much. I felt there was a very good rationale for doing it, and that it preserved the original image I had in mind."

Negative space has positive virtues in art. Whole essays have been written on the dynamic interval—the electric synapse—between God's outstretched finger and Adam's on the Sistine Chapel ceiling. I asked Rowell which he preferred of the intervals between the heaven and earth of his own picture. Without hesitation he answered that he liked his original cleft rock and cloud. "That's why I took it that way. But if I had just stepped back and bent down, I would have gotten a picture with the cloud a little lower. I thought that the alteration was a little bit on the edge, but okay."

Cheetahs. A mother cat reclining on grass, six cubs piled upon her. This cheetah family portrait, according to Rowell, was an Art Wolfe composite of two zoo photographs, one of a mother and single cub, the other of five cubs. Wolfe had digitally removed a zoo fence from the background and reseeded the area with virtual grass. The image had drawn fire at a conference of the North American Nature Photography Association, where an editor from the World Wildlife Fund had objected to it. "The complaint," Rowell said, "was that cheetahs can't have six cubs. Art's defense is that the zoologists who declared this were wrong. Apparently the literature says they can have as many as eight. So Art says, 'Yep, it's good natural history. They can have up to eight.'"

Whether or not six or eight cubs made sense, something was wrong with the photograph. I could not quite put my finger on it. It might have been in the attention of the cats, which seemed divided in an unnatural way. (Two things of considerable and absolutely equal interest seemed to be approaching the group of felines from different directions.) It might have been in the calm of the mother. She did not look like a cheetah inundated by six cubs. She had the relaxed eyes of a mother of one—which was what she was. The more I looked at the picture, the more artificial it appeared.

"In summary," Rowell said, and he pushed the button to advance the carousel. *Bald eagle.* "Totally wild photo, no problem." *Bust of bald eagle, filling frame.* "Totally captive photo. No problem for a lot of markets. Federal Express. Post Office. That's my photo, but it's a captive eagle, and I wouldn't sell it

for a story on wild eagles without putting 'captive' on my slide mount. Some people would." *Eagle soaring against snowy ridge.* "Here's a photo that I manipulated years ago. That was an eagle on a gray sky that I superimposed against a ridge of Mount McKinley—a 'sandwich.' I did it for a slide show about twenty years ago, set to music. I never put it out for publication. Now I wouldn't even create it. I feel it would compromise my work."

Polar bear. A rear view, the bear relaxing on its [15] *belly, facing away across a channel of open water and small icebergs.* "This photo, advertised here in an ad for Tony Stone Images, became very controversial. National Geographic Online, representing the Discovery Channel and the *Explorer* TV series, bought this image from Tony Stone without passing it by the editorial side of the magazine. It appeared in a full-page ad in *National Geographic.* As soon as it was discovered, *National Geographic* pulled the ad. This is a bear in a zoo in Ohio, superimposed digitally against the Lemaire Channel, in Antarctica, where there are no polar bears."

The Arctic is named for its *arctos*, its bear. Its antipodes have never had one. The photograph had reversed the polarity of the planet. I laughed at the boldness, or perhaps it was the oversight, that allowed the photographer to fill this empty Antarctic niche. The bear was a hoax and an oxymoron, but it was funny. The setting, Lemaire Channel, could have fooled me—its icebergs looked Arctic enough. But again I was nagged by something wrong in the picture. The longer I looked at it, the more it seemed to fall apart.

The bear's stubby tail and the dark pads of its rear paws faced the camera. It lay completely oblivious of the cameraman behind. Polar bears are far-ranging predators with wonderful sensory equipment. They inhabit vast solitudes and always know when they have company. In all the photographs of wild polar bears that I have seen (save those taken at Churchill, a town in Manitoba, where the bears are semi-habituated to human beings), the bear's nose is elevated as he tries to get a whiff of the cameraman, or he is moving off uneasily. This supposed Antarctic bear was indifferent to the human being behind it, and that was not natural. The bear's backside and the hams of its legs were matted and stained yellow. The pattern looked peculiar. In sedentary periods wild polar bears are often tinted an attractive old-ivory yellow all over, by their urine, but here the yellow was localized. The bear had dyed itself, I suspected, by sitting for long periods in its urine, before its digital liberation from a concrete slab in Cincinnati and its transport to the wrong pole. Rowell himself had not noticed this pattern. "I think you're right," he said, staring at his screen. "You wouldn't see it like that by open water."

Earthrise. Whiteness of moon in foreground. Across the barren lunar terrain a message scrawled in longhand: "To Tony, I hope you can see this someday. Bill Anders, Apollo 8." "This was taken by Colonel William Anders in 1968," Rowell said. "He held his Hasselblad up to the window and fired away." Rowell, an acquaintance of Anders's, had begged a copy for his son Tony, and the print had arrived with its dedication in longhand, along with a cover note: "Here's a picture your dad asked me to send you that I took on my last vacation."

Earth levitated for a while in the darkened room, against the blackness of eternal space. Khumbu, the golden retriever gone gray, had no interest in earthrise. For dogs, compelling terrestrial images are much closer under the nose. Khumbu put his chin on my thigh and looked soulfully into my eyes for attention. He was highly redolent of old dog, not a bad smell, and I scratched him behind the ear. Khumbu's master, for his part, seemed hypnotized

▶ The earth as photographed by a human being.

by the image. "This is all about lifting the camera and taking a picture of what you see," he said finally. "It's different from a remote picture that you don't quite believe in the same way because there was no human being there behind the camera."

Snapped robotically, NASA photos of earthrise, [20] more detailed and tightly composed, have been published, Rowell said. In his opinion, none has the poetic power or has evoked the sentiment and acclaim that this one has—the shutter tripped by a human finger. Rowell believes, along with many, that Anders's earthrise is epochal, that it is the most important photograph in the history of environmental awareness.

The colonel's earthrise reminded Rowell of the words of another colleague, the Dalai Lama. The two collaborated on the book *My Tibet*—photos by Rowell, text by His Holiness. In 1987, at a symposium of neuroscientists, psychologists, and artificial-intelligence experts, Rowell said, the Dalai Lama was asked how Buddhists validate their perceptions. The scientists wondered, among other things, whether Buddhists accept the existence of external phenomena apart from concepts already in place in their minds. The answer, the Dalai Lama said, was in the Buddhist concept called Extremely Hidden Phenomena. "I know the earth to be a round bluish globe," he explained, "although I have never seen it and have not done any conclusive reasoning about it. I know the earth is round by relying on the words of someone who has seen it and proved it with photographs. First you must prove that the person is reliable by various reasonings—that there is no reason he should tell lies with false photos. After this you understand that the earth is round, although you haven't seen it. This is called inference based upon belief. You have to rely on a person who has already had this kind of experience and has no reason to tell lies."

▶ The earth as photographed by a satellite.

Rowell glanced at me to see if the aptness of this had sunk in. Then he quoted another astronaut, Rusty Schweickart, who had followed Colonel Anders into space. "You are the sensing element for humanity," Schweickart reported on returning. "And that becomes a rather special responsibility." That special responsibility, in Rowell's opinion, is shared by photographers, too.

Cranes taking wing in Africa. Above them an impala leaping. "Final picture," Rowell said. "This is from Ernst Haas's *The Creation*. The impala was in the middle of one of those high bounds. Back then, when *The Creation* was published, this was just a wonderful serendipity. Now the first thing somebody would think is 'Ah, how did he fake it?' And that's what we've lost."

Downstairs, as Rowell and Khumbu herded me toward the door, we paused at a computer monitor in the stockroom. Rowell asked an assistant to call up a particular image for me. The assistant searched rank upon rank of icons. Each icon marked the file of a photograph. The assistant double-clicked on one, and the computer chattered faintly to itself, making its thousands of binary decisions. Then the image formed and clarified. It was a photograph of Khumbu cloned many times, in the manner of Art Wolfe's elephants. A formation of dozens of identical leaping Khumbus filled the sky, and a few Khumbus in the lead were alighting with a splash in a marsh. "This is called *Golden Retrievers Migrating South*," Rowell said, grinning.

"He was more athletic then, wasn't he?" I said, laughing. "And he was more numerous."

This fabrication was a riposte to Wolfe, I understood, and yet, as a friend of Khumbu's, and as someone who had just lost his own sixteen-year-old dog to the indignities of age, I found I liked the picture. It was winningly surrealistic, like something by Magritte or Escher. The apotheosis and replication of Khumbu made Rowell's point nicely, and yet it was somehow stirring.

focus.

1. As you read through Galen Rowell's lesson on ethics, notice the kinds of pictures he includes as examples. What connections can you see among the photographers' motivations for taking their pictures, the types of publications in which the photographs appeared, and Rowell's assessment of the manipulation of the photographs as ethical or unethical?

2. Reread the Dalai Lama's explanation of Extremely Hidden Phenomena in paragraph 21. How might this approach to "the existence of external phenomena apart from concepts already in place in their minds" influence a viewer looking at photographs such as the one used by Senator Joseph McCarthy to discredit his political opponents?

respond.

1. If you had to boil down Brower's argument to one sentence, what would it be? See if you can locate this idea within the essay in the form of a thesis statement.

2. Try your hand at the type of digital photo manipulation that Brower discusses in his article. You might, for example, replace one person's face with another's or make your cat the size of Godzilla. If you do not have an image editor such as Adobe Photoshop or Macromedia Fireworks, you likely can find this software in a campus computer lab. If you own a digital camera, you may have an image editor installed on your computer.

3. Shortly after September 11, 2001, a photo supposedly from a camera found in the World Trade Center wreckage was spammed around the world. A fierce debate arose over the authenticity of the photo. Close observers noted that the plane was coming from the wrong direction and that it was a Boeing 757, not a 767 as was used on American Airlines Flight 11. The image was named Tourist of Death, and the figure in the photo became known as the Tourist Guy. Soon the Tourist of Death image became further manipulated as hundreds of people practiced their

image-editing skills to place Tourist Guy in other historic photos—the crash of the Hindenburg, the D-Day landing, the killing of Lee Harvey Oswald. Go to <www.touristofdeath.com> to view the many manipulated images. What (if anything) do they have in common? Do they all target the same audience, or do they speak to certain subsets of a larger audience? Why did these images proliferate? What functions do they serve? Write an essay analyzing the images inspired by Tourist of Death or another Internet hoax as a cultural phenomenon.

Jennifer Jacobson (b. 1958) is an editor of
the *Chronicle of Higher Education* and an author of
books for children and young adults. Jacobson's
work reflects her commitment to all phases of the
educational process, from early childhood to college.
The following piece, written for the *Chronicle* in 2001,
analyzes the controversy over the foregrounding of
minority students in university admissions brochures.
As you read the article, think about how diversity is
represented in publications put out by your school
and especially about the ethical implications of
digitally manipulating images on Web sites and
brochures that present otherwise factual information.
Please note that we were denied permission to
include an image of the University of Wisconsin
brochure that is the subject of this article.

In Brochures, What You See Isn't Necessarily What You Get

JENNIFER JACOBSON

When Diallo Shabazz was searching for a college several years ago, he thumbed through admissions brochures to find students who looked like him. So Mr. Shabazz, who is black, says he wasn't initially surprised last fall to discover his face on the cover of a brochure for the University of Wisconsin at Madison, where he is a senior.

But then he realized that the photograph showed him amid a sea of white faces at a football game that he had not attended.

University officials apologized to him after admitting that they had pasted his face into the scene to make the crowd look more diverse. But for Mr. Shabazz, the doctoring of the picture wasn't the issue. "It's much easier to falsely portray diversity instead of creating policies and programs—and backing them up with budgets—to actually create diversity on your campus," he says.

With affirmative-action programs under attack at colleges in several states, admissions officials are struggling to find alternate ways to present a picture of diversity to prospective students. For many institutions, it's a difficult task: Minority populations tend to be small and, in many cases, socially segregated from the rest of campus. To work around the problem, a few institutions, like Wisconsin, have resorted to altering images in brochures and videos.

OTHER FORMS OF DECEPTION

Some students and admissions advisers say the deception can go further. Institutions regularly stage photos by gathering students from a rainbow of races and seating them around a cafeteria table. Such pictures are calculated to portray a contentedly diverse student body, one that is proud of its racial harmony.

For example, on the World Wide Web site of the State University of New York at Binghamton, visitors to the home page see three smiling students, one of them black and two white. On the page for prospective students, readers see head shots of six smiling students—one black, two Asian, and three white. And on the page for current students, readers see photos of seven smiling students, two black and five white.

Binghamton students say the photographs belie the racial tensions that have plagued the institution since the beating of Asian-American students by white students last year, and the appearance of swastikas scrawled in residence halls last semester.

John Hachtel, associate vice president for university relations, says Binghamton does not "attempt to depict a particular kind of racial mix" in setting up promotional photos.

The university is quite diverse, he says. About 53 percent of the students are white, 14 percent are Asian or Pacific Islander, 5 percent are black, almost 5 percent are Hispanic, and .2 percent are Native American or Alaskan Native. (The ethnicity of 16 percent is listed as "not known," and 6.7 percent are listed separately as international students.) That very diversity, Mr. Hachtel argues, is what accounts for the recent racial tensions on the campus. "It's only on a very diverse campus that you are going to find issues between cultures and ethnic backgrounds. A nondiverse campus will not lead to those kinds of issues."

But students like Fareed Michelen, a senior and chairman of the Latin American Students Union, say photos reflecting diversity on the university's Web site and in admissions brochures represent an attempt to "artificially" integrate the campus and "pretend we are this great multicultural organization."

Yemisi Yoosuf agrees. "The university boasts its minority composition, but [black students] don't make up a lot of the percentage," says Mr. Yoosuf, a junior who is president of the Black Student Union. "You have Native Americans, Asian Americans and other nonwhites."

PLAYING WITH THE NUMBERS

Michele A. Hernandez, author of *A Is for Admission: The Insider's Guide of Getting Into the Ivy League and Other Top Colleges*, says colleges regularly play with numbers—for example, counting Asian-American students among minorities in a way that does not provide black and Hispanic students with a realistic sense of the total. It's important, she says, for students to visit campuses, see the racial makeup of the student body for themselves, and ask for numbers confirming their observations.

Similar skepticism is appropriate for promotional photographs, says Ms. Hernandez, a former assistant director of admissions at Dartmouth college who runs a consulting service to help students get into top colleges. Institutions that stage photos to show diversity in an effort to attract black and Hispanic students, she argues, "talk down" to those students in a way that says "you're not smart enough to get those numbers."

Such an approach may well backfire, she warns. A Hispanic student with whom she is working, she says, finds the images of campus diversity offensive because they tend to lump black and Hispanic students together even though the two groups "culturally have nothing in common." Her client, she says, "respects the schools that don't throw 15 black kids on the cover."

Some officials say the pictures do matter. "For 15 better or worse, young people looking for colleges make decisions on academic reputation but also on social and cultural variables," says Sharon Harley, acting director of African-American Studies at the University of Maryland at College Park. "They look at the campus and diversity in photos and on the Web."

And when it comes to doctoring photographs, the University of Wisconsin is not alone. At the University of Idaho, a computer technician last fall superimposed the faces of a black student and an Asian student onto the faces of two white students in a picture on the university's Web site.

While some students and professors question whether administrators who rework photos are serious about increasing the diversity of their campuses, at least one college official defends the practice.

Philip R. Breeze, director of university relations at Auburn University at Montgomery, says the doctored images at Idaho and Wisconsin probably showed the true composition of their student bodies.

"Taking photos of 50 students and moving images around in a photo so that you accurately and honestly reflect the demographics of the campus as a whole is far more honest than hiring models with an untouched photo that implies conditions that do not exist," he says.

Asked if Auburn edits photos to show diversity, 20 however, he says, "No." Black students make up about one-third of the university's 4,800 students, and so there is no need to alter photos, he says.

"DISHONEST AND UNFAIR"

Roger B. Clegg, general counsel to the Center for Equal Opportunity, in Washington, an advocacy group that opposes the use of racial preferences, says altering images is not much different from using affirmative action in admissions. "Colleges want to ensure a particular ethnic and racial mix by doctoring photos. Using preferences is dishonest and unfair the same way doctoring photos is dishonest and unfair. They shouldn't be doing either one."

Even institutions caught altering photos don't endorse the practice. Raúl M. Sanchez, special assistant to the president for diversity at Idaho, warns against lumping his institution with the others. "I don't know how much our circumstance here can be representative of anybody else's," he says. "I can't tell you it was pressure on the admissions department. They had nothing to do with what happened."

DEADLINE PRESSURE

Mr. Sanchez attributes the computer technician's decision to alter the photo to deadline pressure: He couldn't find a suitable photo, so he used the technology available to him to change the picture.

If Idaho had wanted to reflect diversity by means of a photo, it could have done so without altering one, Mr. Sanchez says, noting that the university is more diverse than the state as a whole. Minority students account for 8 percent of the university's enrollment, compared with 5 percent of the state's population. Of the technician, Mr. Sanchez says, "the guy feels rotten. He wishes it would all go away."

After the incident, the university created a pol- 25 icy that says employees cannot alter the institution's photos when it comes to race. The university chose not to "lay down an ironclad" policy that says no one can ever alter photos, he says. "That would tie the hands of the people who work with photos for a living." Sometimes, he says, editing a photo—to trim a background or change the lighting, for example—is appropriate, although the recruiting photo wasn't one of them.

Madison, Paul W. Barrows, vice chancellor for student affairs and campus diversity, says colleges want their publications to reflect key themes, diversity among them. But with new technology that makes photo editing a matter of a few mouse clicks, he asks, "Where do you draw the line with the ethics of this?"

To keep any more doctored images out of Madison publications, Patrick Strickler, director of university communications, has told employees in departments that handle communications not to play around with "the integrity of a photograph."

Mr. Shabazz, the student who was pasted into the football crowd, says administrators have met with minority organizations on the campus to discuss ways to make the university more friendly for minority students.

CHANGING THE SYSTEM

Last fall, Mr. Shabazz traveled to a Chicago high school as part of a Wisconsin recruiting trip. He met some students there who decided not to apply to Wisconsin, he says, because of what they saw as the university's false portrayal of diversity. One student asked him: "Why are you here to recruit for the university after what they did to you? What's to stop them from doing the same thing to me?"

Mr. Shabazz told the high-school students that 30 they "should never allow another person's ignorance to cheat you out of getting an education," and that they could "try to change the system from within."

The students didn't know about the meetings that Wisconsin administrators held with minority groups after the incident, he says. They didn't even know that there are 40 such groups on the campus. "All they know was that the nation made them aware this university lied and was convicted in the court of public opinion." The university, he says, now has a chance to "revitalize" its image.

Not all of the incidents of colleges' manipulating photos involve issues of race and ethnicity, and not all of them involve "adding" diversity. At Vanderbilt University, an interview with a gay alumnus was cut from a freshman-orientation video at the beginning of last semester.

Michael Schoenfeld, vice chancellor for public affairs, says the student-affairs office had hired an outside company to make the video. The university deleted the footage, in which the gay alumnus talked about how his fraternity brothers had accepted his sexuality, at the request of the fraternity. "In hindsight, was it the right thing to do? Probably not," Mr. Schoenfeld says. "The student-affairs office acknowledged it should have been handled in a different way. It has pledged it's something that would not happen again."

Jonathan Rollo, a senior, says he's sorry it hap- 35 pened at all. The student-body president of Vanderbilt's Peabody College of human development and education saw the bowdlerized video the night it was shown to freshmen and again in a class taught by Sharon Shields, a professor of human and organizational development, who brings up issues of social justice and diversity. She showed the video to prompt a classroom discussion.

Mr. Rollo says many students, upon learning about the editing, were disappointed and angry that university officials "would treat us like children and manipulate what we need to see."

Mr. Rollo says he felt embarrassed as well for the Lambda Association, the university's gay organization, and considers the editing of the video a "slap in the face" to the group.

"Promoting the Truth"

Ms. Shields, too, condemns the edit. "Universities shouldn't be about the business of promoting falsehood," she says. "We should be about the business of promoting the truth."

Mr. Schoenfeld says that despite the editing, he hopes that students and professors won't question the university's commitment to equity for gay people. He says Vanderbilt was the first private institution in the South to adopt a policy against discrimination based on sexual orientation and the first institution in Tennessee to offer benefits for domestic partners.

Ms. Shields recalls coming upon a recent Vanderbilt admissions brochure that, she says, portrayed only white people on the campus. "As soon I saw it, it was glaring to me that we'd left out important people," she says. The publication has since been taken out of circulation. Ms. Shields acknowledges that Vanderbilt is a predominantly white campus—minority students account for 19 percent of the 10,000 students—but says the brochure nonetheless troubled her. "It wasn't [because] I felt we had to portray racial sensitivity," she explains, "but because we've left people out who are here."

As for the video, Mr. Schoenfeld says he 40 wouldn't put editing out the gay alumnus in the same category as "changing reality" by doctoring brochures. But every time doctoring does happen, he says, it will be exposed. "People are savvy. Ultimately, manipulating the truth never works."

focus.

1. Think back to your decision-making process when you were applying to colleges. Were you able to visit each school, or did you have to rely on Web sites or brochures to get a feel for each place? How much did the published materials influence your decision to apply? to attend?

2. Michele Hernandez argues that doctoring images for the sake of diversity is a form of "talking down" to minority students. Do you agree with her position? Is there any ethical difference between posing a picture (for example, asking white, African American, and Asian American students to sit at the same cafeteria table) and digitally manipulating a photograph? Do you think that one is more morally reprehensible than the other? Why or why not?

respond.

1. Select a time when a particular location on your campus is the busiest, and take as many photographs as you can in 5 minutes. Examine the resulting images. What generalizations can you make about the student body based on these images?

2. Think about family photos, vacation photos, photos in the family album such as the one shown here from a birthday party. Are those photographic representations consistent with your actual, lived reality at those moments? If there is a discrepancy between the lived reality and the image, what accounts for it? Select one of those images and write an essay that compares the reality depicted to the one you remember.

3. Diallo Shabazz, the African American student at the University of Wisconsin who had his face inserted into the crowd at a football game he never attended, says, "It's much easier to falsely portray diversity instead of creating policies and programs—and backing them up with budgets—to actually create diversity on your campus." Does the insertion of images of minority students into brochures and Web pages undermine the motives behind affirmative action? Is it ever acceptable to represent diversity when it doesn't exist? Write an essay that analyzes the ethics of representation, taking into account the fidelity of representations to reality.

Kate Betts (b. 1965) studied European history at
Princeton University and after graduating moved to
Paris, where she ran the Paris bureau of Fairchild
Publications, a company that specializes in retailing
and style. In 1999, she became editor in chief of the
fashion magazine *Harper's Bazaar*, transforming its
look to attract younger readers while attempting to
retain loyal fans. The new look proved controversial,
and Betts was replaced in 2001. She is known for her
insights into the often secretive fashion industry, as
illustrated by this article published in the *New York
Times* in February 2003.

The Man Who Makes
the Pictures Perfect

KATE BETTS

Madonna and J.Lo depend on him. Annie Leibovitz and Steven Meisel won't print a picture without him. Anna Wintour and Graydon Carter shell out many thousands of dollars a year for his services. He's arguably one of the most powerful men in fashion, but he doesn't sit in the front row or wear designer clothes, and you certainly won't find him on the Style network coughing up deep thoughts about Gwen Stefani's Super Bowl outfit.

Come to think of it, though, there is probably no one who has such a close knowledge of Gwen Stefani, down to the pores of her powdered cheek.

This behind-the-scenes magician, more intimate with celebrity flesh than a personal trainer or a masseur, is Pascal Dangin, the digital retoucher for fashion's and Hollywood's most famous photographers. Some refuse to work with anyone else. On the glossy side of the newsstand just this month, he tweaked the covers of *W*, *Harper's Bazaar*, and *Allure*.

In a field where designers, photographers, and stylists want to be celebrated for their every flourish of innovation no matter how dubious—topless models with vacuum cleaners, anyone?—the French-born Mr Dangin, the founder and chief executive of the foremost photo retouching business in the country, Box Studios in New York, cultivates his anonymity.

"I never want to talk about my work, because it's kind of taboo," he said. "The people who benefit from my work do not benefit from me talking about it."

While photo manipulation is more prevalent than ever in this digital age, when many laptops come with software to help get the red out of your mother-in-law's eyes, the extent of retouching practiced by glossy magazines is still little understood by readers. At the same time, insiders offer a shrug of indifference: of course the camera can be made to lie. Do you really think that's Kate Winslet's figure on the cover of British *GQ* this month?

"Hey, everybody wants to look good," said Mr. Dangin (pronounced dahn-ZHANN). "Basically we're selling a product—we're selling an image. To those who say too much retouching, I say you are bogus. This is the world that we're living in. Everything is glorified. I say live in your time."

Although most newspapers, including the *New York Times*, forbid the distortion of news photographs in a lab or on a computer, at fashion magazines it has long been standard to throw in a little digital pixie dust to make a model's eyes bluer, her teeth whiter, her legs slimmer. Periodically, such highly tweaked images stir controversy, proving that the retoucher's skill is still viewed as something of a dark art. Ms. Winslet, who is well known for waxing content about her healthy womanly figure, was at the center of the latest flare-up when she complained of being overly slenderized for the *GQ* cover. "The retouching is excessive," she was quoted as saying in the *Daily Mail*. "I do not look like that, and more importantly, I don't desire to look like that."

Dylan Jones, the editor in chief of British *GQ*, defended the retouching. "I really don't see anything sinister in this," he said by email. "It's been going on for years. Essentially we all want glamour. We all want show business." A second controversy

arose around the body-positive Ms. Winslet when *Women's Wear Daily* reported two weeks ago that her head had been digitally placed on the torso of a slimmer stylist on the cover of the January issue of *Harper's Bazaar*. The report was denied by the magazine and by a spokesman for Ms. Winslet.

That episode suggests that there are some lines 10 that the image manipulators at glossy magazines will not cross. Mr. Dangin has on occasion pieced together a cover photo by putting the model's head on a different picture of her own body, but he rejects the Dr. Frankenstein brand of photo splicing.

"I would not put an actress's head on a stylist's body—no!" he said. He said it would be too hard to make such a composite convincing, and acknowledged that it would also raise an ethical question. "People can get very upset," he said. "They put it in the same pool as human cloning."

Retouching was once an obscure and narrow practice by photographers who would cover skin and body imperfections in their prints using tiny brushes. Now it entails whole new realms, drawing on the power of computer technologies to improve light, color and contrast in photos, not to mention thighs and heads. Mr. Dangin retouches and prints the work of a dozen leading fashion photographers, including Michael Thompson, Mr. Meisel, Craig McDean, Steven Klein, Inez van Lamsweerde, Mario Sorrenti, and David Sims. He also works with a handful of art photographers like Philip-Lorca diCorcia. Some photographers refuse to work with anyone else.

"He is much more than just a technician who removes pimples," said Mr. McDean, who had Mr. Dangin flatten the background and simplify the colors in a Madonna portrait to create a 50s look for a cover of *Vanity Fair* last year. "He's a thinker, too. He's not someone who just pushes a button. There's some kind of soul in it, which is very rare. He can physically express himself through the computer."

The color, flesh tones and bodies aren't the only things tweaked in photos. Sometimes the composition isn't real, either. One example is in last fall's ad campaign for *The Sopranos*. Although it seems that the photographer, Ms. Leibovitz, shot the entire cast around a table, she actually took them separately, and Mr. Dangin assembled the images in his computers.

Photographers and art directors swear by Mr. 15 Dangin's ability to marry a deep knowledge of photography with technology. "Before I met Pascal, I couldn't do so many different kinds of lighting," said Patrick Demarcheller, a prolific shooter of Harper's Bazaar covers and fashion advertising. Because of Mr. Dangin's ability to correct the harsher aspects of dramatic lighting, he said, he has been able to go beyond conventional studio lights. "He has introduced a new brand of photography that didn't exist before," he said. "Without Pascal, a lot of photographers would not exist today."

For all his technological expertise, it is Mr. Dangin's rapport with photographers and his slow, meticulous pace that seem at the center of his success. "Some photographers won't work unless he

One photo, two versions. In the one on the right, the woman has been digitally stretched to appear taller and thinner. Photo by Kip Meyer.

does the retouching and printing," said Raul Martinez, a partner in the advertising firm of A/R Media in New York, who often works with Mr. Meisel. "He has real personal relationships with them, and they trust him."

For somebody who devotes his time to glossing up the images of others—at fees of $500 for an inside magazine page up to $20,000 for a cover image requiring lots of digital cutting and pasting—Mr. Dangin is decidedly unpolished. His tobacco-stained teeth have not been whitened, and despite his stature and success, he wears grungy brown corduroys, a Champion sweatshirt and New Balance sneakers every day. An unruly mass of finger-in-the-socket curls belie his background as a hairdresser.

Watching Mr. Dangin at work at his Box Studios on Broadway near Spring Street, which employs 40 people, is like ducking behind the curtain to see the last stage in the manufacture of film and fashion celebrities. In a pitch-dark loftlike room packed with high-definition computer monitors and light boxes, more than a dozen retouchers hunch over keyboards clicking and pointing and drawing. A huge Oz-like computer server buzzes in the background. The wizard himself sits at a giant triptych of screens. If the one in the middle is the canvas, then the two side screens are like palettes holding the software icons and the files of images.

At any given moment, Mr. Dangin juggles about 10,000 files. Not long ago he was tending to an ad campaign for Cover Girl cosmetics that uses Angela Lindvall, a model; a Leibovitz image to promote the next *Sopranos* season; and a Steven Klein portrait of Madonna for a magazine cover.

"This part is too light, so I am going to basically [20] start to burn it in and bring in more density," Mr. Dangin said, scribbling with a stylus on a computerized drawing pad as he adjusted the color and contrast in a photo by Adam Bartos, an art photographer. "It's about changing light. Think of this as a virtual darkroom, where you would expose parts of the photo to make it denser. Only in a darkroom, that would take five hours, and here we do it in an instant."

In a culture in which image is a major commodity, the paradox of appearing natural on film is nothing new. As far back as the mid-nineteenth century, the photographer Mathew Brady employed retouchers to improve formal portraits. In the early twentieth century, Man Ray used innovative techniques like solarization, and in the 1930s and 40s the Hollywood photographer George Hurrell elevated actresses like Jane Russell and Joan Crawford into icons of glamour by lengthening their eyelashes, smoothing every wrinkle and blemish and highlighting their hair.

Taking a cue from Hurrell, Richard Avedon retouched many society portraits by hand, famously extending the neck of Marella Agnelli in one to make her look literally like a society swan. More recently, artists like Cindy Sherman have used retouching and manipulation to transform identity completely—a process that is now common, but has not always been embraced. In 1997, the fashion photographer David LaChapelle squabbled publicity with one of his subjects, the actress Mira Sorvino, when he transformed her image digitally into a facsimile of Joan Crawford for *Allure*.

These days, anybody can retouch a photo, Web sites like Photo-Brush and the Pixel Foundry sell software that teaches photo-manipulation techniques, which are also described in books like Scott Kelby's *PhotoShop 7: Down and Dirty Tricks*. As a result, almost any photo or image, both personal and public, can be retouched: high school yearbook pictures, family Christmas cards, and online dating head shots.

Which raises the perennial question about Mr. Dangin's work: how much is too much? Is straightening your child's teeth on a Christmas card in the same category as straightening the teeth of a celebrity mother of septuplets, for which *Newsweek* was criticized in the late 1990s?

The only certain answer is that the line between what is in bounds and what is out is a moving one in the digital age. Grabbing a printout from a recent Yves Saint Laurent ad campaign, Mr. Dangin shrugged. "This world is not reality," he said, fingering the print. "It's just paper.

1. Most fashion magazines have been retouching photos for decades. Before the digital age, airbrushes made thighs slimmer, teeth whiter, and wrinkles and blemishes invisible. Computers have made photo retouching more common and more sophisticated. Pascal Dangin says, "To those who say too much retouching, I say you are bogus. This is the world that we're living in. Everything is glorified. I say live in your time." Just because a condition is prevalent—air pollution, for instance—does that mean we should accept it? Examine critically the logic of Dangin's claim. Are the retouchers defining what it means to look good?

2. Major newspapers—including the *New York Times*, where Betts's article was first published—forbid altering news photographs but allow retouching of fashion photos. Where should the line be drawn on which photographs can be altered?

1. Dylan Jones, the editor in chief of British *GQ*, claims there's nothing wrong with digitally slenderizing Kate Winslet on a cover photo, even over her objections. Others, however, blame the fashion industry for promoting body images that few women can achieve, especially when already thin models and actresses are made even thinner. These artificial images, critics claim, are related to eating disorders in thousands of young women. Write an essay that examines the causal connection between fashion images and eating disorders. Illustrate your essay with images of fashion models and of young women suffering from anorexia and other eating disorders.

2. Examine images of men in magazines such as *Men's Health, Flex, Ironman, Muscle Media*, and *Muscle and Fitness*. These magazines present idealized men's bodies that many men find difficult to achieve, even with rigorous exercise and careful diet. In an essay, analyze the diet and fitness advice of a men's magazine. What does the magazine prescribe for building a beautiful body? What dietary supplements do they recommend? Which are considered legal steroids?

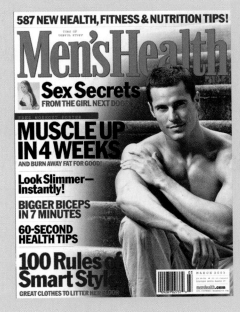

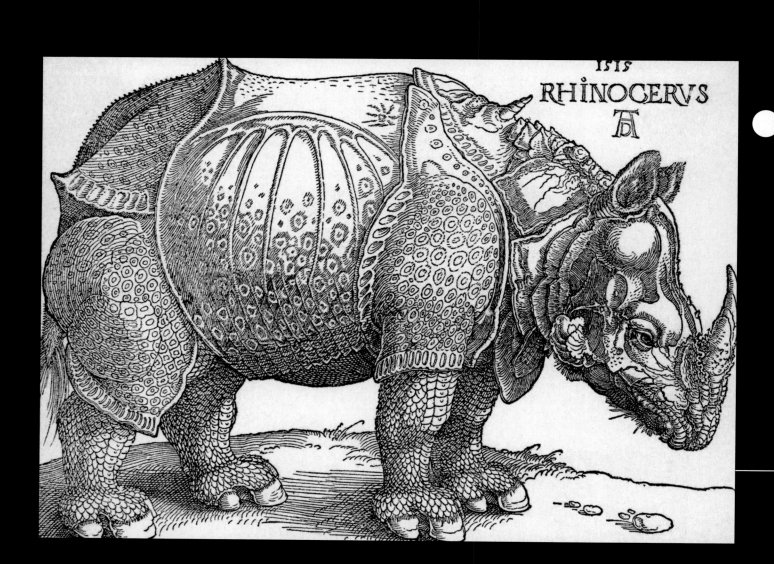

The Boilerplate Rhino

DAVID QUAMMEN

David Quammen (b. 1948) is a nature writer who embraces a unique blend of historical, scientific, and cultural studies. As a veteran contributor to *Outside* magazine, Quammen wrote the "Natural Acts" column, which first appeared in 1981 and has received critical acclaim, including the National Magazine Award for essays and criticism in 1987. Quammen also writes novels and creative nonfiction.

"The Boilerplate Rhino" was originally one of Quammen's "Natural Acts" columns; it is the title piece of his fifth essay collection. It was first published in *Outside* in June 1993. In this essay, Quammen incites his readers to think about nature shows, armchair travel, and the efficacy of art as reflective of life.

The black-footed ferret is now available at Blockbuster Video, yours on a three-evening rental for only two bucks. Also currently in stock are the orangutan, the polar bear, the leopard, the great white shark, the mountain gorilla, the American bison, the duck-billed platypus, and the wombat. The place has its own menagerie. Ignore the shelves labeled DRAMA CLASSICS and COMEDIES and ROMANTIC TEARJERKERS, ignore COPS & ROBBERS and SCHWARZENEGGER and HORROR and SUPER NINTENDO, proceed on toward the back of the store, and there you find it, categorically distinct and conveniently accessible: NATURE. You can pick out a handful of rare and prodigious species, tote them home in your grocery bag or your briefcase. On Tuesdays, take two for the price of one. Obviously I'm talking not about the actual flesh-and-blood creatures but about what passes in our age for the phenomenological equivalent: their images, expertly captured, potently edited, and preserved with the permanence of plastic, which surpasses the permanence of life.

The personnel at Blockbuster will even rent their wares (I have verified this experimentally) to a curmudgeonly Luddite who doesn't own so much as a television, let alone one of those VCR contraptions, and who can therefore only watch *The Mysterious Black-Footed Ferret* in an audiovisual cubicle at his local library, wearing headphones, feeling like a time-spy from the eleventh century. The clerks don't care; they want cash and two ID cards, but actual television-ownership isn't mandatory. They offer also *The Smile of the Walrus*, from Jacques Cousteau, to warm your den at the touch of a few buttons. They provide *Lions of the African Night*, from National Geographic, to roar at you on command. And, sure, they've got rhinos if you want rhinos. You can go birdwatching in Botswana without suffering the jet lag or the shots. You can get a zoo-visitor experience without even crossing town to the zoo. It's the age of takeout, and now the zoo comes to you, each beast caged tractably in a plastic cassette.

This phenomenon, the mass-marketing of video nature, carries an ambivalent mix of implications. The positive ones are straightforward. People learn a fact or three about those endangered ferrets. People enjoy the sense of spectacle. People witness amazing processes and behaviors that they never otherwise could, and as witnesses they acquire, maybe, a certain vested concern for the preservation of wild places and wild beings. The negative implications are less patent and more complicated. Among them: People are lulled, pandered to, hypnotized, and misled. They learn to take nature for granted, as just another form of human amusement, like C-Span or *Monday Night Football*. They become spoiled to the small natural wonders in their local woodlands, since the bigger wonders of Malaysia or Peru are served up more vividly on the tube. They accept the video entertainments as substitutes for, not just reflections of, real living leopards or bears or gorillas. Worst of all, they are enticed to believe that nature as they have seen it—concocted expertly from flickering photographic images—represents nature as it exists.

Of course it doesn't. Images can lie, even photographic images. Time is always compressed, context is often concealed or altered or flouted, in a filmic composition. Nature in reality is more diffuse, more tedious, less satisfactorily dramatic, and often more perishable than a video documentary of some marvelous ecosystem or species, plus in reality there's no heart-filling musical score. Drama is artifice—and natural-history drama no less so than other sorts. Nature as commonly found (without the telephoto lenses, without the cutaway nests, without the editing) is *not* very dramatic. The drab truth is that you could stand under the Amazon canopy for a month, with a good set of binoculars, while the microbes ate your feet, and never catch a single glimpse of copulating monkeys or a snake in the act of swallowing a bird.

Charles Siebert highlighted this truth in a recent issue of *Harper's*. In an essay titled "The Artifice of the Natural," Siebert noted that nature documentaries on television are unnaturally "rapid, focused, and framed," whereas an actual forest is "wide, old, and slow," sublimely indifferent to any human on the lookout for zoological drama. In fact, Siebert argued, the average nature show is actually less like a forest than like a city, "both entities being elaborate human constructs: fast-paced, multi-storied, and artificially lit."

What are the historical roots, Siebert wondered, of the nature-show phenomenon? Where did the mass-market packaging begin? Scanning old tapes at the Museum of Television and Radio, he traced back to the early efforts of Jacques Cousteau, Marlin Perkins, and a few others. Even before the infamously campy Mutual of Omaha's *Wild Kingdom*, as it turns out, Perkins had a TV show called *Zoo Parade*. That was in 1955. And still earlier, in the Thirties, Perkins did a radio show about nature from a station in St. Louis—until a mishap one day with an electric eel, which sent a jolt through him and into his microphone and thereby blew out the station's power.

Siebert's historical search could have gone back even further, if he hadn't chosen to limit himself to such electromagnetic media as television, radio, and eels. One of the first mass-market images of nature was produced almost five centuries ago in the medium of wood. It was part of Gutenberg's revolution, not McLuhan's. It came out of Nuremberg, Germany, in the year 1515.

*   *   *

On May 20, 1515, a rhinoceros arrived in the port of Lisbon, as dolefully and terminally displaced as King Kong in New York. Good lord, what is it? people wondered. No such zoological marvel had been seen in Europe within recent memory—possibly, not since the exotic menageries of imperial Rome. The animal had been sent as a gift from Sultan Muzafar II of Gujarat, in western India, to King Manuel I of Portugal. The king, finding himself in no particular need of a live rhinoceros (which, taxonomy aside, he probably considered a white elephant), saw fit to pass along this unwieldy item to Pope Leo X, but in the course of being shipped onward to Italy it died. Details of its death are sparse and not fully reliable: One account says that the ship sank but that the rhino's corpse was recovered, which sounds somehow more simple than it should. How do you dredge up a drowned rhinoceros from the floor of the ocean? Anyway, instead of a live rhinoceros, the pope received a stuffed (and perhaps soggy) carcass. This was the beast on which the great German artist Albrecht Dürer, up in Nuremberg, based a pen-and-ink drawing that he titled *Rhinoceron*.

Dürer's drawing survives in the British Museum. But that one-of-a-kind artifact isn't what concerns us.

From the drawing, Dürer produced a woodcut, probably executed in pear wood. The carving itself was most likely done by a specialist artisan, a *Formschneyder*, under Dürer's close supervision. From that woodcut block, multiple prints were taken—no one can tell us the exact number, but many—and in this form the image spread across Europe. The dead rhino had intersected with European culture at just the right historical moment to become a pop icon. If it had arrived a hundred years earlier, before Gutenberg's invention and the development of cheap mass-produced paper and the consequent rise of the printing trade, it might have been painted in oils by a medieval allegorist, it might have been memorably drawn in ink or in charcoal, but neither a painted nor a sketched image would have been *published*. Its portrait would have hung in the house of some burgher or in the castle of some prince, precious and singular on its wall, seen by not many eyes. And if the animal had arrived a hundred years later, it would have come too late to inspire one of the prototypic images in the foundational phase of graphic printing. In that case, its likeness would have been just one among hundreds in the published bestiaries of the seventeenth century, exerting no extraordinary force. But instead of being too late or to early, it arrived when it did, perfectly timed to achieve international fame.

Dürer himself never saw the pope's rhinoceros, either while it was alive or as a carcass. He concocted his image secondhand, from a sketch and a description sent to him by letter from Lisbon. Dürer was a consummate draftsman—with a genius hand, a precise eye, and a hungry curiosity toward the natural world that, among Renaissance artists, was second only to Leonardo's. Given his drawing skill and his passion for accuracy, it's only natural to assume that his woodcut would have looked different, and possibly much different, if he had inspected the rhino personally. Probably he'd have drawn the animal as he saw it, and no doubt he'd have seen it pellucidly. Instead he produced a stunning cartoon, a tendentious bit of surrealism with a presciently modern zing, centuries before the birth of, say, Ralph Steadman.[1]

Having heard that the rhinoceros was plated protectively with panels of stiff skin, he gave it a suit of armor. And not just any armor, but armor closely analogous to what a German knight would have worn in the feudal scuffles of Dürer's own era, complete with a gorget at the throat, a breastplate around the midsection, pauldrons[2] for the shoulders, faulds[3] skirting the thighs, and nicely aligned rivets along the plate edges. He canted back the angle of the horn, making it more dangerous as a weapon for hooking and ripping. He applied arabesques of detail, and no small amount of gnarly menace, to the face. For good measure he added a second horn, smaller, pointing forward from the back of the neck. The lower legs he wrapped in chain mail. As Dürer imagined and portrayed it, the rhinoceros was a magnificent aggressor, surly, invulnerable, built to cause terror wherever it strode: a war rhino. His vision, misleading as it was, may have done much to set the tone of European perceptions of rhinos for the next four hundred years.

At the top of the woodcut, in Gothic lettering, Dürer placed an inscription. "After Christ's birth, the year 1513, on May 1, this animal was brought alive to the great and mighty King Emmanuel at Lisbon in Portugal from India," he wrote. "Its color is that of a freckled toad and it is covered by a hard, thick shell. It is of the same size as an elephant but has shorter legs and is well capable of defending itself. On the tip of its nose is a sharp, strong horn which it hones wherever it finds a stone." He further declared that it's the deadly enemy of elephants, which it tears open at the belly with its horn, and that the rhino itself is impervious to being stabbed by a tusk, thanks to its armor. When an elephant lies disemboweled and helpless, the rhinoceros finishes it off by strangulation, Dürer claimed, though he didn't

---

1. Surreal cartoonist who is known as one of the creators of gonzo journalism.

2. Shoulder armor

3. Skirt of metal plates attached to torso armor.

explain how. Amid all the other items of misinformation, his 1513 date was two years too early.

"They say that the Rhinoceros is fast, cunning, and daring," he added. Dürer's rhinoceros, anyway, was forevermore all of these things, even if the pope's rhinoceros hadn't quite been.

One piece of evidence tells us that Dürer him- [15] self intended this image for mass-market publication: the decision to make it a woodcut, as distinct from a copperplate engraving. Both those techniques had come into use for graphic printing at Dürer's time, and he was a master of both. His father, a Nuremberg goldsmith, had taught him as a boy to inscribe delicate patterns onto metal with a fine-pointed burin, and some of Dürer's mature engravings, such as *Knight, Death, and Devil* and *Melencolia I*, are among the most gracefully spooky images of the German Renaissance. Generally, engraving technique offered the advantage of allowing finer lines and more intricate detail than a woodcut. But an engraving also had to be inked and wiped separately for each print, and its finely incised lines tended to wear out rather soon; woodcut prints, on the other hand, could be run off more quickly, using the production-line capacities of a Gutenberg press, and the coarse but sturdy lines of the woodblock held up throughout many repetitions. When an artist chose the woodcut technique in preference to engraving, that choice implied a willingness to compromise the delicacy of each individual print for the sake of producing more copies. It was a familiar trade-off: popular appeal versus subtlety. A woodcut print was a democratic form of art, in those days, cheap enough to be bought and enjoyed by the folks in the humble cottages. Dürer himself was a man of expensive middle-class tastes, with a good head for business, and large-edition woodcuts were one of the ways he made his money.

His rhino woodcut—the carved block itself, not just the image—far outlived him. At least nine separate editions were eventually run from it, each edition comprising unknowably many prints. By the time of the eighth edition, produced by Dutch printers in the seventeenth century, the block showed a crack that slashed through all four of the rhino's legs, plus wormholes in the neck, eyelid, and horn. That it was still being printed, wormholes and crack and all, suggests the exceptional graphic power of Dürer's image. And that image carried even beyond the nine editions; Dürer himself inserted the same rhino as a decorative touch in a huge composite woodcut, *The Triumphal Arch*, done as a commission for the emperor Maximilian. It was also copied by other artists. One of the knock-off versions appeared, soon after Dürer's death, in Konrad von Gesner's volume *Historia Animalium*. Another close copy showed up in a collection of animal and plant drawings assembled by Ulisse Aldrovandi at the end of the century, and still another in the Reverend Edward Topsell's *Historie of Foure-footed Beastes*, published in 1607. When Europeans of that era imagined a rhino, either as a real animal or as a fabulous one, they imagined it according to Dürer. Still later, of course, there were not just plagiarizations but many respectful reprints in books about Dürer's life and work, about the art of the woodcut, about artistic representations of nature in general. From the year 1515 until now, it has probably been the single most familiar image of a rhinoceros among people who have seldom if ever laid eyes on the real thing. In fact, its broad popularity tends to overshadow Dürer's whole body of diverse, wonderful work. Toss the name Albrecht Dürer at a person with some interest in art, ask for a memorable example, and that person is likely to mention the boilerplate rhino.

A similar image even appears—fleetingly, in connection with an old text on Chinese folk medicine, including the uses of rhino horn—in a National Geographic documentary titled *The Rhino War*, now available at Blockbuster Video.

Dürer was fascinated by the natural world, at least as a source of visual images. He created some striking portraits of animals and plants. In most of those cases, he seems to have worked either from live models or from dead specimens, not from imagination or hearsay, and he rendered the real creatures with passionate exactitude. During his first visit to Venice he found things to interest him at the city's fish market, producing a watercolor of a crab so minutely specific that it could stand as a scientific illustration. He also did a splendid lobster. Later he painted a young hare, its eyes bright, its ears erect, its fur textured with such fastidiousness as to anticipate photo-realism, crouching self-consciously as it must have in Dürer's studio. At the height of his powers he did a dead duck, a dead roller (a bird of the family Coraciidae, with iridescent wing feathers of brilliant blue and green), and, still more striking, the wing of a roller, as a disjointed study, sedulously realistic in its treatment of every feather. Even his conventional religious scenes were sometimes festooned with fauna—for instance his *Virgin with a Multitude of Animals*, in which the madonna and child sit surrounded by two owls, two swans, a parrot, a fox, a crab, a frog, and a stag beetle. Not all of his animals, though, were impeccably lifelike. In his early woodcut of Saint Jerome (that's the fellow who, according to pious legend, pulled a thorn from a lion's paw), Dürer's lion is too small, too skinny, with too tiny a head; it looks like a cocker spaniel with an embarrassing summer haircut. But later in life Dürer saw his first living lion, at a zoo in Belgium, after which his lions were vastly more leonine.

Probably his finest work in this vein is a watercolor-and-gouache painting called *The Great Clump of Turf*, which features dandelions and ribwort and meadow grass and a few other herbs, all seen up close and from ground level as though they're a hummock of sizable trees. At first glance it seems a humdrum, uninteresting image, but more careful inspection reveals that Dürer made these little plants into something profound—a world, an ecosystem—by treating them with profound respect. How exactly did he do it? Well, he used a trick of perspective to give them stature, but that wasn't all. He also paid them the compliment of precision.

It might seem incongruous that the same man [20] who painted *The Great Clump of Turf* and the roller's wing and the hare—each one a singular image showing fervent concern for anatomical accuracy—could have also accounted for those nine editions of cartoonish rhino. It seemed incongruous to me, especially after my hour in that library cubicle watching *The Rhino War*, which turns out to be a compelling and clear-sighted film, full of real animals bearing not much resemblance to Albrecht Dürer's notional beast. Matched against those photographic images, Dürer's woodcut looks like fantasy. But hold on, there's another line of sight onto this matter. *The Rhino War* deals only with poaching against the black rhino, *Diceros bicornis*, an African species brought to the verge of extinction by gangs of horn hunters within the past twenty years. Four other rhinoceros species survive elsewhere in the world. Three of those, native to various regions in Asia, are also severely endangered but were beyond the purview of this particular film.

Africa's rhinos have two prominent horns. Dürer's has one. So I consulted a photo in a mammal encyclopedia.

Specifically, I looked at *Rhinoceros unicornis*, the one-horned Indian species, since that's what Muzafar II must have sent from Gujarat to the king of Portugal. Although I had seen *R. unicornis* in the flesh (some years ago, at a reserve in Nepal), I had managed to forget its appearance. What I found now was a peculiar-looking animal, even by rhinoceros standards. It differed drastically from the two smooth-flanked African species. Its stiffened skin seemed to be gathered in slabs—like a suit of armor, yes, complete with breastplate and pauldrons and faulds—and pocked with dermal protuberances resembling rivets. It was surprisingly similar, by God, to the Dürer image. Considering that Dürer worked from hearsay, it was shockingly similar.

This bit of elementary research obliged me to recognize what I should have already known: that the least accurate aspect of Dürer's woodcut is the inscription. His date is wrong; his dermatology is right. His artwork is reasonably faithful, compared to that business about a toad-colored animal in a "thick shell," big as an elephant, cunning and deadly, honing its horn on a stone. His rhinoceros is better than it reads.

That constitutes a chastening reminder for someone like myself, with a bias in favor of the written page and a sour prejudice against mass-market video: a reminder that, although images can be deceptive, they don't stand convicted alone. Writing is just another form of concoction. Words can lie too. You can trust me on this, probably.

focus.

1. How would you describe Quammen's tone in the essay? Is he skeptical? analytical? critical? How does he introduce the topic of Dürer's woodcut, and how does he relate it back to the nature videos at Blockbuster?

2. Quammen says that Dürer's image of the rhinoceros arrived at exactly the right time to achieve international fame. What evidence does Quammen offer to support this assertion?

respond.

1. Do you ever watch television nature shows? How realistic do you find them to be? What leads you to believe that they are—or are not—realistic? Think, for instance, about shows such as *The Crocodile Hunter*. What do such programs have in common with National Geographic's *Explorer*? with IMAX films? How do they differ?

2. Compare this image of a rhinoceros with Dürer's engraving. How accurate is Dürer's interpretation of the rhinoceros, considering he drew it entirely from verbal descriptions and a sketch someone sent him? What do you make of his decision to dress the rhino in armor? How does the presence of the armor speak to Dürer's cultural presuppositions regarding the rhino?

   According to Quammen, Dürer imagined and portrayed the rhinoceros as "a magnificent aggressor, surly, invulnerable, built to cause terror wherever it strode: a war rhino." Do a Web search using the word "rhinoceros." Look for information about its general disposition. Compare Dürer's portrayal with what you learn about the general personality of the rhino. Do the two match up? If not, why do you think Dürer constructed this mythos around the rhino?

3. In the beginning of his essay, Quammen talks about renting nature videos and the differences between lived and vicarious experience. Rent a travel video or DVD about a place you've already been. While you watch the video, make notes on elements that accurately represent your experience and on elements that deviate from your experience. How do the producers of the video want you to think about the travel destination? How is the place portrayed in the video similar to the place you visited and remember? How is it different? What might the motivations of the producers be for representing the place the way they do?

   With all these issues in mind, write an essay analyzing how the travel video constructs a certain reality about its subject. What seems factual? What seems constructed? How is your understanding of the place an image that you have constructed?

Vicki Goldberg has written
several books on photography
and photographers. Recently,
she worked in conjunction with
photographer Christian Coigny
and Vitra, a chair-manufacturing
company, to produce a series of
images of celebrities sitting in Vitra
chairs and compile them into a
collection called *Sittings*. A resident
of New York City, Goldberg serves
as a freelance photography
critic for the *New York Times*
and lectures frequently at the
Metropolitan Museum of Art.
The following article, which first
appeared in the *Times* in October
2001, asks critical questions
regarding both the ethics and
the aesthetics of scientific
photography.

Even Scientific Images Have Trouble Telling the Truth

VICKI GOLDBERG

Scientific pictures are not decoration but knowledge. They support our health, our industry, our search for an understanding of ourselves, our world, and the universe. William M. Ivins Jr., who was, starting in 1916, the first curator of prints at the Metropolitan Museum of Art, later said that science couldn't exist without reproducible images. Modern science certainly cannot: it is difficult even to imagine astronomy advancing solely on words and numbers.

Images reign in a wide swath of science. Most scientists, like most of the rest of us, understand concepts and structures more quickly and thoroughly when they can be visualized; after all, the brain evolved to deal with images rather than abstractions. Some scientific problems cannot even be solved without images. Now digitization and other transformations in image-making technologies are revolutionizing certain sciences and slyly inserting the issues that dog more commonplace photography.

Brilliant and convincing pictures have a kind of celebrity power: they help attract good minds and public support to sciences that produce fine displays. Astronomy is a good example; millions of people pore over the Hubble and Chandra telescopes' revelations from the edge of space. Nanoscience and nanotechnology are similar successes. Dr. George M. Whitesides, Mallinckrodt Professor of Chemistry at Harvard, says that when instruments make structures no bigger than a few hundred billionths of a meter visible, investigators "feel immediately comfortable with their existence." This has contributed to a kind of express-train development of nanoscience, while chemistry and nuclear physics, lacking such mind-opening imagery, have tended to stay on more local tracks.

To many of us who are not in the sciences, pictures like the Hubble images or the Visual Human Project have seemed like the last refuge of photographic "truth" in the current flood of image doubts. A three-day conference at the Massachusetts Institute of Technology in June—"Image and Meaning: Envisioning and Communicating Science and Technology"—almost sneakily suggested that there is no refuge, that scientific images are more subtly but just as surely subject to interpretation, deconstruction and manipulation as the nearest billboard.

Stunning pictures on science pages, though most likely not lies, are not necessarily absolutely faithful copies of molecules or macrophages or quasars. For one thing, such images may have been "improved" to be closer to more closely render the information that was actually there but not entirely caught by the recording camera or other device.

Felice Frankel, an M.I.T. research scientist (and organizer of the Image and Meaning conference), has had to add a color to certain photographs when the photographic instrument did not pick up a tint she could see with her own eyes; the manipulated image was more faithful to visual observation than the unmanipulated. Illustrations may be purposely simplified to make them easier to understand, especially for the lay public. Some published X-ray images of the stars have been adaptively "smoothed," a technique that replaces the value of the intensity of each pixel with the average value of its neighbors, making details easier to see.

Miraculous as microscopes, telescopes, and CAT scans are in their capacity to exceed human vision, human beings still have to interpret the results, and human beings have been known to make mistakes. When the Hubble sent back a picture that was said

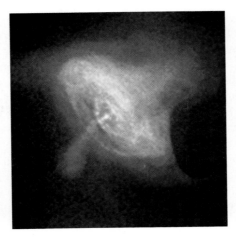

to show a newly discovered planet, the press jumped up and down. A year later, the planet proved not to be a planet after all, but the photograph was exhibited with other scientific photographs at M.I.T. during the conference, and the label still identified it as a planet.

Instruments can't see everything anyway. They make their own adjustments to what they do see, and then the algorithms that convert digital data make other adjustments, so even if the observation didn't change what was observed (and Heisenberg assured us that it did) it may change the way it looks. An object looks very different under different modes of observation; consider an X-ray of Uncle Harry's skull compared with a portrait of him. The Crab Nebula changes shape when "seen" by instruments using different parts of the electromagnetic spectrum: it appears bell-shaped to X-ray observation, as an irregular cloud under optical examination, and as an even more irregular cloud in an examination, and as an even more irregular cloud in an infrared picture. When you're asked to draw the Crab Nebula on the final exam, what will it look like?

Medicine has been turned inside out by new imaging techniques. At the M.I.T. conference, Dr. Richard Satava of the Yale University School of Medicine predicted that one day we will be able to have holograms of our entire inner space printed on a card the size of a credit card. He already does. But John Abele founder-chairman of Boston Scientific, a medical device manufacturer, says such images, like other medical images, contain extraneous artifacts. Not that a tea kettle shows up where your heart should be but a tumorlike spot might put in an appearance. Radiologists know this; their business includes telling spots, and tumors apart. Mr. Abele, noting that medical imaging is improving, advises that you wait as long as you can to get sick.

Drawings and diagrams have always been more 10 subject to distortion than photographs, but digital imaging has made distortion both easier and more alluring. It is now possible to construct images that look perfectly real without enough data to corrobo-

▶ What you see depends on the means you use to see it. The Crab Nebula, photographed by optical light (left), X-ray (center), and infrared light (right). Photos from Chandra/NASA.

rate them, increasing the risk of overrendering. Mr. Abele says that color graphics make overinterpretation all too easy, allowing facile translation of ambiguous data into pictures that provoke an instant aha! Articles are occasionally illustrated with images representing a guess about the appearance of invisible objects and events, though no one has any real idea what they look like or any hope of finding out in the near future.

The true color of objects is also elusive. Some color schemes have fairly ancient and possibly capricious traditions. In 1865, when the chemist August Wilhelm von Hoffmann gave a public lecture in England, he showed models of the way molecules combined, using croquet balls and thin rods. Chemists making atomic models today still use the colors of Hoffmann's croquet balls for the elements he illustrated. Other kinds of scientific coloration may be equally arbitrary, though seldom quite so British.

Added color turns up often, as do colored pictures of things that have no color at all. Color printouts of three-dimensional CAT scans and MRI's assign different colors to different levels, much as topographic maps do, to make reading what's behind or less elevated easier. Radiologists know perfectly well that your skeleton is not orange and green and gold.

What's called "false color" is often added to black-and-white pictures from outer space according to various formulas. Some derive from the gases and mineral elements in the pictures. Others try to approximate what could be seen if the light were bright enough to see color but not so bright that everything simply looked white, an unlikely set of circumstances. The optical accuracy of such formulas cannot be checked until someone can get millions of light-years out into space and take a look around.

Representations are not simply cultural efflorescences or the image soup we swim in but crucial to our knowledge and existence. If scientific imaging and images are imperfect, so are most of our tools, and we work with the best we've got until we devise better. If color in scientific illustration is often a matter of convention, convention rules in more common places, too; traffic lights, for example, blink yellow, a color that has no inherent connection to slowness or caution at all. If certain scientific photographs have been manipulated in some way to make them easier to read or more beautiful, well, there's another nail in the coffin of photography's truthfulness, which has been moribund so long it's hard to mourn by now.

And yet the reports of photography's death [15] have been greatly exaggerated. Scientists continue to attach cameras to microscopes, telescopes, endoscopes, and accelerators in search of elusive information. Dr. Dan Werthimer, chief scientist of the SETI@home project, which analyses radio astronomy data for signals that might come from extraterrestrial life, says that most scientists think such communication will come through images.

Images already fill not just our lives but our universe. Earthlings have intentionally sent a few pictures, of DNA, amino acids, that sort of thing, journeying into space, but in fact we have unintentionally inundated the universe with images. Dr. Werthimer points out that television signals broadcast not in a straight line to your screen but in every direction at once. Leaving earth, they travel at the speed of light, going on approximately forever. They get weaker and weaker as they go, but that just means you'd need a big antenna to pick them up if you were truly far away. Think of it: Milton Berle, *Leave It to Beaver*, MTV, and *Midnight Blue* are coursing to the farthest stars even as you are reading this.

focus.

1. Examine the three photographs of the Crab Nebula (p. 363). Describe them using the concepts set out in Chapter 1, including unity, arrangement, and emphasis. How do these qualities contribute to the way we read each picture? to the way we read the three photos as a whole series?

2. In explaining the various qualities and associations people attribute to colors, Goldberg uses the example of a yellow light, saying that there is no inherent connection between the color yellow and cautionary behavior. What associations do you have with certain colors? How might you feel if you had an MRI or a CAT scan done and part of the image came back red? black? Would the color scheme of the image affect your response to it?

respond.

1. Examine these molecular images of gin, amaretto, ~~and a mint julep~~, respectively, taken from the Molecular Expressions Web site created by Florida State University <www.microscopy.fsu.edu/micro/gallery/cocktails/cocktail.html.> Pay attention to the color scheme and patterns in these images. Would it change the way you read the picture if you knew that the different elements that comprise the image had been dyed to stand out more clearly? Think about the relationship between science and art. People often think these two fields are diametrically opposed. How are they similar? How are they different?

2. Periodically, we hear about the excavation of newly discovered graves or the uncovering of bodies buried long ago. Anthropologists and forensic scientists perform a series of assessments on the found remains and make assumptions on the life of that person based on those findings. Here is a description from a PBS Web site about the discovery of a Stone Age corpse.

Return of the Iceman. Cutting-edge science and archaeology are reconstructing the life and culture of the Iceman—the 5,000-year-old frozen corpse found buried in the ice of the Alps. By analyzing every inch of the Iceman's body and the tools and equipment found with it, scientists are piecing together the most complete picture yet of the late Stone Age in this part of Europe. X-ray, CAT scan, and microscopic analysis of this spectacular find is revealing where the Iceman lived, what he ate, and how he may have died; nuclear physics reveals that the Iceman's hair was contaminated with arsenic and copper, suggesting he was involved in copper production centuries before it was known to exist in the region. <www.pbs.org/wgbh/nova/listseason/25.htm#2516>

How might the observations of the Iceman, and the conclusions about his life based on them, be a product of contemporary assumptions regarding that period?

Most national newspapers have a science section at least one day a week. Find an article in a newspaper reporting a scientific discovery. Write an essay analyzing the assumptions in the article. How much is the reader expected to know? How is the significance of the discovery described? What comparisons are made?

Molecular view of gin.

Molecular view of amaretto.

Oversimulated Suburbia

DAVID BROOKS

David Brooks (b. 1961) is the author of *Bobos in Paradise: The New Upper Class and How They Got There*. He is a senior editor at the *Weekly Standard*; publishes in *Newsweek, Atlantic Monthly*, and the *New York Times Magazine;* and serves as a commentator on National Public Radio and CNN. Trained as a police reporter for the *Chicago Tribune* and the *Chicago Sun Times,* Brooks expanded his beat later in his career to cover such regions as Russia and the Middle East.

The following piece, published in the *New York Times Magazine* in November 2002, investigates the phenomenon of *The Sims* and other reality video games, examining the allure and cultural implications of a pastime in which, "as in life, you just keep doing the dishes until you die." Brooks calls into question the commercial values of the game, in which players must lavishly outfit themselves and their homes, and asks whether there's a greater possibility for happy endings in a cybersociety than there is in reality.

I don't know if it strikes you as odd that of all the arenas of human endeavor, the one that has produced the best-selling computer game of all time *is* the American suburb. There are other games about intergalactic warfare, supersonic-jet dogfights, and inner-city car theft, but none of them attract the same fanatical following—and no game attracts any sort of following among women—as *The Sims*™.

You install *The Sims* on your computer and you begin the game, and what do you see? A subdivision. There's a little ranch home over there, a colonial over there, a larger McMansion up the hill. And the object of the game? Suburban conquest in its rawest form. You've got to get the kids scrubbed and fed by the time the school bus comes around in the morning. You have to select the right coffee table to go with your love seat. You have to remember to turn off the TV if you want to take a nap, because the noise will keep you up. There's no winning and losing in *The Sims*. No points, no end. In the game, as in life, you just keep doing the dishes until you die.

It's all about time management. You want to throw a dinner party for your friends, and you'd also like to do some gardening, but you've got to take out the garbage and pick up the paper from the front yard, and you notice your bladder is alarmingly full and you won't be at your best unless you head to the bathroom to relieve yourself. This is the epic heroism of everyday life! The most mundane tasks—the ones that actually bore the hell out of you in reality—come at you in the computer game with relentless insistence, and if you are going to be a happy Sim, master of your tract home, lord of your lawn, sultan of your suburb, you have to get organized. You have to impose order on chaos. You have to stay cool and go with the flow. In this way you can achieve split-level greatness.

The Sims is the brainchild of Will Wright. In the early 1980s, Wright was a programmer for a company that made conventional bullets-and-bombs PC games. For one game, Wright was told to design some enemy islands for warplanes to destroy. He discovered he was more interested in the islands—with refineries, buildings and streets—than the bombers, so he developed a computer game, *SimCity*, that lets players build their own cities. His employer, Broderbund, resisted the idea, so he went off to help found a company and in 1989 introduced the fantastically successful *SimCity*™ line of games.

Wright went on to design *SimEarth*™, *SimHealth*™, and *SimTower*™, and, influenced by the work of the architectural theorist Christopher Alexander (the author of *A Pattern Language: Towns, Buildings, Construction*), he decided to build a game in which players would try to design the perfect home. He created abstract characters to live in the homes, but he quickly discovered that the characters were more fun than the residences. *The Sims* was released in February 2000; soon thereafter it was followed by expansion packs that allow you to take your characters, or Sims, out on dates, to resort hotels or nightclubs. Last year, Sims-related games occupied 5 of the top 10 spots on the computer-game best-seller chart. (Keep in mind, when weighing the social importance of these things, that in the United States, computer- and video-game revenues are greater than movie box-office receipts. Almost 20 million copies of *The Sims* and its add-ons have been sold.)

And next month, an online version of *The Sims* goes on sale ($50 for the game; $10 per month in subscription fees). In other words, in addition to the regular suburbia all around us, there will be a massive new cybersociety, filled with little computer-generated people with a passion for Barcaloungers.

The Sims allows you to create your own characters, and the first thing many players do is base characters on themselves and their families. You can choose personality traits, skin shades, and wardrobes—all to reincarnate you and your loved ones onscreen. Then you have to buy things for them. As with any good bourgeois society, Sims society is built around interior decorating. You have to furnish your home, and the game itself offers a dazzling array of dining-room-table sets, recliners for every price point, party balloons, and sconces.

But, of course, as in American life generally, a mind-numbing array of choices is never enough. On the Internet are hundreds, if not thousands, of sites put up by freelancers who have designed clothing, furnishings, and fashion accessories that you can download and import into your Sims game. There is Mall of the Sims, with more than 50 stores, where you can browse for paintings for your Sims walls and swimwear for your Sims selves. There is a Sims Thrift Mart, Yuppie Sims, and Historic Sims Houses, for those tired of the game's mostly contemporary architecture options. The designers sometimes charge a fee for their products; others, like philanthropic Ralph Laurens, make free Sims necklaces, Sims reading lamps, Sims tattoos, lingerie, and carpets just for the joy of creating new fashions.

And see how the public bubbles with enthusiasm! In Sims sites devoted to fashion discussions, you find yourself among people in a shopping frenzy. Authentic Victorian wallpaper is now available! Here's a new site with pet gyms for your little Sims gerbils to run around in! "Oh! And something very very very very very very special!" one Sims nut enthuses on <partysims.com>. "A brand-new portable-TV collection! . . . The base was made from a person named 'm.' . . . Big thanks and praise to you!"

You give a bunch of mostly young and, more 10 often than not, female Sims players the chance through a make-believe computer world to do anything they want, to explore any reality or set of interactions, and what do they do first? They consume! They nest and decorate! It's not exactly a materialistic fever they're stoking, because none of the Sims stuff is actually material. Instead it's a virtual hedonism that consumes them, a delicious set of pleasures and sensations that apparently come from imagining what floorings would go with what wall surfaces, from selecting blouses and boleros, from mixing and matching and combining. Human beings, at least in our culture, truly are consuming creatures.

But they are also social creatures. On the official Sims site, thousands of Sims lovers have posted Sims novellas—a sort of folk literature that future historians, zeitgeist hunters, and museum curators are going to go for in a big way. These novellas look like storyboards, with pictures of Sims interiors and characters, above written stories and dialogue. A typical novella may stretch for 64 to 200 pictures and thousands of words. Some of them are just *Architectural Digest* in digital form, involving dinner parties and room-by-room house tours. But most of the novellas are more substantial, and after you've read through a hundred or so of these things, they all blend into one vast modern cultural landscape in which *Oprah* meets *Friends*, *Terms of Endearment* and MTV's *Real World*.

Here's a bit from a story about a teenage single mom who lives with her alcoholic father, Shane, who beats her child, May:

> "Who the hell do you think you are!!!!" I yelled at Shane after telling May to go in the bedroom. "What the hell are you talking about?!" Shane yelled. "I saw you hit May you bastard!" . . . Shane just glared at me.

At the end of the story the single mom meets a hunky boyfriend who beats up the dad near the backyard swing set.

Some of the stories end badly. It occurs to some players that they don't have to play by the rules of normal society, so they start killing people. They invite neighbors over to their backyard pools and then pull up the exit ladders and watch them drown. Or they kill off husbands. But the striking thing about these stories is that most of them do end happily, the abusive relationships, dysfunctional families, drug and alcohol addictions are overcome and careers are put on track, just like at the ending of all those *Behind the Music* rockumentaries. Interestingly, the stories generally don't seem to regard marriage as the happily-ever-after ideal. Instead, cliques are the key to paradise. In story after story, the happy denouement comes when the main character settles into her new home, furnishes it to her taste and then invites 5 to 10 people over, and they surround her with companionship and celebrate her triumphs.

In this way, too, the Sims world reflects, antici-15 pates and parodies the real world. Specifically, it reflects the social inversion that has taken place over the past decade. If you came of age before, say, 1985, then your social life probably followed the 1950s pattern: you had a group of friends and also a relationship with your special boyfriend or girlfriend that was understood to be higher and more intense than that with the rest of the gang. There was a distinct line between "going out" and not "going out."

But for many American young people, the friendship relationship is more important than the sexual relationship. That's the model you see in the Sims world and the Sims literature. People go out in groups, rather than on one-on-one dates. In the new pattern, no one sits around by the phone waiting for the boy to ask the girl out, which is nice, but on the other hand, every serious or possibly serious relationship is plagued by ambiguity. There's a pervasive level of sexual tension, but also a new sort of anxiety, because without the formal dating rituals, it's hard to know where anyone stands.

Will Wright says that one of the things that has amazed him most about the online Sims—more than 35,000 people have been testing the system before its official launch—is the passionate energy people put into acquiring and cultivating roommates. People set up a home and then invite groups of people to come live and share resources with them. These social pods are like yuppie kibbutzim in which every woman is Jennifer Aniston and every guy is Matthew Perry, and so each anomic individual is surrounded in all directions by a supportive clique of happy singles for flirting and reinforcement. If you grew up in the bowling-alone world, maybe this is your idea of heaven.

So far, there are two basic types of players. First, there are the highly driven players obsessed with making Sims money and becoming masters of the Sims universe. (Already one player has become the Donald Trump of the online Sims world, acquiring enough money and property to open a string of coffee shops, stores and clubs.) Then there is another set of players who are mostly interested in building intimacies and relationships. (Draw your own sexist conclusions about which sort of person creates which type of Sim.) These people are interested in creating bonds, giving hugs, and building a clique. In the Sims world, of course, you can be as obnoxious as you want to be, with no real cost, but Wright says he's been impressed by the spirit of attentive camaraderie that so far prevails. "People are polite and social with each other," he says. (While there are many fantastic monsters and other bizarre personas available to them, most players are content to create normal, humanlike Sims beings.) There is no government yet in the online *Sims* game. It's a Hobbesian state of nature. And yet most people are cooperative and friendly—perhaps slightly more flamboyant than the average person you see in the Safeway, but not much.

The relationship players tend to create what Wright calls a mythos. They start with names like Backseat Betty, Tokyo Rose, the Lady of Prose, and Dean Martinez Bravo and create a back story to explain their characters. They want their Sims lives to be legible to the characters around them, so the other characters know how to approach and relate to them. The Sims players who thrive, according to Wright, are the ones who can build the abstract computer characters into distinct personalities. They can project a clear persona while also reading the moods of the other Sims.

The online world, which can accommodate a [20] million players, is a vast society with Internet cafes, investment banks, B & B's, parties, pizzerias, and homes, apartments, and condos. Aside from making money, the main activity is schmoozing. One player complained recently that he created a beauty pageant but that a character named Cheerleader Sue came in dressed as a hillbilly and ruined the talent competition with a flatulent version of "Camptown Races"; he had to block Cheerleader Sue from his environment. The online game allows you to register your displeasure with others by putting them in wrestling holds or by stomping on them. (This is only symbolic and doesn't kill them.) You can also die by your own hand—by starving or drowning yourself, at which point you wander around as a ghost until another player agrees to resurrect you.

But dealing grief is relatively rare. Many people compete to make the Top 100 Most Liked list. That means trying to invite hundreds of players over to your house to make friends, sometimes by having parties, quiz-show games, or offering bribes. (Every 24 hours, the game dispenses money to players depending on how many people have visited their homes.) If you walk into, say, somebody's backyard barbecue, you'll find a dozen Sims hanging out in the Jacuzzi or dancing by the stereo. The male characters are all ripped, and the female characters have bikini-perfect bodies, inevitably with humongous breasts. Mostly they're exchanging banal pleasantries. "This barbecue is such a good way to start the season!" enthuses one young woman in a short skirt with breasts that would have her tipping over if she existed in real life. "Burgers and hot dogs, grilled how you like 'em!" announces the host at the grill. "Sounds mouth-watering, but I know they'll just go straight to my thighs," says an African American Sim.

This isn't exactly Dostoyevsky material, so you head over to a futuristic nightclub with another clique of beautiful people, steel floors and weird twenty-third-century molded furniture that looks like Frank Gehry crossed with the design sensibility of Woody Allen's *Sleeper*. But again you detect a gap between the amazing visual sophistication of the place and the barely literate conversation. One beautiful guy is standing in the middle of the room saying, "Boy, these long silences are almost unbearable." So you move on to find a woman, again in a bikini, saying, "I need something to lift me up," and a *Saturday Night Fever* disco man with his shirt open to his navel responds, "I think I can provide that lift, young lady."

Another devastating come-on line.

I confess I sometimes don't know whether to be happy or depressed when I dip into Sims world.

Sometimes you get the sense that these Sims fanatics are compensating online for the needs that aren't met in their real lives. If you read through the Sims discussion rooms, you find a lot of people who seem to spend a lot of time alone in their rooms thinking, often not terribly positively, about their own lives. "My family has been having a lot of problems lately," one teenager writes. "My sisters . . . have been fighting nonstop, which puts my mother in a bad mood, so she nags everyone, which puts me in a bad mood, and then my dad comes home drunk every night, which puts everyone in a worse mood. . . . I'll do anything to get away from home."

Others use it as the one place they can be in charge. "Hi, I'm a mom of four very busy boys, 16, 13, 11, and 4. I'm always on the run with basketball. The Sims keep me sane, and they are my downtime."

But the other and more positive sensation you get in Sims world is that some mass creative process is going on, like the writing of a joint novel with millions of collaborative and competitive authors. We generally don't think that John Updike or Saul Bellow or Cynthia Ozick are pathetic because they escape from reality into richly populated fantasy worlds. We regard that process of creativity as something that enriches a life and yields deeper understandings about the real world. And the Sims players are doing something like that at their keyboards. The game is a superstructure for fantasy. The players become emotionally involved with their characters, celebrating their friendships and mourning them when they die. They engage in long debates about the virtual morality of Sims world and Sims fate. When Will Wright introduced a plague into the game, characters who bought a guinea pig but who didn't clean its cage got sick and sometimes died. The Sims fanatics had to figure out how to deal with this "reality."

Their fantasy, when you step back and look at it, is a remarkably realistic fantasy. The Sims is the most realistic computer game by far, but it is also more realistic than most contemporary novels that get produced by writing workshops. Unlike the fictional worlds that flow from the precious prose academies, the Sims world has the feel of real suburban life. It has the same emphasis on money making, shopping, coupling, and party throwing. The *Sims* characters have real-estate fantasies, just as real people do. They have consumer longings. And most of all, they have this desperate need to carve out a place for themselves amid the sprawl.

Unlike people, say, in a traditional Italian village, Sims characters have weak bonds—if any—to extended family or past generations, and they feel this intense need to tie themselves to others, to create some local community in which they can be happy. And all the shopping and decorating and party giving and bonding is part of that quest—the need to create your own roots in a mobile and individualistic world. That doesn't sound so strange for anybody living in modern America. Indeed, it's kind of inspiring. The creative process isn't just for art students and design professionals. It's alive out there amid the subdivisions.

focus.

1. Reread paragraph 9. Pay attention to Brooks's word choices, his punctuation, and the way he structures sentences. How do these mechanical choices contribute to his overall tone? What one word would you choose to classify Brooks's tone in this paragraph?

2. Brooks identifies two basic types of Sims players: those who seek material acquisitions and those who try to make friends. If you've played any of *The Sims* series, which kind of player are you? If not, which kind of player do you imagine yourself to be? How do people in real life function in ways similar to Sims players? How do they function differently?

3. Read the excerpt from the Sims novella in paragraph 12. Do you think stories like this fill any specific social function? If so, what? Does Sims fiction of this sort offer an important creative outlet for people? How do Sims stories differ from other outlets, such as art, journals, or therapy?

respond.

1. In his 1994 book *Simulacra and Simulation* (written before the heyday of reality shows), Jean Baudrilliard wrote, "TV is watching us." How true is this statement? Why have reality shows become so popular? Is it more interesting to watch real people than it is to watch fictional characters? Think about reality television shows and video games such as *The Sims.* How real are any of them? Create a chart that plots reality shows and video games on a continuum from more real to less real. Then write a paragraph about each show and game that explains why you consider it more or less real.

2. Brooks says that Sims fanatics may be "compensating online for needs that aren't met in their real lives," and in fact one advertising slogan for *The Sims* is "Be somebody. Else." Write an essay that analyzes the attraction of being someone else. What are the advantages and disadvantages? How much freedom do you have in creating an alternate self in *The Sims*?

picture this

constructing realities

Create an advertisement for an organization or group that you're a member of—a dorm, team, sorority, singing group, or religious organization. The purpose of the ad is to tell an audience what this group is or stands for as well as to give some sense of its character. You'll need to decide who your audience is and where the ad will be published in order to determine how to best write and design your ad.

1. Start by thinking about how you want to portray the group. In other words, what reality do you want to construct? You might think in terms of adjectives: Is it a serious group? creative? fun? attractive? wacky? something else?

2. You'll probably want to include an image of some kind—a photo, a symbol, some other graphic. If there's an image already available for you to use, think about what it projects and whether that's the kind of impression you want to create.

3. Next, you'll need to do some writing. Think carefully about what you want to say about the group and also about what your words and tone might suggest. You'll need to compose a headline—and, again, to think about what first impression it makes.

4. Finally, you'll need to design your ad to look "good" and, as important, to project the image about the group that you wish. Think carefully about what typeface(s) and font(s) you use.

gallery
of
images

constructing realities

① *Paris, Eiffel Tower*. Photo contact print by Thomas Kellner, 1977. Thomas Kellner creates photographs that consist of many fragmented views of buildings that are cultural icons. He starts by taking an entire roll of film of the building from different angles and then making a contact print, a proof sheet of single-frame images. The fragmented image that results from this process includes multiple views pieced together to form a whole.

② *Flying Goldfish*. Installation and photograph by Sandy Skogland, 1981. Sandy Skogland's sees her photographs
    as a kind of "film in one frame"—staged scenes in which the characters do not move or speak. They begin as
    installations, which she designs, constructs, and stages with figures who assume certain poses and gestures.
    Her work is often dreamlike, combining naturalism with bizarre colors and objects. The installation is
    photographed and exhibited simultaneously, causing viewers to reflect on the nature of photographic truth.

③ *London Tube Stop*. Photograph by Joel DeGrande. Using QuickTime and Photoshop computer programs, Joel DeGrande stitches together photographs taken in precisely calibrated increments to form a complete 360-degree image. This image then can be viewed in QuickTime as a moving image—or it can be cropped and flattened into a panoramic photograph as shown here. Time and space are thus combined and compressed into a single moment that is perceived as a snapshot. The image becomes more abstract as it is flattened, as we see simultaneously what is in front of us and behind us. The train on the left side is the same one we see on the right. The two tunnels are actually the same tunnel with light at one end, darkness at the other.

"I was trained to take images that were carefully worked out in my mind even prior to setting up the camera. Working "in the round" has released me from the preconceived image; the process is now fluid, with surprises right up to the final print. I never know what will be the main focal point until the end."

—Joel DeGrande

4 *Flight*. Photograph by Sam Mapp, 2002. Piecing together fifteen slices of two identical photographs, Sam Mapp created a kinetic photograph, one with movement. He allows the seams to show, showing us how the image was constructed. Mapp thus takes the compressed moment of a single snapshot and with the use of repetition extends time, thereby creating the illusion of movement.

5 *Seventh Avenue, New York City.* Photograph by Eli Reed, 1986. At first glance, Ronald Reagan appears to be standing on Seventh Avenue and actually walking towards us. In fact, he is made of cardboard, though he looks quite real in the midst of the very real pedestrians walking by him. You might say the cardboard figure is a constructed reality—as is this photograph.

⑥ *Photobooth*. Photos collected by Babbette Hines. The photobooth was created in 1925 by a Siberian immigrant named Anatol Josepho, and marketed as a way to make photography cheaply available to the masses as Ford did with automobiles. The device was an instant success and has remained popular to this day, inspiring and allowing us to carefully construct images of ourselves. As we can see from the child's photographs in the sampling of photobooth pictures shown here, only when we become conscious of our ability to create a reality in our recorded image, does the photo-strip take on the varied and posed look we associate with the photobooth.

"It doesn't matter whether you are in a train station, on a busy street, or in the middle of an amusement park. Nor does it matter whether you have deliberately sought out the booth to record a specific moment or happened upon one unexpectedly. What matters is that you are both photographer and subject. Alone in the booth, you forgo the behaviors and attitudes expected when a camera is forced upon you. You cannot be coaxed into position; you cannot be commanded to smile. You can be sexy or goofy or tough. You can even pretend to be happier than you really are, and you get eight (or at least four) chances to do it. And if, when the picture emerges after the interminable wait, you are not pleased with the results, if it doesn't tell the story you want, there is no proof that it ever existed.

A picture is worth a thousand words, knowing that words spoken are often false. Memory and imagination merge with fact and transform a single moment into an entire story, and eventually, all we will remember is the moment defined and distilled in the picture. When our memories are no longer accessible as actual memories, when they are simply stories that we tell, we will look at ourselves and show our friends and will say, "See here, this is how I was." It doesn't matter if the situation represented changed dramatically the very next day, that the lover we were so cozy with has broken our hearts, or that we have grown old and no longer resemble our youthful selves. In the photobooth picture, unlike any other portrait or photograph, truth and fiction commingle. In a photobooth we choose the moment and the way in which we represent ourselves. We choose our truth."

—Babette Hines, from Photobooth

picturing argument

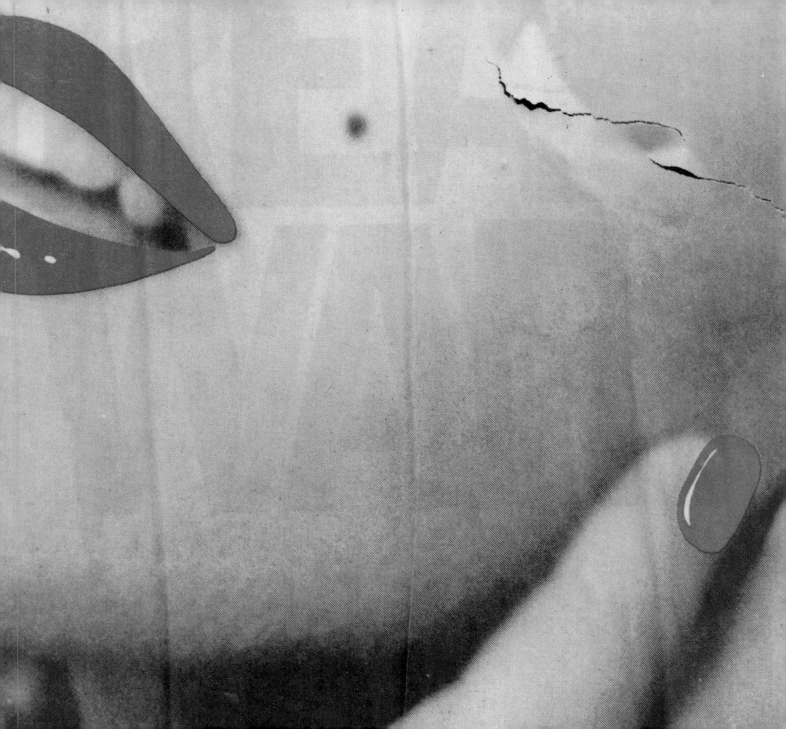

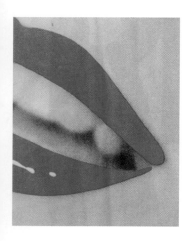

If you have ever seen the before-and-after photos standard in weight-loss and body-building ads, then you have seen—and read—a visual argument. Like written arguments, visual arguments make claims, stake out positions, or offer points of view. A before-and-after ad for a weight-loss product, for example, makes a claim: If you use this product, you'll have the same results as the person in the pictures. First-person testimony—"I quickly lost 30 lbs of bodyfat and got into the best shape of my life"—is often added, to support the claim and reinforce what the reader can see.

The visual evidence, however, is the heart of the argument, which is a straight-forward product claim: You can *see* what has happened to one person—and, by extension, what you can expect from the product—by just looking at the evidence. The "before" photo becomes part of the logic that leads to the usually larger, brighter "after" photo of a buffed and lean model. The reasoning goes something like this: If this guy can get into that kind of shape, this product can work for anybody.

Many visual arguments, especially in advertising, work the same way. They show results or warn of consequences. Sometimes that warning is expressed through a visual metaphor, such as in this 1980s antidrug poster, in which sniffing cocaine is likened to putting a gun up your nose. It isn't subtle, but

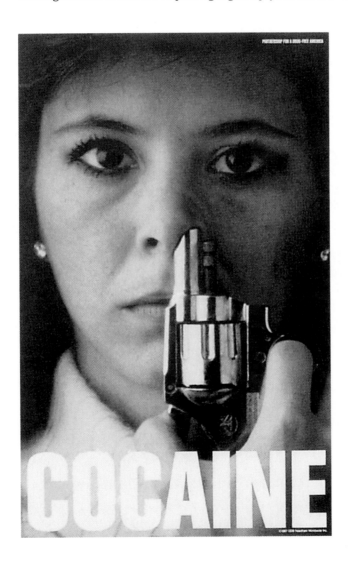

▶ Ad sponsored by the
Partnership for a Drug-
Free America

it is easy to read. Certainly, readers are not confused about the argument being made. How many people are actually persuaded by such heavy-handed tactics is another issue.

One charge often made about visual forms of persuasion is that they oversimplify and too easily boil down an argument to pro or con, black or white. In fact, a direct and uncompromising position is exactly what some designers are after in the arguments they construct. When the Episcopal Church ran the ad reproduced here, they used a device common in visual argument—juxtaposition—in order to make their position clear. This ad asks us to make a choice between two clear options, Santa or Jesus:

image conscious

Carefully read the Episcopal Church ad and, considering the question it poses, write a brief statement summarizing the ad's argument. In what ways is the argument more complex than it at first appears?

▶ Ad sponsored by the Episcopal Church.

386

"Whose birthday is it, anyway?" Juxtapositioning is also what makes the before-and-after formula work in weight-loss ads. As readers, we are asked to choose which of the two bodies we would like to have. Visual argument often asks us to think quickly, make a choice, notice a difference, or take a stand. Yet, visual arguments, like written arguments, can be simple or complex. They can also be serious, comic, or satirical. The Adbusters postcard here uses irony to challenge consumers to think about what void in their lives they are trying to fill with mindless purchases.

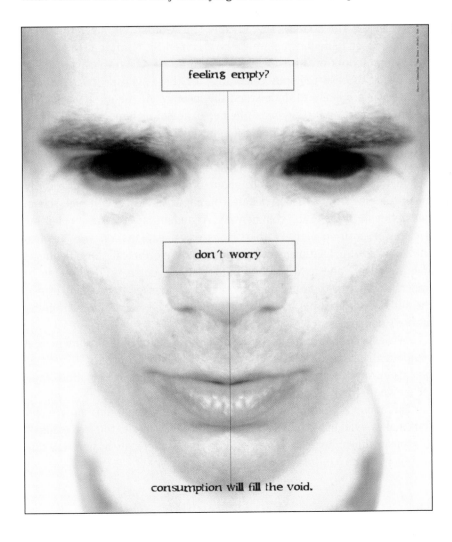

▶ Postcard distributed by Adbusters <www.adbusters.org>

We use arguments of various sorts to persuade readers of the value of some claim or position. When you present a claim or state a position you should assume that not everyone is going to accept that position without question. An argument must present reasons for an audience to regard its claim as one at least worth considering. Quite often, ad designers use visuals to convince readers without having to put the argument into words.

We can see the construction of a visual argument in the Episcopal Church Christmas ad. Once readers are reminded that Christmas is about religion and not presents, the ad team assumes, they will rethink the ways they celebrate the holiday. The ad copy (the words) reinforces this message but doesn't add much more to the argument. It is, after all, a message that will not work on all readers. Some—those not convinced that Christmas needs to be a religious celebration or those who do not celebrate Christmas—are likely to understand the meaning of the message but not be willing to act on it. They won't be persuaded of its importance.

The choices all writers and designers make depend on who they imagine their audience to be, what they want to convey, what their purpose is, and what medium and genre they select to convey the argument.

In this book, when we talk about argument, we don't necessarily mean the kind of pro-or-con debate you might associate with high school debate teams or television commentary. Argument often means presenting a claim or position along with reasons or an explanation why readers should accept the legitimacy of that position. We often call this a deliberative argument, one in which the author stakes out a way of seeing or understanding the topic at hand. In order for a message to have any effect, the audience at least has to accept the possibility of seeing things from the author's point of view.

We expect that sort of argument in advertising. But argument is a component whenever information is presented visually. Think, for example, about how a map works. In one sense, maps display information. They tell us where things are and how to get there.

But a map also visually constructs a way of understanding a place and thus makes a deliberative argument. Notice, for example, the two maps of Wisconsin shown here. Each map outlines the same territory, but very different areas and interests are defined and identified, within that territory, depending on what the mapmaker wants us to understand about the history of the state.

Mapmakers make their claims clear by drawing boundaries and by choosing what to leave in and what to leave out. After advertising, maps are one of the most common kinds of visual arguments we see in our daily lives. In fact, many travel and tourist maps, such as the 1936 map of Beverly Shores, Indiana, reprinted on the next page, actually *are* advertisements, identifying only certain hotels or restaurants and marking out tourist attractions such as museums, zoos, and historic locations. In other words, they argue for seeing a place in a particular way—as an interesting place to visit, or as a convenient place to stay.

▶ Map showing ethnic patterns in Wisconsin, ca. 1940.

▶ Map showing Native American settlement in Wisconsin, ca. 1830.

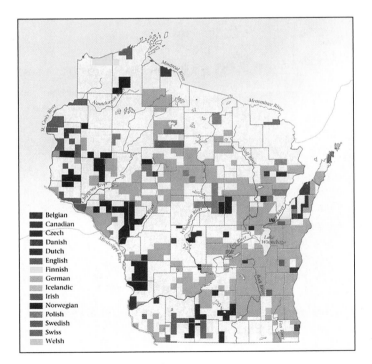

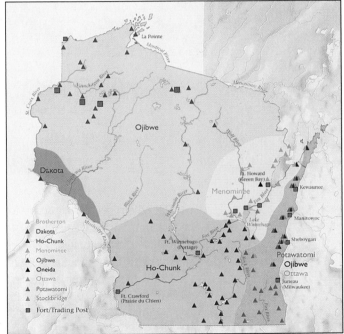

▶ A map of Beverly Shores, Indiana, showing the recreational possibilities of the town. Designed by the illustrator Helen Aldrich Swenson in 1936.

The advertiser's job, too, is to persuade potential customers to see a product in a particular way. Consider the Chrysler ad reprinted here. The ad presents its argument as a kind of equation that equals driving a Chrysler with love of some sort. It is meant to be read as "The open road minus a highway patrolman plus a Chrysler equals happiness."

It is doubtful that readers will take the ad as seriously as a math problem, but the advertiser very likely doesn't expect that kind of a reading. Instead, the ad asks readers to consider that it would be pleasurable to drive a powerful automobile (specifically, a Chrysler) down an open road if there were no one there to issue a speeding ticket. Not everyone will agree, but this particular advertisement is not aimed at readers who would seriously question the argument. This particular ad ran in *Outside* magazine, a publication addressed to readers who like adventure and, perhaps, speed, danger, and luxury. With that potential audience, the advertiser can assume that many readers might be attracted to their position.

An ad for the same product, placed in a publication aimed at a different audience, demands a different argument. See, for example, how the equation is refigured for *Newsweek*, a magazine read by a broader audience, including people likely to have families and busy, middle-class lifestyles: As in the first ad, the argument is primarily visual, partially because Chrysler is familiar enough without words and partially because the advertiser is selling an image, not a logical argument. The expanded explanation of the central equation (Drive = Love) changes somewhat each time the advertiser aims at a different audience, but the image of the open road and the Chrysler vehicle is very much the same in each ad.

▶ Chrysler "drive = love" ad from *Outside* magazine, 2002.

▶ Chrysler "drive = love" ad from *Newsweek*, 2002.

The arguments made in advertising rarely rely on visual elements alone. Almost always they combine images with words, and often the words shape the way we read the images, as in the ads shown here. In each of these ads, the images are key elements of the argument. The American Civil Liberties Union uses a picture of the signers of the Bill of Rights above a photo of Attorney General John Ashcroft to argue that Ashcroft is attempting to rewrite the Bill of Rights, a document that historically defines American freedom. Ashcroft's image, which appears confrontational and angry, is set as a contrast to the dignified print of the founders of the nation.

The images alone, however, cannot make the argument offered in this ad. Captions in large bold type label "The Author" and "The Editor." In smaller print, the ad makes a more explicit argument, but the immediate and the most emotional argument is made in the two images with their captions.

The ad featuring the photograph of Albert Einstein makes an argument of authority. This is a very familiar argument strategy in advertising. Famous persons often offer authority to a product or organization simply by lending their names and faces. In the case of the TIAA-CREF ad shown here, readers of *Harper's Magazine*, where it appeared, would certainly recognize Einstein as an instant icon for intelligence. The photo is in sepia, giving it the quality of a historic photograph. As for the words, they simply tell readers that the company has been around for more than eighty years and has been working with smart people that entire time.

Notice, however, what the designers have done with typeface sizes. The words "Albert Einstein" and "never wasted time thinking" are much larger and bolder than the other words, suggesting this ad is about to tell us something about the great man we never suspected. Instead, this is probably a tactic to make readers stop and read the rest of the text. The visual argument is "If this company was good enough for Albert Einstein, isn't it good enough for you?" The written text makes a fuller argument than that, of course—one that represents the company as a stable one working with educators over a long time.

image conscious

Locate an ad for a product that is likely to appeal to different audiences (soap, cars, coffee). How do the ad's visuals make their appeal to a specific audience? How would the visuals have to change if this ad were aimed at a very different audience?

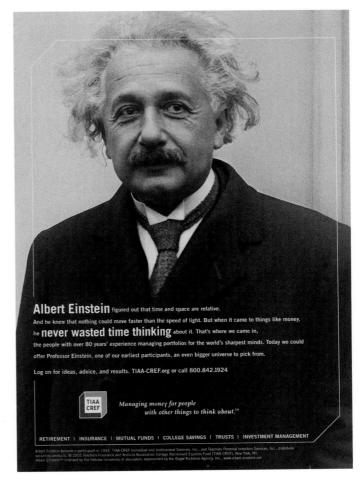

▶ Ad sponsored by the American Civil Liberties Union, 2003.

Both of these ads appeal to emotion. The ACLU ad appeals to our assumed loyalty to the U.S. Bill of Rights and is surely hoping to raise outrage, whereas the TIAA-CREF ad appeals to our desire to be associated with a great man. In each case, the written text is crucial to our understanding of the argument, but the images make the first and, perhaps, most powerful impression.

▶ Ad for the Teachers Insurance and Annuity Association–College Retirement Equities Fund, 2003.

From the moment the camera was invented, photography took on an importance that other visual media did not have. The camera could capture what was in front of it more accurately than any previous technology. Many hailed the camera as a machine that could reproduce scientific and objective truth as it appears in nature. They didn't think of photography as art. They thought of it as science.

We know today that photographic truth is fleeting, that pictures are easily manipulated, and that what the camera shows depends on what the person behind the camera decides to photograph and how that image is handled. Yet, one role that photography continues to play is to prove theories about the physical world. Some of the earliest experiments with the camera were photos taken to capture physical movement in time.

The photos of Harold Edgerton, Eadweard Muybridge, and others constitute a particular kind of argument, using pictures as evidence that an event occurred in a particular way. The Edgerton photo series of a milk drop is one famous example, providing visual evidence of what happens when a drop of milk hits a surface. Today we see time-lapse films of flowers opening, ice fields melting in an Arctic spring, sunflowers turning to follow the light—all of which constitute a kind of argument that movement is occurring whether or not we can see it with the naked eye.

Other photos have been used to settle arguments. Muybridge, for example, took a series of photos of horses running to settle a bet with Leland Stanford over whether or not a running horse's feet are ever all up in the air at the same time (they are). His photos then changed other visual depictions of horses; before the Muybridge horse series, Degas and other painters had depicted running horses with their four feet spread out in different directions—a very un-horse-like gait.

▶ Eadweard Muybridge's photos showing that a horse's feet can be all in the air at the same time, 1872.

Documentary photography continues this tradition of the photo as evidence. Early photos by social activist Jacob Riis, for example, argued for a change in tenement housing in New York City at the turn of the twentieth century. During the Great Depression of the 1930s, U.S. government photographers such as Marion Post Wolcott, Dorothea Lange, Walker Evans, and Arthur Rothstein documented the Dust Bowl, migration west, tenant farming, and small-town life—images that helped the Roosevelt administration argue for New Deal policies. In the 1960s, Danny Lyons documented the Civil Rights movement in Albany, Georgia, for white northerners who knew little of the realities of segregation. In these examples, images both made arguments and provided evidence for those arguments. The photograph thus made a claim and, in some cases, asked readers to accept the camera as dispassionate witness

▶ *Untitled*, by Dorothea Lange, 1937. Unemployed family from Texas camped out on a river bottom near Hottville, California.

This chapter offers a range of visual arguments—maps, book covers, posters, photographs, advertisements—to use both as prompts for discussion and analysis and as models for your own visual arguments. In any visual argument, you need to take into account what it is you want to argue, what medium and genre are appropriate, what audience you wish to address, and what visual and verbal elements you need in order to present a readable and a credible argument. In other words, you will want to consider many of the same things in a visual argument that you would in a verbal argument. See the chart on page 397 for a list of questions you'll want to consider in making a visual argument.

You're probably not a professional photographer or designer, and you might not even consider yourself very artistic. Still, you can make visual arguments using whatever skills and materials you have at hand. The key is to let the visual carry as much of the message as possible. The more familiar an image is, the more quickly your audience will get your meaning. If you are making an original design, think about what you must include to make your meaning as clear as possible. You might need to juxtapose one image with another or to add words that emphasize or clarify your position.

Think of a visual argument as a way to make your position stand out in a world saturated with information. Your goal is to make both an immediate and a long-lasting impact.

s n a p s h o t

Although you might not think of them in this way, the photographs in real estate ads function as visual arguments. They argue that this is a place you will want to buy—a good place to raise a family, perhaps, or to entertain, to retire, or something else. Look in your local papers and on the Internet for real estate ads that include images of the property. What arguments do these images make? Create your own ad in which you make an argument about a place for sale or rent. Think about what you want the visual to convey and about what written words you need to go along with the visual.

- What do you plan to argue? (What is your claim? your position?)

- How would you describe your audience? What do they know about your subject, and why would they care about it? How are they likely to respond to your position?

- What evidence or reasons will you offer to convince your audience to take your argument seriously?

- Why choose a visual argument? What, if anything, can you accomplish with a visual argument that you cannot accomplish with a verbal argument?

- Where is your text likely to appear?

- What medium and genre will you use for your argument? Why?

- What will be the balance between verbal and visual? Can you make your argument with no words at all? with only a few words?

- What is the basic argument? What is the claim, the position, or the point of view proposed in the text you are examining?

- What seems to be the purpose of this argument? Is it asking you to do something? to think differently about something?

- Who is the target audience? How do you know?

- What genre of visual is it—a poster? a cartoon? a public service ad? a commercial ad? a photograph? a billboard?

- Where does (or will) this argument appear?

- Is there anything in the image or words that surprises you, makes you laugh, makes you think differently?

- What visual elements help you read the argument? Is there juxtapositioning? visual metaphors? visual evidence?

- What else do you know about this visual? Does it remind you of something else? Is it a common logo or symbol?

- Are there any words? Are they used to state the main argument or to support the argument made by the visual?

Elaine Reichek is a New York artist who has shown her work extensively in museums and galleries throughout the world. She works in several different media, including embroidery, weaving, and photocollage. The 1991 image reproduced here is a photocollage. Speaking to an interviewer about this image, Reichek explained its title and her use of old movie scenes that form a circle around the central figure:

> A lot of white people are familiar with the use of the word "oreo" among African-Americans to apply to someone who's black on the outside, white on the inside, like the cookie. Native Americans use "apple" for the same thing—someone who's red on the outside, white on the inside. So that's what *Red Delicious* is about. The central image is Wright of Derby's painting *Grieving Indian Widow*. It supposedly shows a Native American woman, though she could be anyone really—she certainly could be white. She has this little headdress on that's like a cocktail hat, and she's sitting on a rock in a sort of Grecian pose with one breast bare. It's the mythology of the noble savage. The painting is deeply romantic, and pictorially its models are Greek revival, neoclassical. I surrounded the woman with stills from B-movies in which an Indian is doing something horrible to a white woman—movie style. They float around her in a circle, like the stars in the Paramount logo. And for me it had to do with how the "other" is always perceived as threatening "our" women. It's all a male construction.

This picture and commentary are from the photography magazine *Aperture*.

Red Delicious

ELAINE REICHEK

"The trouble with photography is that it gives you the illusion that it's possible to see purely. In a limited way, the camera catches so accurately what's in front of it that you think that's all there is to say. In fact, of course, the very idea that that's all there is to say is part of an attitude, a cultural stance, a politics, an ideology, a whole mental structure of which the camera is only a small part. In the work I do with photographs—choosing them, coloring them (or not), copying them into other media—I try to reveal that structure of thought: an iceberg with the photograph tiny at its tip. I want to be the woman who put the kink in the straightness of photography."

—ELAINE REICHEK

1. What argument does the photocollage make? What in the text conveys that argument?

2. In her commentary, Reichek says that photography doesn't always show us what we want to see. What does she mean by that? How might a medium such as photocollage work better for expressing what an artist is trying to say than a single photograph would?

3. How might photocollage "put a kink in the straightness of photography," as Reichek says she wants to do?

1. Write an essay on Reichek's *Red Delicious* in which you first explain the argument she is making and then explain what in the photocollage supports that argument. In your essay, take into account Reichek's discussion of this work. Who would you say is Reichek's audience? Are additional readings of this image possible? What are they?

2. Using *Red Delicious* as a model, create a photocollage of your own. You might start with a familiar image and then surround it with images that force your audience read the original in a different way.

   If you are familiar with programs such as Photoshop, you can create the argument as a digital design, but you can also make it using scissors and glue. Decide on a topic, your argument, the central image, your primary audience, your materials, and the title. The title is important for a photocollage because it helps viewers understand how you want them to read the image.

3. Once you have completed your collage, show it to five different viewers. You can use other students, but it will also be useful to show your visual to people outside the class who aren't thinking in terms of visual argument. Ask your viewers what they think the collage is saying. What is it about? Does it make an argument? What difficulties do they have understanding your argument?

   Once you have gathered these responses and suggestions, revise your collage and write an explanation of the changes you made in response to your audience.

Jesse Levine is a graphic designer whose Turnabout Map has become a classic example of using design to overturn our normal way of seeing things. In the world map most Americans are used to seeing, north is at the top. North America and Europe figure prominently. We have grown up seeing that map displayed on our classroom walls, on posters, in newspapers, in textbooks, and in atlases. For most of us, that map represents what we think the world looks like. We don't think of it as an argument for one way of seeing the world. We simply take it for granted. Levine's Turnabout Map forces us to question that way of seeing the world.

"Since 'on top,' 'over,' and 'above' are equated with superiority, while 'down there,' 'beneath,' and 'below' imply the reverse," Levine argues, we can get a new understanding of the world if we simply reverse the way we normally position the Americas.

Turnabout Map—
A New World of Understanding

JESSE LEVINE

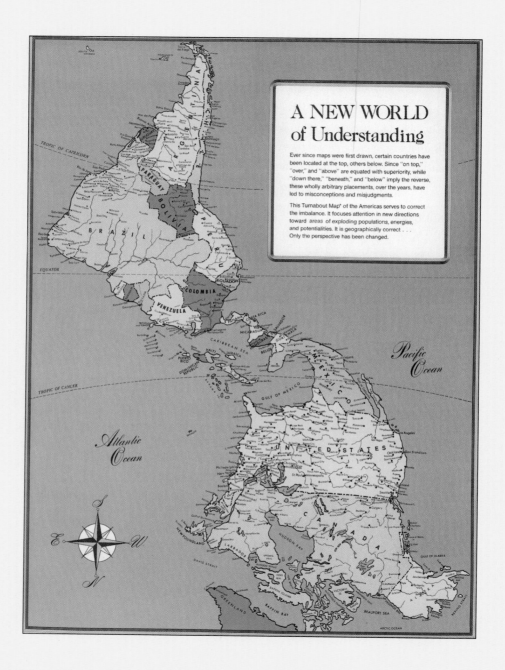

A NEW WORLD
of Understanding

Ever since maps were first drawn, certain countries have been located at the top, others below. Since "on top," "over," and "above" are equated with superiority, while "down there," "beneath," and "below" imply the reverse, these wholly arbitrary placements, over the years, have led to misconceptions and misjudgments.

This Turnabout Map* of the Americas serves to correct the imbalance. It focuses attention in new directions toward areas of exploding populations, energies, and potentialities. It is geographically correct . . . Only the perspective has been changed.

focus.

1. Levine's map was designed in 1982. What do you know about the political relations among North and Central and South America at that time? What does Levine's map argue about those relationships? If you were not able to research the political activity of the late 1970s and early 1980s, what would you guess about those relationships based on your reading of Levine's map?

2. Why do you think Levine felt he needed to explain his reasons for turning the traditional map upside down? How might you read this map if it did not contain the explanation?

3. To what extent has Levine accomplished his purpose—to provide a new perspective—by reorienting the map of the Americas?

respond.

1. Considering political events today, design a map of the world that argues that relations between regions or nations currently in conflict should change. This could be any sort of conflict—struggles in the Middle East, ongoing disputes between Britain and Ireland, arguments over free trade agreements or globalization of the marketplace—any conflict that involves ways of seeing national or international relationships.

   In creating your map, you can use any existing map and reconfigure it to make your visual argument. As with Levine's map, include a brief legend explaining your design choices.

2. No map can show everything that's there. The cartographer must choose details such as which towns to include on a map. Many American small towns that were once on the route to cities or tourist destinations are now easily bypassed on the highways and are literally "off the map." Their removal means they are even less likely to draw travelers or tourist dollars. Towns work very hard to make sure that they are not taken off the map.

   Get a map of an area you know well. After you have looked at it carefully, write a brief analysis of how that map

represents the place. What choices did the cartographer make? What is highlighted? What is left off? Redesign the map to argue for a different way of seeing the same place.

3. Earlier in this chapter are two maps of Wisconsin that argue for two ways of seeing that state. Make a map of your own state that argues for one way of seeing it. You might focus on agriculture, industry, transportation, superhighways, back roads, higher education, age demographics, fast-food restaurants, discount stores. This will take research, so choose a topic you can find information on, decide how you will represent each region (for instance, is it going to be a serious or satiric map?), and then produce it.

Michaela Sullivan is a staff designer at Houghton Mifflin. In 1998, she designed the book cover shown here for *King Leopold's Ghost*, a book by Adam Hochschild about Leopold II of Belgium. The old saying "You can't tell a book by its cover" is often true. Many book-cover designs don't tell us what we might actually find inside. Yet a book jacket is meant as an advertisement. After all, we buy most books before we have read them. Books must vie for our attention on display racks or on Internet bookstore sites, many of which show the book cover and little else. The cover, then, must persuade us to buy the book by convincing us that we want to read what is inside. A cover such as Sullivan's can also reflect the argument of the book. Sullivan uses a simple technique—placing one image behind another in order to suggest that the two images have something to do with one another—to make a complicated argument. In this case, the official state portrait of Leopold II of Belgium, who colonized the Congo and initiated the horrors of the ivory and rubber trades in that region, is placed over a photo of mutilated Congolese children. These children, Sullivan suggests, haunt Leopold's memory; his portrait is more complete by adding the realities of Leopold's rule.

King Leopold's Ghost

MICHAELA SULLIVAN

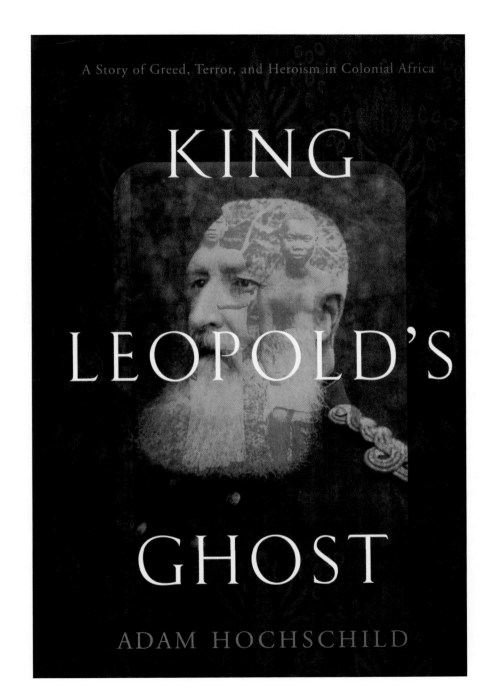

1. How would the book cover's argument change if Sullivan had not used the photo of Congolese children in her design—if, instead, she simply reprinted Leopold's official state portrait?

2. Choose a textbook from one of your classes and discuss with a group of students what argument the cover design makes about the book. Is it meant to seem hip? serious? Something else? Does the design appeal more to the students or to the instructor who chose the book for your course? What in the design makes you read it the way you do?

3. With a group of students, examine the book covers reprinted here. From looking at the cover design, what do you expect to be in the book? Who is the audience for this book? From what you can determine, is there an argument or a position being staked out in the cover art that you would expect to be reflected in the content of the book? What, if anything, does the cover remind you of?

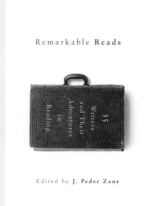

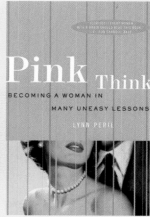

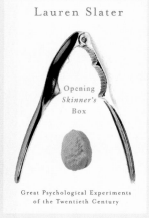

respond.

1. Examine the following two cover designs for the same novel, Edward Carey's *Observatory Mansions*. The second is a redesign of the first. According to the design firm, Pylon Design, Inc., the first version "failed to capture the disturbing content of this novel. The client felt that it could be better executed. We agreed. With the help of Gary Clement, a Toronto-based illustrator, Pylon pulled it off. Our concept, a portrayal of the main character's personal inventory, was painstakingly brought to life by Gary's illustration talent and careful handwriting."

   In a 2–3 page analysis of these two designs, explain what they convey about the book. Why might the designers identify the second as conveying "disturbing content"?

2. Choose a favorite book and redesign the cover to better convey what you believe is the central argument of the book. Consider the audience. Is this a book for young people or for adults? What do you want potential readers to think about this book? Is there a scene or an idea you can convey with a simple image?

3. When you have completed your book design, write an explanation of what you were trying to convey and what choices you made to create your argument. How did you address your target audience? Why do you think they will understand your argument? What features have you used to communicate to a particular kind of reader?

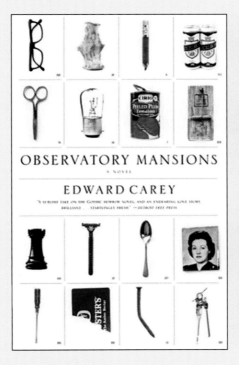

Jason Berry is an investigative journalist living and writing in Louisiana. He has written several books, including *Lead Us Not into Temptation*, a history of clergy sex abuse, and *Louisiana Faces: Images from a Renaissance,* with photographs by Philip Gould. **Richard Misrach** is a photographer who has spent much of his life photographing the American desert, revealing the effects of industry on the landscape. The photograph in this essay was taken in 1998 along the Louisiana shoreline of the Mississippi River. The essay first appeared in 2001 in the photography magazine *Aperture*.

Documentary photography historically has offered powerful visual evidence to support arguments about the environment, social and political issues, and more. Of course, every documentary photograph is created by a photographer who has a point of view—someone who very likely sees an opportunity both to show what is there and to make a good picture. In other words, though the documentary photograph makes its argument through visual evidence, that argument—like any argument—is a product of both the technology (the camera) and the author (the photographer).

In the essay that follows, Jason Berry examines the role of photography in uncovering environmental disasters.

Cancer Alley: The Poisoning of the American South

JASON BERRY
PHOTOGRAPHY BY RICHARD MISRACH

"Baton Rouge was clothed in flowers, like a bride— no, much more so; like a greenhouse. For we were in the absolute South now," wrote Mark Twain of the vistas from a riverboat in his 1883 classic *Life on the Mississippi*. "From Baton Rouge to New Orleans," he continued, "the great sugar-plantations border both sides of the river all the way, and stretch their league-wide levels back to the dim forest of bearded cypress in the rear. The broad river lying between the two rows becomes a sort of spacious street."

Twain caught the ninety-mile river corridor between the old Capitol and New Orleans at a poignant moment. Plantations still harvested prof- its in cotton and sugarcane; the black field workers, no longer slaves, were sharecroppers or virtual serfs. The river flowed through a land riddled with injustice. Yet there was beauty in the waterway and surrounding landscape, and beauty—although burdened with an unsavory history—in those old houses of "the absolute South," with their porticoes and pillared balconies.

By the 1940s, when Clarence John Laughlin trained his lens upon the area, some of the mansions had been torn down and others lay in ruins. The wrecked buildings riveted his eye as much as the several dozen that were still preserved (then starting to shift from farming to tourist sites, which most remain today). A haunting sense of loss suffuses the black-and-white surrealism in Laughlin's remarkable book *Ghosts Along the Mississippi*.

Between the time of Twain's reportage and Laughlin's elegiac photographs from the mid-twentieth century, oil and petrochemical producers bought up vast pieces of land along the river and began grafting an industrial economy over the old agricultural estates. The refineries and plants—like the derricks that dot the Cajun prairie and the oil-production platforms in Louisiana coastal waters off the Gulf of Mexico—boosted the economies of communities once mired in poverty. The downside has been a political mentality blind to the ravages of pollution.

ORIGINS OF CANCER ALLEY

Standard Oil opened a refinery in 1909 on the fringes of Baton Rouge. In 1929 Governor Huey P. Long erected the new Capitol, a thirty-four-story Art Deco tower near the Standard plant. Today that political temple stands out in high relief from the expanded grid of pumping stacks and smoke clouds where Exxon (Standard's successor) functions like a city-within-the-city. The Capitol and the massive oil complex issuing pungent clouds have melded into an awesome symbol of Louisiana politics: pollution as the price of power.

Providence Plantation, which dated to the 1720s, was in the river town of Des Allemands, and on its grounds was a massive tree known as the Locke Breaux Live Oak, which was 36 feet around and 101 feet high, with a limb span of 172 feet. That majestic tree, estimated to be over three hundred years old, died from exposure to pollution in 1968: the new owner of its site, Hooker Chemical, had it cut up and removed.

The human toll has been even more harsh.

By the 1980s, according to the Louisiana Office of Conservation, thousands of oil-waste pits, many leaching toxic chemicals, were scattered across Louisiana; hundreds of them were seeping into areas of the fertile rice belt in Cajun country. As awareness spread about groundwater contamination and diseases in communities along the river's industrial corridor, activists began calling the area "Cancer Alley."

Although Louisiana ranks in the top 10 percent of states in terms of its cancer mortality rate, petrochemical interests dismiss the term "Cancer Alley" as factually unsupported, a provocation. Black irony coats their charge.

The Louisiana Chemical Association provided base funding for the state Tumor Registry, which assembles the data on cancers. The registry is undertaken by a division of the Louisiana State University Medical Center, which is a beneficiary of donations from polluting industries. Louisiana's Tumor Registry, unlike those in most other states, offers no reliable data on incidences of childhood cancer, or incidences by parish (county), or incidences on a yearly basis. It reports trends only in larger geographic groupings; as a result, disease clusters cannot be pinpointed. Rare forms of cancer can't be tracked geographically. Much information gathered by physicians who treat cancer patients is anecdotal.

And that, in the opinion of Dr. Patricia Williams, is just the way business and petrochemical lobbyists want it. "Without reliable data, no one

can link disease patterns to pollution," says Williams, who is herself a professor at the LSU Medical School, and is at the forefront of attempts to change the system.

"We're being denied the raw data and it's unconscionable," says Williams. "Embryonic tumors are not being reported as they are diagnosed. Raw data, by parish, would allow prevention programs. If you see a particular trend of brain cancers, you could begin to sort out what's going on. . . . The same [holds true] with cancer clusters."

Despite the state's history of being at or near the top of statistical lists in categories of toxic emissions, plaintiff attorneys have a great deal of trouble getting medical data to prove the impact of pollution in a given community.

* * *

Like Clarence John Laughlin before him, Richard Misrach captures the tones of a culture in spiritual twilight—clinging to a past beauty in the old mansions and icons of Catholicism—now facing a darkness brought about by big oil. Misrach's use of color sets him apart from Laughlin stylistically, as does his striking sense of juxtapositions: the petrochemical specters shadowing fields, ponds, buildings, cemeteries, and basketball courts. Misrach's commitment to discovering the ravaged landscape, while conceptually similar to Laughlin's, is rooted in the land itself. His longterm exploration of the American West and its defilement, the epic *Desert Cantos*, are relentlessly straightforward. The *Bravo 20* series of the late 1980s—photographs of Nevada's disturbingly stunning bombing ranges—allow the terrain to create its own dark metaphors. Misrach's work reveals the primary emblems and moods of these frightening landscapes; the Louisiana images are thus as mysterious as they are horrific.

CITIZENS TAKE A STAND

Clarence Laughlin was a romantic who saw industry in symbolic terms—machine against man. In 1980, he took a firm stand at a news conference in New Orleans, lashing out against a plan to put the world's largest toxic-waste incinerator next to the historic Houmas House plantation, in Ascension Parish, midway along the river corridor south of Baton Rouge. A California-based company called Industrial Tank (I.T.) had begun with a $350,000 grant from the state government in Baton Rouge for a site feasibility study. I.T. recommended the construction of a massive disposal complex on a piece of land that was a proven flood plain, below sea level, in an already congested industrial road fronting the Mississippi River. In a move that reeked of corrupt politics, state officials then awarded I.T. the necessary permits to build the complex—whose feasibility I.T. had just been paid to assess. (In fact, the company had put money down on the land before it even got the permits.)

Reports soon surfaced that I.T. had pollution problems at its California sites and was utterly inexperienced in managing a project of the scope envisioned in Louisiana. A citizens' group filed suit against I.T. and the state. In 1984, the state Supreme Court threw out the permits, killing the project. By then, activists were challenging industry over other conflicts.

DYNAMICS OF CHANGE

Amos Favorite, a seventy-eight-year-old black man, is now retired after many years in the union at Ormet Aluminum. Favorite grew up speaking the Creole French patois in the town of Vacherie, where Fats Domino was born. He remembers when ponds

▶ *West Bank Mississippi River, near Dow Chemical plant, Plaquemine, Louisiana, 1998.* Photo by Richard Misrach.

were blue. As a teenager he moved to nearby Geismar, where he has lived ever since.

"This was a good place to live at one time," says Favorite. "All the meat was wild game. I was raised on rabbits, squirrels, and deer." He hated work in the fields, however, and when he came home from infantry in World War II, Favorite bought a dozen acres of Geismar plantation, which was being sold off at thirty-five dollars an acre. The town is named for the family that owned the estate. Favorite's nine children grew up on his acreage; one of his sons was building a handsome two-story house next door to Amos Favorite's this past August.

One of his daughters, artist Malika Favorite, was the first black child to desegregate the local white school. Because of that, two KKK members tried to dynamite the family home. Before they could set the charge, Amos Favorite took his shotgun and started blasting. "I gave 'em the red ass, yes I did," he laughs. "They went runnin' to the sheriff, but that sheriff didn't do nothin' to me."

That was in 1968. A few years later, Favorite 20 began to realize that people were getting sick from wells that drew water from the local aquifer, and he started speaking out against Ascension Parish's sacred cow: industry. BASF, the largest chemical company in the world, and Vulcan, which produces perchloroethylene (the chemical that goes into dry cleaning fluid), have plants in the area.

Despite opposition from management at thirteen major plants in Geismar, including BASF and Vulcan, Favorite won support from union members in those industries for his attempt to establish a public water system and separate district for Geismar. Favorite found a valuable ally in Willie Fontenot, the environmental investigator in the state attorney general's office. Fontenot has made a career of helping communities organize and gather research against polluters and unresponsive state agencies.

"The local government in Ascension had failed to provide adequate water," says Fontenot. "Amos Favorite and the Labor Neighbor project [a cross section of activists from various walks of life] broke the impasse and got the Baton Rouge water company to extend piping and set up a distribution system in Ascension to supplant the old private wells. . . . It was a pretty big victory for a ragtag citizens' group."

The most recent "ragtag" victory came in the town of Convent, where a company called Shintech wanted to build a huge chemical plant in an area of low-income black residents. Tulane University's Environmental Law Clinic helped the citizens challenge the state's operating permits, citing new EPA standards to guard against environmental racism. Shintech pulled out, and found another site, rather than risk being the first major test case of EPA's guidelines. The law clinic took a pounding from Governor Mike Foster and the State Supreme Court, which issued a ruling that severely restricts law students from working with community groups on environmental cases.

The people who live and work in this region of the Mississippi take a long view of their struggle. "The pendulum is going to swing," says Dr. Williams, who lives in LaPlace, twenty miles upriver from New Orleans. "Pollution is such a problem that people are becoming aware of cancers in their friends. They're becoming suspicious. Ten or fifteen years from now, what has happened to big tobacco companies is going to happen to industries that are polluting here." A surge of civil-damage suits against industry is inevitable, she predicts, "because there has been such a concerted effort to conceal what's happened."

focus.

1. Berry opens his essay with a quote from Mark Twain. Why does he use this quote? How does it set up his description of Cancer Alley?

2. Misrach's photo "documents"—provides evidence for—pollution along the Mississippi. It is also quite beautiful. Considering the contrast between its content (pollution) and the beauty of its form (the mist rising out of the river, for example), what argument does this image make about Cancer Alley?

3. How does Misrach's photo add to or help shape Berry's argument? In what ways would Berry's argument have to change if there were no photo?

respond.

1. In his article, Berry compares Misrach's photos of the Louisiana shoreline to Clarence John Laughlin's photos from a book called *Ghosts Along the Mississippi*. See Laughlin's *The Besieging Wilderness, Number Two*, reprinted on page 417. After examining the Laughlin and Misrach photos, write an explanation of the comparison Berry is making between the two photographers. How are they similar? In what ways is their work very different? What argument does each make? Address your explanation to your fellow students.

2. Create a photographic record of an environmental issue in your area and write a companion article, using Berry's as a model. Notice that Berry considers the Louisiana shoreline in several contexts: the great plantations of Mark Twain's day, the ruined mansions of the 1940s, and the refineries and industrial plants of Cancer Alley. Try to explore different contexts in your article using your photographs to show the place as it is now and using your words to give your readers a larger, more historic view of the place as it once was.

3. One way that environmental organizations advance their arguments is through ad campaigns. Look at the ad created above by a student and one reprinted at left about reducing pollution. It makes a very simple argument: One easy way to reduce pollution is by drinking from reusable cups.

Choose an issue that interests you and create an ad with a simple argument like this one, using a headline that addresses readers directly ("Take one cup to reduce pollution") and an image your audience will easily recognize.

Shirley Ann Grau is a Louisiana-born author of several novels and collections of short stories. Her novel *The Keepers of the House* was awarded a Pulitzer Prize for fiction. Photographer **Clarence John Laughlin** (1905–1985) spent most of his career in and around New Orleans, where he photographed abandoned mansions, overgrown cemeteries, and the ruins of what has come to be called the Old South. Throughout his life, he experimented with a number of ways to tell the stories of these places and the people who once lived there. Many of his photos use double exposures or include mysterious figures in windows or among fallen stones to capture haunting images of Louisiana.

The following essay is Grau's contribution to *Haunter of Ruins*, a collection of photos by Laughlin. For Grau, photographs such as Laughlin's are memories of a past that has been displaced by modern inventions and a faster lifestyle.

Memory, Mint Juleps, and My Grandfather

SHIRLEY ANN GRAU
PHOTOGRAPHY BY CLARENCE JOHN LAUGHLIN

Memory, my grandfather used to say, is a most amazing thing. It is what makes a human being human. It is what links one generation to another. Common memories are the cement of civilization.

Whenever he began talking like that, it meant that he was about to launch into one of his long disquisitions. (Tirades, my grandmother called them; ruminative soliloquies, he said.) He first poured himself a highball, added sugar until there was a half inch deposit on the bottom of the glass. Then he went into the kitchen garden to pick a long sprig of mint for top garnish. If it was late in the year, if there had been a hard frost and the mint had shriveled or vanished completely, he would stand contemplatively for a few minutes, stubbing at the clump with his toe. "I will keep this under glass next year." He never did, of course. He never even thought of it again until the next time he wanted a fragrant green decoration.

Anyway, there was no room in his small greenhouse. It was jammed—bench, shelf, floor, and even ceiling—with horticultural enthusiasms. There was a special kumquat bush, as stubby and round as a fat man. And an eight-foot-tall avocado tree grown from a pit. It was pruned every year and then hauled out into the summer sun by a sweating three-man crew; it actually did produce fruit, hard and dry and quite inedible. A bougainvillea vine, leggy and thorny with occasional raggedy clusters of brilliant pink flowers, dangled from the rafters overhead. And all the small pots—row on row of scrawny plants, dozens and dozens of them, the waifs and strays of the botanical world. My grandfather's lifelong ambition was to discover an unknown species, some bit of green that would carry his name into the obscure lists in reference books. The pursuit of that dream led him to search the corners of old pastures and the kudzu-covered chimneys of burned-out farmhouses, even litter-filled city lots. The cuttings and clippings, the seeds and bulbs, and corms and rhizomes all came into his greenhouse, to be housed in neat numbered rows and inspected carefully, if sporadically. They were all failures; not one proved a suitable vehicle for his immortality. Most sulked and dwindled in their pots until they were finally swept away by one of the periodic epidemics of insects or virus that swept through the small space. "I am," he declared loudly to anyone who would listen, "a magician. For me plants grow back into the ground and disappear. . . ."

One small compact yellow iris showed brilliant yellow flowers, but it was soon identified as a well-known wild variety. A mysterious shoot of rosebush from an abandoned garden sulked for three years before producing the blooms that identified it as Lady Banksia. Not in the least discouraged, he went on searching. And, of course, year after year he forgot to pot his own garden's mint for wintering over. The great power of human memory that he extolled so eloquently did not include such small homey housekeeping details.

Faced with the complete absence of mint, my 5 grandfather shrugged and lifted his eyes to the sky, dramatically, a man in despair. On one such occasion, he spotted me watching him. He beckoned me over and delivered to a bewildered ten-year-old a complicated explanation of the concept of Tyche, or

Fate, among the ancient Greeks. I didn't understand a single word, but I was immensely flattered.

Slowly, ponderously, with the air of an elephant moving through the brush, my grandfather left the herb garden for the house, the kitchen, and the refrigerator.

A refrigerator, not an icebox. A mechanical marvel that was his pride and joy, a yellowish bow-legged structure with a condenser coil like a crown on top, that wheezed and purred and produced strange-tasting air-bubble-flecked ice cubes.

(My grandmother still kept an icebox, large and sleek and newly purchased from Sears, on the back porch. The iceman still came twice a week to slip his heavy burlap-wrapped block into the upper compartment. He stayed for a moment or two, foot propped on the top step, to tell my grandmother the latest neighborhood gossip, while she gave him her selections for the day's horse racing at various tracks around the country. He placed the bets with a mysterious bookie known only as Mr. Andrew.)

My grandfather ignored the icebox, went straight to the refrigerator, and checked the contents carefully, as if he expected a bunch of mint to appear miraculously. Finally, with a deep theatrical sigh, he removed a sprig of parsley from the bunch that was always kept, wrapped in a damp cloth, on the second shelf. He then tucked the long-stemmed bit of green into his drink, adjusted the angle to the proper rakish tilt. He was ready.

He settled himself on the front porch, in a cane 10 rocker specially made to accommodate his long legs. Chairside there was a low round table on which my grandmother kept a small bunch of flowers or a sweet potato vine or a bit of ivy. Whatever it was, my grandfather always put it on the floor, carelessly, not caring if trailing vines were crushed under the rockers. He rode his chair hard, feet crashing down each time, chair moving across the porch as if it had wheels. He'd worn tracks into the floor; they crisscrossed back and forth across the gray painted boards.

There, whatever the weather, in his chair on his porch, he had his drink—toddy, he called it. (And the glass, he insisted, was a proper toddy glass, from Ireland.) In cold months the porch was enclosed by an elaborate set of hinged windows, awkward heavy panels that took several days to install. During warm weather those panels were stored under the house in neat three-deep piles. There was plenty of room for them there—it was an old-fashioned house, built high off the ground. Its dim sheltered spaces provided convenient storage for adults. For children the entire area was a mysterious playground, cool in summer, cold in winter, smelling always of the heavy rich sweet earth. In summer my cats and dogs and I explored the tangled jumble of pipes and wiring and hid out, bandits in our secret cave, to watch the feet of passersby. In winter sacks of oysters were kept there, and bags of potatoes and onions. And once, weeks before Christmas, I found my special present: a red and silver two-wheel bike, partially assembled, still in its box.

After a few moments the rocking slowed. The chair had moved itself next to the porch rail, the glass with its garnish of mint or parsley was half empty. And the neighborhood children had arrived. There were always six or eight of them, more during summer vacation, most of all during the Christmas holidays. Boys and girls ready to hear a story.

He always started the same way, with a question. "Answer me this. When you young people came up the front steps a minute ago, you walked right by a cat. What color was he? Don't anybody turn around. . . . You didn't notice? Well then, what color is this house painted? No, it's not gray. You're just guessing because you don't know. I ought to send you home. . . . If you can't remember, how do you know you've been here? Maybe you aren't here. Think of that. Maybe you're not sitting on this porch, maybe you didn't come up the steps past the cat. Maybe this house isn't here at all. If you don't remember, you might just as well stay home, stay in bed, because you aren't really seeing anything or thinking anything or being anywhere."

Then, warmed by his own peroration, he began to tell stories. He had the diction of an old-fashioned Shakespearean actor. (Some of the children thought he had come from a distant, exotic place, so artificial were those dulcet voice tones.) His whispers could be heard down the block, his shouts shook the pigeons from their roosts under the eaves.

They were good stories; they were wonderful stories. They were filled with action and adventure, with daring exploits and hairbreadth escapes. And they were always told in the first person. [15]

He was a good actor. He made us children hear the creak of the timbers on the *Mayflower*, smell the stench of the bilge, shudder at the first sight of the low gray empty coast. . . . Or he'd tell of a Mormon family, Utah-bound by wagon train from Missouri to a winter spent in a sod house and a plague of snakes in the spring. . . . Or he'd become a sea captain encountering a ghost ship on a stormy night off Cape Hatteras. . . . In a flash he might change into Paul Bunyan or Alligator Joe and set us laughing with his outrageous bragging tall tales. . . . Sometimes he sang lilting Irish songs with endless verses and a cheerful "Singsong Kitty" refrain. Other times his songs were those of a black man working on the Ohio River, calling on the morning star to witness his endless labor. . . .

The afternoon raced past. It was suppertime, mothers were calling children home, some by name, some by a clapping of hands, one by loud blasts on a police whistle. The children vanished as quietly and as quickly as they had arrived. My grandfather pulled a spoon from his vest pocket and began eating the sugar from the bottom of his toddy glass. From the dining room behind us came a clatter of china, rattle of silverware, small chink of ice in glasses. In its timely, well-ordered fashion, the day was ending. All up and down the street windows were turning blank reflections to the setting sun. A sad time, the way all endings are sad.

"Are the stories true?" I'd always ask.

"All stories are true," my grandfather said, "if you believe them."

"I'll remember them," I promised. [20]

"Of course you will," he said.

focus.

1. Grau begins her essay by talking about memory. In what ways do photographs such as Laughlin's both spark and shape our memories?

2. Images present a way of seeing the world and, in that way, present an argument about what we see. Look at Laughlin's photo and then at Misrach's (see p. 412). What argument or way of seeing is being presented about the places in the photos?

3. Grau's essay appears in a book about Laughlin's photography, but she never mentions his work. How does her story of her grandfather help readers understand or respond to Laughlin's photos?

respond.

1. Laughlin once wrote that he disliked "the use of the camera as a mere recording instrument." He was trying, he said, "to create purely visual poetry, and to use objects as symbols of states of mind." Using any of the photographs in this book, write a 1–2 page response to Laughlin's statement. In what way can photography create poetry? How can objects represent states of mind? When is a photograph a mere recording, and when is it something more? Make sure you refer specifically to the photographs in your response.

2. Create your own way of visually representing a place. It can be a place you grew up in, the place you are living now, a place you remember in a partic- ular way, or a place you would like others to see in a particular way. First, take photographs or choose existing photographs of the place that fit your idea or argument about how you want your audience to see the place. Write an essay to accompany these photos. The length of your essay depends on what you want your readers to know about the place and how you have represented it in your photos. Decide who your audience will be. Do you want to address friends? family? tourists? students? an industry or superstore that wants to build in this area? Keep both argument and audience in mind as you choose photos and write your essay.

picture this

picturing argument

When we think of visual argument, we most likely think of the kinds of images shown in this chapter—advertisements, public service appeals, documentary photography. Yet, even very simple visuals, such as the photos many families use as holiday greetings, make an argument. They often ask us to see a family in a certain way—happy, thriving, together, beautiful.

Look, for example, at the greetings reproduced here. In one, a couple sits smiling with their young daughter. Next to the photo, they've added the words "Merry Christmas and Happy New Year." In another, Rolling Oaks Goldens poses a litter of golden retriever puppies peeking over the side of a hay wagon.

Happy Holidays

Merry Christmas + Happy New Year!

From Steve, Vanessa, and Charlotte

Season's Greetings with love, Marilyn, John & Willie

SEASON'S GREETINGS
·2002·

From all of us at
RollingOaks Goldens

www.rollingoaks.com

Read these greetings carefully. What argument is being made? What details in the images help create the argument? How do the words in the greetings reinforce or make the argument clear?

Then, make a greeting of your own, for a holiday or some other occasion. It should argue for how you want yourself or your family to be seen.

Place your image on card stock.

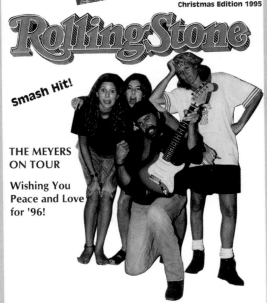

Christmas Edition 1995

Rolling Stone

Smash Hit!

THE MEYERS ON TOUR

Wishing You Peace and Love for '96!

Merry Christmas 2001   Greg Pfarr

gallery
of
images

picturing argument

① *Fragile*, by Neil Ryder Hoos, 1993. Neil Ryder Hoos looks for narratives in posters and ads and billboards and other such public texts. He photographs his images with an editorial eye, often juxtaposing many layers of text to emphasize what he wishes the image to convey.

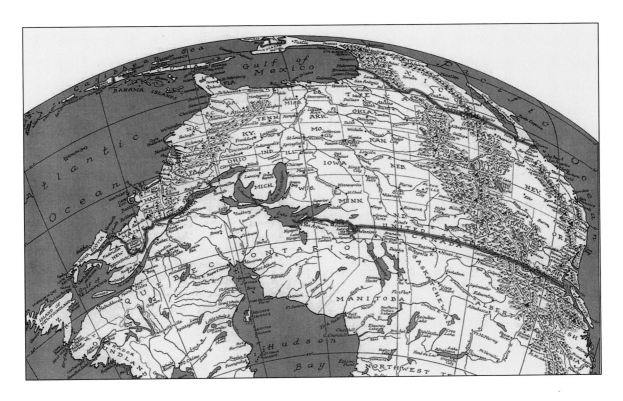

② *The U.S.A. as Seen from Canada*, World Eagle. Most maps position nations north-south, assuming the North Pole to be at the top and the South Pole at the bottom. Look what happens when you reverse that perspective.

③ Corolla Toyota Ad,
designed by Saatchi
and Saatchi, 1997. The
ad is somewhat unusual
in attempting to make
an abstract, invisible
concept—safety—
visible and not even
showing the car it is
trying to sell.

Corolla. For overprotective parents.

Dual airbags, self-tensioning seat belts, collapsible steering column, energy-absorbing reinforcements in the roof-side rails and pillars, side impact protection beams, rigid passenger safety cell, ABS and shatter-resistant glass. TOYOTA

④ Ad for the Chiropractic Association of South Africa. This ad asks a simple question: Does This Hurt? By positioning the type sideways, it also leads readers to the answer.

⑤ *Untitled* (School, Cumberland Mountain Farms, near Scottsboro, Alabama).
Photo by Carl Mydans, 1936, taken for the Farm Security Administration.

6 *Untitled* (Son of a tenant famer, Greensboro, Alabama).
Photo by Jack Delano, 1941, taken for the Farm Security Administration.

Life's different when you dance.

FRED ASTAIRE
DANCE STUDIOS

designing texts

▶ Body language tells us what's going on in these two photographs. Like people, texts have body language, which is expressed through design.

Whenever we set out to write something, we have in mind certain goals. We might want to share our thoughts with others, report new or unfamiliar information, analyze how something works, convince someone to take action, spin a tale. When we create images and other visual texts, we are motivated by many similar purposes: to document an event, present factual information, record memories, persuade others to believe or to do something.

Our purposes control which genres we choose and what we decide to say or show. Equally important, they affect how we say it and how we design it. How we design and present a text gives character to our content: it can enhance, clarify, or soften our message. It can also affect our audience: when we read, design gives us an immediate impression, just as visual information helps us an impression when we meet a person for the first time. How is she dressed? Is he smiling? Is she standing up straight? Although they can be misleading, such impressions have meaning.

Our initial reaction to a text is similarly shaped by visual cues. The design of a text influences how we understand the content, both by focusing and organizing that content and by giving it a certain look. A memorable design even helps us retain content by fixing in our mind a picture of the material.

All texts have a look and feel that contribute to their meaning, in addition to the words they include. Like people, texts have a body language that often communicates more than what they actually say. In a primarily verbal text, typeface, type size, font, color, and even layout and capitalization all make a difference in how we read the text.

Design 1

CHAPTER ONE

The Arrest / Conversation with Frau Grubach Then Fräulein Bürstner

SOMEONE must have traduced Joseph K., for without having done anything wrong he was arrested one fine morning. His landlady's cook, who always brought him his breakfast at eight o'clock, failed to appear on this occasion. That had never happened before. K. waited for a little while longer, watching from his pillow the old

3

design 1. By George Salter. Text body in 11.5 pt. Linotype Scotch. Chapter title is calligraphy by the designer. Illustration used as graphic device.

Design 2

THE TRIAL

The arrest : Conversation with Frau Grubach, then Fräulein Bürstner

13

Someone must have traduced Joseph K., for without having done anything wrong he was arrested one fine morning. His landlady's cook, who always brought him his breakfast at eight o'clock, failed to appear on this occasion. That had never happened before. K. waited for a little while longer, watching from his pillow the old lady opposite, who seemed to be peering at him with a curiosity unusual even for her, but then, feeling both put out and hungry, he rang the bell. At once there was a knock at the door and a man entered whom he had never seen before in the house. He was slim and yet well knit, he wore a closely fitting black suit, which was furnished with all sorts of pleats, pockets, buckles, and buttons, as well as a belt, like a tourist's outfit, and in consequence

design 2. By Marshall Lee. Text body in 10 pt. Linotype Devinne. Chapter title in Berthold Standard Medium. Book title used as graphic element.

Design 3

THE ARREST

Someone must have traduced Joseph K., for without having done anything wrong he was arrested one fine morning. His landlady's cook, who always brought him his breakfast at eight o'clock, failed to appear on this occasion. That had never happened before. K. waited for a little while longer, watching from his pillow the old lady opposite, who seemed to be peering at him with a curiosity unusual even for her, but then, feeling both put out and hungry, he rang the bell. At once there was a knock at the door and a man entered whom he had never seen before in the house. He was slim and yet well knit, he wore a closely fitting black suit, which was furnished with all sorts of pleats, pockets, buckles, and buttons, as well as a belt, like a tourist's outfit, and in consequence looked eminently practical, though one could not quite tell what actual purpose it served. "Who are you?" asked K., sitting half upright in his bed. But the man ignored the question, as though his appearance needed no explanation, and merely said: "Did you ring?" "Anna is to bring me my breakfast," said K., and then studied the fellow, silently and carefully, trying to make out who he could be. The man did not submit to this scrutiny for very long, but turned to the door and opened it slightly so as to report to someone who was evidently standing just behind it: "He says Anna is to bring him his breakfast." A short guffaw from the next room came in answer; and it rather sounded as if several people had joined in. Although the strange man could not have learned anything from it that he did not know already, he now said to K., as if passing on a statement: "It can't be done." "This is news indeed," cried K., springing out of bed and quickly pulling on his trousers. "I must see what people these are next door, and how Frau Grubach can account to me for such behavior." Yet it occurred to him at once that he should not have said this aloud and that by doing so he had in a way admitted the stranger's right to superintend his actions; still, that did not seem important to him at the moment. The stranger, however, took his words in some such sense, for he asked: "Hadn't you better stay here?" "I shall neither stay here nor let you address me until you have introduced yourself." "I meant

8

THE ARREST

CONVERSATION WITH FRAU GRUBACH

THEN FRÄULEIN BÜRSTNER

K

design 3. By Carl Zahn. Text body in 8 pt. Helvetica. Chapter title on preceding page in Helvetica (shown in inset above). Letter "K" for Kafka used as graphic device.

▶ In 1968, Hammermill Paper published *The Trial of Six Designers*, for which six graphic designers were asked to design Franz Kafka's *The Trial*, using the same book size but the typeface and arrangement of their own choosing. Three chapter-opening designs are shown here. Note how the tone changes based on the typeface, arrangement of elements, and even the size of the margins.

Written messages may start with words, but rarely if ever do they end there. The words are written or designed to look a certain way, and their look almost always affects how they are read—or sometimes even whether they are read at all. Consider one example of how design can affect a written message.

When Sarah Huang moved to Lakewood, she was at first delighted to see the many deer roaming around. But after seeing several dead deer along the road and almost hitting a deer herself one evening on an unlit road, she had second thoughts. When she noticed two small ticks on her leg—and realized she could get Lyme disease—she began to think of the deer as a problem.

Soon thereafter, she noticed the bags of deer corn outside her local grocery store and realized, with a start, that people in the community were making the deer problem worse by feeding them. She decided then and there to write an opinion piece about the situation for the neighborhood newsletter. The editor of the newsletter told her that she could have a half page, approximately three hundred words.

The article ran, but Sarah had the feeling that few people read it. Then she noticed the small rack for community brochures at the grocery store, right next to the deer corn. The people who buy deer corn might notice a brochure about deer—and they were the ones she needed to reach. She decided to reformat her article as a brochure.

Before printing out the brochures, Sarah showed her draft to a friend who was an art major. She was surprised by her friend's response: "The deer on the cover of your brochure wants to be petted. I thought you were trying to discourage people from feeding them. And no one is going to wade through all those words."

Sarah tried again. She changed her title to a question, thinking it might get more people's attention: "Too Many Deer?" And she replaced the photo of the cute deer with one of deer grazing in a backyard that better demonstrated the problem. She then inserted color headings to make it easy to see the problem, the possible solutions, and what needed to be done; reran the unsuccessful solutions as a bulleted list; and added a photo of a tick to dramatize the threat of Lyme disease. She made the title much larger, to grab shoppers' attention.

The Deer Problem in Lakewood

White-tailed deer have become a frequent sight in Lakewood. While these graceful creatures are a delight to watch, the abundance of deer has become overwhelming. Even though the deer have eaten many of our flowers, shrubs, and trees, they are obviously malnourished.

Overpopulation leads to many collisions of deer and vehicles. Deer also carry ticks that spread Lyme disease, which can be fatal to humans. In the suburbs of New York City and Boston, the number of cases of Lyme disease has risen dramatically since 1998, the result of an out-of-control deer population. The disease has spread throughout the Midwest, including our community.

Other communities overrun with deer have tried to find solutions short of killing the deer. Trapping and relocating deer seems like an obvious alternative, but the solution is costly, and most deer die during the process or shortly after they are relocated to new places.

Wild animal contraceptives have been tried in Ohio and Kentucky, but without success. Deer learn to avoid the bait that carries the contraceptive, and high doses are required for the contraceptive to be effective. Deer herds are now so large that it is extremely difficult to vaccinate most of a herd. Longer hunting seasons can reduce the number of deer in rural areas, but hunting deer is not possible when they give birth and raise their young in the front yards of our houses.

No management plan will work until the deer population is brought down to sustainable limits. We have no options for relocating deer. Consequently, trapping deer with immediate euthanasia is the only practical solution. Allowing deer to die of starvation or as road kill denies our responsibility. We have no ethical choice but to manage the deer population until we can find a nonlethal means to control their explosive birth rate.

Ragged right text produces a sloppy edge around photograph.

Image of deer quite appealing. Does not convey the correct message for this article.

The revised
brochure.

More compact
brochure size allows
readers to take
publication with them.

Front cover asks
simple question and
provides an image to
support the question.
Simple bold type
contrasts with image.

Back cover provides
phone number for
more information and
a photo which makes
the phone number
easy to remember.

For information call:
1-800-123-Deer

Too
Many
Deer?

Back Cover

Front cover

Photograph of multiple deer in suburban landscape visually supports claim made by author

Overpopulation Is Bad for Deer

White-tailed deer have become a frequent sight in Lakewood. While these graceful creatures are a delight to watch, the abundance of deer has become overwhelming. Even though the deer have eaten many of our flowers, shrubs, and trees, they are obviously malnourished. Overpopulation leads to many collisions of deer and vehicles.

The Threat of Lyme Disease

Deer also carry ticks that spread Lyme disease, which can be fatal to humans. In the suburbs of New York City and Boston, the number of cases of Lyme disease has risen dramatically since 1998, the result of an out-of-control deer population. The disease has spread throughout the Midwest, and now only six of the fifty states are free of Lyme disease.

Deer tick actual size and magnified

Solutions that Have Been Tried

- Trapping and relocating deer is costly, and most deer die during the process or shortly after they are relocated.

- Wild animal contraceptives have been tried without success because deer learn to avoid the bait that carries the contraceptive, and high doses are required for the contraceptive to be effective.

- Longer hunting seasons can reduce the number of deer in rural areas, but deer hunting is not possible when they give birth and raise their young in our front yards.

What We Must Do

No plan will work until the deer population is brought down to sustainable limits. We have no way of relocating deer. Thus, trapping them with immediate euthanasia is the only practical solution. Allowing deer to die of starvation or as road kill denies our responsibility. Our most ethical choice is to manage the deer population until we can find a nonlethal means to control their explosive birth rate.

Headings in boldface and color provide contrast to the text.

Bulleted list breaks up text into easy-to-understand units

Photographs of deer tick emphasizes the problem of disease associated with a large deer population. Caption explains the size differences shown in the images

Inside left page   Inside right page

Once a writer has a purpose in mind, the first design decision is to choose a genre. Sarah Huang began by writing an article, which did not require her to think much about design because that was a decision made by the newspaper, not the writer. She needed only to limit her text to three hundred words, and so her primary decisions were about content. Given the space restrictions, she planned carefully what facts she would present. She also thought carefully about her tone. Knowing that some of her neighbors would be upset by her proposal to euthanatize deer, she needed to convince her readers that she was concerned about the health of people and deer alike.

When she decided to create a brochure, however, she had to make many decisions about design, starting with size and format. These decisions were guided by her knowledge of her audience (thus the large red title, to catch their attention) and goals. Her computer offered her many design options—the ability to scan in photos, create bulleted lists, and so on—and she kept her readers and purpose in mind as she made her design choices. Had she chosen another genre—a poster or a Web site—her design options would have been different.

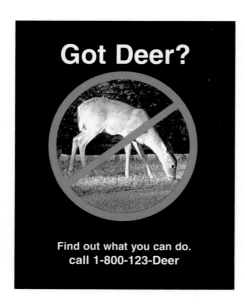

Before computers, people wrote by hand or on a typewriter, and most typewriters offered only one style and size of type. Type was an issue for printers and designers, not writers. Today we can choose from hundreds of typefaces—Times Roman, Courier, Bodoni, Futura, Edwardian Script, and so on. This section discusses some of the many decisions writers now have to make about the use of type.

THINKING RHETORICALLY ABOUT TYPE Typography is an art form. It is a way we deliver a message to others, and it can be used as a means of self-expression. As such, it is one way we add tone and style to our written words. The printed word is in essence visible speech. Just as one would not choose to whisper when delivering a speech at a political rally, one would not choose the *visual equivalent* for a political poster that will be read from a distance. One would instead choose a simple, clear, and **bold** type-face—the visual equivalent of strong direct speech.

Our choice of typeface depends on the TONE we intend—whether we want our text to look serious, playful, traditional, trendy, or so on. Here is one text set in three very different typefaces. How does the type affect the way you read the text?

Script typefaces (such as Nuptial Script, above) are often used on awards and invitations. They convey a formal look, but they also make long stretches of text hard to read.

Deer also carry ticks that spread Lyme disease, which can be fatal to humans. In the suburbs of New York City and Boston, the number of cases of Lyme disease has risen dramatically since 1998, the result of an out-of-control deer population.

Type in boldface capital letters conveys formality, but the tone is much less friendly than script typefaces. Trade Gothic Bold, below, seems better suited for a warning label than for an essay.

DEER ALSO CARRY TICKS THAT SPREAD LYME DISEASE, WHICH CAN BE FATAL TO HUMANS. IN THE SUBURBS OF NEW YORK CITY AND BOSTON, THE NUMBER OF CASES OF LYME DISEASE HAS RISEN DRAMATICALLY SINCE 1998, THE RESULT OF AN OUT-OF-CONTROL DEER POPULATION.

VALLEY

WIDE/NARROW

SHARP

dull

Whimsical
Reserved

liquid
SOLID

DiS CON NECT

▌ The examples above created by students at Ivy Tech in 2002 show how typefaces can convey meaning.

Typefaces such as Comic Sans, below, appear far less serious and convey an informal tone.

Deer also carry ticks that spread Lyme disease, which can be fatal to humans. In the suburbs of New York City and Boston, the number of cases of Lyme disease has risen dramatically since 1998, the result of an out-of-control deer population.

Sometimes type is even used to convey meaning, as in the examples shown on this page. You'll often see type used this way in advertising and on book and CD covers, though you probably won't have many occasions to use type this way in your academic work.

▌ On book covers typefaces are typically selected to reinforce the image and content of a book.

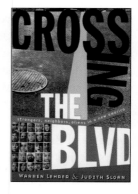

Garamond Light
Garamond Light Italic
Garamond Book
Garamond Book Italic
Garamond Bold
Garamond Bold Italic
Garamond Ultra

▶ Different fonts in one typeface.

TYPEFACES AND FONTS A TYPEFACE is a family of type design. Each typeface has various FONTS—italic, bold, condensed, extended, and so on. Most typefaces include, at a minimum, fonts for boldface and italics. Type is measured in points, with each point the equivalent of $\frac{1}{72}$ of an inch.

Typefaces are classified as *serif* (type with short cross-lines at the ends of letters) or *sans serif* (type without cross lines). The paragraph you are reading is set in 10 pt. *Foundry Form*. This book uses two main typefaces: *Foundry Form Serif* and *Foundry Form Sans*. Both come in various fonts—bold, italic, medium, and book, to name a few. This paragraph, for example, uses *Foundry Form Serif Book*. The heading that begins the paragraph is set in *Foundry Form Sans Boldface*. This typeface was chosen for its clear, contemporary style and because it has a variety of different fonts and also a matching sans serif typeface. This choice allows us to use matching but contrasting type for different elements, hopefully resulting in a book that looks good and that is easy to navigate. In addition, we've used a third typeface by the name of *Impact*, which is used for just that reason for chapter titles, gallery headings, and the title of several special features.

Boldface and italics have particular uses in academic writing. Italics are used to indicate the names of books, magazines, newspapers, plays, films, paintings, sculptures, and other works of art. Sometimes italics are used to create emphasis, as Nancy Carpenter does on page 171, for example, when she writes *I know she's not going to buy that hat*. It is usually advisable to use italics sparingly for purposes of emphasis, however—a little goes a long way. Boldface is used mostly for headings, though you will see it sometimes used to highlight key words in textbooks.

THE ANATOMY OF TYPE

Typefaces are generally categorized as **serif** or **sans serif**. The serifs are the crossbars or "feet" that appear at the bottom or top of the main strokes of a letter.

serif

serif   sans serif

Fonts that are taller than usual in proportion to their widths are called **condensed**.

condensed typeface
(Trade Gothic Condensed)

Fonts that are wider in proportion to their height are called **expanded** or **extended**.

box

expanded typeface
(Trade Gothic Extended)

▶ All type is not the same. Here are examples of serif typefaces (left) and sans serif typefaces (right). All these examples are set in 9 pt type, but some appear larger than others because their lower case letters are larger.

This is an example of Garamond Book.

This is an example of Times Roman.

This is an example of Goudy Old Style.

This is an example of Palatino.

This is an example of New Baskerville.

This is an example of Bodoni.

This is an example of Ariel.

This is an example of Techno.

This is an example of Comic Sans.

This is an example of Helvetica.

This is an example of Trade Gothic Condensed.

This is an example of Kabel Medium.

LINE SPACING   Most word-processing programs allow us to choose the line spacing of our texts. Final drafts of academic papers should generally be double-spaced, whereas letters and memos are usually single-spaced. Reports and other genres may have other requirements; it's best to check what's expected if you're not sure. Adobe Photoshop and other programs follow professional typesetting terminology and refer to the space between the lines as "leading." Whatever it's called, this space is an important factor in a text's look and readability. Lines that are too close together—or too far apart—slow down readers, because it's more difficult for the eye to find the beginning of the next line. In general, it's best to make the leading 2 points greater than the size of type: 10 pt. type, for example, commonly has 12 pt. leading. The following examples show 10 pt. *Times* type with different spacing between lines.

Lines Too Far Apart

If the lines of type on the page are too far apart, the text will look smaller, and the text on the page will visually look lighter. However, if you are writing for a class and expect to write corrections on this copy, generous leading is advisable. This text is set in 10 point Times with 20 point leading which simulates double spacing.

Appropriate Line Spacing

When the lines of type are correctly proportioned in relation to the size of the type, the reader can read with ease. This text is set in 10 point Times with 12 point leading. This follows the general rule that leading set 2 points greater than the text size. There is enough space between the lines to read each line clearly and yet the reader doesn't have to search for the next line.

Lines Too Close

When lines are set too close to each other, the page looks too dense and the reader finds it difficult to find the beginning of the next line when reading. The text size appears to be larger than the same size type with more space between the lines. This type is set in 10 point Times with 10 points of leading.

JUSTIFICATION   Lines of type are JUSTIFIED if they are flush with the left-hand margin, the right-hand margin, or both. Most writing is justified on the left margin—even handwriting. Word-processing programs give us the option of justifying the right margin or leaving it uneven, or "ragged." At first glance, a justified right margin looks cleaner, but it is not necessarily easier to read as a result. In order to justify the right margin, the space between words and in some cases even the space between letters must be varied. If this variation is too great, justified type can become difficult to read.

Ragged-right type is easier to read as long as it's not too ragged. If line lengths vary too much, the eye has difficulty moving from one line to the next. When you insert images into your written text, with the text running around an image, it is best to justify the type so that it follows the shape of the image.

▶ It's not a good idea to insert a photo on the right side of text set ragged right. See how much better it looks when the same text is set justified.

▶ Type justified in narrow measure creates "rivers" of space between the words

BAD SPACING. In order to justify the right margin, the space between words and in some cases even the space between letters must be varied. If this variation is too great, justified type can become difficult to read as it creates rivers of space. To correct this problem, one must decrease the size of type or increase the length of line.

The Deer Problem in Lakewood

White-tailed deer have become a frequent sight in Lakewood. While these graceful creatures are a delight to watch, the abundance of deer has become overwhelming. Even though the deer have eaten many of our flowers, shrubs, and trees, they are obviously malnourished.

Overpopulation leads to many collisions of deer and vehicles. Deer also carry ticks that spread Lyme disease, which can be fatal to humans. In the suburbs of New York City and Boston, the number of cases of Lyme disease has risen dramatically since 1998, the result of an out-of-control deer population. The disease has spread throughout the Midwest, including our community.

Other communities overrun with deer have tried to find solutions short of killing the deer. Trapping and relocating deer seems like an obvious alternative, but the solution is costly, and most deer die during the process or shortly after they are relocated to new places.

Wild animal contraceptives have been tried in Ohio and Kentucky, but without success. Deer learn to avoid the bait that carries the contraceptive, and high doses are required for the contraceptive to be effective. Deer herds are now so large that it is extremely difficult to vaccinate most of a herd. Longer hunting seasons can reduce the number of deer in rural areas, but hunting deer is not possible when they give birth and raise their young in the front yards of our houses.

No management plan will work until the deer population is brought down to sustainable limits. We have no options for relocating deer. Consequently, trapping deer with immediate euthanasia is the only practical solution. Allowing deer to die of starvation or as road kill denies our responsibility. We have no ethical choice but to manage the deer population until we can find a nonlethal means to control their explosive birth rate.

The Deer Problem in Lakewood

White-tailed deer have become a frequent sight in Lakewood. While these graceful creatures are a delight to watch, the abundance of deer has become overwhelming. Even though the deer have eaten many of our flowers, shrubs, and trees, they are obviously malnourished.

Overpopulation leads to many collisions of deer and vehicles. Deer also carry ticks that spread Lyme disease, which can be fatal to humans. In the suburbs of New York City and Boston, the number of cases of Lyme disease has risen dramatically since 1998, the result of an out-of-control deer population. The disease has spread throughout the Midwest, including our community.

Other communities overrun with deer have tried to find solutions short of killing the deer. Trapping and relocating deer seems like an obvious alternative, but the solution is costly, and most deer die during the process or shortly after they are relocated to new places.

Wild animal contraceptives have been tried in Ohio and Kentucky, but without success. Deer learn to avoid the bait that carries the contraceptive, and high doses are required for the contraceptive to be effective. Deer herds are now so large that it is extremely difficult to vaccinate most of a herd. Longer hunting seasons can reduce the number of deer in rural areas, but hunting deer is not possible when they give birth and raise their young in the front yards of our houses.

No management plan will work until the deer population is brought down to sustainable limits. We have no options for relocating deer. Consequently, trapping deer with immediate euthanasia is the only practical solution. Allowing deer to die of starvation or as road kill denies our responsibility. We have no ethical choice but to manage the deer population until we can find a nonlethal means to control their explosive birth rate.

COLOR Text can be lighter or darker, depending on the font and the spacing between letters, words, and lines. A font with thick lines will appear to be bolder and darker than one with thin lines. Text will also appear darker if there is less space between lines, and lighter when there is more.

Text can also be printed in color. Variety in the color of text helps readers distinguish one element from another. Sometimes examples printed in color are easier to spot because they contrast with the black type on the page. Likewise, setting headings in color helps readers to see the basic outline of a text without reading the entire piece. You'll want to think about what colors you use—red provides greater contrast than blue, orange or hot pink are fun but not always appropriate.

▶ Layouts from this book showing how color can differentiate one type of text from another—dark blue for the *Snapshot* excercise, red for the *Gallery* heading.

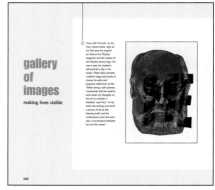

▶ This "quilt" of typefaces demonstrates the many shades of gray found in "black" type—and shows how different typefaces and fonts can be lighter or darker.

- What is the appropriate look for your purpose and audience? Is it formal? informal? whimsical? edgy? something else?

- What is your genre, and does it require a particular style of type? If it includes headings and lists, should they be in the same font as the rest of your text, or should they be in boldface or italics to make them more prominent?

- In what medium are you writing, and does it have any type requirements? If you are writing online, you'll probably want to choose a sans serif typeface, and you may be expected to put some of your text in lists.

- How is your text organized? Does anything need to be highlighted— headings? key words? epigraphs? examples?

- If you're writing for an assignment, does it have any requirements that affect your use of type? Length requirements, for instance, sometimes mean you need to use smaller or larger type.

- If you're using more than one typeface, font, or color, do you use them consistently?. In most cases it's best to use no more than two different typefaces. If you have more than one kind of heading, the more important ones should be more prominent—and thus boldface or larger (or both). If you print headings in color, be sure they're all in the same color.

No matter how many elements a text has, they have to be arranged in some way. Readers expect elements that are similar to be grouped together and to be set off from other, different elements. There are certain patterns that help us to navigate a page—indents signal a new paragraph, bullets mark a list, color or boldface words above a paragraph are probably a heading.

Below is a Yellow Pages ad for a landscape services company. Though it lists all the different services the company provides, apparently no one thought about how to group or organize these services. The result is a long, diffuse list; a potential customer thumbing through the Yellow Pages won't easily see what services Down to Earth provides.

The first task in redesigning this ad is to determine how the services are related to one another. Some involve landscape design, others involve installation, and still others involve maintenance. They should be sorted accordingly and placed under headings. The original ad has a lot of blank space, called WHITE SPACE, but the space does not set off the information. In the redesigned ad, the services are organized into three groups, and bold face headings, bullets, and space between the separate services and the three groups make the ad easy to read.

Down to Earth

Build retaining walls
Tree trimming and removal
Water gardens
Consultation
Install patios and walkways
Grass and shrub installation
Yard mowing and edging
Pest control
Landscape lighting
Install sprinkler systems
Drawings and plans

Down to Earth

DESIGN
- Consultation
- Landscape drawings and plans

INSTALLATION
- Sprinkler systems
- Patios and walkways
- Retaining walls
- Landscape lighting
- Water gardens
- Grass and shrubs

MAINTENANCE
- Tree trimming and removal
- Yard mowing and edging
- Pest control

Proximity gives us important clues about the relationship between design elements. Look at business card A. The name at the center of the card is the visual focus, but none of the other information has any kind of visual relationship. One solution is to center everything and simply list the information in some kind of order. Another strategy is to align elements, either left or right, which can be more interesting.

image conscious

Collect a few business cards and study the way they organize information. Where is the primary focus, and how is it achieved? What image do the cards project, and how does the use of type and other graphics create that impression?

(619) 409-2741	1010 Point Drive
	Chula Vista, CA 91910

Isabella Sanchez

Down to Earth	Landscape Architect

Card A

The layout in card B is easier to read than that in card A. In card A, the eye jumps from corner to corner to retrieve information. Card B centers the type in a balanced format and presents the text in the order we wish it to read. It groups the owner and her title together and separates the name of the company to stand by itself. It gives the company name emphasis by increasing its size and weight and by adding color. Card C maintains this order but centers the type on the right. The type is balanced visually by the addition of a logo on the left.

Isabella Sanchez
Landscape Architect

Down to Earth

(619) 409-2741
1010 Point Drive
Chula Vista, CA 91910

Card B

Isabella Sanchez
Landscape Architect

Down to Earth

(619) 409-2741
1010 Point Drive
Chula Vista, CA 91910

Card C

PAGE DESIGN Many word-processing programs specify a format for basic page design, including page size, margins, justification, and paragraph indents. You may wish to follow the default settings for these items or you may want to design your own pages to suit your content and reflect the tone you wish to present to your audience. If you decide to design your own material, you need to consider several things.

1. *Choose the orientation and size of your page.* The first decision you need to make is the size of the page. You'll need to evaluate the amount and type of material. Most academic work requires 8½ × 11" paper in a vertical, or "portrait," orientation. Horizontal, or "landscape," orientation works better when you need to have multiple columns of text or when many photos or charts have horizontal proportions. This book uses a horizontal format because of these needs.

2. *Organize text into appropriate units.* Sometimes you'll want to put everything in paragraph form, but some information might be better conveyed as a list, or in a table or chart. Some genres require certain elements—an abstract, a list of works cited, and so on.

3. *Present material according to its importance.* The main body of your text is probably the most important part, so you should consider carefully the length of line, size of type, and space between lines. Headings should go at the beginning of the sections they introduce. Remember that Western cultures are accustomed to reading top to bottom, left to right.

   Group related materials together. Illustrations and charts need to be referred to in the main text and should be positioned near their text reference. Captions need to be near the illustrations they accompany. If you have material that needs to be set off from the main text, consider indenting it with space above and below, framing it with a box, or using a different typeface.

4. *Use white space to organize and separate the various parts of your text.* Add extra space above headings; around photos, charts, and graphs; and between captions and other text. Make sure your margins are adequate: readers should be able to hold the page without covering any text with their thumbs.

5. *If you are required to follow MLA or some other academic style, be aware of what it requires.* Some styles have particular requirements about margins, indents, reference lists, and other things.

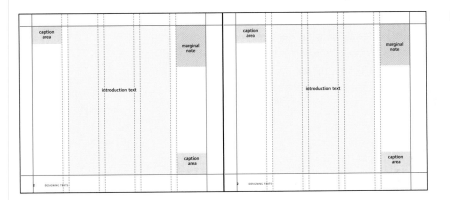

▶ Professional designers use a grid to design pages. The 5-column grid used in this book provides many ways to present words and images on the page.

image conscious

Look at the designs of several pages of one magazine. Can you determine a grid used in the layout of a particular article? How does this grid organize the texts? Does the grid affect the overall look and tone of the article?

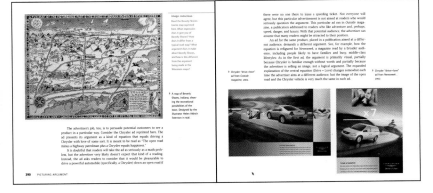

▶ Default grids on word processing programs are typically very simple, as shown below.

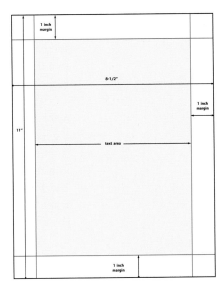

HEADINGS   Most longer texts and many shorter ones include headings, which provide an at-a-glance overview, helping readers to find specific information and making the overall structure of a text easier to follow and remember. Headings visually indicate the major sections of a text. For example, a brochure designed to inform college students about tattoos might have the following headings:

Deciding on a Tattoo
Finding a Studio
Considering the Long Term
Anticipating Pain
Caring for a Tattoo

Alternatively, such a brochure might have headings that anticipate the questions its readers are likely to have about the subject:

Why Get a Tattoo?
How Can You Find a Reputable Studio?
How Permanent Is a Tattoo?
Does It Hurt?
How Much Do Tattoos Cost?
How Do You Take Care of a Tattoo?

To be effective, headings must stand out from the rest of the text, so often they are set in type that is larger, bold, or in color. If you set your headings in a different typeface from your main text, be consistent and avoid using more than two typefaces throughout.

The selection of a typeface for the headings can also reflect the character of the content. In the first list of headings above, the written wording is more formal and impersonal in character; the second list of questions is more personal and friendly. The first headings would probably be better in a roman font in capital letters, the latter in an italic font in upper and lower case to emphasize that they are questions. Keep in mind length when deciding how to style headings. Capitals make short headings look stronger but can make lengthy headings cumbersome and difficult to read.

Adding space above and below the heading is another way of making headings stand out. Add more space above a heading than below so that

DECIDING ON A TATTOO

When you look in the mirror, do you think that you need a "little something" to make you stand out from the rest of the crowd? Would some sort of personal adornment be a reflection of your personality and individuality? Perhaps a tattoo would satisfy these goals. It can be as discreet as you want it to be. But it is important to find a professional studio, one that is reputable and can meet your needs.

FINDING A STUDIO

The most important decision you can make other than deciding on the design of your tattoo is finding a reputable studio. Referrals are important. Ask friends who have had tattoos if they can recommend a studio. Ask them if the facilities were clean and the staff followed hygienic practices. Call the Better Business Bureau or consumer watchgroups to make sure there haven't been any complaints filed against the studio. Finally, visit the studio, interview the artist, review samples of his or her work. Ask about any possible problems.

Why Get a Tattoo?

When you look in the mirror, do you think that you need a "little something" to make you stand out from the rest of the crowd? Would some sort of personal adornment be a reflection of your personality and individuality? Perhaps a tattoo would satisfy these goals. It can be as discreet as you want it to be. But it is important to find a professional studio, one that is reputable and can meet your needs.

How Can You Find a Reputable Studio?

The most important decision you can make other than deciding on the design of your tattoo is finding a reputable studio. Referrals are important. Ask friends who have had tattoos if they can recommend a studio. Ask them if the facilities were clean and the staff followed hygienic practices. Call the Better Business Bureau or consumer watchgroups to make sure there haven't been any complaints filed against the studio. Finally, visit the studio, interview the artist, review samples of his or her work. Ask about any possible problems.

▶ The style of your design shapes your message. The headings are different in these two examples, notice how much more formal the example on the left seems to the eye. In contrast, the example on the right appears more informal and interactive because the right margin is ragged, the headings are converted to questions, and the headings are set in color in upper- and lower-case *sans serif* type.

the heading is visually linked to the material that follows. Keeping the size and spacing consistent will establish a pattern for readers to follow, similar to cadence in a song or rap. Once the pattern or rhythm is established, we know to look for it and we expect it. Such patterning contributes to the unity and flow of the design.

LISTS   Like headings, lists visually set off information. They can be numbered or bulleted and they usually have extra space between items as well as above and below the entire list to separate it from the other text.

Word-processing programs make it easy to create lists, but you should use lists only when you have a reason for setting off information rather than presenting it in a paragraph. The following list, for example, could be written as a single sentence, but setting it up as a list makes the points easier to see and remember.

GOOD DESIGN

- directs the reader
- provides clear emphasis
- conveys the writer's message
- makes the text memorable
- sets an appropriate tone
- builds the writer's credibility
- helps persuade the reader to take the text seriously

IMAGES AND OTHER GRAPHICS

IMAGES Computers, digital cameras, inexpensive printers, and the Web have made it easy for us to work with images and to include them in our writing. These technologies do not tell us when to use images, however, or for what purposes. Pictures, drawings, and other graphics can have a powerful impact on readers. They can support or emphasize a point and make concrete the ideas expressed in words. They can be used to introduce additional details and even to add other viewpoints.

Most important, you should not use images as mere decoration. Every image in some way should support your argument. The first step in using images is selection. You might choose certain images to gain attention or to set a tone, but the majority of the images you use should be used to illustrate content. And they need to be fresh. Overused or overly familiar images will not get readers' attention. If you have reason to include an image of the Eiffel Tower or the Golden Gate Bridge, for example, they had better be photographed in new ways if you want your readers to pay attention.

When you decide that you need a particular image, the next step is to find or create it. If you use someone else's images, including those you find on the Web, you need to obtain permission from the owner and to credit the image just as you would a quotation.

You can add your own photographs to your text electronically by using a digital camera or by scanning them. You also can literally glue them onto a page, but digital technologies have become inexpensive and easy to use (and available in many campus computer labs). Images in a digital format can be edited with software designed for this purpose. Professionals use sophisticated programs such as Adobe Photoshop and Macromedia Fireworks, but many computers now come with image editors, or you can download shareware from the Web. If you own a digital camera, it probably includes some type of image editor.

One of the most useful features of an image editor is the cropping tool, which allows you to select part of an image and discard the rest. You can crop out distracting or unneeded detail and thus create a stronger focus on the important part of an image. Cropping can also reduce file size, creating images that load faster on a Web site.

image conscious

Find an article that interests you in a magazine or newspaper. If your article includes images, what do they contribute to the argument? If there are no images, imagine some that would be appropriate. What would they contribute to the effectiveness of the article?

▶ One photo cropped two different ways. See how the signs at the top of the image on the left are distracting if the subject of the photo is the cameraman.

▶ Right: By taking the same photograph and selectively cropping and enlarging segments of it, a single image can produce a photo essay. The key is to look closely at your images. Often you'll find more than the subject that led you to take the photo.

The BIG Game

By taking the same photograph and selectively cropping and enlarging segments of it, a single image can produce a photo essay. The key is to look closely at your images. Often you'll find more than the subject that led you to take the photo.

CHARTS AND GRAPHS   Charts and graphs are diagrams that plot relationships that are more difficult to understanding using words alone. They present facts effectively and make them easy to see. It would take paragraphs to describe the information presented in a typical chart or graph. These graphic forms can enliven a paper that consists mainly of written words—and call attention to information that may get lost when embedded in text.

A good diagram shows more than data; it makes clear at a glance the significance of the data. The message is conveyed by the arrangement of the data, by the proportions shown, and by the labels that accompany the diagram. The title states a claim, the diagram with labels shows proof, and the caption gives a summary of the significance of the diagram. In effect a diagram presents a visual and verbal argument.

Many people use the words "chart" and "graph" interchangeably, but their meanings are distinct. GRAPHS are plotted using coordinates on x and y axes. CHARTS are not plotted. Popular spreadsheet applications such as Microsoft Excel and Lotus 1-2-3 allow you to make charts and graphs by typing the data into a workbook and selecting the type of graph or chart. The program then creates the chart or graph. You still are responsible for labeling the chart or graph, and you have to ensure that it is legible.

BAR GRAPHS are useful for comparing numerical data. Bar graphs can be vertical or horizontal, flat or two-dimensional. Sometimes they are even pictorial, as in the beer graph shown here ?

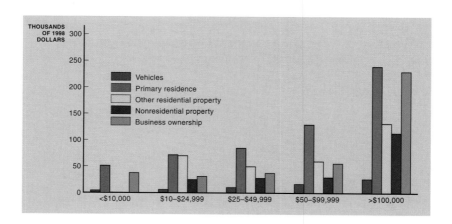

THOUSANDS OF 1998 DOLLARS

Vehicles
Primary residence
Other residential property
Nonresidential property
Business ownership

<$10,000 $10–$24,999 $25–$49,999 $50–$99,999   >$100,000

▶ Bar graph showing median family holdings of nonfinancial assets by income.

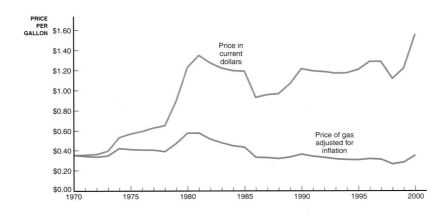

LINE GRAPHS are good for displaying changes in data that occur across time. One data set can be displayed with a single line. Two or more data sets allow comparisons at particular points in time, as shown here.

PIE CHARTS provide a quick overview of the relationship of parts to a whole. The pieces of a pie chart must add up to 100 percent. Pie charts generally are limited to about six or seven slices, because if the slices become too small, they are difficult to label and recognize.

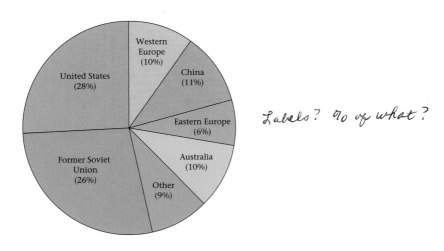

Labels? % of what?

EVALUATING DESIGN

Evaluating a design involves much more than making a judgment about how attractive or unattractive a text is. A product is well designed if it performs the function for which it was made and if it satisfies the needs of the user. Think of things that you own or are thinking about buying—an MP3 player, perhaps. After you decide how much you want to spend, the next consideration is likely to be sound quality. If the sound quality is lacking, the product fails. But there are other considerations besides sound quality and price. If the controls are complicated, you may not use it. If it's too heavy to carry in a pocket, you probably won't take it with you as often as you might like. Furthermore, you don't want to carry around an *ugly* MP3 player. A well-designed MP3 player brings all of these considerations into a harmonious balance.

A well-designed text works the same way, serving the various needs of its intended user. Recall the example at the beginning of this chapter in which one writer converted a newspaper article into a brochure. Her motivation was not that a brochure would be more attractive but rather that it was a genre that would better suit her purpose and especially her audience. If we were to evaluate her design, we would need to consider how well it serves her purpose, audience, genre, and message. How attractive it is to look at matters, but it's only one of many elements in a good design. Evaluating a design requires that we take into account the context in which a text will be read or viewed.

snapshot

Sometimes you can completely change a photo by cropping it. The photo here, for example, shows a young girl and her mom standing in front of a pizzeria. The signs for the pizzeria and for the driving school and income-tax business next door add texture to the photo, making it a scene from the late 1940s. Cropping out the signs focuses the photo more on mother and daughter; cropping out mom makes it a more timeless image of a little girl.

Find a photo that interests you and crop it to create three different pictures. You can scan your photo and crop it electronically as explained on page 455, or you can make photocopies and crop with scissors. Consider what each version "says" and how cropping changes the way the photo is read.

Audience, Purpose, Genre, and Medium

- Who is the intended *audience*? Will the overall look of the design appeal to them? How does the design serve their needs? Electronic texts should suit the needs of the user (for example, a Web site that requires high bandwidth is not going to work for readers who connect to the Internet with a telephone modem).

- What is the primary *purpose* of the text—to entertain? provide information? persuade readers to take some action? Does the design suit the purpose?

- What is the *genre*? Does the design serve the conventions of that genre? A brochure, for example, needs an attention-getting title.

- What is the *medium*? Does the design accommodate its requirements? Images that will be posted on the Web, for example, should not be too big or they could take too long to open.

Organization

- Does the design serve the organization? Does it make the main parts visible and the main points clear?

- Are headings inserted in the right places? If there is more than one level of headings, will readers be able to see and understand the difference between first- and second-level headings?

- Is there any information that should be set off as a list?

Readability

- Is the typeface attractive and readable? Is the font appropriate for the medium?

- Are the margins sufficient?

Readability

- Are there any statistics or other data that would be easier to read in a chart, graph, or table?

- Is high-contrast text, including boldface and all caps, brief enough to be legible? If not, either revise the text or change the font.

Images and Other Graphics

- What do images and other graphics contribute? Do they illustrate a concept? highlight an important point? show something that is difficult to describe in words alone? If the images and other graphics are only decorative, consider removing them.

- Are images and other graphics the right size—big enough to read or to see the important detail?

- Do images have an obvious focus? Will readers see the part that matters? If not, consider if you can crop the image.

- Are the charts, graphs, maps, or other graphics clear and informative? Do they have titles and captions? Are they referred to in the main text?

Layout

- Is the basic layout effective? Is the overall look appropriate to the genre, purpose, and audience?

- Is there adequate white space around headings, images, and other key elements?

- If color is used, is it appropriate to the audience and purpose? Does color direct emphasis where it belongs? Are too many colors used?

Paula Scher (b. 1968) is a professional graphic designer, a partner at Pentagram Design, in New York. She began her career as an art director for Atlantic Records and has worked for *Time* magazine and has taught at Cooper Union's School of Visual Arts. She is also a writer and was nominated for the American Book Award for Best Compilation of Written and Graphic Material for her 1981 book *The Honeymoon Book: A Tribute to the Last Ritual of Sexual Innocence*.

The piece here appeared on the op-ed page of the *New York Times* in the wake of the "hanging chad" controversy in the 2000 presidential election, when a confusing ballot in Palm Beach County, Florida, caused many votes to be miscast or ruled invalid— and literally "not to count," Scher's op-ed piece consists of the actual Palm Beach ballot, annotated to show how bad design confused voters.

Defective Equipment: The Palm Beach County Ballot

PAULA SCHER

DEFECTIVE EQUIPMENT: The Palm Beach County Ballot

The divider line between Republican and Democrat appears to be pointing to the second dot, suggesting it is the correct one for a Democratic vote.

The arrows look decorative, not functional.

Bush is first on the ballot, and the punch dot for the Republicans is also first. This is good design, making it highly unlikely that a Bush voter would make an error.

The Democrats are listed second, but the correct punch dot for them is third. Since it is logical to assume that one punches the second dot on the ballot to vote for them, this is unsuccessful design.

*1 This is the logical place for the dots corresponding to the second column of party listings. (Florida law actually specifies that voters must mark the box to the right of the ballot. The county election officials foolishly violated this law.)

*2 Since the English language is read from left to right, it is natural to expect that the dot will appear after the name. The sudden shift in the pattern – putting the dots for the right column on the left – is likely to confuse voters.**

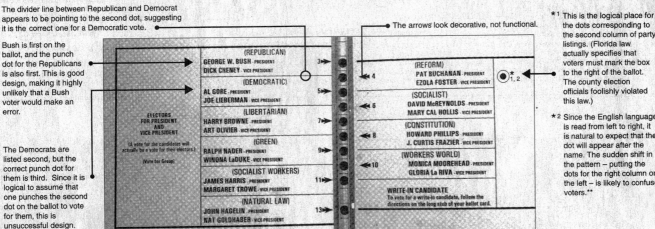

** Many official bodies and corporations approve products or documents that are incompetently designed. When a design causes problems for a significant number of people, even if it was "approved," the product is usually recalled, and sometimes reparations are made.

1. Notice the order in which the political parties are listed on the ballot. How do you think this order was determined? How might it suggest some kind of hierarchy?

2. Written English is read from left to right, top to bottom. How does this ballot *not* suit readers of English? How could it be improved?

1. Examine the layout of the ballot. What gets emphasis? Look at the positioning of the vertical and horizontal lines and the placement of the dots and arrows. Consider the various sizes of type—and notice that most of it is in all capital letters. See how the candidates' names are positioned—some aligned to the left, some not. How are the candidates treated the same? How are they treated differently? What might be the party affiliation of the designer?

2. Here are ballots from three nations: Costa Rica, Ethiopia, and Peru. Compare the Palm Beach County ballot to the ballots from other nations (you can find additional examples with a Web search for "election ballot"). How does ballot design influence voting? Why do some ballots contain only the images of party symbols? Why do others contain photographs of candidates?

Ballot from Costa Rica

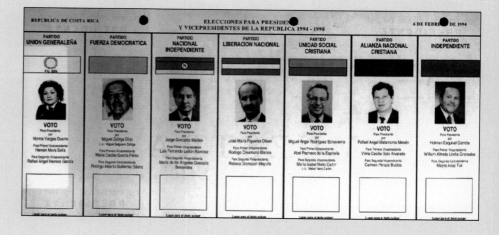

Ballot from Ethiopia

Ballot from Peru

3. Design your own ballot. Pay attention to the elements of design—typeface and font, layout, images and other graphics. Is your ballot intuitive—will voters understand easily how to use it?

After you've designed your ballot, write an essay describing its features. How does it compare with other ballots? What issues did you consider in its design?

A New Poland, No Joke

SARAH BOXER

Hitting on the idea of the kite was "like finding gold in the street," Szymon Gutkowski says. Gutkowski is the managing director of DDB Corporate Profiles, an advertising agency in Warsaw. A kite, he says, connotes youth, freedom, playfulness, and hope "in any language, any country." It floats gracefully above nations and politics. "It's extremely positive." And soon it may become Poland's national logo.

Last year, Poland's Ministry of Foreign Affairs hired DDB Corporate Profiles, a branch of the global agency DDB, to design a logo that could be used to promote tourism and trade. This summer, the company unveiled its design: a red-and-white kite whose tail is held by a dancing stick figure that doubles as the K in the word "Polska." The Polska lettering is thick, red, and curvaceous, a nod to the emblem of the Solidarity movement. The red-and-white design on the kite is a four-square checkered pattern, reminiscent of the emblem on Polish warplanes.

You might wonder why Poland needs a logo. It already has a nice flag, a band of white resting on a band of red, and an emblem, the white eagle. The problem is that the eagle is too traditional and too common. (Germany, Russia, and the United States all have eagles as national emblems.) And "flags have nationalist, military, or political connotations," Wally Olins, a British branding consultant, says. The kite is post-political. It represents a break from the past, Olins adds. "It is joyful, modern."

And commercial. Like the Nike swoosh or McDonald's golden arches, the kite is an advertisement. It says: Come here. Buy our stuff. Eat our food. We're not grim. We're fun. "We want to target the worldwide consumer. We want to show we are a young, dynamic country," Gutkowski says, adding that "politicians now realize that a country is a brand." And as with any other brand, people have associations, good or bad, with the nations they know. But can you change people's minds by repackaging, rebranding a nation?

In 1999, Olins's old company, Wolff Olins, proposed that Germany, the land of beer, Hitler, and lederhosen, could be transformed in the eyes of the world into a warm and friendly nation "by replacing black in the current national colors with the European blue." The tip was not taken.

A few years earlier, Wolff Olins had made another suggestion—that Great Britain, a stuffy nation with a queen, a palace, and rain, could seem like a more hip and happening place if it erased the "Great" from its name and ditched the Union Jack. "We feel that the Union Jack is no longer representative of a modern Britain," Wolff Olins's Web site proclaimed, because "it stands for imperialism in many parts of the world." In 1998, the British rebranding effort was taken up by Prime Minister Tony Blair's much derided "Cool Britannia" campaign. A pop version of "God Save the Queen" greeted the queen at a meeting of the Commonwealth. And British Airways infamously decided to replace the Union Jack colors on its planes' tail fins with psychedelic, multicultural designs.

Why does anyone think national rebranding works? Because of Spain. Two decades ago, Joan Miro designed a splashy, sunny national emblem to promote tourism. Thanks in part to the España logo, Spain is no longer associated just with Franco, the Spanish Civil War, and Don Quixote. It is a country of wine (Rioja), moves (Pedro Almodóvar), and art (Miró).

But in the case of Poland, rebranding is different because the idea came from the government. After years of Communist rule, Poland, rushing to emulate what it sees as modern Western ways, has put itself in the hands of DDB Corporate Profiles, an

ad agency whose greatest local success to date has been a beer campaign.

Last summer, the agency started thinking about what kind of brand Poland should be, but first it had to find out what kind of brand the country already was. Anna Koszur, the brand consulting director of DDB Corporate Profiles, assembled groups of foreigners to free associate about Poland. Their responses included gray, cold, vodka, poor, white, unsmiling, unfriendly, sad, boring, hard-living, fast-driving, hard-working, car-stealing, argumentative, creative, chauvinistic, chaotic, conservative, romantic, sentimental, anti-Semitic, Catholic, Walesa, Solidarity, Auschwitz, Chopin.

"What they thought about Poland is that they 10 were quite afraid of it," Gutkowski says.

Poles don't have a very good image of themselves either. When Koszur brought Poles into focus groups, they rated themselves brave, romantic, patriotic, and strong, but also irrational, impatient, disorganized, and argumentative; they said they love blood, martyrdom, and alcohol. How to turn the tide?

The design process took about a year. First came a logo of a white eagle, representing Poland, surrounded by the yellow stars of the European Union. Then came a logo with three different colored blocks—red, yellow and blue—with white stars inside each one. The stars kept multiplying, a sign that the designers were fixated on showing Poland among the European nations. The unspoken hope was that Poland could escape Eastern Europe by joining the European Union. (The slogan for the rebranding campaign is "Poland: Europe Is Bigger.") At one point, the K of Polska was drawn as a white star. At another point, the artist drew a blue horn of plenty with yellow stars and fire coming out of it. The Ministry of Foreign Affairs asked, What is it, a snake?

Finally, riffing on the theme of liberation rather than European union, Wojciech Mierowski, the creative director of Brand Nature Access, the branding arm of DDB Corporate Profiles, drew a kite. At first he formed the kite's tail out of white stars on a blue background. Then he shaped it like the Vistula River. Next he had the kite's tail cross the shape of Poland and wrote the name Polska under it. Finally the K of the Polska grabbed hold of the tail of the kite. The ministry loved it. It was youthful, fun and, well, not already claimed.

Many countries have commercial or tourist logos. Canada has a maple leaf. Hungary has a heart. Holland has a tulip. Estonia has a yellow sun with bands of blue, black, and white beneath. But no one has a kite. "It was out there to be taken," Gutkowski says. What's more, it was deemed an appropriate heir to the Solidarity logo. Gutkowski says, "A dancing group of people flying a kite with Poland's colors" has taken the place of protesters carrying a bloody flag.

What do foreigners think of the new logo? A brief survey of Americans yielded these responses: Charlie Brown with his kite stuck in a tree, Thing One and Thing Two in "The Cat in the Hat," Ben Franklin in the lightning storm, and the brush-off "Go fly a kite." Not a peep about Poland. And not unambiguously good associations.

"It's bourgeois," Lawrence Weschler, the director of the New York Institute for the Humanities, who wrote a paean to the Solidarity logo years ago, says. "It's capitalist. It says life is a holiday." And that dancing K, he added, is derivative. Franz Kafka used it in his drawings of Joseph K.

Tom Geismar, a partner at the graphic design firm Chermayeff & Geismar, which created the NBC peacock, says that the new logo "is sort of fussy—the kite and the string."

Rafal Olbinski, a Polish-born artist who works in the United States, says, "The kite is uplifting, but maybe too childish" for a nation that is 1,000 years old. It also ignores Poland's tradition of surreal posters, those dark and elliptical designs created to befuddle Communist censors.

Maybe design isn't everything though. After all, logos "take on the meaning of the things they represent," Geismar says.

Think of the swastika. It began in India as a [20] symbol of good fortune. In the early 20th century, it appeared on beer bottles and girls' club magazines. It was a great design. Then came Hitler. Or think of the hammer and sickle. That wasn't a very strong design, Olins says, but it became a very powerful image. In both cases, the logo's meaning was pounded in. The Nazis and the Soviets saturated their nations with these symbols and regulated how and when they were used. Albert Speer, Hitler's creative director, made sure the swastika would appear "on aircraft, racing cars, everything." Olins says.

"It's hard to get consistency without a dictatorship," he adds, almost wistfully.

Will the Polish kite take off? Who knows? But regardless, Poland has broken some strange new ground with its logo. It's not just that the government of Poland has spearheaded the rebranding process, but also what the logo itself implies. What sets the kite apart from all other logos is that it is painfully, almost pathetically, honest about what is expected from it. The hope is that the kite will lift Poland up and let it float gently away from its past and toward the prosperity of Europe.

"Why has Poland depicted itself as a day at the beach?" Weschler asks. "I don't know. Maybe if you lived its history, you might want a day at the beach."

▶ The kite logo was commissioned by the Polish government to change the image of Poland.

focus.

1. Write down ten adjectives that you think describe a kite. Do you agree with Szymon Gutkowski's assertion that a kite connotes playfulness and hope? What about an eagle? What makes a kite "post-political" and an eagle politically loaded?

2. Consider Tom Geismar's claim that logos "take on the meaning of the things they represent." Pick two logos you're familiar with. Have they taken on the identities of the products or companies they represent? If so, how?

respond.

1. "A country is a brand," according to Szymon Gutkowski. What is the function of a brand in advertising? Where did the term "brand" originally come from? When you think of branding, do you think specifically of consumer goods, such as sneakers, or can the term be extended?

   How might a country function as a brand? What would be the purpose of branding a country? Think about the United States—is it already a brand? Or does it need to create a brand? What symbols are already associated with America? Do they serve to market it to tourists? to increase a sense of national pride? Are they successful in doing so?

   Write an essay on the branding of countries. Is a country inherently a brand, or does a brand have to be constructed and promoted?

2. Design a brand for your school or town. Make a list of all the associations surrounding your place of choice. Then pick a graphic that might symbolize the positive things about it. Identify appropriate words and incorporate them into your logo.

3. This tourist poster is by Australian artist Ken Done. Done's art, though not a

THE KEN DONE GALLERY, THE ROCKS, SYDNEY. ∩∩∩

brand per se, has become popular with Australian residents and visiting tourists and has helped shape the world's perception of Australia. Examine this poster carefully for its content. How does it contribute to your perception of Australia? What does it emphasize about Australia? If you've never been there, how might you imagine Australia to be, based on this poster? How might art such as Done's posters serve to "sell" a country? How does your state (or school) brand itself? How legitimate is the brand image? Write an essay evaluating this brand. Include examples of the image.

Tibor Kalman (1949–1999) immigrated to the United States from Hungary at the age of seven. As a young journalism student, he worked at a Barnes and Noble bookstore in New York City. One day, the window-display designer called in sick, leaving Kalman the task of arranging the display. The opportunity shifted Kalman's interest from the printed word to design. In 1979, he founded the innovative design firm M&Co.

The following piece was originally published in 1987 in *I.D. Magazine,* a journal read by professional designers. In it Kalman analyzes corporate logos, critically questioning the way in which advertisers graphically design written text to make it marketable. He follows the questions by placing corporate logos in a flow chart that illustrates how they might be redesigned.

What's Happening to Logos?

TIBOR KALMAN

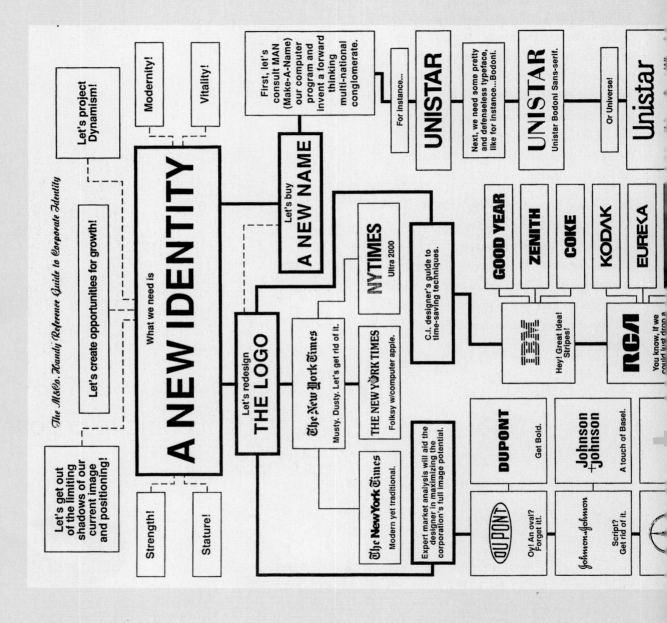

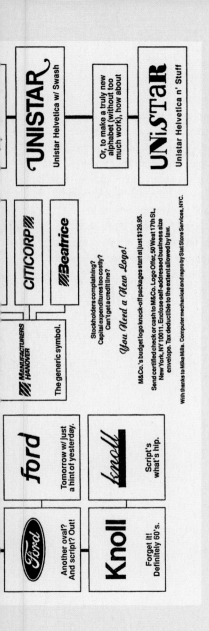

WHAT'S happening to logos? Why do they look just like one another? Why do the new ones always seem to look worse than the old ones?

WEREN'T logos originally designed to distinguish one product or company from another? Didn't they once give a sense of a company's character or direction or point of view?

DO designers of logos encourage corporations to have distinct, meaningful marks? Would it make much difference if the Fortune 500 just had their names set in Helvetica bold? Would we know more about the companies? Or less? Or just as much?

DO corporations want nebulous non-identity identities? Is it easier for designers to sell non-identities than identities? Do the designers of these logos actually like them? What do corporations get for the six-figure fees they pay?

WHY does everyone like the IBM logo more than the Sears logo? Is is because the IBM logo was designed in 1962 and Sears in 1984? Why is one better than the other? What's the difference between the two?

DO old logos seem nicer than new ones just because they're more familiar? Or are most redesigned logos just undistinguished? Or ugly?

WHY do some companies, after evaluation, choose to continue using their "old" logos? What is the image we get of a company that uses a fifty-year-old logo? Why are some companies capable of updating or reorganizing their identities while keeping the essential elements intact?

WHY do some designers apply the same design "tricks" to various clients? Is it because the design doesn't really matter?

WHY do so many logos look alike? Do logos need to mean anything? Are the differences in designs more important than the similarities?

WHY is it that some companies never seem to change their logos? Do they look dated?

IS IT TRUE, as rumor has it, that GE is redesigning its logo? Will it be a lot different? Does it matter?

CAN YOU TELL what companies do from their logos? Can you guess why they picked their logos?

focus.

1. Notice that Kalman composed his article as a list of questions, starting with the title. Why do you think he wrote it this way? Why do you suppose he set the first word of each paragraph in bold caps?

2. Why do you think Kalman displays the logos in a corporate flow chart? What point is he making?

respond.

1. Look up the words "logo" and "logos" in the *Oxford English Dictionary*. An online version may be available on your library's Web site, or you can find it in the reference section of the library. Note down what each word meant at different points in history. You'll find that "logo" in the sense that Kalman uses the word is short for "logogram," so look up the longer term as well.

   Write a summary charting the evolution of the Greek word "logos" from its earliest recorded use to the modern concept of the commercial logo. What do the definitions have in common? How have they changed? Are they two sides of the same coin? Or has the meaning changed entirely?

2. Logos are more prominent today than when Kalman published "What's Happening to Logos?" in 1987. Note all the logos you see at a concert or sports event, including those of official sponsors and those worn by spectators. How do these logos distinguish similar products? What else are they saying besides the brand name?

3. Notice the typography of two magazines that target the same audience. How does the typeface influence the look of a magazine? For example, what does the typography of *InStyle* say about the magazine? How is the look of *InStyle* different from *Vogue*? How might *InStyle* be redesigned for men? Write an essay comparing the look of two magazines, including visual examples to illustrate your comparison.

Ellen Lupton and **J. Abbott Miller** collaborate as writers, graphic designers, and teachers at the Maryland Institute College of Art in Baltimore. Dedicated to examining the cultural role of design and the transmission of the written word, Lupton and Miller have collectively and independently received numerous awards for their work, most notably the Chrysler Design Award and the New York Magazine Award.

First published in 1996 in Lupton and Miller's book *Design Writing Research: Writing on Graphic Design*, "McPaper" argues that *USA Today*'s introduction of televisionlike graphics into print newspapers has revolutionized the way we receive and digest news.

McPaper: *USA Today* and the Journalism of Hope

ELLEN LUPTON AND J. ABBOTT MILLER

Newspapers have been one of graphic design's most immutable genres. Change has historically been resisted, unwelcome, and calculated to be so gradual as to be imperceptible. A strident departure from convention occurred with the 1982 launch of *USA Today*. The design of this new paper responded to competition from television and magazines, which had become a major source of news for the American public.

Born of marketing surveys and opinion polls, *USA Today* is a product engineered for consumption by the largest possible audience. In 1995, The Gannett Corporation's *USA Today* was the second-largest newspaper in the U.S. Each day, the paper's mission is printed at the top of the editorial page: "*USA Today* hopes to serve as a forum for better understanding and unity to help make the U.S.A. truly one nation." First uttered by Al Neuharth at the paper's 1982 debut, these words are a mixture of lofty goals and sales pitch: national unity = national media = national markets. The subject of

USA Today is domestic and, to a lesser extent, international news that affects the nation. While papers like *The New York Times*, the nation's "paper of record," and *The Los Angeles Times* are also national in scope, they are still anchored to specific metropolitan areas. Since its inception, *USA Today* has taken the broadness of its desired market as an editorial agenda. "National unity" is a persistent theme of the paper, articulated through Gallup polls, opinion surveys, and stories focused on Washington, D.C., Hollywood, and Smalltown, U.S.A.—locales that serve, metonymically, as slices of the larger American pie chart. Without the theme of national unity, *USA Today* has little to offer readers normally served by local journalism. While the scope of its coverage is not dissimilar to that found in network television news programming, it is still unusual in the traditionally decentralized realm of newspapers.

In design terms, *USA Today* is not so much a "revolution" as a clever combination of lessons learned from magazines, film, and television over the last three decades. Its adaptive, synthetic approach to design has yielded a look that is both surprising and utterly familiar: the paper resembles a full-color printout of a half-hour of network news and commercials. The novelty consists in seeing it in hard copy. While judgments about its design have varied, *USA Today* provoked a sense of inevitability when it emerged, a feeling that, sooner or later, television would force such a change, and the gray sobriety of "the news" would suddenly have the colorful, diffuse, high-speed impact of TV. *USA Today*'s relationship to television has been deliberately cultivated. Full-color photographs are framed with drawings of TVs, early advertising campaigns dubbed the publication "the first modern newspa-per for *readers* who grew up as *viewers*," and the *USA Today* vending machines were consciously designed to look like televisions.

While there is a semiotic correspondence between the coarse resolution of the video image and the grainy dot pattern of four-color printing, it is the speed and sound of television that have influenced the paper's graphic style. The editors recognize that the logic of the soundbite, exemplified in the terse diction of Peter Jennings and Ted Koppel, has diminished the attention span of readers. More than the "look" of television, the authoritative, condensed *speech* of the TV anchor begot the style of *USA Today*. A ring of authority comes from minimizing details and eradicating qualifying or parenthetical statements. When asked to evaluate *USA Today*'s influence on other newspapers, Richard Curtis, managing editor of graphics and photography, cited the paper's clipped writing style, which allows it to cover more news in less space.

USA Today's multi-colored data graphics and full-color photography have been widely imitated. This pictorial emphasis makes *USA Today* suspect among readers and journalists who regard newspapers as a textual medium, that, *when necessary*, may resort to photographs and illustrative graphics. *USA Today* crosses genres freely, incorporating the breezy tone of newscaster speech with the illustrative style of TV weather maps.

Many of the features that make *USA Today* exceptional among newspapers are elements characteristic of other media. The style of the paper's information graphics and typography has been culled from the pages of *Time* and *Newsweek*. Walter Bernard's 1977 redesign of *Time*, which provoked *Newsweek* to change its own graphic style—culminating in Roger Black's 1985 redesign—reshaped the editorial identity of magazines. According to Black, "*USA Today* probably would not be possible without *Time*." Although information graphics had been a standard feature in both *Time* and *Newsweek*, they were usually unimaginative, crude in execution, and limited in number. The pop data graphics for *Time*, begun in 1978 by Nigel Holmes, heavily influenced *USA Today*'s house style.

The *Time* and *Newsweek* redesigns brought visually flamboyant and conceptually elaborate information graphics to the fore of newsweekly journalism, which in turn influenced other print media. A number of publications with a picture-graphic bias attest to an "infotainment" zeitgeist that has influenced design since the early 1980s. Noteworthy examples include Access Press, a publisher of guidebooks established in 1980 by Richard Saul Wurman. The *Access* series emphasized the role of information graphics in books on travel, medicine, and sports. At the other end of the spectrum were the baroque charts and diagrams of *Spy* magazine, launched in

▶ *USA Today*'s first issue, in 1982, showed the "brighter side" that the paper would consistently emphasize. See, for example, the headline: "Miracle: 327 survive, 55 die."

▶ The *USA Today* logo is one of its most important graphic elements. The sans serif type punching through a blue field distinguishes it from the black-letter treatments of traditional newspaper logos. Numerous versions were developed, including those shown here, before arriving at the final one. Masthead design by Young & Rubicam, New York.

1986. *Spy*'s techniques of graphic parody reflected a fascination with both naïve and sophisticated modes of information graphics.

While the mass appeal of *Time* and *Newsweek* make them clear predecessors of *USA Today*, the newspaper industry was responding to its own imperative to say less and show more. *USA Today* followed in the footsteps of many newspapers throughout the country—notably the *Morning Call*, *The Chicago Tribune*, the Orange County *Register*, and *The Miami Herald*—which were increasingly reporting the news through didactic graphics, large photographs, and illustrations arranged in magazine-inspired layouts. Many of the changes that occurred at *The New York Times* in the late 1970s, under art director and assistant managing editor Louis Silverstein, indicated a paradigm shift in American news media. Between 1976 and 1978, Silverstein introduced daily themed sections such as "Science Times," "Home," and "The Living Section." The bold treatment of large illustrations and photographs reinforced the magazine-like quality of the sections and set them apart from the still-sober look of the main section.

USA Today also responded to the expansion of television news, marked by the establishment of CNN in 1980. Programs such as *60 Minutes, 20/20, Nightline, Prime Time Live*, and the *MacNeil/Lehrer Newshour* indicated a trend toward "primetiming" the news. Tabloid TV programs, such as *Hard Copy, Rescue 911, Unsolved Mysteries,* and *America's Most Wanted*, provide the same unabashed conflation of news and entertainment as *USA Today*.

USA Today's reporting implicitly equates objec- 10 tivity with simplicity and brevity. This equation is made clear in *The Making of McPaper*, an in-house history of *USA Today*. Throughout the book, the reader is reminded of the editors' ruthless demands for the simplest presentation of facts. The trademark terseness of *USA Today*'s writing style is partly an effect of production: the news must fit into the 56-page maximum capacity shared by all of the paper's 36 print sites (33 in the U.S., one in Hong Kong, one in Singapore, and one in Switzerland). Thus, *USA Today* is a fixed matrix that the news must be carefully tailored to accommodate. The clipped writing style results from the gap between a small "news-hold" and a broad agenda.

The pursuit of brevity was institutionalized at the paper with monthly "McNugget Awards" for "tight, clear, fact-filled stories." Brevity, clarity, and objectivity are noble goals, but when chosen over other determinants of good journalism, such as comprehensiveness and quality of interpretation, they are incomplete criteria. Moreover, while the writing at *USA Today* is ritually purged of detail and intricacy, the information graphics are complexly rendered and loaded with gratuitous color and illusionistic tonal gradations. This transformation of abstract data into detailed tableaux appears at odds with the brevity of the articles. Yet when asked if the paper had an overall goal in producing its graphics, Richard Curtis cited "simplicity and clarity." He attributed the colorful stylization of the graphics to an effort to provide entertainment and decoration as well as information. This attitude is shared by Nigel Holmes, whose graphics for *Time* familiarize data by converting abstract numbers into iconic forms.

The graphic designer and political scientist Edward Tufte, in his landmark books *The Visual Display of Quantitative Information* and *Envisioning Information*, has argued for data graphics whose visual presentation is the product of a content-based approach to color and form. Color, according to Tufte, should be used to convey concrete distinctions; the amount of ink expended in a chart or diagram should be weighed against the amount of information conveyed. Such criteria play no part in the graphics of *USA Today, Newsweek, Time*, and other newsweeklies. In *Visual Display*, Tufte specifically criticized a *Time* graphic because its pictorial conceit misrepresented the statistic it purported to elucidate.[1] Such pictorial conceits are a staple among *USA Today*'s fifteen full-time graphic journalists.

The design principles outlined by Tufte, with their concern for method and objectivity, recall the rigor and purity associated with Swiss modernism. This rigor was also part of Otto Neurath's Isotype movement, which held that information graphics can attain a communicative effect superior—not merely parallel—to the written word. Beginning in the 1920s, Neurath sought a vocabulary of schematic symbols that would operate with alphabetic consistency. Stylistically, Neurath's silhouette forms had a typographic clarity and regularity that aligned them with the reduced imagery of much of modernist graphic design. While the Isotype movement was more narrowly focused than the scope of graphics Tufte is concerned with, both can be located within a Modernist-Rationalist lineage that eschews decorative forms and colors in favor of what could be called "prose graphics."

The graphic journalists at *USA Today* and the mass-circulation newsweeklies, on the other hand, have a more eclectic, Pop-inspired approach, parallel to the sign-based architecture of Robert Venturi, Steven Izenour, and Denise Scott Brown. Their line-

age can be traced to the Push Pin Studios, with their distinctly Postmodern approach: pragmatic, anti-systematic, populist, deliberately inconsistent, and playful. The *USA Today* style has much in common with the synthetic blending of cartoon styles and conventions typical of Push Pin illustrator Seymour Chwast's work. The figures that populate many *USA Today* graphics are a kind of hybrid between Otto Neurath's severe "information man" and the more approachable Elmer Fudd: they are info-toons for the infotainment age. Hollywood's translation of cartoons into the "real life" of cinema—from *Superman* (1978) and *Who Framed Roger Rabbit?* (1988) to *Batman* (1989) and *Dick Tracy* (1990)—has accompanied the incorporation of cartoons into the "real life" of the news. While Neurath and Tufte represent the values of "prose graphics," *USA Today* and its magazine progenitors promote "theatrical graphics," which spotlight the illustrative, decorative, and emotive potential of data. A serious drawback is that "theatrical graphics" can put an editorial spin on the data being presented. A caricature of an Arab in one of Holmes's graphics for *Time* made the data itself largely irrelevant: the hostility of the image overwhelmed the statistics being presented. Apart from such stylized representations, graphics that are apparently "objective" or straightforward may have complex inflections. For example, in the pictograms in Access Press's book *Medical Access* (1985), the icon that represents "man" is adapted from the 1974 U.S. Department of Transportation symbols that populate airports, restrooms, and lob-

1. Tufte reproduces a *Time* chart of crude-oil exports represented with drawings of barrels and shows that the volumetric amount suggested by the image is at odds with the data. Tufte, *The Visual Display of Quantitative Information* (Cheshire, CT: Graphics Press, 1983).

▶ *USA Today* graphics are a hybrid between the Information Man of the 1920s and Elmer Fudd. The figure on the right is the 1990 Everyman who presents statistics that "shape the nation." Everyman is drawn by Keith Carter; Elmer Fudd copyright 1990 Warner Brothers.

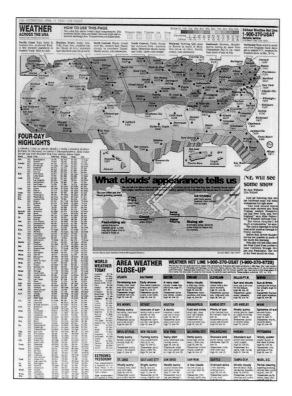

The colorful weather map is the most widely imitated feature of *USA Today*. It is a graphic translation of a TV weather map, without pulsating suns or encroaching storm fronts. Art director, Richard A. Curtis.

statistics are not willfully misrepresented in the information graphics of *USA Today*, the treatment of them as info-toons discourages the sustained analysis this mode of communication can offer. One of the virtues of information graphics is that, unlike narrative forms, they may be read analytically from different vantage points, yielding different insights. Yet in the case of many of *USA Today's* graphics, the multiple content of the data is tied to one simplistic image, which typically indicates only the broadest message of the data, such as *rise/fall, few/many*. The pictorial devices used in the graphics counter-productively anchor the data to one dominant narrative.

While more attention is now given to graphics in news media—with a consequent expansion of opportunity for designers—there is at the same time a narrowing of the kind of information designers and illustrators are called upon to convey. Increasingly, mainstream journalism is exchanging editorial cartoonists, who have traditionally been expected to express their own opinions, for "graphic journalists," whose job is to express the opinions of others, gathered through Gallup polls and reader surveys. Most of the graphics is *USA Today* deal with statistics aimed to show the range of public opinion toward a particular issue—to represent everyone, and yet no one in particular. The historian Warren Susmann has observed that George Gallup's American Institute of Public Opinion, founded in 1935, was pivotal in the culture of the 1930s for "the discovery and molding of dominant cultural patterns . . . [and] for their reinforcement." The predominance of opinion-survey graphics in *USA Today* is indicative of the paper's vested interest in the theme of national unity, a theme that favors consensus.

USA Today claims that readers buy the paper an

bies. The symbol for "woman," however, is differentiated from her male counterpart not only by the clichéd curvature of her hips and breasts in silhouette, but also by interior lines that outline her face, indicate her nipples, and suggest her hairstyle. These cartoon-like signs of femininity belie the supposed objectivity of the Access Press style.

Many of *USA Today's* graphics illustrate the tension between journalistic ideals of objectivity and the sometimes conflicting demands for entertainment, "human interest," and decoration. Although

average of 3.5 times a week and typically read it in combination with another newspaper. Thus *USA Today* constitutes only one part of a reader's daily intake of news. This fact, frequently offered as a defense in answer to *USA Today*'s critics, raises serious questions. Why should the paper attempt to be exhaustive in its coverage when people have all sorts of other news sources? Why should it attempt to be comprehensive in its international reporting when other papers do that better? Why shouldn't it emphasize good news when other newspapers are filled with bad news? *USA Today* defines and positions itself in *opposition* to mainstream journalism. It is stridently *not* comprehensive; instead, it is eager to provide what founder Al Neuharth calls a "journalism of hope." In doing so it positions it its competitors as overly serious, argumentative, gloomy, and gray.

"Positioning" is, of course, a marketing term, and *USA Today* has found a large and profitable market by differentiating itself, visually and editorially, from goods that fall into the same category. Curtis succinctly explained the paper's source of distinction: "We use graphics a lot, they use graphics a little. We write short stories, they write long stories. We think of ourselves as lively, upbeat, positive." This incorporation of marketing strategies into the paper's editorial stance raises a number of questions: What happens when a newspaper embraces, not merely accepts, that it is not a primary, or even comprehensive, news source? How does this affect what is deemed newsworthy or what constitutes balanced coverage? What happens to a newspaper (a textual medium) when it is modeled after television (a visual medium)?

The high circulation numbers of *USA Today*, particularly among young readers, indicate that *USA Today* will survive. Its popularity proves that graphic journalists have an increasingly large role to play in the visually saturated contexts of contemporary journalism. Serious magazines and newspapers that fail to take heed of *USA Today*'s popularity, and are even scornful of its emphasis on the visual, will find themselves cast as retrograde and even reactionary. The challenge for designers, publishers, and editors is how to wed state-of-the-art information graphics to a progressive, critical editorial agenda, rather than to the all-purpose marketing opportunity that is *USA Today*.

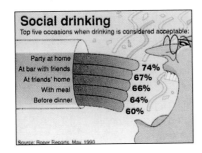

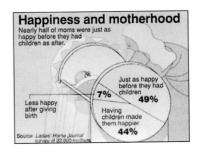

▶ Statistical data are often presented graphically, centered on one simplistic image.

focus.

1. *USA Today* is marketed as "the first modern newspaper for readers who grew up as viewers." Think about the ways in which you received local and national news growing up. Did your parents read the newspaper? watch TV? listen to the radio? How do you learn about what is going on in the world now? How does your way compare with your parents'?

2. The influence of television on *USA Today* has been controversial from the beginning. Critics have accused *USA Today*'s editors of being more interested in entertainment than in reporting the news. The editors of *USA Today* have replied that not every newspaper needs to be serious or exhaustive in its coverage. They make no apologies for their lack of analysis and their emphasis on short articles and graphics that report "happy" news. Does news reporting necessarily fall into two categories—gray, dense, and sober analysis versus colorful, fluffy, lightweight reporting? Can news be reported in visually appealing ways and still contain in-depth analysis? Find some examples from newspapers you read to support your answer.

respond.

1. Compare either the print or the Web versions of the *New York Times* <www.nytimes.com> and *USA Today* <www.usatoday.com>. Note the elements of each newspaper's front page, including the headlines, the presence or absence of graphics, the typefaces and font, and the types of articles that are featured. Make notes.

Write an essay that compares the rhetorical features on the two papers's front pages. Think particularly about issues of audience. To whom is each periodical marketed? Do the two papers serve the same functions for the reading public or do their purposes differ? What are the strengths of each paper? What are their weaknesses? How are the issues of audience reflected in the layout and design of each paper?

2. Find an article in *USA Today* that presents information both verbally and visually. Write a short analysis examining what is presented in the verbal explanation and what is included in the visual explanation. Are any of the same facts presented in both? Does either work better? Imagine the article as only verbal. Would you find it easier to read? harder? Why? What if it were entirely visual?

Jim Heimann (b. 1948) is a graphic designer, illustrator, and teacher. His books include *Car Hops and Curb Service* and he is a contributor to the *Los Angeles Times*, *Rolling Stone*, and other periodicals. He teaches at the Art Center College of Design in Pasadena, California, and he has had graphic work displayed in galleries worldwide.

The following graphics are taken from Heimann's most recent book, *May I Take Your Order? American Menu Design, 1920–1960*. Restaurant menus were once all handwritten, usually on a chalkboard. Developments in printing changed this, and in 1834 Delmonico's in New York introduced the first printed menu. Gradually menus became more elaborate, and by the 1930s menus functioned to whet appetites, explain food entries, create a mood, and sell food. Restaurant menus since then reflect their times, showing patriotism in the 1940s, and images of atomic power and space travel in the 1950s. TV and fast food in the 1960s inspired even more innovative graphics to capture busy diners. Many restaurants continue to develop careful graphic identities (see M&Co's designs for Restaurant Florent in Chapter 1) and to reflect their particular moment in time.

Included here are the cover and table of contents from *May I Take Your Order?* along with several menus from the 1920s to the 1960s. As you look at these materials, think about how menus function as arguments targeting us as diners and consumers.

May I Take Your Order?

JIM HEIMANN

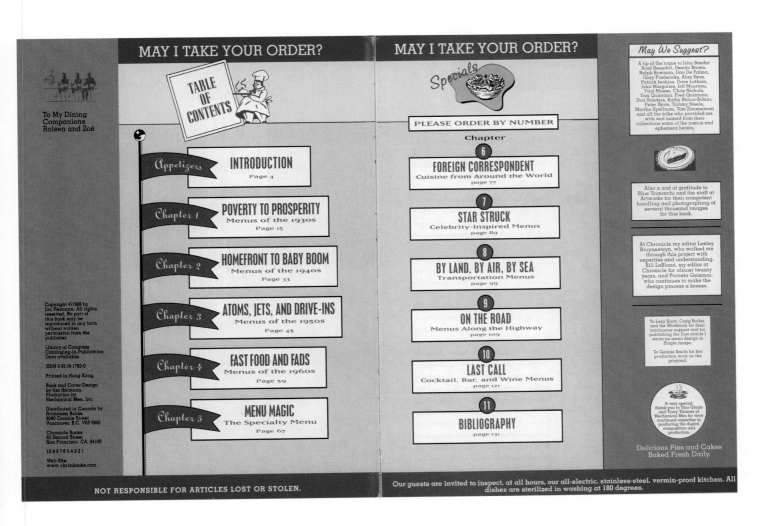

May We Suggest?

A tip of the toque to John Baeder, Brad Benedict, Desoto Brown, Ralph Bowman, Dan De Palma, Gary Fredericks, Alan Hess, Patrick Jenkins, Dave Lathom, John Margolies, Jeff Moureau, Paul Mussa, Chris Nichols, Tom Quintana, Fred Quintana, Don Sanders, Kathy Staico-Schorr, Peter Shire, Tommy Steele, Martha Spellman, Tom Zimmerman and all the folks who provided me with and loaned from their collections some of the menus and ephemera herein.

Also a nod of gratitude to Blue Trimarchi and the staff at Artworks for their competent handling and photographing of several thousand images for this book.

At Chronicle my editor Lesley Bruynesteyn, who walked me through this project with expertise and understanding, Bill LeBlond, my editor at Chronicle for almost twenty years, and Pamela Geismar, who continues to make the design process a breeze.

To Larry Scott, Craig Butler, and the Workbook for their continuous support and for publishing the first article I wrote on menu design in Single Image.

To Genine Smith for her production work on the proposal.

A very special thank-you to Tina Glaub and Tracy Thomas of Mechanical Men for their continued expertise in producing the digital composition and production.

Delicious Pies and Cakes Baked Fresh Daily.

To My Dining Companions Roleen and Zoë

Copyright ©1998 by Jim Heimann. All rights reserved. No part of this book may be reproduced in any form without written permission from the publisher.

Library of Congress Cataloging-In-Publication Data available.

ISBN 0-8118-1783-0

Printed in Hong Kong.

Book and Cover Design by Jim Heimann. Production by Mechanical Men, Inc.

Distributed in Canada by Raincoast Books 8680 Cambie Street Vancouver, B.C. V6P 6M9

Chronicle Books 85 Second Street San Francisco, CA. 94105

10 9 8 7 6 5 4 3 2 1

Web Site: www.chronbooks.com

TABLE OF CONTENTS

Specials

PLEASE ORDER BY NUMBER

Chapter

NOT RESPONSIBLE FOR ARTICLES LOST OR STOLEN.

Our guests are invited to inspect, at all hours, our all-electric, stainless-steel, vermin-proof kitchen. All dishes are sterilized in washing at 180 degrees.

1935

1925

1938

1945

Menu covers from the 1920s through the 1960s.

1953

1960s

1950s

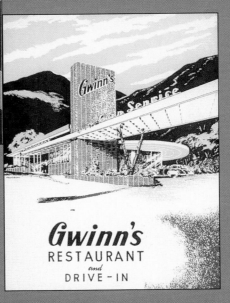

1954

The Howard Johnson's chain of restaurants once catered mostly to motorists.

▶ Maps showing the
restaurant's location and
the local landmarks were once
a popular menu tradition.

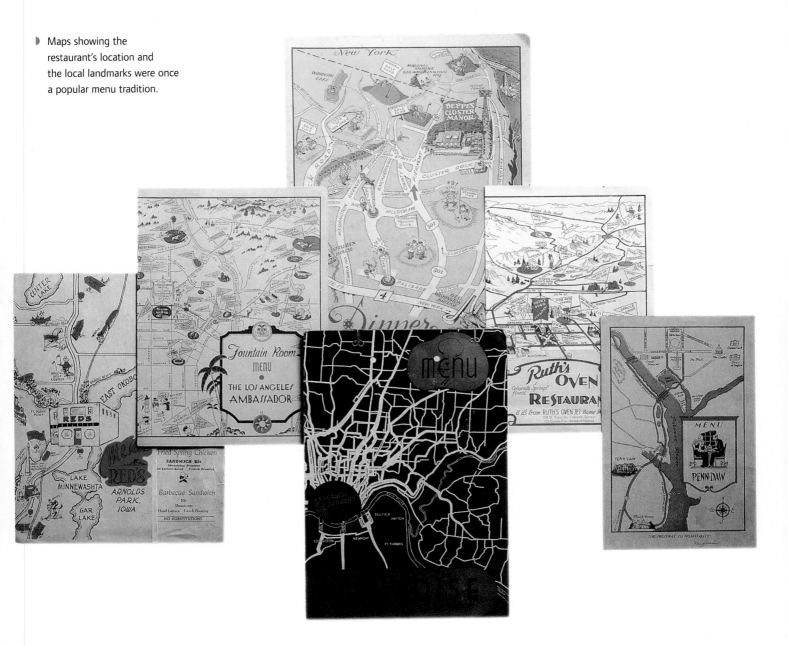

focus.

1. Notice the typeface and font in which the title of *May I Take Your Order?* is written. What kind of restaurant does it suggest? What else does the cover design lead you to expect in this book? Why do you think these particular colors were selected?

2. Read the disclaimers at the bottom of the Table of Contents. What would their function be on a real menu? What is their function on this mock menu?

respond.

1. Collect menus from several restaurants, either in print or from the Web. Study the design of each one. What is the basic look—traditional? elegant? hip? exotic? something else? How do the typography, the graphics, the layout, and the use of color create each look? Consider also the words, including the name of the restaurant. What do they tell you about its style? What argument do they make for eating at the restaurant?

Think of yourself as a hungry consumer. If you had to choose one of these establishments based on its menu alone, which factors would contribute to your decision? Write an essay that analyzes and then compares the rhetorical strategies of two menus.

2. Try your hand at designing your own menu. First, you'll have to decide on the kind of restaurant—a sports bar? a coffee house? a pizzeria?—and the clientele you hope to attract—college students? families? You'll need to figure out what will be on your menu, what look you want, and how you can appeal to your audience. Decide on a name for your restaurant. Next, make a sketch of the menu. Think about what typeface(s) and fonts are appropriate, what background and other colors you should use, and what clip art or other graphics would enhance your text. Then create your menu using word-processing software.

3. In the past, when smoking was an accepted part of the public dining experience, restaurants used matchbooks as a form of self-promotion. In fact, the custom caught on to such a large extent that couples getting married would often give away their own version at the wedding reception. In today's health-conscious world it is no longer an accepted practice. Take this opportunity to turn the old custom into a current one by designing a matchbook cover as an anti-smoking ad. Pay attention to the way the matchbook cover folds when you write your text and design your cover.

picture this

designing texts

Write a brief film review for an audience of fellow students. You'll need to say whether you think the film is good or bad, supporting your opinion with examples from the movie. Also, since you can't assume your readers will have seen the film, you'll need to give a brief summary of the plot.

Next, design your review for publication in a campus newspaper or magazine. For this purpose, you'll need to enlarge your title to look like a headline, and you may want to use a particularly telling sentence highlighted in some way. You'll want to illustrate your review with screenshots from the film, which you can download from the Web or literally cut and paste from print sources.

The screenshots are critical to convey what the movie is about. Your readers will imagine the film from your words and the images you select.

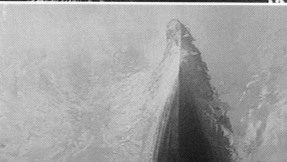

▷ Four different frames from the movie *The Piano.*

▶ Four different frames from the movie *Apocolypse Now*.

Finally, design a poster for the film—again, for an audience of your peers. It should be on 8½ × 11" paper, appropriate for posting on a bulletin board, and should include the name of the film, a photo or other graphic, maybe some quotes from critics, and a very short synopsis. You'll need to design a text that will attract someone's attention from a short distance—maybe by using a large headline or a striking image.

Complete this exercise by thinking about the design requirements for a text that someone will sit down and read versus a text that needs to catch someone's attention from a distance. How are they different? How are they the same?

gallery of images

designing texts

① *Bring in Da Noise, Bring in Da Funk,* poster design by Paula Scher of Pentagram Design. Scher is known for her great ability to illustrate and convey emotion with type. "Letterforms have character," she once said. "Letter-forms have weight, so designing with typography is like creating a montage. You're putting elements together in a specific way that creates a certain dynamic, and the words themselves help illustrate the point. You're using scale, color, texture to create an impression....If I'm doing a poster for a play, I've got to convey the spirit of the show and a sense of what the play is about. Part of design is creating order, and some of design is evoking spirit."

(2) Ad designed for Hewitt Associates, a global outsourcing and consulting firm. Typography is used here to represent both the figures in the image and their thoughts. The figures in this ad are made up of type; in the poster on the facing page, the background is made up of type. Note the difference between the two.

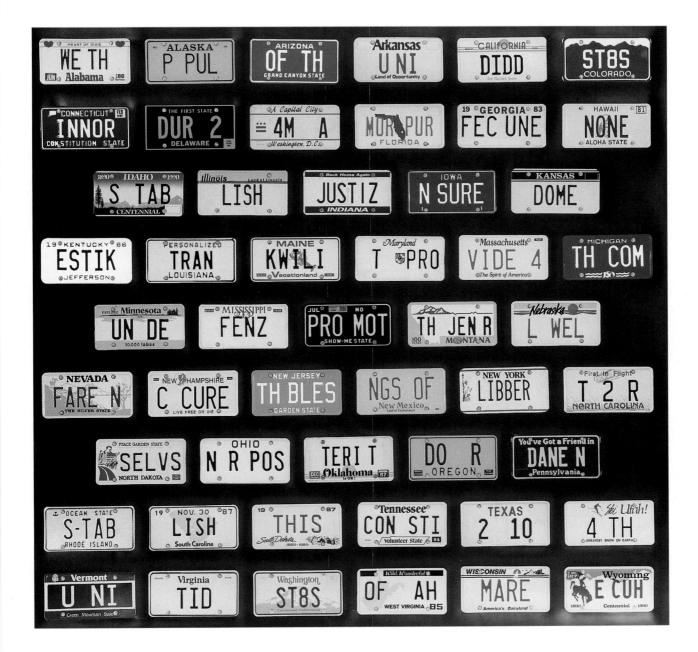

499

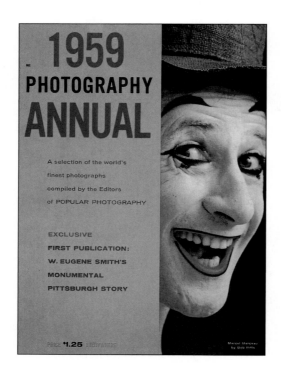

⑤ In 1955 the photographer Eugene Smith was commissioned to spend three weeks taking photographs for a book commemorating the bicentennial of Pittsburgh. He stayed a year and took seventeen thousand photographs. Only a small number of the photographs were ever used. In 1959, *Popular Photography* magazine gave Smith the opportunity to reproduce some of these photographs and also gave him the rare opportunity to create his own layouts. It allows us to see into the vision he had when taking the images. In later years, Smith often returned to this version of his Pittsburgh work as an example of his "many layered" approach to editing. Of the opening picture of the steelworker, which happened to be one of the last photos he made in Pittsburgh, Smith said, "I needed a picture of man submerged underneath industry, but not lost." The following is part of the essay that was published in *Popular Photography.* In this essay, Smith tells a story about Pittsburgh— the story he discovered while taking the pictures.

PITTSBURGH

Juanita Lee Smith

W. EUGENE SMITH'S
MONUMENTAL
POEM TO A CITY

Out of ten thousand looks at a city, out of countless nights without sleep and days without rest, out of a deep sympathy and a wide understanding, a great photographer has brought forth a magnificent epic in pictures. W. Eugene Smith's *Pittsburgh* has been whispered around photography's inner circles for two years, discussed discreetly among picture editors, much admired by the very few who have seen parts of it.

Smith wanted more from *Pittsburgh* than just generous display in a big magazine. He had firm convictions about the organization and presentation of the pictures, and he had many things to say in words as well. He had felt for a long time that a photographer ought not to lose control over his work as soon as the prints were made. He had, in fact, left the staff of the biggest U. S. picture magazine in a defense of that principle. He was determined that *Pittsburgh* should establish it firmly.

Magazine editors were avidly interested. They were unanimous in praise of *Pittsburgh*. But one after another declined Smith's terms: presentation satisfactory to him—which virtually meant layouts and text by Smith. Some frankly refused to abdicate these editorial functions; some sadly passed the buck to uninspired managements over their heads. *Life* went so far as to make several versions of layouts—each, it said, embodying Smith's ideas—but none was acceptable to him.

PHOTOGRAPHY ANNUAL's editors, having seen much of *Pittsburgh*, and hearing that the story was not yet scheduled for publication, approached Gene Smith with a proposal as revolutionary as his own demand: *Pittsburgh* would have at least 32 pages, and Smith would have full freedom in layout and text. What you see in these pages—expanded now to 38—is all W. Eugene Smith, pictures, layout, and text. The sole reservation is that at the time of the completion of the layout, illness and other emergencies prevented his preparing the written words as richly and fully as he would have liked.

Smith spent most of his time for more than two years on the Pittsburgh project, beginning with six months in 1955 and ending with a brief return to the city late in 1957. And in the largest sense he is not yet finished with Pittsburgh; he still feels a "terrible lingering urgency" that there is more to do, and he expects to return for a few days at a time to walk the city's streets and absorb more of its life.

The story originated with an assignment by historian Stefan Lorant, who wanted some illustrations for a book he was preparing. He had been intrigued by Smith's *Spanish Village* essay, and commissioned Smith, who had just resigned from *Life* in a dispute over presentation of his *Schweitzer* story.

Gene moved to Pittsburgh where Lorant had found an apartment for him, and went to work. When he had finished the assignment, he found that he had only begun something much greater: the "long poem" to the city, the consuming effort to define and communicate a personal view of Pittsburgh.

He moved to another apartment, converted a bathroom into a darkroom without nailing anything to a wall, and went out into the heart of the city that was to be his home for long months, and to occupy his heart and mind for longer still. He does not yet know how many hours he actually spent in processing the 10,000 negatives he shot, but it was usual for him to work in the darkroom for as many as 30 uninterrupted hours. In one session he remembers developing 43 rolls of film in a single immersion—both fast and fine-grain.

Smith did little printing while in Pittsburgh; some proof prints were made by a friend in New York and mailed back to him, but most of the 7,000 5x7 proof prints from which the story was built were made *continued on page 220*

continued on page 220

96

97

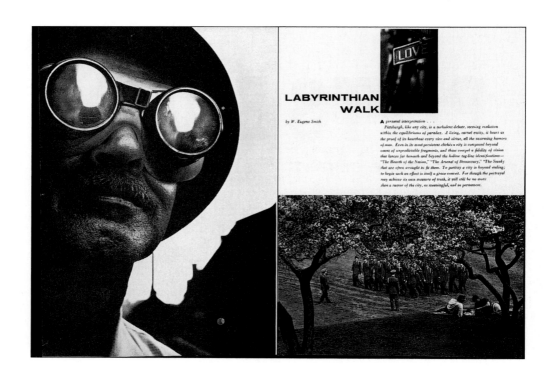

LABYRINTHIAN WALK

by W. Eugene Smith

A personal interpretation . . .

Pittsburgh, like any city, is a turbulent debate, teeming revolution within the equilibriums of paradox. A living, carnal entity, it bears as the proof of its heartbeat every vice and virtue, all the swarming humors of man. Even in its most persistent clichés a city is composed beyond count of unpredictable fragments, and these compel a fidelity of vision that lances far beneath and beyond the hollow tag-line identifications—"The Hearth of the Nation," "The Arsenal of Democracy," "The Smoky" that are often wrought to fit them. To portray a city is beyond ending; to begin such an effort is itself a grave conceit. For though the portrayal may achieve its own measure of truth, it will still be no more than a rumor of the city, as meaningful, and as permanent.

Of cathedrals, inclines and a sight of the moon

The first complaint about smoke was in 1804. Its disturbed author petitioned the City Council to "remedy the nuisance." But that remedy, frequently legislated, was long in coming. For almost 100 years the people of Pittsburgh lived under a heavy black roof that smothered the landscape, extinguished the horizon, and made the moon an omen of disaster. For only when the huge, flaming factories were idle could the heavens be glimpsed. Then the moon meant strike, depression, hardship.

Now—sometimes—it is different. Though still smudged by delays and defects, Pittsburgh's smoke control has restored considerable purity to the air, distance to the sight. Not since the chimneys began to vomit up their black infection have the jutting hills, crowned at their summits by cathedrals of worship and learning, stood so sharply against the sky. Now at last the moon has recovered its magic.

University of Pittsburgh's "Cathedral," St. Paul's spires landmark Oakland area. . . . Mighty climbs to worker's homes are thoroughly characteristic . . . . The moon could symbolize confidence backing creation of new skyline.

Exclusions and inclusions

Some, the exalted, huddle in splendor. Under canopies of deference, carpeted away from the laboring city, they breathe an air that is filtered through privilege, savor a setting where even the shadows are elite. Only distinction enters these precincts, only power, only the likeness destined to weight the library wall with stern and varnished nobility.

Thus the mighty, and thus also—thus hired in private, thus roosted off behind lookouts and clanging admonition—the payroll of that might. Alien accent, union button, beer on a raw plank and two-bit bet on the hole-card—this no less than glistening opulence is for members only. Forted on the city, the two camps guarded, and few the conducts granted to pass between.

Yet at the core, down at the coiling depths of pulse and instinct, what difference here except in furnishing? No difference: all are everywhere enrolled in a club from which there is no expulsion save in the last fluttering breath. Some arenas post no sentries; on some grounds the outlines blur; and who knows what hungers mingle at night, after the ball game, while islands glow from distant windows?

Social clubs of many nationalities ask to see your membership card.

The Duquesne Club—most exclusive, staid sanctuary of the highest of hierarchy.

To dine at the restaurant of the Pittsburgh Playhouse you must belong.

102

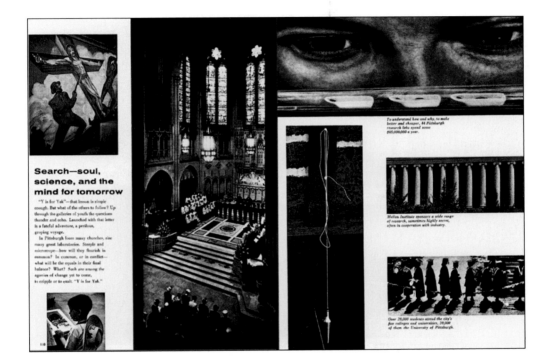

Search—soul, science, and the mind for tomorrow

"Y is for Yak"—that lesson is simple enough. But what of the others to follow? Up through the galleries of youth the questions thunder and echo. Launched with that letter is a fateful adventure, a perilous, groping voyage.

In Pittsburgh loom many churches, rise many great laboratories. Simple and microscope—how will they flourish in essence? In common, or in conflict—what will be the equals in their final balance? What? Such are among the agonies of change yet to come, to cripple or to exalt "Y is for Yak."

To understand how and why, to make better and cheaper, 84 Pittsburgh research labs spend some $05,000,000 a year.

Mellon Institute sponsors a wide range of research, sometimes highly secret, often in cooperation with industry.

Over 20,000 students attend the city's five colleges and universities, 20,000 of them the University of Pittsburgh.

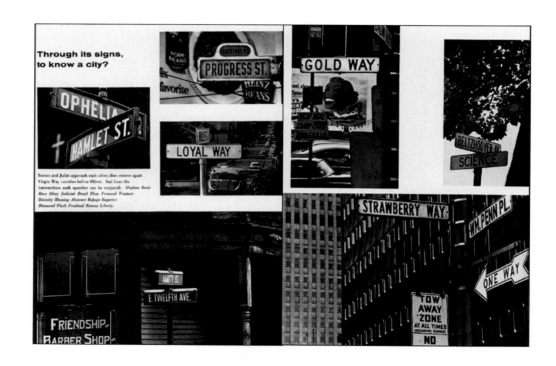

Through its signs,
to know a city?

OPHELIA
HAMLET ST.

Romeo and Juliet approach each other, then swerve apart.
Virgin Way vanishes before Oliver. And from the
intersections such speeches can be conjured: *Orphan Basic
Race Obey Judicial Bread Plea Forward Venture
Divinity Blessing Abstract Refuge Superior
Diamond Flush Freeland Rescue Liberty.*

Carnegie Museum is dusty but sound; Pittsburgh's educational TV station is more imaginative, and permitted a lamp to marry.

Cultural still lifes

Author John Gunther, in a book called *Inside U.S.A.*, once lavished more than 3,600 words of text on the subject of Pittsburgh's industrial exploits. To its cultural life, however, he conspicuously devoted only six curt sentences.

No injustice, this. Pittsburgh, America's 12th ranking city, is not nor has it ever been a sanctuary for the arts. One of its most historic citizens, in fact, coke king Henry Clay Frick, was once described by a waspish art dealer as "an intellectual spittoon."

Pittsburgh's professional theater is in distress, all but vanished, although the Carnegie Tech School of Drama is a notable one, eyed with respect by experts throughout the country. Museums are static; they need fresh injections of money, spirit and ideas. Writers move away. Musical fare, however—concerts, ballet and summer light opera—is generally excellent. The Pittsburgh Symphony Orchestra has recently earned a special distinction, but is without a truly suitable place to play. This lack the city, in typically grandiloquent style, proposes to correct. Plans have been drawn for an epic new Civic and Cultural Center, which will house in one super arena several different theaters, galleries, and auditoriums. Baseball will not be accommodated. Wrestling will.

Caryden of tradition Carnegie Tech Art students use statue as sandwichman.

Near Forbes Field is "Honus" Wagner, whose team was once great.

A less formalized audience: chalk on pavement, Sherman Avenue and North Diamond.

ad copy   The words in a print advertisement: any description of the product, the product name, or the product catchphrase. Ad copy is distinguished from the visual elements of the ad, so when you examine a print ad, you may need to consider both the visuals and the ad copy, the words in the ad.

analysis   The process of examining any text— visual, verbal, oral—to explain how it works. Analysis involves taking a text apart to see how its various parts function in relation to one another.

arrangement   In writing, arrangement refers to the selection and ordering of parts of an essay or story. In visual design, arrangement refers to the selection and placement or ordering of elements (e.g., words, images, white space) within the visual composition. See also *composition* and *white space*.

balance   In writing as well as in visual design, balance refers to a state of equilibrium. We often refer to a "balanced" discussion meaning that a writer or speaker attempts to represent fairly more than one side of an issue. In visual design, balance refers to a harmonious or pleasing arrangement of parts or elements.

bar graph   A diagram that plots information, usually used to compare numerical data. Bar graphs can be vertical or horizontal, flat or two-dimensional, and even pictorial.

broader context   The social, historical, cultural, and economic influences surrounding a text.

callout   An explanatory label for an illustration or other element in the text, often connected with a line pointing to the material it is meant to explain. See also *pull quotes*.

caption   A description or identification that accompanies a photograph or graphic, usually a brief phrase or a few short sentences. In newspapers and news magazines, captions are sometimes called cut-lines.

chart   A diagram that provides information visually. Unlike graphs, charts are not plotted.

claim   In argument, a statement that expresses a belief or position. The claim on its own will not be sufficient to carry an argument. Claims are usually accompanied by reasons meant to convince a reader or listener of the validity or worth of the claim. A claim is sometimes also called an assertion.

closed form   In the composition of an image, where the entire image is inside the visual frame and the viewer's attention is focused within the picture.

collage   In visual arts, a type of composition consisting of a variety of images, objects, and/or materials arranged together—sometimes overlapping—and pasted on a flat surface. These images, objects, or materials on their own might initially seem unrelated, but the point of the collage composition is to show how these separate and different images or objects are connected to convey a central idea or make a statement. Except in experimental writing, the term *collage* is rarely used to describe written compositions.

composition   A term common in many fields including writing, the visual arts, music, and even cooking. It refers to the selection and arrangement of material to create something new (i.e., an essay, a painting, a symphony, a dish).

cropping   In the visual arts, the process of cutting out the unwanted parts of an image. This is a term typically used in photography.

documentary   Normally referring to film, television, or photography, a documentary is meant to be a nonfiction rendition of an event, era, or series of events based on documents or records. A documentary film often consists of news films or photographs brought together to tell the story of an event. Film documentary might be narrated in voice-over so that it seems very objective. Documentary photographs are often—though not always—black and white and offered as evidence that an event really happened in the way it has been described in the story.

emphasis   Prominence or special attention to a particular detail or part of a composition to bring it to a reader's or viewer's attention. For example, boldface type on a page places emphasis on the words that are boldfaced.

font   The style of a typeface. For example, Times, Times New Roman, and Arrus, are all typeface styles. You can usually find different fonts listed under the font menu in your word-processing program. The font you choose will contribute to meaning as well as tone and so designers pay careful attention to the fonts they choose for different texts.

framing   In visual design, the border around an image or page layout. Visual artists talk about arranging objects within a frame, in much the same way we place a photograph within a frame—choosing the style of the frame to fit the photograph. But a frame is more than a physical object, it is a sense of limited space. If you look through a camera lens, for example, you will be able to "frame" your subject differently depending on whether you use a close-up or landscape orientation, where you place the subject with reference to the center of the frame, and how much of the background you include. Framing also refers to written compositions. When a writer provides structure to give shape to an argument, we call that "framing" the argument.

genre   A term common in the arts, it refers to a specific type or category of production. For example, films are often divided into several genres—western, horror, action, romantic comedy, etc. Television programming includes such genres as soap operas, talk shows, reality TV, sit-com, and drama series.

graph   A diagram that plots information using coordinates on x and y axes.

icon   Originally, icons were images of sacred persons. The visual representation stood in for the actual person and became an aid to worship. Today, the term is attached to any personage whose image has taken on symbolic significance within cultural circles. Elvis, for example, is an icon of early rock and roll. The image of Martin Luther King, Jr., giving his "I Have a Dream" speech in front of the Lincoln Monument is iconic for the Civil Rights Movement.

immediate context   Of a text, the combination of author, subject, and audience.

intertextuality   The referencing of one text inside another. Television texts do this all of the time when they create period programs like *That 70s Show or American Dreams,* in which clips of older programs are inserted into the text of the new show. Intertextuality is also at play in many forms of communication including advertising, film, and photography. Intertextual references only work well when the audience is likely to recognize them.

justified text   Type set so that the text runs even on both right and left margins. This is typical in newspaper columns and most textbook page layouts.

juxtapositioning   The act of putting objects close together or side-by-side to signal a relationship. Two photos juxtaposed might indicate contrast, movement in time, or similarity. Advertisers often use juxtapositioning to compare one product with another to show a product's effectiveness.

line graph   A diagram that plots information, usually used to compare changes in data that occur across time.

medium/media   The materials or technologies through which ideas are translated or made into cultural productions. In the visual arts, *medium* might refer to marble, oil paints, or watercolor, for example. In communication, the medium might be television, film, or digital technologies. *Media* is the plural of *medium* but is often used as singular when referring to communication technologies. Because *medium* suggests something ideas or thoughts pass through, we often talk of ideas or attitudes being interpreted by or developed through the media.

metaphor   A figure of speech in which a word, or phrase, is substituted for another to create a comparison. Visual arts as well as verbal art forms make use of metaphor.

open form   In the composition of an image, where the image extends or in some way points beyond the visual frame, leading viewers to think about what lies beyond the image.

page layout   The way a page of any sort is designed. *Layout* is often used to refer to newspaper page design.

perspective   In writing as well as in visual arts, perspective refers to the position from which a reader or viewer sees a subject. In the visual arts, perspective was an invention of Renaissance painters that allowed artists to give the illusion of depth on a flat surface, by using geometric models to make objects appear farther away or to make a road seem to disappear into the distance. By designating a van-

ishing point, linear perspective directs a viewer's eye and, thus, determines how a viewer will see the world represented by the painting. In the same way, *perspective* also refers to a writer's ability to determine how a reader will understand an argument or sympathize with a character depending on the perspective presented in the writing.

photo essay   A collection of photographs selected and arranged to tell a story or make a point. In the 1940s, *Life* magazine made the photo essay a popular form for magazines. The creators of *Life* made it clear that a photo essay should be readable (beginning, middle, and end) from the photos alone without much or any text to accompany them. Photo essays have been especially popular with documentary photographers.

photojournalism   News reporting through photographs or film footage shot on location showing the events taking place.

pie chart   A visual representation of statistical information highlighting the proportion of a segment in relation to a whole.

point of view   The position from which a story is told or argument is made. See also *perspective*.

proportion   A part considered in relationship to the whole. Visual designers pay attention to the proportion of the page taken up with white space, with visuals, and with words. Whatever takes up the largest proportion of a space is what is given the most emphasis. Writers also consider proportion when they make decisions about which topics should be covered and at what length. See also *emphasis* and *page layout*.

pull quote   A brief phrase (not necessarily an actual quotation) from the body text, enlarged and set off from the text with rules, a box, and/or a screen. For some readers, pull quotes actually determine how an article is read because they tend to distill the article into a few words and act as a summary of or guide through the longer article.

sans serif   A typeface, such as Helvetica or Arrus, that has no serifs. See also *serif*.

serif   In a typeface, a counterstroke on letterforms, projecting from the ends of the main strokes. For example, Times or Century School is a serifed typeface. See also *sans serif*.

stereotype   A generalized characterization about a group. For example, the phrase, "He drives like a woman," relies on the characterization of all women as one kind of a person—a bad driver. Stereotypes are oversimplified beliefs that ignore individuality or difference.

symbol   A word or image that represents an idea or ideal. For example, a nation's flag, often is taken to stand for the entire country and its ideals.

tone   Although the term is normally associated with sound, *tone* also refers to the manner of a writer's expression—angry, strident, fair, even—and is conveyed by the writer's choice of words and style of presentation. Visual art also uses the term *tone* to refer to how an image or visual design expresses mood or attitude through such elements as color, balance, layout, and choice of image.

typeface   The set of characters created by a type designer, including uppercase and lowercase alphabetical characters, numbers, punctuation, and special characters such as dingbats. A single typeface contains many fonts, at different sizes and styles. See also *font*.

verbal   Of or relating to words, expressed in words alone.

white space   In visual design, white space is the space where the figure and any accompanying language is absent—in artwork, usually the background; in a publication, the parts of the page not occupied by type or graphics.

Every effort has been made to gain permissions for images used in *Picturing Texts*. Unless otherwise noted, all images not cited in this section have been provided by the editor and authors of this publication. Please contact the publishers with any updated information.

INTRODUCTION

3: Document elaborated with the support of the French Ministry of Culture and Communication, Regional Direction for Cultural Affairs - Rhône-Alpes, Regional Department of Archaeology. **6:** *Top:* Courtesy the Library of Congress; *Bottom:* Courtesy the Library of Congress. **7:** Courtesy the Library of Congress. **8:** Elliott Erwitt/Magnum Photos. **10:** Design: David Carson. **11:** *Left:* McCann-Erickson Frankfurt; *Right:* Diagram from Pressman, Andy. *Architectural Design Portable Handbook: A Guide to Excellent Practices.* NY: McGraw-Hill, 2001. **12:** *Top:* Image: Steve Meyer; *Bottom:* Crispin Porter & Bogusky, Miami, 1996. **13:** *Top and Bottom:* Steve Meyer. **16:** Courtesy Ronald Feldman Fine Arts. **18–19:** From *Long Time Coming: A Photographic Portrait of America, 1935–1943,* by Michael Lesy, copyright 2002 W. W. Norton & Company, New York. Photographs courtesy of the Library of Congress Prints and Photographs Division.

CHAPTER 1

21: Neil Ryder Hoos. **24:** *Left:* Courtesy of the National Park Service; *Right:* © MapEasy, Inc. 2003, www.mapeasy.com. **26:** Courtesy the Library of Congress. **27:** *Left:* Photography Gallery Fund. Photo: Greg Williams reproduction, The Art Institute of Chicago. *Right:* Courtesy Levi Strauss & Co. and Levi's® SILVERTAB® **28:** Dover publications. **30:** The Martin Agency Charlotte, NC. **31:** Margaret Bourke-White/Time Life Pictures/Getty Images. **32:** *Left:* Courtesy the Library of Congress; *Bottom:*

TBWA Hunt Lascaris, Johannesburg, 2000. **33:** Courtesy the Library of Congress. **34:** Dun & Bradstreet Software. **35:** Michael Stipe. **36:** Courtesy www.adbusters.org. **37:** Copyright 1985, American Cancer Society, Inc. Reprinted with permission. **38:** Ullstein Birnback. **39:** *Top:* Museo Nacional Centro de Arte Reina Sofia, Madrid, Spain. © The Estate of Pablo Picasso/Artists Rights Society (ARS), New York. Photo from Art Resource, NY; *Bottom:* Courtesy the Library of Congress. **40:** *Bottom Left:* David Oakley, copywriter, and John Boone, art director. The Martin Agency Charlotte, NC; *Right:* Design: Shigeo Fukuda. **41:** *Cutouts,* 1956, Copyright the Estate of Harry Callahan, courtesy Pace/MacGill Gallery, New York. **42:** Palmer Jarvis DDB, Vancouver, British Columbia, Canada. **43:** James Nachtwey/VII. **44:** Margaret Sartor. **45:** Frank Horvat. **46:** The Thomas Walther Collection. **47:** O. Winston Link. **48:** From *Earth, Portrait of a Planet,* Stephen Marshak, W. W. Norton & Company, 2001. **49:** *Top and Bottom:* From *Earth, Portrait of a Planet,* Stephen Marshak, W. W. Norton & Company, 2001. **50:** From *Earth, Portrait of a Planet,* Stephen Marshak, W. W. Norton & Company, 2001. **51:** *Top:* © Yann Arthus-Bertrand/CORBIS; *Bottom:* From *Earth, Portrait of a Planet,* Stephen Marshak, W. W. Norton & Company, 2001. **52:** Courtesy Michael Ian. **53:** Sam Mapp. **54:** *Top Left:* Cover of *Stiff: The Curious Lives of Human Cadavers,* Mary Roach, W. W. Norton, 2003; *Bottom Left:* Cover of *The Last Magician: A Novel,* Janette Turner Hospital, W. W. Norton & Company, 2003; *Bottom Right:* Cover of *In My Father's Footsteps: A Memoir,* Sebastian Matthews, W. W. Norton & Company, 2004. **55:** Benjamin Kracauer. **67:** © Layne Kennedy/CORBIS. **69–76:** From *Reinventing Comics: How Imagination and Technology are Revolutionizing an Art Form,* Scott McCloud, HarperCollins, 2000. **77:** Benjamin Kracauer. **80:** "Restaurant Florent Ad Campaign" from *Tibor,* edited by Peter Hall and Michail Bierut, Princeton Architectural Press, NY, 1998.

81: "Restaurant Florent Ad Campaign" from *Tibor*, edited by Peter Hall and Michail Bierut, Princeton Architectural Press, NY, 1998. **82:** *Top and Bottom:* "Restaurant Florent Ad Campaign" from *Tibor*, edited by Peter Hall and Michail Bierut, Princeton Architectural Press, NY, 1998. **83:** "Restaurant Florent Ad Campaign" from *Tibor*, edited by Peter Hall and Michail Bierut, Princeton Architectural Press, NY, 1998. **86 and 88:** Jessica Helfand, "Squaring the Circle" originally published in *Eye* Magazine, Fall 2001. Essay was later expanded into book form: *Reinventing the Wheel* (Winterhouse Editions/ Princeton Architectural Press, 2002). © 2001 Jessica Helfand. **91:** Peter Gwillim Kreitler Collection. **92:** *Left:* Courtesy Another Poster for Peace, Design by Kimberly Cross; *Bottom Right:* Courtesy the Library of Congress. **93:** *Top Left:* Neil Ryder Hoos. **93:** Benjamin Kracauer.

CHAPTER 2

97: Neil Ryder Hoos. **99:** *Left:* © 2001 The Record (Bergen County, NJ), Thomas E. Franklin, Staff Photographer/Corbis/SABA; *Right:* © Corbis. **105:** © Corbis. **106:** Photo: Neil Ryder Hoos. **107:** Courtesy John Porter and Kim Yi. **108:** *Left and Right:* © Corbis. **110:** © 1992 Benetton Group S.p.A., Photo: T. Frare, Concept: O. Toscani. **112:** Nora Mapp. **117:** Friends of American Art Collection. Reproduction, The Art Institute of Chicago. **124:** Roland Charles/Courtesy Deborah Charles. **125:** Photographer unknown, from *Snapshots: The Photography of Everyday Life at the San Francisco Museum of Modern Art.* **127:** Copyright Joel Sternfeld. Courtesy Pace/MacGill Gallery, New York. **131:** The Museum of Modern Art, New York, NY/© Digital Image © The Museum of Modern Art/Licensed by SCALA/Art Resource, NY. **144:** © Archivo Iconografico, S.A./Corbis. **146:** Photo by Yashuhiro Ishimoto; from *Yashuhiro Ishimoto: A Tale of Two Cities* by Colin Westerbeck. Catalogue published by the Art Institute of Chicago,

1999. **147:** Untitled (Jaspar County, Iowa), by John Vachon. From *Long Time Coming: A Photographic Portrait of America*, 1935–1943, by Michael Lesy, copyright 2002 W. W. Norton & Company, New York. Photographs courtesy of the Library of Congress Prints and Photographs Division. **148:** Warren Wheeler. **149:** Anna Gaskell. Courtesy The Guggenheim Museum.

CHAPTER 3

151: Neil Ryder Hoos. **152:** Photo detail: Neil Ryder Hoos. **153:** Alexander Goodall Diary, MS 12075, Australian Manuscripts Collection, State Library of Victoria. **155:** National Museum, Port Said, Egypt. **156–157:** Cheryl Ball. **159:** Eric Rodenbeck, http://www.stamen.com. **160–162** Archives of American Art Smithsonian Institution. **163:** Joseph Squier. **165:** Jacalyn Lopez Garcia. **166:** *Top:* Bowen Zunino; *Bottom:* Carolina Arellano. **170:** From *Crowns: Portraits of Black Women in Church Hats*, Michael Chunningham, Doubleday, 2000. Photo: Michael Cunningham. **173:** From *SPILLING OPEN* by Sabrina Ward Harrison, copyright © 1999 by Sabrina Ward Harrison. Used by permission of Villard Books, a division of Random House, Inc. **176:** Courtesy of Carrie Mae Weems. **184:** Benjamin Kracauer. **190–191:** Courtesy: Mary Boone Gallery, New York. **192:** *Top:* Courtesy Planned Parenthood ® Global Partners. **193:** A *Message from Men*, 2001, by Cynthia and Richard Selfe. **195–206:** Images from "What's Wrong With This Picture?" from *Home Movies and Other Necessary Fictions*, Michelle Citron. University of Minnesota Press. Copyright 1999 by the Regents of the University of Minnesota. **208:** Photograph from *Harvard Works Because We Do*, (The Quantuck Lane Press, 2003) copyright 2003 by Greg Halpern. All rights reserved. **212:** Photograph from *Harvard Works Because We Do*, (The Quantuck Lane Press, 2003) copyright 2003 by Greg Halpern. All rights reserved. **213:** Photograph from *Harvard Works*

Because We Do, (The Quantuck Lane Press, 2003) copyright 2003 by Greg Halpern. All rights reserved. **214:** Photograph from *Harvard Works Because We Do*, (The Quantuck Lane Press, 2003) copyright 2003 by Greg Halpern. All rights reserved. **216:** of Charlotte Greenough.
217: From *Visual Literacy* by Judith Wilde and Richard Wilde. © Judith Wilde and Richard Wilde. Published by Watson-Guptill publications, New York, NY. www.watsonguptill.com. **219:** Charlotte Greenough. **220–221:** Courtesy Arthur Paul.
222: Courtesy Jack Leigh Gallery. **223:** From *Long Time Coming: A Photographic Portrait of America*, 1935–1943, by Michael Lesy, copyright 2002 W. W. Norton & Company, New York. Photographs courtesy of the Library of Congress Prints and Photographs Division. **224:** AFP PHOTO/JIJI PRESS.
225: Daniel Galvez, © 1983. **226:** *Left:* Amherst College Archives and Special Collections; *Right:* Todd-Bingham Picture Collection, Manuscripts and Archives, Yale University Library. **227:** Courtesy: Sean Kelly Gallery, New York.

CHAPTER 4

229: Neil Ryder Hoos. **230:** Private Collection of Quentin Peterson. **231:** Carolina Arellano.
233: Jennifer Bartell. **234:** Library of Congress Prints and Photographs Division Washington, DC 20540 USA. **238:** Préfecture de Police, tous droits réservés. **239** *Top Left:* Federal Bureau of Investigation Ten Most Wanted Web site; *Right:* AP Worldwide Photos. **240:** Courtesy of BoondocksNet.com. **244:** © 2002 The *New Yorker* Collection from cartoonbank.com. All Rights Reserved. **245:** © Marvel Comics. **246:** © Marvel Comics. **248:** Benjamin Kracauer. **250:** Harry Wilson. **261:** Katherine Carlson. **263:** Copyright Duane Michals. Courtesy Pace/MacGill Gallery, New York. **264:** Benjamin Kracauer. **266:** Will Counts. **268:** Will Counts. **272:** *Left: The Belle of the Yakimas*: Photo: E.S. Curtis/Image courtesy Sepia International, Inc. New York City; *Right: The Belle of the Deccan Plateau*: Photo: Annu Palakunnathu Matthew/Image courtesy Sepia International, Inc. New York City. **273:** *Left: Navajo Smile*: Photo: E.S. Curtis/Image courtesy Sepia International, Inc. New York City; *Right: Malayalee Smile*: Photo: Annu Palakunnathu Matthew/Image courtesy Sepia International, Inc. New York City **274:** *Left: Noble Savage*: Photo: E.S. Curtis. Northwestern University Library, Evanston, IL/Image courtesy Sepia International, Inc. New York City; *Right: Savage Noble*: Photo: Annu Palakunnathu Matthew. Northwestern University Library, Evanston, IL/Image courtesy Sepia International, Inc. New York City. **280:** From Pieterse, Jan Nederveen. *Black on White*, New Haven: Yale University Press, 1992. **283:** © 2003 Peter Menzel. **285:** © 2003 Peter Menzel. **286:** Nora Mapp. **293–298:** Story by Cynthia L. Selfe and Marilyn M. Cooper.
301: From *Visual Literacy* by Judith Wilde and Richard Wilde. © Judith Wilde and Richard Wilde. Published by Watson-Guptill Publications, New York, NY. www.watsonguptill.com **302:** From *Comic Book Bad Guys and Gals* by Christopher Hart (1998). Published by Watson-Guptill Publications, New York, NY. www.watsonguptill.com. **304:** Katie Hannah.
305: Melea Seward. **306:** © Colin Anderson/Corbis. **307:** Shannon Taggart/courtesy Blind Spot Artist. **308–309:** Pawan Kumar/AFP/Getty Images. **310:** Jamie Berson. **311:** *Little Girls with Their Dolls and Buggies, Caldwell, Idaho*, Russell Lee, 1941, from *Long Time Coming: A Photographic Portrait of America*, 1935–1943, by Michael Lesy, copyright 2002 W. W. Norton & Company, New York. Photographs courtesy of the Library of Congress Prints and Photographs Division. **312:** Ad developed by the Pro-Choice Public Education Project. **313:** From the series Postcards from Camp, 1999–2000, acrylic on canvas. Exhibited in The 46th Biennial Exhibition: Media/Metaphor, Courtesy of the Artist© Ben Sakoguchi. **314:** James VanDerZee, © Donna Mussenden VanDerZee. **315:** *Negro*

Women near Earle, Arkansas, Dorothea Lange, 1936, from *Long Time Coming: A Photographic Portrait of America,* 1935–1943, by Michael Lesy, copyright 2002 W. W. Norton & Company, New York. Photographs courtesy of the Library of Congress Prints and Photographs Division.

CHAPTER 5

317: Neil Ryder Hoos.   **319:** Frame from Robert Zemeckis's *Forrest Gump:* © Paramount Pictures/1994.   **321:** All images rom *The Commissar Vanishes,* Henry Holt, 1997.   **322:** Jamie Berzon.
325: Alabama Department of Archives and History, Montgomery, Alabama.   **328:** Museo del Prado, Madrid. Photo: Scala/Art Resource, NY.
329: Frames from Wachowski & Wachowski's *The Matrix,* 1999: © Warner Brothers/1999.   **336:** NASA/ Courtesy Mountain Light Phototgraphy.
337: NASA.   **338:** Galen Rowell/Mountain Light.
339: Tourist of Death Web site: http://www. touristofdeath.com/.   **345:** Benjamin Kracauer.
348: Rune Hellestad/Corbis.   **349:** Courtesy Kip Meyer.   **351:** Courtesy *Men's Health Magazine.*
352: © Bettmann/Corbis.   **361:** Courtesy NASA.
362: Photos Courtesy NASA.   **365:** Images: Michael W. Davidson at Florida State University.
374: Thomas Kellner, Paris, Tour Eiffel 2#10, 1997.
375: © Christie's Images/CORBIS.   **376–377:** Joel De Grande.**378:** Sam Mapp.   **379:** Eli Reed/Magnum Photos.   **381:** From *Photobooth,* Babbette Hines, Princeton Architectural Press, 2002. *Far Left:* Emily Kracauer

CHAPTER 6

383: Neil Ryder Hoos.   **384:** Photo detail: Neil Ryder Hoos.   **385:** Courtesy: Partnership for a Drug-Free America.   **386:** © Church Ad Project.
387: Courtesy www.adbusters.org.   **389:** *Left and Right:* Woodward, David, Robert Ostergren, Onno

Brouwer, Steven Hoelscher and Joshua Hane. Cultural Map of Wisconsin. © 1996. Reprinted by permission of The University of Wisconsin Press.   **391:** *Left and Right:* Courtesy of DaimlerChrysler Corporation.   **393:** *Left:* Courtesy: the American Civil Liberties Union.   **393:** *Right:* Albert Einstein (TM) HUJ, Represented by The Roger Richman Agency, Inc., www.albert-einstein.net.   **394:** Edweard Muybridge's horses. Photo: Corbis.   **395:** Courtesy Library of Congress.   **396:** Benjamin Kracauer.   **397:** Courtesy Library of Congress.   **398:** Courtesy Library of Congress.   **401:** Courtesy Nicole Klagsbrun Gallery.   **404:** Copyright 1982, 1990 by Jesse Levine.   **409:** *King Leopold's Ghost* by Adam Hochschild. Copyright © 1998 by Adam Hochschild. Used by permission of Houghton Mifflin Company. All rights reserved.   **408:** *Top Left:* Cover of *The Curious Case of Benjamin Button Apt. 3 W,* Gabriel Brownstein, W. W. Norton, 2003; *Top Middle:* Cover of *Remarkable Reads,* Edited by J. Peder Zane W. W. Norton & Company, 2004; *Top Left:* Cover of *A Kind of Flying,* Ron Carlson, W. W. Norton & Company, 2003; *Bottom Left: The Green Hour,* Frederic Tuten, W. W. Norton & Company, 2003; *Bottom Middle: Pink Think,* Lynn Peril, W. W. Norton & Company, 2002; *Bottom Right:* Cover of *Opening Skinner's Box: Great Psychological Experiments of the Twentieth Century,* Lauren Slater, W. W. Norton & Company, 2004.   **409:** "Jacket Cover," from *Observatory Mansions* by Edward Carey, copyright © 2000 by Edward Carey. Illustrations © 2000 by Edward Carey. Used by permission of Crown Publishers, a division of Random House, Inc.   **412:** Copyright Richard Misrach 1998.   **415:** *Left:* Courtesy of Environmental Defense. *Right:* Matthew Hodgman   **417:** © The Historic New Orleans Collection.   **421:** Benjamin Kracauer.   **422:** Vanessa Drake-Johnson and Steve Dunn.   **423:** *Bottom Left:* Image: Susie and Steve Meyer. *Bottom Right:* Gregory Pfarr.   **424:** Neil Ryder Hoos.   **425:** © World Eagle.   **426:** Saatchi & Saatchi, Singapore.   **427:** Courtesy the Chiropractic

Association of South Africa.   **428:** Courtesy Library of Congress.   **429:** Courtesy Library of Congress.   **430:** Courtesy Fred Astaire Dance Studios.   **431:** Courtesy the German committee for UNICEF

CHAPTER 7

433: Neil Ryder Hoos.   **435:** Images Courtesy Hammermill Paper Co.   **437–440:** Design: Sarah Huang.   **442:** *Top Left:* Cover of *Napoleon's Women*, Christopher Hibbert, W. W. Norton & Company, forthcoming; *Top Middle:* Cover of *Crossing the BLVD: Strangers, Neighbors, Aliens in a New America*, Warren Lehrer, Judith Sloan, W. W. Norton & Company, 2003; *Top Right:* Cover of *Holocaust, a History*, Deborah Dwork, W. W. Norton & Company, 2003; *Bottom Left:* Cover of *Dear Mrs. Lindbergh: a Novel*, Kathleen Hughes, W. W. Norton & Company, 2003; *Bottom Middle:* Cover of *Simply Einstein*, Richard Wolfson, W. W. Norton & Company, 2003; *Bottom Right:* Cover of *Wings*, Tom D. Crouch, W. W. Norton & Company, 2003.   **442:** Typefaces on left: Corianne Daman, Bryan Fisher, Shaun Gingerich, and Andy Wagoner.   **458:** From *Economics*, Third Edition, Joseph E. Stiglitz and Carl E. Walsh, W. W. Norton & Company, 2002.   **459:** *Top:* From *Earth, Portrait of a Planet*, Stephen Marshak, W. W. Norton & Company, 2001; *Bottom:* From *Economics*, Third Edition, Joseph E. Stiglitz and Carl E. Walsh, W. W. Norton & Company, 2002.   **461:** Rise Axelrod.   **462:** Benjamin Kracauer.   **465:** Design: Paula Scher.   **472:** Courtesy The Ken Done Gallery.   **479:** Abbott Miller: from *Design Writing Research: Writing on Graphic Design* by Miller, Abbott and Lupton, Ellen. Copyright © 1996: pp. 143–155. Reprinted by permission of Abbott Miller.   **481:** Abbott Miller: from *Design Writing Research: Writing on Graphic Design* by Miller, Abbott and Lupton, Ellen. Copyright © 1996: pp. 143–155. Reprinted by permission of Abbott Miller.   **482:** Abbott Miller: from *Design Writing Research:*

Writing on Graphic Design by Miller, Abbott and Lupton, Ellen. Copyright © 1996: pp. 143–155. Reprinted by permission of Abbott Miller.   **483:** Abbott Miller: from *Design Writing Research: Writing on Graphic Design* by Miller, Abbott and Lupton, Ellen. Copyright © 1996: pp. 143–155. Reprinted by permission of Abbott Miller.   **485:** Graphic: Nora Mapp.   **486–492:** Courtesy Jim Heimann.   **494:** Frames from Jane Campion's *The Piano*, 1993: © Miramax Films.   **495:** Frames from Francis Ford Coppola's *Apocalypse Now*, 1979: © Paramount Studio.   **496:** Title: "Bring in 'Da Noise, Bring in 'Da Funk" Broadway poster campaign for The Public Theater, 1996. Design: Paula Scher/Pentagram Photo: Richard Avedon.   **497:** Hewitt.   **498:** Nicolas Faure.   **499:** Smithsonian American Art Museum, Washington, DC. Copyright Smithsonian American Art Museum, Washinton, DC/ Art Resource, NY   **500–507:** Selections from "Pittsburgh: W. Eugene Smith's Monumental Poem to the City" from Popular Photography's Photography Annual 1959, from *Dream Street: W. Eugene Smith's Pittsburgh Project*, Edited by Sam Stephenson, copyright 2001 by Sam Stephenson, the Center for Documentary Studies, and the Heirs of W. Eugene Smith. All photographs appearing in *Dream Street* are copyright The Heirs of W. Eugene Smith Collection and W. Eugene Smith Archive, Center for Creative Photography; Carnegie Museum of Art, Pittsburgh, Lorant Collection/Gift of the Carnegie Library. All rights reserved.

TEXT PERMISSIONS

Joseph Bathanti: "Your Mum and Dad" from *The Sun* Magazine. Copyright © 2000. Permission granted by author.

Jason Berry: "Cancer Alley: The Poisoning of the American South" from *Aperture* Magazine. Reprinted with the permission of the author.

Joyce Carol Oates: "Edward Hopper's *Nighthawks, 1942*" from *The Time Traveler* by Joyce Carol Oates, Copyright © 1983, 1984, 1985, 1986, 1987, 1988, 1989 by The Ontario Review, Inc. Used by permission of Dutton, a division of Penguin Group (USA) Inc.

David Quammen: This originally appeared in *The Boilerplate Rhino*, reprinted by permission of David Quammen. All rights reserved. Copyright © 2000 by David Quammen.

Helen Starkweather: "Crisis at Central High" from Smithsonian Magazine (February 2002) pp. 19–20. Reprinted with the permission of *Smithsonian* Magazine.

Mitchell Stephens: "By Means of the Visible" in *The Rise of the Image, The Fall of The Word*. Copyright © 1998. Reprinted by permission of Oxford University *Press*.

Mark Strand: from *Hopper* by Mark Strand, copyright © 1994, 2001 by Mark Strand. Used by permission of Alfred A. Knopf, a division of Random House, Inc.

Marita Sturken: "Practices of Looking" from Practices of Looking: An Introduction to Visual Culture. Copyright © 2000. Reprinted by permission of Oxford University Press.

John Szarkowski: Reprinted by permission from *Looking at Photographs: 100 Pictures from the Collection of The Museum of Modern Art* © 1973 The Museum of Modern Art.

ABOUT THE AUTHORS

The four authors of **Picturing Texts** include three composition specialists and one professional book designer. **Lester Faigley** teaches at the University of Texas, Austin. Known for his scholarship about visual discourse and electronic technologies, he was the 1996 chair of CCCC and the winner of the 1992 MLA Shaughnessy Prize and CCCC Outstanding Book Award. **Diana George** teaches at Michigan Technological University. She is known for her scholarship about visual texts in the composition classroom and was the winner of the 1998 CCCC Braddock Award. **Anna Palchik** is an award-winning book designer with a background in fine arts and art education. For the past twenty-five years, she has specialized in designing composition textbooks. **Cynthia Selfe** teaches at Michigan Technological University. Known for her work on writing in electronic environments, she was the 1998 chair of CCCC and the winner of the 1996 EDUCOM Medal for Innovative Teaching with Technology.